INSIGHT ⊙ GUIDES

PORTUGAL

PLAN & BOOK
YOUR TAILOR-MADE TRIP

BRAZIL **CHILE** **ECUADOR**

TAILOR-MADE TRIPS & UNIQUE EXPERIENCES CREATED BY LOCAL TRAVEL EXPERTS AT INSIGHTGUIDES.COM/HOLIDAYS

Insight Guides has been inspiring travellers with high-quality travel content for over 45 years. As well as our popular guidebooks, we now offer the opportunity to book tailor-made private trips completely personalised to your needs and interests. By connecting with one of our local experts, you will directly benefit from their expertise and local know-how, helping you create memories that will last a lifetime.

HOW INSIGHTGUIDES.COM/HOLIDAYS WORKS

STEP 1
Pick your dream destination and submit an enquiry, or modify an existing itinerary if you prefer.

STEP 2
Fill in a short form, sharing details of your travel plans and preferences with a local expert.

STEP 3
Your local expert will create your personalised itinerary, which you can amend until you are completely satisfied.

STEP 4
Book securely online. Pack your bags and enjoy your holiday! Your local expert will be available to answer questions during your trip.

BENEFITS OF PLANNING & BOOKING AT INSIGHTGUIDES.COM/HOLIDAYS

PLANNED BY LOCAL EXPERTS
The Insight Guides local experts are hand-picked, based on their experience in the travel industry and their impeccable standards of customer service.

SAVE TIME & MONEY
When a local expert plans your trip, you save time and money when you book, even during high season. You won't be charged for using a credit card either.

TAILOR-MADE TRIPS
Book with Insight Guides, and you will be in complete control of the planning process, from the initial selections to amending your final itinerary.

BOOK & TRAVEL STRESS-FREE
Enjoy stress-free travel when you use the Insight Guides secure online booking platform. All bookings come with a money-back guarantee.

WHAT OTHER TRAVELLERS THINK ABOUT TRIPS BOOKED AT INSIGHTGUIDES.COM/HOLIDAYS

Trip to Portugal

Every step of the planning process and the trip itself was effortless and exceptional. Our special interests, preferences and requests were accommodated resulting in a trip that exceeded our expectations.

Corinne, USA ★★★★★

Trip to Vietnam

The organization was superb, the drivers professional, and accommodation quite comfortable. I was well taken care of! My thanks to your colleagues who helped make my trip to Vietnam such a great experience. My only regret is that I couldn't spend more time in the country.

Heather ★★★★★

DON'T MISS OUT
BOOK NOW AT
INSIGHTGUIDES.COM/HOLIDAYS

CONTENTS

Introduction

The Best of Portugal 8
Land by the Sea 21
The Portuguese 23

History & features

Decisive Dates 30
Ancient Lusitania 33
A Nation is Born 41
   🔍 Castles in the Air 45
The English Connection 46
Empire Building 49
   🔍 Luís de Camões 57
The Conquerors are Conquered 59
Revolution and Evolution 67
   🔍 Salazar 73
Saints, Miracles and Shrines 77
Travellers' Tales 82
Fado 85
Portuguese Food 89
Wines of Portugal 97
   🔍 Port Dynasties 101
📷 Festivals for All Seasons 102
Portuguese Architecture 107
Portuguese Art Through the Ages 114
Pousadas and Manor Houses 120
Natural Portugal 125

Places

Introduction 137
■ LISBON 143
📷 Azulejos: A National Emblem 162
■ ESTORIL AND CASCAIS 165
■ SINTRA 171
■ SETÚBAL AND THE ARRÁBIDA
    PENINSULA 177
■ ALGARVE 183
■ ÉVORA AND ALENTEJO 199
📷 Preserving Arts and Crafts 220

- ESTREMADURA AND RIBATEJO **223**
- COIMBRA **235**
- SIDE TRIPS FROM COIMBRA **243**
- BEIRA ALTA AND BEIRA BAIXA............ **251**
- PORTO **259**
  - 🔍 Barcos rabelos **265**
- THE DOURO VALLEY................................. **267**
  - 📷 Port Wine, The Douro's Treasure **276**
- COSTA VERDE AND THE MINHO........... **279**
- TRÁS-OS-MONTES................................. **291**
- MADEIRA.. **301**
- THE AZORES **311**

Travel tips

TRANSPORT
Getting there **320**
Getting around **321**

A – Z
Accessible travel **323**
Admission charges **323**
Accommodation **323**
Budgeting for your trip **323**
Children.. **323**
Climate.. **324**
Crime and safety **324**
Customs regulations **324**
Eating out **324**
Electricity **324**
Embassies **325**
Emergencies **325**
Etiquette... **325**
Festivals and holidays................................ **325**
Health and medical care............................ **326**
LGBTQ+ travellers **326**
Media **326**
Money... **327**
Nightlife **327**
Opening hours... **328**
Postal services **328**
Religious services **328**
Shopping **328**
Sports... **328**
Telephones **329**
Tourist information **329**

Tour operators and travel agents **330**
Visas and passports..................................... **330**
Website and apps... **330**
Weights and measures **330**
Women travellers... **330**

LANGUAGE
Getting by **331**
Basic communication **331**
Eating and drinking in a restaurant............ **332**
Menu decoder **332**
Health.. **332**
Sightseeing **333**
Shopping **333**
Travelling **333**
Numbers **333**

FURTHER READING
Portuguese works.. **334**
Books about Portugal **334**
Other Insight Guides **334**

Maps
Overview **6**
Portugal **138**
Lisbon... **140**
Central Lisbon **146**
Estoril, Cascais, Sintra and Setúbal.......... **166**
Sintra Vila.. **172**
Algarve **184**
Evora and Alentejo **200**
Evora **203**
Estremadura and Ribatejo......................... **224**
Coimbra **236**
Side Trips from Coimbra............................ **244**
Beira Alta and Beira Baixa......................... **252**
Porto... **260**
The Douro Valley **268**
Costa Verde and the Minho **280**
Trás-os-Montes **292**
Madeira **302**
The Azores **312**

LEGEND
🔍 Insight on
📷 Photo story

7

RIBATEJO

ESTORIL AND CASCAIS

SINTRA

LISBON

SETÚBAL AND THE ARRÁBIDA PENINSULA

ÉVORA AND ALENTEJO

ALGARVE

Portugal

THE BEST OF PORTUGAL: TOP ATTRACTIONS

△ **Algarve**. This region has the greatest choice of beaches and warmest waters, from the semi-wild beaches on the windy west coast, like Monte Clerigo, to the more sheltered stretches around Lagos hemmed in by gorgeous rock-framed, sandy coves. See page 183.

▽ **Sintra**. Once a cool summer residence for kings, Sintra is a magical town that has kept the character that proved a lure for poets and rich foreigners alike. Its beautiful royal palace, splendid *quintas* (estates), the extraordinary Pena palace, and some good museums all add lustre. See page 171.

△ **Évora**. Gleaming above the Alentejo plains, Évora traverses the ages with amazing megaliths nearby, a glorious Roman temple, spectacular churches, shops under ancient arcades, and great food and lodgings. See page 203.

△ **Reserva Natural das Berlengas**. This protected archipelago 10km (6 miles) offshore from Peniche on the west coast is characterised by a dramatic rocky terrain, home to thousands of nesting sea birds, especially guillemots. See page 232.

TOP ATTRACTIONS | 9

△ **Vila Nova de Milfontes**. The most charming of the Alentejo seaside resorts, Vila Nova de Milfontes is a white-washed, laid-back town close to some lovely golden sand beaches. See page 215.

▽ **Porto**. This glorious city has a beguilingly pretty river front, wonderful *azulejos*, a cutting-edge Casa da Musica and lots of lively places to eat, drink and sip port. See page 259.

△ **Lisbon**. The Portuguese capital is stunningly rich in historic sights, led by the great Jerónimos monastery at Belém. Picturesque neighbourhoods, like Moorish Alfama or the Bairro Alto, are architecturally pleasing and full of colour, music and good places to eat. See page 143.

△ **The Alentejo Wine Route**. This route offers a chance to explore the ancient bleached landscape of the Alentejo. See page 201.

△ **The Convento do Cristo, Tomar**. This UNESCO World Heritage Site is a dazzling Manueline maze of winding passageways, irregular cloisters and extraordinary carvings, centred around the mystical sixteen-sided Templar church. See page 225.

△ **University town, Coimbra**. Once Portugal's medieval capital, Coimbra combines beautiful ancient buildings and a sense of tradition with a buzzy atmosphere courtesy of the student population, dressed in their traditional black capes. See page 235.

THE BEST OF PORTUGAL: EDITOR'S CHOICE

The high-perched Castelo de Almourol.

ONLY IN PORTUGAL

The Douro Valley. This arresting valley is the birthplace of Portugal's famous port wines – landscaped vineyards stripe the river's steep slopes. Start your tour at ancient Porto or the port-wine lodges of Vila Nova de Gaia opposite, and work your way through the valley. Or you can sit back and enjoy a cruise from Porto's colourful Ribeira, lasting several hours or several days. See page 267.

Pousadas. A specialty of the country, a *pousada* is a type of accommodation that makes for a memorable stay. They are national establishments and are usually located in historic castles or converted convents, with a simple yet charming style including high ceilings, stone walls and sometimes even swimming pools and air conditioning. There are plenty to choose from all around the country. See page 120.

Fado. Meaning fate or destiny, fado is Portugal's most renowned music – intense, soulful singing accompanied usually by a 12-stringed Portuguese guitar. In Lisbon you can hear it at its best in the Bairro Alto or Alfama. In Coimbra it is usually black-cloaked male students who sing fado. See page 85.

BEST CASTLES AND ANCIENT SITES

São Jorge (St George). With its long history and dominant hilltop position, Lisbon's São Jorge takes pride of place. The city views are spectacular, there's a citadel to explore, birds to spot, a restaurant, and quite often an exhibition or an event. See page 151.

Foz Côa. A UNESCO World Heritage Site, this archaeological park is found in the Douro Valley region. With the largest area of palaeolithic engravings in Europe, it is one of the surprises in a country rich in historic treasures, and the area includes a beautiful museum. See page 272.

Guimarães. This 10th-century castle is the "cradle of Portugal" where the nation's first king, Afonso Henriques, was born in 1110. The restored castle walls and towers remain impressive. See page 287.

Almourol. Set on a river island, Almourol castle has an enchanting atmosphere. Built (or possibly rebuilt) by Gualdim Pais, the founder of the Templar city of Tomar, it is haunted by legends. See page 224.

Conímbriga. Near Coimbra, this site of marvellous Roman ruins and mosaics is complemented by an excellent museum. See page 243.

The Douro Valley.

BEST FESTAS AND SPECTACLES

An Easter procession in Lisbon.

Viana do Castelo's festa. This three-day *festa* in August is queen of the folk fairs. Vivid embroidered costumes and "brides" in black adorned in gold jewellery are the highlight of a stunning festival of traditional music, dancing and parades. See page 283.

The Festas dos Santos Populares. This festival held in June celebrates Lisbon's favourite saints with parades, feasting and wine. The aroma of grilled sausages and sardines hangs over Alfama during this fun, friendly festival. See page 103.

Escola Portuguesa de Arte Equestre shows. Classic displays of stylish horsemanship by the school's *equitadores* (horse riders) are a treat. For shows, the Alter Real horses are beribboned and the riders dressed in courtly costumes and tricorne hats. The *escola* performs every Wednesday (May–July, Sept and Oct) at Henrique Calado Riding Ring. See page 172.

The Colete Encarnada (Red Waistcoat). The Ribatejo's favourite *festa* takes place in July and October in Vila Franca de Xira, northeast of Lisbon. The red waistcoats are those of *campinos* or herdsmen who tend to the region's bulls, cattle and horses all year. You can bypass the bullfights and still be richly entertained by local colour, bullrunning, riding and herding contests. See page 223.

Carnival. The pre-Lenten celebration is practised each February in several towns, but most charmingly in Loulé in the Algarve. Children parade in costumes; adults on themed floats toss sweets – or bags of flour – into the crowds. See page 102.

Ilha de Tavira beach.

BEST BEACHES

Ilha de Tavira. Accessible by ferry from Tavira, this beach-ringed island off the Algarve is unspoilt, beautiful, and rarely overcrowded. See page 189.

Praia Dona Ana. There are some wonderful beaches around Lagos in the Algarve, which has dramatically beautiful rock formations lining the coast, and this is one of the most attractive. See page 193.

Praia do Guincho. This long, white-sanded beach in Cascais is easy to access from the capital and a favourite of windsurfers. See page 169.

Praia da Rocha. Close to Portimao in the Algarve, dramatic cliffs provide a spectacular backdrop to this pretty beach. See page 192.

Praia de Mira. Backed by the forested nature reserve Mata Nacional das Dunas de Mira, this is a picturesque, white-sanded beach. See page 248.

Almograve. The Alentejan coast, edged by the Atlantic, is short but attractive, and Vila Nova da Milfontes is one of its loveliest spots. See page 216.

BEST MOUNTAIN PARKS

The Serra da Estréla. There's enough snow for gentle skiing in winter and wonderful herb-scented pastures for shepherds' flocks in spring and summer – providing Portugal's finest *serra* cheese. See page 253.

Parque Nacional Peneda-Gerês. This national park is wild, grand and great for hiking. It covers 720 sq km (278 sq miles) with peaks up to Nervosa at 1,545 metres (5,070ft). The park includes tiny granite villages like Soajo. See page 286.

The Serra da Arrábida. Cliffs plunging into blue sea give this *serra* an extra dimension. Its great natural beauty is enhanced in spring by a dazzling array of wild flowers. The Arrábida area is also known for a savoury cheese, Azeitão. See page 180.

Parque Nacional Peneda-Gerês.

THE BEST OF PORTUGAL: PLAN & BOOK YOUR TAILOR-MADE TRIP

Portugal is a country rich in natural diversity: golden beaches line the coast, while inland is lush with forests, vineyards and towering mountains. And although its cosmopolitan cities may be embracing the 21st century with gusto, they're also steeped in history, with medieval castles and grandiose cathedrals to be admired, as well as the famous blue-and-white *azulejo* tilework.

△ **Day 1, Porto**. Porto is one of the oldest cities in the country and among its most vibrant. Start at the Praça da Liberdade, a magnificent square, and head south, taking in the cathedral (Sé do Porto) where the cloisters are lined with *azulejo* – the classic blue-and-white Portuguese tiles. Spend your evening in Ribeira, an atmospheric district on the Douro river.

△ **Day 2, The Douro Valley**. The waterfront – Cais da Ribeira – is the ideal spot from which to embark on a leisurely boat trip to Pinhão, through the Douro Valley. The photogenic valley is the birthplace of Port and terraced vineyards stretch out on either side of the riverbank. The journey takes the best part of a day, so you'll breakfast and lunch aboard as you soak up the scenery.

▽ **Day 3, Pinhão and its surrounds**. Pinhão is a good starting point for a circular half-day tour of the region's traditional villages and wineries. Take the drive at a leisurely pace, passing through São João da Pesqueira, Linhares, Tua and Alijo, and admiring the Valeira dam along the way. Back at Pinhão, head for the station with its ornamental tiles depicting *vendimia* (wine harvest) and hop on a train back to Porto.

TAILOR-MADE TRIPS | 13

△ **Day 4, Queluz**. Rise early and head south from Porto to Sintra, a town of lush forests, fairytale castles and exotic gardens. En route, stop at Queluz where the Palacio is often compared to the Palace of Versailles with its lavishly decorated throne room, Hall of Mirrors and French-style gardens.

▽ **Day 5, The palaces of Sintra**. Swing by Sintra's Café Saudade and fortify yourself with its famous queijadas (small, fragrant cakes). A short stroll will bring you to the Palacio Nacional, with its two extraordinary chimney cones. Next, make your way to the Palacio Nacional da Pena; it's a steep climb but worth it for the forested grounds alone, with their hidden pathways, ornate fountains and sweeping views.

△ **Day 6, Lisbon**. Trains depart regularly from Sintra to Lisbon, with a journey time of under one hour. Head straight for the Baixa district, in the heart of the city, with its historic architecture; then jump forward a few centuries at MUDE, the excellent modern design museum. If you've time, hop in a cab to the UNESCO-listed 16th-century Mosteiro dos Jerónimos before dining in the buzzy Bairro Alto quarter.

▽ **Day 7, Alfama district**. Take the tram to the towering Castelo de Sao Jorge and walk the ramparts. Afterwards, feast on a traditional *bacalhau* (salted cod) stew at one of the restaurants that line the cobblestone streets of the ancient Moorish quarter Alfama, before making your way to the magnificent 12th-century cathedral, a must-see in the city.

You can plan and book this trip with Insight Guides, or we can help you create your own. Whether you're after adventure or a family-friendly holiday, we have a trip for you, with all the activities you enjoy doing and the sights you want to see. All our trips are devised by local experts who get the most out of the destination. Visit **www.insightguides.com/holidays** to chat with one of our local travel experts.

Azulejo tiles adorn the exterior of the Chapel of Souls, Porto.

View of Douro valley and its vineyards.

The white sands of Praia de Carvoeiro.

Narrow lane in Alte.

LAND BY THE SEA

Portugal's diverse landscapes – from world-class beaches to dramatic mountain peaks – set it apart from the rest of Europe.

Accordion player in traditional dress, Viana do Castelo.

Portugal is a land on the edge, "where land ends and sea begins", as the 16th-century epic poet Luís Vaz de Camões put it.

It is a small country, encompassing an area of 92,100 sq km (33,550 sq miles) – a bit bigger than Austria – but has a stunning diversity of lovely landscapes: long white beaches and pretty coves; ranges of rolling hills and mountains, the central Serra da Estrela (Mountains of the Stars) being the highest; numerous rivers, including the Tagus and the Douro; and, in the southern central area, Alentejo's broad plain, which is patched with cork oaks and olive plantations.

The Algarve offers 160km (100 miles) of sweeping coastline, and for many this is the quintessential Portuguese holiday destination. Azure seas, rocky inlets and golden sands have long drawn visitors here, who are well catered for with holiday apartments, luxury golf courses and a variety of activities.

For the beach-weary, Lisbon – Portugal's sophisticated capital city – has fast become one of Europe's top city destinations. With a cosmopolitan vibe and hip style sitting alongside quaint winding alleys, striking Moorish architecture and traditional fado music, Lisbon has buckets of character and charm. Here, like in so many other areas of Portugal, you can feel the tension between old and new. Historic customs, vibrant festivals, and – in more remote regions – traditional methods of baking, spinning and farming are still very much alive.

Wine cellar in Porto.

Portugal is relatively easy to travel around and, given its size, you won't necessarily have to sacrifice one stop off to make room for another. A single trip can include a visit to some of Portugal's stunning hilltop castles, dramatic mountain valleys and vast agricultural plains.

Crowning Portugal's natural beauty for much of the year are blue skies and glowing sunshine: an agreeable climate of hot summers and chilly but never freezing winters. It's a temperate country, in mood as in weather. The characteristics of its people (numbering about 10.3 million) tend towards gentleness, courteousness, hospitality and tolerance – with a pronounced and stubborn streak of fatalism.

Portugal offers everything a visitor could want, from the tireless energy of the clubs and bars of Lisbon to sleepy rural villages where time seems to have stood still.

Cork art at a market in the Algarve.

THE PORTUGUESE

While a passion for coffee and cakes is a national characteristic to which visitors can instantly relate, other traits are a little more complex.

Traditionally characterised as easy-going, smiling and good-natured but imbued with an inner *saudade*, a tricky-to-define quality that equates to nostalgia or melancholy, the Portuguese (as a whole) tend to come across as a gentle, cordial people. They certainly offer a relaxed welcome to foreign visitors, whether they are seeking sunny beaches, medieval architecture, the beauties of the countryside, or the local food and wines. In addition, generations of international exploration, connections with former colonies, and immigration from abroad have made this a much more cosmopolitan country than you might expect – in Lisbon and the Algarve, at least.

REGIONAL CHARACTERISTICS

The Portuguese population is one of the most homogeneous in Europe; however, the country displays distinct variations from region to region, and in particular between north and south. There are historically some physical differences in the people: in the north, traditional Iberian characteristics like dark hair and eyes have been imbued with Celtic blood, while in the south, Jewish, Moorish and African ancestries are prominent. The more sparsely populated north is generally more conservative, both politically and culturally, and is the bastion of Portuguese Catholicism. The south has a tradition of liberalism and adaptation. The two different temperaments – the warm Mediterranean and cool Atlantic – wash over each other. The people are as varied as their land. There is a saying that "Coimbra studies while Braga prays, Porto works while Lisbon plays".

INTERNAL DIFFERENCES

There are other internal differences, too. Portugal had the fastest expanding economy in the

Detail from traditional folk costume for women.

> Of its 10.4 million-strong population, around two-thirds of the Portuguese live in the coastal areas, with the north far less populated.

European Union 10 years after joining, but in the early 2000s it was one of the least healthy economies in the EU. However, unpopular austerity measures introduced by the government helped to curb Portugal's deficit, bring unemployment down and restore a steady GDP growth (1.7 percent in 2024). Notwithstanding, like other countries in Europe, Portugal is attempting a tricky balancing act between decreasing the budget deficit, avoiding discontent, and promoting growth. The robust state of the Portuguese economy is cause for optimism: new builds continue to go up and global technologies continue to expand Portugal's horizons.

Seemingly removed from the mercurial economic tides are the bucolic backways of Trás-os-Montes and the Beiras, among the windmills, the cobbled roads, and horse-drawn farmers' carts. These rural communities remain almost defiantly untouched, with the men in their flat caps chatting in the town square. Venturing here you may well feel that you have stepped back in time. Rural people generally distrust Lisbon and all that it stands for: social turmoil, taxes, bureaucracy, centralised education. They would rather keep their distance. Able to sustain themselves by their harvests, they have little interest in inflation or trade deficits. They are self-reliant. Religious festivals are taken very seriously and can last for several days, especially in the Minho province and the Azores Islands, with celebrations including solemn processions, traditional dances and fireworks.

This was once an extremely patriarchal soci-

Fado in Tasca do Chico, Bairro Alto, Lisbon.

⊙ COMING HOME

Traditionally Portugal was a country of emigration, where the very young and the old were left behind while wage-earners went abroad to work and send money home. However, in the 1990s, as Portugal boomed and EU capital brought new life to the country, many professional workers – doctors, lawyers and so on – arrived from Brazil and elsewhere, bringing with them their different tastes and lifestyles. Portugal also received an influx of migrant workers from Eastern Europe in an interesting reversal of earlier times. But with the economic crisis the situation has reversed once again, with 31,000 people leaving in 2023: the majority being young graduates.

ety – women only gained the vote in 1975 – and there has been great progress in terms of the position of women. Many urban women hold important jobs, and the lifestyle of younger generations in the cities is usually similar to that of their counterparts in other European countries. But despite legal equality, attitudes are slow to change, particularly in rural areas.

In many ways, the rhythm of Portuguese life is slow and habits cautious. This is less to do with Latin temperament or the climate than with the effects of the Salazar era and its aftermath; many people returning from the colonies had a deeply traumatic time in the clashes between new left and old right.

However, there's a more forward-looking feel to

Portugal's cities. Cutting-edge architecture now co-exists with the gorgeous old buildings of Lisbon and Porto, and the cities are also significantly multicultural. Portugal has long been notable for emigration, with Portuguese people living all over the world, in South America, Africa, India and China. More than four million Portuguese citizens still live abroad, most of whom emigrated in the early and mid-20th century, settling mainly in France, Germany, Switzerland, Luxembourg (curiously, 16 percent of the population there are of Portuguese descent), the United States, Canada, Brazil, and Venezuela. The majority of the Portuguese population in the United States is from the Azores islands, as are many of the Portuguese who settled in Canada.

In the 1970s the tide turned, and there was an influx of people from the former Portuguese colonies, especially Brazil, Angola and Cape Verde, bringing their influence to bear particularly in Lisbon and Algarve. Other communities include Goans from India and Chinese from Macau. The Afro-Portuguese music clubs in Lisbon are some of the capital's funkiest venues; this is one of the best places in Europe to hear afrobeats, afrohouse and amapiano. Mariza, the current queen of fado, was born in Mozambique, and one of her most emotional songs is *O Gente da Minha Terra* (Oh People of my Country) – which expresses a very Portuguese sentiment in a very bittersweet, Portuguese way: the love of this staunchly patriotic land, a place of poets and sailors.

With the economic crisis and biting austerity of the early 21st century, once again the flow turned outwards. Young Portuguese are heading abroad – in many cases reversing the trend and making their way to Portugal's former colonies in Angola and Brazil – in search of opportunities and a brighter future. The shrinking population has led to calls from the government welcoming foreign migrants, which could see the Portuguese population become more diverse.

WORK

In keeping with the slowdown of the global economy and conditions elsewhere in the world, unemployment in Portugal rose steadily in the early 21st century, peaking at 18 percent in 2013. It has decreased dramatically since then, sitting at 6.5 percent in 2023. The figure is at its highest among the under-24 age group. As people move to find work in the cities, and the birth rate remains low, villages are rapidly depopulating – some appear to be inhabited only by elderly widows. The urban population accounts for more than 65 percent of the national total, which is a considerable shift.

Portuguese farmer tilling his field.

In industry and commerce there are a few conglomerates, but the large majority of companies are small- and medium-sized businesses employing, for the most part, fewer than 10 people. Textiles and shoes are the top manufactured products and are excellent value for tourists.

With a long coastline, Portugal's fishing industry remains steady but it is not a high-paying trade. Agriculture has never been more than basically productive, despite the country's rustic image. Portugal's olive oil production, for example, just meets its own needs. About 5 percent of

Shopping for hats.

the workforce is in agriculture, which produces less than 2 percent of the GDP. Despite appalling annual fires, forestry is profitable, with cork still a major harvest. Port wine from the Douro Valley is among Portugal's most famous products, but table wines from many newly designated areas are reaching new peaks of quality. Tourism contributes a high proportion of foreign earnings and around two-thirds of the workforce is in the service sector.

FAMILY TIES

The family unit is a bedrock of Portuguese society, but this is now also beginning to change, with a decline in the birth rate (1.38 is now the national average) resulting in an ageing population.

However, the Portuguese adore babies and small children, as you will notice while out and in restaurants.

Portugal is a predominantly Roman Catholic country (around 80 percent), with a few Protestant communities, and a few Jewish and Muslim ones as well. One interesting group is the so-called *Marranos*, Jews who converted during the 16th- and 17th-century persecutions, and who retain some Jewish rituals, sometimes in combination with a nominal Catholicism. Catholicism in Portugal tends towards the colourful and mystical, bound up with local superstitions, ancient traditions and pre-Christian practices. Popular beliefs involve the phases of the moon and the threat of the evil eye. It is the tradition that older rural women dress in black after the death of their husbands for about seven years, and many wear it for the rest of their lives.

A CHANGING SOCIETY

As you travel around Portugal, it becomes increasingly obvious that this is a country that hangs in the balance between the old ways and the new. You can go from the graceful formality and strict religious conformity of a traditional village, where life seems to have remained unchanged for hundreds of years, to a sleek modernist art gallery or a nightclub that flings its doors open at 5am so that punters can dance their way through to the following afternoon. You can wander from an ironic, arty bar in Lisbon's Bairro Alto to a nearby hole-in-the-wall drinking den selling cherry brandy to gnarled old-timers.

This is a nation that is fiercely proud of its identity and traditions, but is not averse to change. Considering that Portugal was a country living under a dictatorship until 1973, it is extraordinary to think that it is one of the few places worldwide where the policy on illegal drugs is aimed at rehabilitation rather than retribution – drugs were decriminalised here in 2001, and the problem is regarded as a public health issue (those found in possession of less than 10 days' supply are offered treatment rather than incarcerated).

These elements – of worldliness versus the parochial, of exploration overseas versus the timelessness of life in a tiny whitewashed village – point to some of the contradictions that will remain part of the beguiling complexity of this mesmerising country.

Celebrating the Festa de São João.

The evolution of Portugal's flag.

1147

1227

1497

1762

1385

1834

DECISIVE DATES

EARLY DAYS

9th–6th centuries BC
Phoenician and Greek traders establish settlements.

5th century BC
Carthaginians in control of the Iberian peninsula.

130 BC
Roman conquest of Lusitania, modern-day Portugal.

4th century AD
Christianity spreads.

AD 419
The Germanic Suevi arrive; vanquished by the Visigoths over the next 50 years.

711
African Moors occupy Iberia.

718
Victory by the Christians over the Moors at Covadonga starts the reconquest.

11th–12th centuries
A complex round of civil wars between Henri of Burgundy and his cousin Raymond.

RECONQUEST AND NATIONHOOD

1143
Afonso Henriques is declared first king of Portugal, but is not recognised by Pope Lucius II.

1147
Henriques captures Lisbon.

1179
Afonso Henriques is finally recognised by Pope Alexander III as king.

A statue of the D. Fernando, the 2nd Duke of Braganca at Braganca.

1249
Moors expelled from Algarve.

1260
Afonso III transfers capital from Coimbra to Lisbon.

1279–1325
Reign of King Dinis.

1297
Treaty of Alcañices establishes Portugal's borders.

1348
Plague ravages Lisbon.

1373
First Anglo-Portuguese Alliance signed.

1385
Defeat of Castilians. João I becomes king, commencing the House of Avis.

THE AGE OF DISCOVERIES

1415
Ceuta, North Africa, is taken by Portuguese force. Madeira encountered.

1427
Azores encountered.

1434
Gil Eanes explores parts of West Africa.

1481
João II ascends the throne.

1487
Bartolomeu Dias rounds Cape of Good Hope.

1492
Around 60,000 Jews expelled from Spain flee to Portugal.

1494
Treaty of Tordesillas: Portugal and Spain divide up the New World.

1497–98
Explorer Vasco da Gama opens a sea route to India.

1500
Pedro Alvares Cabral encounters Brazil.

1510
Conquest of Goa.

1519–22
Ferdinand Magellan circumnavigates the globe.

1536
Holy Inquisition is introduced.

1557
Trading post opens in Macau.

1580
Portugal falls under Spanish rule.

1640
Spanish overthrown; Duke of Bragança becomes João IV.

CHRONOLOGY

1668
Treaty of Lisbon; Spain recognises Portugal's independence. Early

1700s
Gold is discovered in Brazil.

1755
The Great Earthquake devastates Lisbon.

1777
Maria I becomes queen.

1807
France invades; royal family leaves for Brazil.

1808
The Peninsular War.

1820
Liberal revolution.

1822
New liberal constitution ends the Inquisition. Brazil proclaims independence.

1829–34
Miguelist Wars between factions led by brothers Miguel and Pedro. The latter wins and becomes Pedro IV in 1834.

1834–1908
Rise of political parties, Septembrists (Liberals) and Chartists (Conservatives).

1908
King Carlos and Crown Prince are shot dead in Lisbon. Manuel II ascends the throne.

1910
Portugal becomes a republic; Manuel II exiled.

1910–26
Political turmoil, military coups and assassinations.

SALAZAR AND AFTER

1926
Military coup overthrows democratic government and brings General Carmona to power.

1932
Salazar becomes PM and rules as dictator until 1968.

1939–1945
World War II: Portugal is neutral.

1955
Portugal allowed to join the UN.

1961
Angolan uprising brutally crushed. Goa lost to Indian control.

1970
Death of Salazar. Marcelo Caetano is now prime minister.

1974
Young Captains' Revolution restores democracy. Armed Forces Movement governs until 1976. African colonies made independent.

1976
Socialist Mario Soares becomes prime minister.

1979
Coalition of the right in power.

1986
Portugal joins the European Economic Community (EEC).

1999
Macau reverts to Chinese control.

2005
Socialists sweep to victory in general elections. Jose Sócrates sworn in as PM.

Portugal's president, Marcelo Rebelo de Sousa, in 2020.

2013
Portugal's highest court strikes down some of the 2013 budget's austerity measures. The economy slowly picks up.

2016
Social Democrat Marcelo Rebelo de Sousa becomes the new president. Portuguese football squad wins Euro 2016 tournament. Forest fires hit Algarve region and Madeira.

2020
The COVID-19 pandemic sweeps the nation; a day of national mourning in November commemorates those who died from the virus.

2023
The Portuguese government bans new Airbnb licenses due to a boom in tourism alongside housing shortages and increasing rents. Prime Minister António Costa resigns following an investigation into alleged corruption by members of his government.

2024
The Democratic Alliance wins a majority in the Portuguese legislative election.

A dolmen (burial chamber) in the Alentejo flatlands.

ANCIENT LUSITANIA

For centuries, successive waves of invaders swept over the peninsula. The Moors held on longest, even after Afonso Henriques became Portugal's first king.

Portugal, with borders already established by the 13th century, is one of the oldest nations in Europe. Despite its small size, its impact on global history has been powerful and its influences visible in many places across the world. Over the centuries it has colonised and lost an empire, relinquished and regained its cherished autonomy and, since the 1974 revolution that ended decades of dictatorship, formed new ties with some of its former colonies.

A rich prehistoric culture has left its traces throughout Portugal. There is evidence of the earliest stages of human evolution among a large number of megalithic sites. The variety and quantity of these finds have led many scholars to a theory that cultural diffusion came primarily from overseas. Opponents of this notion claim that this is unlikely, as most of the megalithic sites are far from the coastline. They think the population grew via natural land routes of settlement which, unsurprisingly, correspond to the paths invaders have taken throughout Portugal's history: across the Rio Minho from the north and over the Alentejo flatlands from the south.

In any case, by the 2nd millennium BC, social organisation consisted of scattered *castros* – garrisoned hilltop villages that suggest warfare between tribes. The people subsisted on goat-herding and primitive agriculture, and clad themselves in woollen cloaks.

In the south, tribes came under the influence of Phoenician trade settlements in the 9th century BC, and Greek ones in the 6th century BC, both on the coast and inland, where metals were mined. Only at this late point is there evidence of a significant fishing economy among the indigenous people. Perhaps before then the

The ancient standing stones at Almendres, Évora, is the largest existing group of structured menhirs in the Iberian Peninsula.

> Evidence of 2nd millennium BC Portuguese society can be seen in the form of few constructions that still stand, for example at the Citânia de Briteiros near Guimarães.

rough-hewn and storm-beaten Atlantic coast was too intimidating for their small boats. During the 5th century BC, the Carthaginians wrested control of the Iberian peninsula from these earlier traders, but lost it to the Roman Empire in the Second Punic War.

WARS OF CONQUESTS

The Romans called the peninsula Hispania Ulterior. Here, as elsewhere in the empire, they combined their economic exploitation with cultural upheaval. They were not traders, after all, but conquerors, who set about the business of founding cities, building roads and reorganising territories. They also implemented governmental and judicial systems.

The locals resisted. The largest and most intransigent group were the Lusitani, who lived north of the Rio Tejo (Tagus), and after whom the region was given its name, Lusitania. Bitter guerrilla fighting was intermittent for two centuries. The most renowned rebel was a shepherd named Viriathus, who led uprisings until he was assassinated in 139 BC by three treacherous comrades who had been bribed by the Romans. It was during these wars of conquest that Roman troops are said to have refused to cross the Rio Lima, believing it to be the *Lethe*, the mythical River of Forgetfulness. Their commander, the story goes, had to cross the river alone, then call each soldier by name to prove that the dip had not affected his memory. The death of Viriathus took the heart out of the revolt, although the Lusitanian uprisings were not finally quelled until 72 BC.

In 61 BC, Julius Caesar governed the province from Olisipo (as Lisbon was then called). Cities were established and colonised at Évora, Beja, Santarém and elsewhere. Roads linked the north and south, and Lisbon became an important administrative centre, at the hub of the Romans' local road network linking the major population centres. These centres and routes have waned in importance, but many – most notably the capital, Lisbon – are still geographic focal points.

Before their empire eventually fell, the Romans had infused the area with their language, legal system, currency, agriculture and, eventually, with Christianity. The organisation of *latifundios* – great, landed estates – was particularly significant as it brought large-scale farming to the area for the first time.

With the conversion of the late Roman emperors (Constantine, who issued an Edict of Tolerance in AD 331, was the first Christian emperor), the tenets and organisation of Christianity spread throughout the fading empire. Bishoprics were established in a number of cities, Braga and Évora among them. As the church expanded, it usurped the administrative power that had been developed by the empire at the height of its strength.

Heretical Christian doctrines held sway in Portugal during the 3rd and 4th centuries. In the early

A sculpture found in Lisbon's Roman theatre.

ANCIENT LUSITANIA

5th century various groups of barbarians occupied the land. The Alani and Vandals each settled for a short time, but by 419 the Suevi were in sole, if not steady, possession of Galicia, and from there they conquered Lusitania and most of the Iberian peninsula. The Suevi apparently assimilated easily with the existing Hispano-Roman population, but the tide turned with the fall of Rome and the arrival of the Visigoths.

For the next half century, military conquest inevitably meant religious conversion. In 448, Rechiarius, the king of a diminished Suevi empire, converted to Catholicism, perhaps hoping to elicit aid from Rome in battling against the Visigoths, who were nominally Christian but clung to vestiges of heretical beliefs. When Rechiarius was killed in 457, the Suevi kingdom survived, led by his son, Masdra. The latter's son, Remismund, succeeded him and in 465 renounced Christianity, probably hoping to appease the Visigoths. But by 550, the growing power of the Catholic Church had produced a new round of conversions, led by St Martin of Dume. The remnants of the Suevi were politically extinguished in 585.

Roman temple in Evora.

INVADERS FROM THE SOUTH

Visigoth rule, under an elective monarchy, was not seriously challenged until the Moors – Muslims from North Africa – arrived on the south coast in 711 and began their expansion northwards. The Moors were following the instructions of their leader, the Prophet Mohammed (who died in 632), to wage a holy war (*jihad*) against non-believers. However, like the Christian Crusades that followed (see page 36), their advances were increasingly concerned with empire building.

The Visigoths were defeated at the Battle of Jerez, and Lisbon soon fell into Muslim hands. Southern Portugal became part of Muslim Spain, loosely organised under the Córdoba caliph – caliphs were successors of the Prophet, regional rulers created under the Umayyad dynasty (650–749).

To the Moors, this land was known as Al-Gharb (the West), from which was derived the modern name Algarve. The Moors soon ruled all of Portugal, and Christianity was forced north of the Minho, where it lay gathering strength for the *reconquest* – the *Reconquista*.

A NATION IN PROSPECT

Stirrings of the *Reconquista* are believed to have started as early as 718 at Covadonga in Asturias, where the Christians defeated a small force of Moors. Galicia became a battleground over the next century and a half. The kings of Asturias-León made ever-increasing excursions into Galicia and beyond. Slowly, towns fell before the Christian armies: Porto in 868, Coimbra in 878, and by 955 the King of León, Ordona III, had engineered a raid on Lisbon. Most of the victories below the Douro, however, were transient ones, amounting to nothing more than successful raids, as the territory was seldom held for more than a season or two. Under the Emir of Córdoba, Muslims in Portugal lived in relative peace, introducing irrigation systems and water mills as well as wheat, rice, oranges and saffron. Shipbuilding was active, copper and silver mines were exploited, Roman roads expanded and towns were planned. There was religious tolerance and the arts flourished. Muslim stuccowork and glazed tiles, called *azulejos*, were a lasting contribution to the nation's architectural style.

Although the local culture was strong, the authority of Córdoba began to wear thin and small kingdoms called *taifas* gained local control. Decentralisation led to internal dissent, partly caused by the rise of the Sufi religious

HISTORY & FEATURES

> The most famous Sufi poet was Omar Khayyám (1048–1120), whose Rubaiyat, in which women and wine are given mystical significance, was translated into English by the Victorian poet Edward Fitzgerald.

sect. Sufism was considered a subversive and heretical kind of mysticism, but it gained popularity in reaction to the rationalism of conventional Islamic beliefs. These internal divisions allowed Christian forces to push the frontier lines down from the north, but they also permitted radical Muslim military groups such as the Almoravids and the Almohads to rise rapidly to power.

The Almoravids, who had built an empire in Africa, spread northwards. After helping the Islamic rulers in the peninsula to force the Christians back, they unified the *taifas* under their own rule. By 1095 they had succeeded in installing an austere military system and harsh government. They were soon followed by the still more fanatical Almohads and the simmering *Reconquista* took on the aspect of a Holy War for both Christians and Muslims.

Afonso Henriques, first king of Portugal.

THE SPLIT WITH SPAIN

Portugal's separateness from Spain, with which it shares a border, has been attributed to various causes, from the original boundaries between indigenous tribes to the land held by the Suevi against the Visigothic advances. However, it was during the Christian reconquest of Iberia that Portugal first truly asserted its independent stance and its leaders gained their sense of national destiny.

Late in the 9th century, the area between the Lima and Douro rivers, a territory which became known as Portucale, was divided under unstable feudal states, and came under the control of the Kingdom of León.

Fernando I of León was the great consolidating force in northern Spain during the 11th century. As part of his policy of centralising authority, he tried to diminish Portugal's power by dismantling it and dividing it into different provinces under separate governors. When Fernando's successor Alfonso VI took over the kingdoms of León, Castile, Galicia and Portugal, he declared himself "emperor", putting himself above kings. It may have been the lure of the title "king", which the emperor had unwittingly made available, that inspired Afonso Henriques, in the 12th century, to battle, deal and connive for the autonomy of his particular *terra*, Portugal.

FEUDING COUSINS

Afonso Henriques was the son of Henri of Burgundy and his wife Teresa. Henri was among a number of French knights who had arrived

⚔ MILITARY ORDERS

The crusades produced an unusual kind of soldier – that is, those belonging to the military orders created by St Bernard of Clairvaux in 1128. The Knights Templar was the first such order; they were followed by the Knights of St John (the Hospitallers), established in Rhodes, then by the Teutonic Order and the Spanish Knights of Calatrava. Originally, their role was to fight for the true faith while obeying monastic rules of poverty, chastity and obedience. Soon, however, the spoils of war became more important than the spread of Christianity. The orders were rewarded with land grants and many soldiers grew wealthy and powerful – the Templars, in fact, became prestigious bankers.

in the late 11th century to fight the infidels. They were mostly second and third sons, who, under the prevailing system of male primogeniture – which meant that the eldest son inherited property and titles – were left with no real inheritance. If they wanted land and riches, they usually had to travel abroad to gain those things themselves.

Henri's cousin Raymond, who, like Henri, was a fourth son, also came south. After proving his heroism in battle, Raymond married Alfonso VI's eldest daughter Urraca, and was granted the territories of Galicia and Coimbra. When Henri married Teresa, who was Alfonso's favourite (although illegitimate) daughter, he was given the territory of Portugal. With the death of Raymond and Alfonso VI, Urraca inherited that crown, but her second marriage, to Alfonso I of Aragon, also set in motion a complex round of civil wars.

During this period, Henri of Burgundy made significant strides towards gaining autonomy for the state of Portugal. The most important of these was the support he offered to the archbishops of Braga in a dispute with those of Toledo, the principal seat of Spain.

In 1126 Urraca died and her son, Alfonso Raimundez, became Emperor Alfonso VII. When Henri died, his widow, Teresa, ruled Portugal as regent for her son, Afonso Henriques. Without wasting much time in mourning, she took a Galician count, Fernão Peres, as a lover, displeasing some of the nobility as well as her son. Continuing her husband's policies, Teresa schemed successfully to maintain Portugal's independence, but in 1127 she submitted to Alfonso VII's dominion after her army's defeat.

A year later 18-year-old Afonso Henriques led a rebellion against his mother, ending her rule at the battle of São Mamede, near their castle in Guimarães.

An 18th-century engraving showing Afonso rallying his troops at the conquest of Lisbon in 1147.

A KING IS CROWNED

Over the next decade, Afonso Henriques vied with his emperor cousin for ultimate control of Portugal. After a brilliant military victory over the Moors in the Battle of Ourique in 1139, he began to refer to himself as king. In 1143, the Treaty of Zamora was signed between the two cousins, wherein Alfonso VII gave Afonso Henriques the title of King of Portugal in exchange for feudal ties of military aid and loyalty.

Afonso Henriques sought to fix the title more firmly by seeking recognition from Rome. Pope Lucius II refused, keeping to a policy of supporting Iberian union in the hope of stemming the tide of Islam. It was only in 1179 that Pope Alexander III, in exchange for a yearly tribute and

HISTORY & FEATURES

> One result of the crusades – which began in 1096 and lasted for more than 150 years – was the founding of powerful military-religious organisations such as the Knights Templar and the Hospitallers (see page 36).

various other privileges, finally granted recognition of the Portuguese kingdom. By that late date, papal acceptance served only to formalise an entity that was not only well established but growing. Afonso Henriques had enlisted the aid of crusaders and beaten back the Moors, adding his conquests to the emerging nation. Santarém and Lisbon were both taken in 1147; the first by surprise attack, the second in a siege that was supported by French, English, Flemish and German crusaders who were passing through Portugal on their way to the Holy Land, to fight what we now know as the Second Crusade.

The inestimable assistance of these 164 shiploads of men was extremely fortuitous; it very nearly fell through when Afonso Henriques pronounced that he expected them to fight only for Christianity and not for earthly rewards. This was not the way the crusaders believed holy wars should be fought. The English and Germans walked out, and the king quickly compromised, offering loot and land in exchange for military service.

Saint Catherine commemorated by azulejos.

THE WESTERN CRUSADE

The Bishop of Braga also offered aid in recruiting foreign crusaders, providing theological assurance that their enemies in the south would be heathens, and therefore no different from those they would be fighting in the Holy Land – convincing crusaders that one batch of infidels was as good as another was crucial to the *Reconquista*.

Afonso Henriques's confessor, however, questioned the diversion of troops from the crusade, and the story is told that on the way to Santarém – with crusaders in tow – the king, believing his confessor to be right, was besieged by guilt. He was also, understandably, anxious because of the Moorish stronghold's reputation for impregnability. To soothe his torment, he vowed that he would build an abbey at Alcobaça (some 90km/55 miles southwest of Coimbra) in honour of the Virgin if the attack was successful. The battle was won, and Afonso Henriques laid the foundation stone of the promised building the following year. The imposing abbey still stands (see page 228).

In 1170, Afonso Henriques fought his last battle, at Badajoz. The powerful Almohads had enlisted the aid of Fernando II of León, who felt that the Portuguese were recapturing not only the Moorish-held land, but territory that was by right a part of León.

The most renowned of Afonso Henriques' military cohorts was Geraldo Geraldes, a local adventurer dubbed O Sem Pavor (The Fearless) for his brilliant raids into Muslim territory. This popular hero had won a string of epic victories, but at Badajoz the combination of Moorish and Leonese forces was too much for both Geraldes and his king. The ageing Afonso Henriques broke his leg and was captured. His release came only after he had surrendered hard-won castles and territories to enemy parties. His retreat allowed the Moors to entrench their forces along the battle zone.

The founding king of Portugal's days of victory were over, with the *Reconquista* still a century away. Yet, with Henriques' monarchy, a country was born. Whether it was through an act of political will or not, the independence and individuality of the Portuguese nation was forever determined.

Azulejos depicting victory in the Battle of Ourique (1139).

OURIQUE

King Dinis, depicted in a 17th-century screen.

A NATION IS BORN

With the final expulsion of the Moors, Portugal steadily established a kingdom under the House of Burgundy.

For a century after the death of Afonso Henriques in 1185, the first order of business was the slow riddance of the remaining, and still feisty, Moors. The *Reconquista*, now virtually sanctioned by the Church with various papal bulls and indulgences as a "western crusade", was very much under way.

The Knights Templar had arrived in Portugal when they stopped on their way to Palestine in 1128. They were soon followed by other military-religious orders – the Hospitallers and the Knights of Calatrava and Santiago – who all clung to religion as a justification for their war-mongering and for their massive accumulation of land and loot.

However, the western crusade remained controversial. In Palestine the dividing line between Christians and infidels was clearly drawn, but southern Iberia had intermingled Muslim, Christian and Jewish people in economic, cultural and political spheres. In 1197, papal indulgences were even promised in a war against Alfonso IX of León, a Christian, though at that time an ally of the Muslims.

The war proceeded steadily, if slowly. The first kings of the Burgundian line after Afonso Henriques continued to press the borders southwards. Under Sancho II, the eastern Algarve and Alentejo were incorporated in the burgeoning nation. By 1249, during the reign of Afonso III, the western Algarve and Faro had fallen. By 1260 Afonso had moved the capital south from Coimbra to Lisbon. These boundaries – much like today's – were finally recognised by Castile in the Treaty of Alcañices in 1297.

SOCIAL TRANSFORMATION

The *Reconquista* brought Portugal fundamental social transformation. The lands of the south,

The 13th-century cross of Sancho I.

having been reclaimed, now had to be populated. In order to do this, the Burgundian kings needed to balance their centralised, essentially military power with popular and financial support. The need for such support forced successive kings to consult the *cortes*, local assemblies of nobles, clergy and, later, mercantile classes. At the *cortes* of Leiria (1254), Afonso III conceded the right of municipal representation in taxation and other economic issues. For the most part, the *cortes* were gathered whenever the king needed to raise money. When later monarchs used trade and their own military orders to reap independent profits, the *cortes* fell into disuse.

Another result of the *Reconquista*, with the expansion of properties and the need for labourers, was an increase in social mobility among the lower classes. Distinctions fell away among various levels of serfs as farm workers became a scarcer and more valuable commodity. Another effect was the early divergence of the northern and southern cultures. The south was a culture of tolerance, marked by refinement and urbanity, while northern culture retained a certain arrogance, the attitude of invaders. Differences between the two, many argue, remain today.

The Church rode the *Reconquista* to riches. The various military-monastic orders were granted vast areas of land in return for military assistance. Furthermore, Church and clergy were free from taxation, and were granted the right to collect tithes from the population. Their power was such that it soon threatened the monarchy. Afonso II was the first ruler to defy the Church by attempting to curb its acquisition of property. His efforts generally failed, as did those of his successor, Sancho II, who was finally excommunicated and dethroned in 1245 for his insistence on royal prerogatives.

THE POET KING

It was the reign of Dinis, known both as "the farmer king" and "the poet king", that truly cemented Portuguese independence and the power of the monarchy. After briefly joining Aragon in a war against Castile, Dinis ushered in a long period of peace and progress. He encouraged learning and literature, establishing the first university in 1288, initially in Lisbon, then transferred to Coimbra. Portuguese, having distinguished itself from its Latin roots and from Castilian (which became Spanish), was established as the language of the troubadour culture, and the official language of law and state.

The troubadour culture – poetry and music spread by peripatetic minstrels – was greatly influential. Drawing on French tradition and Moorish influences, Portuguese troubadours created a native literature. These song-poems of love and satire were often written by nobles, among them, of course, Dinis himself. Other forms of literary expression lagged far behind.

Dinis's rule also brought political progress. Landmark agreements were made to seal peace with Castile (the Treaty of Alcañices, 1297) and the clergy (the Concordat of 1289). The latter agreement was a major victory for royal jurisdiction in matters of property. Dinis also fortified the frontier, building some 50 castles.

ECONOMIC ADVANCES

By now a monetary economy was well established, internally as well as for international trade. Agricultural production was more and more geared towards markets, although self-sufficient farming did not disappear. Dinis encouraged the expansion of the economic system with large fairs – trading centres that encouraged internal trade. He chartered 48 such fairs, more than all the other Portuguese kings combined. This concentration of trade also, not coincidentally, allowed for more systematic taxation.

The only section of the economy to lag behind was industrial production. Dinis, and later kings, were counter-productive in resisting the idea of corporations. Craftsmen tended to work on their own, and thus confined themselves to

Inside Tomar's Convento do Cristo.

> In his role of "farmer king" Dinis reformed the agricultural system and initiated programmes that encouraged the export of olive oil, grain, wine and other foodstuffs.

A NATION IS BORN

local markets and limited quantities, although some goldsmithing, shipbuilding, and pottery was done in commercial quantities. Perhaps the most significant of Dinis's accomplishments was the disbanding of the Knights Templar in 1312. The order was under fire throughout Europe, and its demise was imminent. Dinis's triumph was to retain its wealth within the country and prevent the Church from appropriating it. In 1317 he founded the Order of Our Lord Jesus Christ, which placed the former possessions of the Knights Templar under royal control.

PLAGUES AND CRISES

Afonso IV succeeded Dinis. His administration was less secure and hostilities with Castile waxed and waned. More significantly, his reign was burdened with the Black Death. The first bout devastated the country, particularly the urban centres, in 1348–9. Throughout the next century the pestilence returned again and again, causing depopulation and despondency. Concurrently, various demographic and economic crises were undermining the nation. The attraction of urban centres left the interior underpopulated, causing inflation in

The tomb of Pedro I in the monastery at Alcobaça.

⊙ THE STORY OF PEDRO AND INÊS

Betrothed to Constanza, a Spanish princess, Pedro, son of Afonso IV, fell in love with her lady-in-waiting, Inês de Castro, a member of a powerful Castilian family. She was banished in 1340, but returned upon the death of the princess in 1345. The threat of a Castilian heir was intolerable to Afonso, so, under pressure from three of his noblemen, he agreed to her assassination, then immediately withdrew consent. In 1355, taking matters into their own hands, the nobles murdered Inês in the grounds of what is now Quinta da Lágrimas (House of Tears) in Coimbra (see page 240). Pedro was inconsolable. Two years later, when he assumed the throne on his father's death, he tracked down his lover's assassins, caught two of them, and had their hearts torn out. He then ordered the exhumation of Inês, whose body was dressed in royal robes and placed next to him on the throne. Each member of the court was forced to pay homage by kissing her decomposed hand. She was finally entombed in Alcobaça Monastery along with Pedro, who insisted their tombs were placed foot to foot so that, on the Day of Judgement, the first thing they would see would be each other. Both tombs carry the same inscription *Até o Fim do Mundo* – "Until the End of the World".

This dramatic and touching story of love and revenge has been an inspiration to generations of Portuguese writers and poets.

food prices. Successive monarchs tried to regulate population movements but were ineffectual. The deadening influence of economic stagnation dragged on until the coming of the maritime empire.

The reign of Pedro I was marked by peaceful coexistence with Castile. Social and political growth flourished as the country recovered from the convulsions of the Black Death. However, the increasing power of the nobles, the clergy and the emergent bourgeoisie, all represented in the *cortes,* would later break loose in active social discontent during the reign of his son, Fernando I. It was this social unrest, coupled with Portuguese commitment to total independence from Castile, that would finally bring down the House of Burgundy.

Fernando tried to unite Portugal and Castile, engaging the country in a series of unpopular and unsuccessful wars. France and England joined the turmoil, using the Iberian peninsula as a theatre for the Hundred Years' War. In 1373, Fernando signed an Anglo-Portuguese alliance with John of Gaunt, who had married a Spanish princess (see page 46). The same year, Enrique II of Castile attacked Lisbon, burning and pillaging the city. To add to the confusion, the "Great Schism" divided the Catholic Church under opposing popes from 1378, and Fernando changed loyalties frequently. Wars ravaged the country, leaving the populace tired and angry.

Fernando further alienated his subjects with his unpopular marriage to Leonor Teles, who was perceived to represent the landed gentry. Riots broke out at the wedding and again in 1383 when Fernando died, leaving his widow (aided by her lover, the Galician count João Fernandez Andeiro) to rule as queen mother.

Andeiro was assassinated within weeks by João, illegitimate son of Pedro I. In the ensuing civil war, Leonor had the support of most of the nobles and clergy, while João relied upon that of the middle class. He depended upon the deepening resentment the people felt towards Castile – where Leonor had fled after Andeiro's death – and rode this growing wave to victory. The final military conflict was the Battle of Aljubarrota (1385), a decisive victory for João's troops, despite being outnumbered.

The subsequent rule of João I, founder of the House of Avis, one of the military-religious orders, represented a new political beginning. The unsteady Anglo-Portuguese alliance was cemented by the Treaty of Windsor in 1386, a document cited as recently as World War II, when Britain invoked it to gain fuelling stations in the Azores. João I brought stability, but the change of order was not a social revolution. New political representation was established by the mercantile class, but it soon became clear that only the names had changed. The landed aristocracy still held the real power, and the new dynasty was much like the old.

The carved figures of Batalha Abbey.

⊙ THE BATTLE OF ALJUBARROTA

Many stories surround the Battle of Aljubarrota. Nuno Alvares Pereira, captain of João's army, was ravaged by thirst when leading his forces into battle, and swore no traveller would ever go thirsty there again. Since 1385 a pitcher of water has been placed daily in a niche of the Aljubarrota chapel of São Jorge. João, too, made a vow: to build a church in the Virgin's honour if his outnumbered army was victorious. As the enemy fled, João hurled his lance into the air to pick the spot where the monastery of Batalha would be built. He must have had a very strong arm, because the battlefield is 16km (10 miles) from the monastery.

CASTLES IN THE AIR

Portugal is home to hundreds of castles and forts, which have stood watch over its plains and valleys for centuries.

Most of Portugal's many castles were either built or rebuilt between the 12th and 14th centuries. King Dinis (1279–1325) alone began the construction or expansion of more than 50 fortresses. Perhaps he should have been called "the king of the castle" along with his other titles: "the poet king" and "the farmer king". His legacy can be seen throughout Portugal, but he concentrated his efforts mainly along the eastern boundary. He strengthened the towns of Guarda, Penedo, Penamacor, Castelo Mendo, Pinhel and others, attempting to secure the area from the threat posed by Castile. He was well rewarded: the Treaty of Alcañices, signed in 1297, initiated a period of peace and stability between the two countries.

Dinis provided the money for the castles, and even specified the exact measurements of walls and towers. They were of a particularly fine construction, with designs not found on other buildings. Some of the towers were slender and elegant; many balconies were elaborate, with detailed machicolations. Dinis often gave a specific character and grandeur to the structures, as in the 15 towers he had built at Numão, or the Torre do Galo (Cockerel Tower) at Freixo de Espada à Cinta, with its beautiful seven faces.

PREPARING FOR WAR

Many castles were built on the sites of earlier forts: Moorish, Visigothic, Roman, or even earlier. It is interesting to note the developments in warfare as they are reflected in physical features of Portugal's castles. Long wooden verandahs, for example, were attached to the castles' walls in early days. Later these verandahs were covered with animal hides to prevent, or at least inhibit, them being burned by flaming arrows, but these too were abandoned at the end of the 13th century.

By this time, the carved stone balconies were being used for defensive purposes, with machicolations which allowed the defending forces to repel attackers as they attempted to scale the castle walls. (Machicolation is the name given to a space between corbels, or in the floor of a balcony, from which boiling oil or other substances could be poured or dropped onto the enemy.)

The most significant change came with the advent of gunpowder and artillery. The heavy cannons required thicker walls, sloped to resist the more powerful projectiles. Thicker walls also meant that the ramparts, running along the tops of the walls, could be wider, and enabled the heavy artillery to be perched on top. Arrow slits, a common feature in castles, were rounded to accommodate the new artillery, then abandoned as impractical.

Almourol Castle stands on Almourol island.

All Portugal's castles – many still sound, some in semi-ruin – are dramatically sited. Among the best are Lamego, in the Douro Valley (see page 270); Almourol, the most romantic of all, set on its own tiny island in the Rio Tejo (Tagus) and the subject of many myths (see page 224); and, of course, Guimarães, the birthplace (c. 1110) of Portugal's first king, Afonso Henriques. Guimarães is one of Portugal's oldest castles, having been built in the 10th century and restored many times. Early in the 19th century the castle was used as a debtors' prison. It underwent extensive renovation in the 1940s (see page 287).

Most castles are open to visitors; some have been converted to hotels, while others stand ignored in empty fields. Solid though their construction may have been, do be careful when visiting the semi-ruined ones; you don't want to end your visit trapped under a piece of falling masonry.

HISTORY & FEATURES

THE ENGLISH CONNECTION

A much-loved English queen in Portugal, firm military alliances, and mutually beneficial trade have all helped cement the Anglo-Portuguese relationship over the centuries.

In 1147 a band of crusaders – English, German, French and Flemish – broke their journey in Porto en route to the Holy Land (some by choice, while others may have been shipwrecked). They were persuaded by the new king of Portugal, Afonso Henriques, to join him in an expedition to seize Lisbon from the Moors. Chronicles of the time praised the beauties of Lisbon as seen by the English crusaders. Its fertile countryside, lush with figs and vines, epitomised the seductive pleasures of the south, and encouraged many Englishmen to settle there. The first Bishop of Lisbon, Gilbert of Hastings, was English.

The 17-week siege of the city ended in victory for the Christian forces, and was much celebrated. Much later it became the subject of a poem by William Mickle, the 18th-century translator of Luís de Camões (see page 57), who is considered Portugal's greatest poet:
*The hills and lawns to English valour given
What time the Arab Moors from Spain were driven,
Before the banners of the cross subdued,
When Lisbon's towers were bathed in Moorish blood
By Gloster's Lance – Romantic days that yield
Of gallant deeds a wide luxuriant field
Dear to the Muse that loves the fairy plains
Where ancient honour wild and ardent reigns.*

The Portuguese themselves had less happy memories of the crusaders from the north,

John I, King of Portugal marries Philippa of Lancaster.

whom they considered a loud and drunken lot, given more to piracy than to piety. But the English, with their superior numbers and martial skills, would long feel a condescending pride in their Portuguese achievement, expecting gratitude and deference from their southern allies.

TREATIES AND ALLIANCES

Kingdoms were there for the taking. In 1371, John of Gaunt, Duke of Lancaster, hoped to ensure one for himself by marrying the ex-Infanta Constance, the elder of two surviving daughters of the murdered King Pedro the Cruel of Castile. Gaunt then firmly believed himself to be the rightful king of Castile. To double the family's claim, his brother married Constance's

> *Admired by the Portuguese, generous, kind, high-minded Philippa slowly transformed the king. João, a notorious womaniser, became faithful to Philippa and ended his days translating religious books.*

younger sister. But there remained one problem: the incumbent king of Castile needed to be convinced. John of Gaunt enlisted the help of Fernando of Portugal, and after rounds of courtship, lavish entertaining and the bestowal of favours, an alliance was signed in 1373 by which the two nations agreed to help one another against all enemies.

In 1385, the youthful Dom João ascended the Portuguese throne with English help, and John of Gaunt felt the time was right to go to Castile to establish his royal claims. Along with his wife Constance, two daughters (26-year-old Philippa from his first marriage, and Katherine), a couple of his illegitimate children and an army, John of Gaunt set up court in the north, in Santiago de Compostela. He met the king and the earlier alliance was formalised as the Treaty of Windsor. In return King João was offered the hand of the devout and virtuous Philippa. They married in Porto and the city celebrated lavishly.

THE ENGLISH QUEEN

Philippa was a remarkable queen. By surrounding herself in court with an English retinue, she encouraged merchants from England to come in pursuit of trade. Children were born of the marriage at regular intervals, six in all, alternately named after their English and Portuguese families. All five princes were highly gifted and excelled during their lifetimes. Henry, known later as Henry the Navigator, became the most famous of them all through his contribution to Portuguese exploration of the world. Philippa died of the plague in 1415, at the age of 51, and was mourned throughout the country.

WELLINGTON RIDES IN

Contact between these two Atlantic nations remained close. Following the period of Spanish domination of Portugal, the old alliance with England was reinstated by Charles I (1642), Oliver Cromwell (1654) and finally by the Treaty of 1661, by which Charles II married Catherine of Bragança. Combined Anglo-Portuguese armies were not unusual: they were in action on a number of occasions, fighting each other's battles. The most heavily recorded is the Peninsular War in the Napoleonic era. Sir Arthur Wellesley, who became the Duke of Wellington, commanded the British troops and built the famous defensive Lines of Torres Vedras, which effectively repelled the French and won the war for Portugal.

THE WINE TRADE

Throughout the history of trade between these two countries, textiles made their way to Lisbon and Porto, but there was usually wine in the hold on the return trip. During the second half of the 17th century, increasing factors of British firms settled in Viana do Castelo, Monção and Porto, and selected the wines for shipping home. Porto soon became the centre of the wine trade (see

Wellington and Sir William Carr Beresford at Salamanca in July of 1812.

page 259). Names like Taylor, Croft, Cockburn, Symington, Sandeman and Graham became established, and by the 19th century these families were busy buying their own *quintas* (manor houses) along the banks of the Douro.

The trade in port wine flourished through wars, civil dissent and fierce regulation, and the British made a valuable contribution, such as Baron Joseph James Forrester, who helped improve port safety standards, and also mapped the Rio Douro, in which he eventually drowned in 1862.

Born out of mutual need, the Anglo-Portuguese friendship has been touched by romance, passion, piety, greed, hope and despair, and yet has endured intact for almost a millennium.

A Japanese screen commemorates the arrival of Portuguese traders.

EMPIRE BUILDING

Under the House of Avis, Portugal matured as a nation. The golden age of discoveries began, bringing untold wealth to the Church and the Crown.

João I ruled from 1385 to 1433, fending off the demands of a resurgent nobility by installing his legitimate sons Duarte, Pedro, Henry, Fernão and João in powerful positions as the leaders of military-religious orders – Henry the Navigator, for example, headed the wealthy Order of Christ. It was under João I that Portugal first began to look across the seas for solutions to internal economic and political problems.

João's successor, Duarte, initially continued with overseas expansion, but drew back after a disastrous failed attack on Tangiers in 1437. The following year Duarte died, precipitating a brief civil war to determine who would act as regent to his young son, who became Afonso V.

Two of Afonso's uncles were particularly trusted advisers: Henry the Navigator, who was in the forefront of exploration and conquest, and yet another Afonso, the Duke of Bragança, leader of the newly strengthened nobility. Each was granted a large share of independent power. King Afonso himself remained above the administrative fray. He was not particularly inept, but he was a chivalric leader in an era where politics had been sullied by the growing power of mercantiles and low nobility, and he was out of tune with the times. Afonso concerned himself largely with martial glory, which he found crusading in North Africa. In 1471 he took Tangiers. Another of his accomplishments was the minting of the first *cruzado,* the gold coin that became a symbol of the wealth flowing in from the voyages.

In 1475 dispute over the crown of Castile led to civil discord. Afonso married his niece, Joana, one of the claimants, and thus united Portugal and Castile under his monarchy. He invaded in support of his wife's claims, and occupied León, but failed to hold his ground. Defeated by the

Henry the Navigator, son of John I of Portugal.

> Trade and exploration, it was then thought, would serve both to occupy the nobility and to boost commerce.

forces of Ferdinand of Aragón and Isabela of Castile, he tried to enlist the aid of French king Louis XI in support of his claims to the Castilian throne, travelling to France to make a personal plea. He arrived in the midst of Louis XI's tumultuous rivalry with the Duke of Burgundy and proved a hapless diplomat, alienating both sides.

Frustrated, he announced his intention to abdicate his throne to go on a pilgrimage to the

Holy Land, but even this quixotic voyage was thwarted. Louis prevented him from embarking, and the despondent Afonso was sent back to his homeland. His son, the future João II, allowed Afonso to resume his nominal position, and rule was shared until the older man's death in 1481.

OVERSEAS EXPANSION

The 15th century was the era when colonisation began in earnest, but no one had any idea of the empire that was to come. The existing policy was a mixture of crusading ideals, curiosity and, of course, profit. Charting the world was a secondary matter to João II – less important, for example, than the acquisition of spices, or the search for the odd figure who was known as Prester John.

A mythical priest and king, Prester John was supposed to have been the leader of a vast and powerful Christian empire located somewhere in the continent of Africa. His legend was elaborated with tales of a kingdom that was an earthly paradise peopled with a bizarre menagerie of chimeras and mythical characters. Strange as it seems, this tale had an enormous influence on early colonisation of Africa. In fact, in 1455, after the Portuguese had established their dominance all along the northern coast, a papal bull granted them the sole right to conquest of all of Africa except those parts ruled by Prester John. It was only later, by the early 16th century, that Portugal's explorers began to realise that spices and gold were more tangible goals, and the voyages in and around Ethiopia were replaced by more profitable itineraries.

The most sinister act of the seafarers was the slaughter of the "infidel". Attacking Muslims gave the voyages all the benefits of a crusade: the effort was legitimised, and the Church lent its financial resources along with spiritual support. The sanctions of Rome, like the papal bull of 1455, would become an important factor when maritime competition intensified.

Economic and social growth undoubtedly motivated the voyages. There was a shortage of gold all over Europe, and without it, coinage was severely debased and the growth of commerce stunted. Gold from Africa, the Americas and India eventually did find its way into the coffers of Lisbon, but it also proved to be a debilitating obsession, diverting attention from surer if less spectacular sources of profit. These lesser goals were nevertheless an impetus for exploration from the start. Fishing boats had circled further and further out in search of more richly stocked waters. Moroccan grain, sugar, spices, woods, dyestuffs and of course slaves – for

Lisbon's Padrao dos Descobrimentos celebrates Portuguese explorers from the Age of Discovery.

human lives were stacked alongside these other commodities – were all highly prized.

HENRY THE NAVIGATOR

Before any exploration could begin, of course, the technical aspects of navigation had to be mastered and improved. Navigators familiar with the Pole Star, dead reckoning and the compass began to establish their position with the quadrant, the astrolabe adapted for sea use, and a simple cross-staff from which they calculated latitude. Celestial tables and so-called *portolano* charts, basic maps, became ever more detailed. Ships, too, radically changed – neatest of all was the nimble caravel, derived from the heftier cargo-carrying *caravela* of the Rio Douro. Prince Henry, who was born in Porto, would have known it well.

The prince was dubbed Henry the Navigator and is credited with masterminding the discoveries from a centre of navigation in Sagres at Cabo de São Vicente in Algarve, where he surrounded himself with astronomers and shipbuilders. His sponsorship and enthusiasm were profoundly influential, and the research material he assembled was unrivalled (much of it contributed by his brother, Pedro, a true wanderer who sent Henry every relevant map and book he could find). But discovering the world – the Portuguese were the first Europeans to find two-thirds of it – was beyond the scope of any one man, and there must be other, unsung, heroes.

With many hands at the tillers, the enterprise was not always well coordinated. The main goal was to press the crusade forward and to advance knowledge of navigation and the oceans. Maps were accurate enough to suggest that there were islands in the unknown Sea of Darkness, and land beyond it, but it needed courage and determination to sail into oceans that legend had filled with fearsome monsters.

Pedro Alvares Cabral lands in Brazil.

EPIC VOYAGES

It is easy to see why popular history might accord undue credit to an individual like Henry. The Age of Discoveries was, at the time, billed as an era for heroes and adventurers, and also for the rebirth of chivalric ideals. Fearless mariners sailed off into unknown realms. Their voyages were imbued with intentions they considered noble: the greater glory of the Church, the advancement of knowledge, and the benefit of their nation.

Popular history also makes unverifiable, but plausible, claims that Portuguese mariners were the first Europeans in America. Among explorers who sailed from the Azores were members of the Corte Real family, who explored the North American coast in the 1470s. One of

HISTORY & FEATURES

them, Miguel, may have been marooned there.

The first "hero" of the era was Gil Eanes. Madeira and the Azores, along with the north of Africa, had been charted. The islands had begun to be colonised. The fabulous tales of the edge of the world and the various horrors of the southern seas were soon connected with the stormy promontory of Cape Bojador, on the west coast of Africa, which became a symbolic boundary. Finally, in 1434, Gil Eanes, a pilot commissioned by Henry the Navigator, broke the barrier. He found more coastline and safe waters, and returned to Portugal triumphant, bringing wild plants plucked from the land beyond. The next year he led voyages further down Africa's coast, and the way was opened for the many who followed. They searched primarily for the legendary Rio do Ouro (River of Gold). Eventually some of the precious ore was found.

> The Portuguese began fishing for cod (bacalhau) in Newfoundland's Grand Banks shortly after Columbus's voyage of discovery. It soon became a very popular dish.

In 1482, Portuguese ships explored the mouth of the Congo. Five years later, Bartolomeu Dias rounded the Cape of Good Hope. So intense did the competition between Spain and Portugal become that in 1494 papal intervention resulted in the famous Treaty of Tordesillas, which divided the newly discovered and the still unknown lands between the two countries. It granted Portugal the lands east of a line of demarcation 592km (370 miles) west of the Azores, which put Brazil (then unknown to the West, but encountered by Pedro Alvares Cabral in 1500) within Portugal's sphere.

From 1497–9, Vasco da Gama sailed to Calicut (Calcutta) in India and back – with great loss of life – immediately throwing Portugal into competition with Muslim and Venetian spice traders. In 1519–22, Fernão de Magalhães (anglicised to Ferdinand Magellan), a Portuguese serving Spain, led the first voyage to circumnavigate the

A statue of Vasco de Gama.

⊘ HENRY THE HERO?

Prince Henry the Navigator's primary goal, rather than to discover uncharted territory, was controlling the North African coast. He never travelled farther than Morocco, where he had taken Ceuta in 1415, and gained his lifelong interest in colonisation. Contemporary chronicles portray Henry devoting most of his time to squeezing profits out of his various tithes, monopolies and privileges.

However, the riches uncovered by his expeditions were undeniable, whatever his motivation. It was an expedition initiated by Henry the Navigator that, quite accidentally, discovered Madeira and the Azores. In 1415, two ships were blown off course and landed on an uninhabited island, which they named Madeira (meaning "wood") because it was thickly forested. The first of the nine Azores (Açores) islands was discovered a dozen years later, the others over a period of 25 years. Henry proved to be an efficient coloniser, introducing wheat, vines and sugar cane to Madeira, and organising the settlement of the Azores, which later became recognised ports of call for sailors en route to and from the Americas.

Later in life increasing reports of wondrous and far-off places inspired Henry to give these discoveries his full attention. Yet throughout his life he ploughed much of his profits back into the enterprises, which were a costly business, and died in debt.

globe, although he died before it was completed.

The expeditions opened the seaways, but there were battles to be fought to establish trading posts in Africa and the Caribbean. Arabs, protecting their own trade interests, fought the Portuguese wherever they could. The Portuguese, of course, were still intent on eradicating such infidels from the face of the earth. So although Portugal originally had no intentions of land conquest, by simply striving to establish and maintain a monopoly of the high seas, they were constantly at war.

COLONIES

The leader of these voyages of colonisation to the East was Governor Afonso de Albuquerque, the founding father of the empire in Asia. His victories allowed garrisoned ports and fortresses to be built in key locations. Goa, in India, colonised in 1510, became the centre for all operations. Malacca (now in Malaysia) fell in 1511 and served as the East Indies hub, while Ormuz came under Portuguese control in 1515, proving the ideal seat from which to dominate the Persian Gulf. Later, in 1557, Macau was established on a kind of permanent lease with China, extending Portugal's reach to South-East Asia.

Portugal claimed to administer these new holdings under a basic policy of colonisation rather than exploitation. All the major cities, Goa in particular, were converted by architecture and government into European towns. Interracial marriages were encouraged and Catholic missions established.

The growth of Goa was indeed, extraordinary. By 1540, there were 10,000 households of European descent and the town was the seat of a bishopric. However, these few much-changed cities and the battles of the Caribbean were in marked contrast to the general policy of peaceful coexistence that Portugal adopted wherever it could. In Africa, Brazil, and the various islands and archipelagos, they tried to set up trading stations without interfering with local customs or politics.

It is, however, the exceptions that proved the most interesting. In the Congo, for example, where a number of missions were established, many people were quite taken with their European visitors, though they could provide little of interest to the traders. Once the Congolese were exposed to certain Western practices, they embraced them rapidly. They took to Christianity, and imitated the manners and fashions of the Portuguese. Their first Christian monarch dropped the title "Nzinga a Nkuwu" and renamed himself João I. His son took the name Afonso, and from that point until the 17th century the land was ruled by a succession of native Henriques, Pedros and Franciscos.

Despite providing the tragic "commodities" of ivory and slaves, the Congo was not of central economic importance to the Portuguese, who were too busy reaping bounty elsewhere. Spices were carried from the east, gold was found in

Afonso de Albuquerque, painted by an unknown artist, c.1509.

Ghana and other parts of Africa, sugar and wine were brought from Madeira, while sugar and dye-stuffs came from Brazil.

The wealth reaped overseas made for a stable economy, but it did not make Portugal rich. Enterprising individuals and the monarchy – taking its royal fifth of all trade revenues – flourished, but even they eventually found it difficult to build or hold on to their fortunes.

At its beginning, the "empire" demanded little from its diminutive fatherland. Like other small trading centres in Italy and the later Dutch empire, organisation and central authority were more important than mere size. Furthermore, the early expeditions required little manpower. It was only later, when they found themselves trying to enforce the worldwide trade monopoly, that the sparseness of Portugal's population began to tell. It has also been suggested that a crucial deficiency was Portugal's lack of a middle class. Quashed by royal and noble dominance of commerce, it might have provided qualified and educated planners, pilots and administrators.

In explaining the empire's failure, some have pointed to widespread corruption or to the foreign control of profits garnered from Portuguese expeditions. How great an effect they had is arguable. Certainly the religious efforts that went hand in hand with Portuguese voyages did not make the wheels of commerce spin any more freely. Whether persecuting Muslims, or trying to force Christianity down the throats of local populations, the Portuguese wasted time and diverted their focus from the business at hand.

Whatever the causes, potential benefits of the burgeoning overseas trade were not being reaped. Deflation in Europe stifled trade. Domestic agricultural production, hampered by a lack of manpower, lagged occasionally, which caused serious shortages of meat and grain. Even the Crown was in debt as the cost of the trading empire rose higher than its revenues. It was, of course, many years before these flaws and inadequacies truly sank the empire.

DOMESTIC LIFE

Before the slide began, the lucrative age of empire brought sufficient peace and prosperity for Portugal to sustain great eras of artistic and humanist achievement. João II had taken over from his father, the unreliable Afonso V, in 1481. Revitalising the throne, he managed to take up where Henry the Navigator, who died in 1460, left off. João turned away from the nobility, minimising their rights and calling on the *cortes* for support. A conspiracy soon gathered against him, but he learned of the central traitors soon enough to strike back. In 1484, the Duke of Bragança was tried and beheaded. When other members of the nobility fled the country, their titles and holdings reverted to the Crown.

Azulejo of a Portuguese expedition ship.

⊘ JEWISH POPULATION IN PORTUGAL

A Jewish population had, by the 15th century, lived peaceably in Portugal for a thousand years or more. With high levels of education, the contribution of Jewish people to the economy and progress of the country was invaluable. It was Jews who opened Portugal's first printing presses; the first 11 books published in Portugal were written in Hebrew. Abraham Zacuto, astronomer and mathematician, published the *Almanach Perpetuum*, which contained tables enabling mariners to determine latitude by declination of the sun. The *Almanach* was translated into Latin and became the basis of a system used by the Portuguese for many years. In 1492, Spain, having rid itself of the Moors, was equally determined to expel Jews from its soil, and some 60,000 found a new home in Portugal. However, when King Manuel married Princess Isabella of Spain in 1497, he was forced, as a condition of marriage, to act against the Jews. Realising their value to the country, he was reluctant to expel them so he offered them the option of baptism as "New Christians" (enforced conversion to Christianity), with a 20-year period of "grace" before their faith would be tested. Many refused outright, and those who accepted found that they were still not treated as equals. Prejudice and intolerance were quick to burgeon into full-scale repression as the Inquisition took hold.

The Duke of Viseu, who was both cousin and brother-in-law to the king, unwisely mounted a second plot, and was stabbed by the king himself. Another group fled the country, and João II was left in full command. The prestige and authority that these tactics bestowed on the monarchy would stand undiminished for centuries. However, João's successor, Manuel I, who came to the throne in 1495, had to find a balance between the ferocity of his predecessor and the confused idealism of Afonso V.

This he accomplished through diplomatic and far-sighted administration. The estates of the noble families were largely restored, though this did not restore their political power. Judicial and tax reforms worked to bring authority to government on both the national and local levels. A postal system was instituted. Public services such as hospitals were centralised. Essentially, Manuel lifted the power of the monarchy above both the nobles and the *cortes*, launching the first era of enlightened absolutism.

THE IMPORTANCE OF EDUCATION

Manuel also fostered contacts with proponents of Renaissance humanism, which was then spreading throughout Europe. There were many trading, religious and cultural contacts with Italy in particular, and young Portuguese men began to seek education abroad, at universities in France or Spain.

Manuel tried to buy Paris's renowned St Barbara College, and, although he failed, it became a centre for Portuguese students. By 1487 a printing press had been established in Lisbon. Portugal entered the 16th century with a rush of new cultural currents and ideas.

New colleges and educational reforms were basic elements of the new century's progress. Teaching methods were modernised and the curriculum expanded. The students were drawn from a larger pool, including aristocrats and members of the wealthy bourgeoisie, in addition to young men from the religious orders.

These changes were not without crises. The University of Lisbon had a cultural and political influence that threatened the Crown. It was difficult to impinge on its traditional autonomy, but Manuel, as part of his process of centralisation, tried to force change through economic and legal pressure.

Finding great resistance, he turned to the idea of founding a new university elsewhere, without success. João III, who came to the throne in 1521, on his father's death, continued these efforts, later giving control of national education to the Jesuits and moving the university to Coimbra, where its permanent home was established. It was a victory for the monarchy. There would be no university in Lisbon until 1911.

Nonetheless, the century inspired a broad-ranging intellectual vigour. Some of the works produced were directly attributable to the expe-

João III, in a portrait by Cristovão Lopes.

ditions of discovery. Travel books, with both scientific and cultural themes, were a rich vein: Tomé Pires, for example, wrote *Suma Oriental* in 1550, describing his voyages to the East.

Portugal's main contributions to the intellectual ferment of the Renaissance were in science, particularly navigation, astronomy, mathematics and geography. This was not the mere accumulation of facts from foreign places: they amounted to a kind of sceptical empiricism, a science based on experience. Having disproved a dozen theories about the shape, limits and contours of the earth, Portuguese intellectuals felt free to question the other dogmas of antiquity.

New writers and new sciences were emerging but there was no real Reformation in Portugal,

> *João III continued Manuel's expansion of the trading empire and of royal authority, but his most significant act was the establishment of the Inquisition in Portugal.*

where there was an antipathy towards Germanic philosophies. Nevertheless, the Counter-Reformation cast a pall of religious conformism over learning and creativity. In addition, the political threat to Portuguese autonomy – the future union with Spain was already an undercurrent – hung over all these academic achievements.

"Heretics" are led to their death by fire in an auto-da-fé procession.

PORTUGUESE INQUISITION

João III ruled from 1521 to 1557. The Inquisition had by now become established in Spain, where it had been enforced with vigour after the Moors had been expelled in 1492 by the "Catholic Monarchs", Isabel and Ferdinand. The papacy knew there was no real need for it, no menaces to the unity of faith, so resisted its introduction. But João III was more fanatical than the pope and he used every diplomatic intrigue at his disposal to get his way. Finally, in 1536, he won approval for a limited version of the Inquisition, but within a dozen years these limitations had been lifted and its full force arrived.

João III had turned away from the current humanist influences of Europe towards religious fanaticism, and the power and the bureaucracy of the Inquisition expanded rapidly. Its main target was the converted Jews known as New Christians. What had been intended as a tool of the monarchy soon took on a direction and authority of its own. The Inquisitor-Generals, who took their orders from Rome, had the right of excommunication and soon wielded an influence far beyond their legal authority.

The impact of the Inquisition, with its rigid orthodoxy, vengeful judiciary and general intolerance, was deadening to both culture and commerce. Many of the bourgeois leaders of trade were targets. In those uncertain times, epic poet Luís de Camões and the great 16th-century playwright Gil Vicente became renowned for their works in the Portuguese language.

The Inquisition's power continued under King Sebastião, who came to the throne in 1568, when he was 14 years old. An unstable king, with a dangerous streak of misplaced chivalry, Sebastião took upon himself a crusade against the Moors of North Africa. A lack of funds prevented him from undertaking the task for many years. In the meantime he surrounded himself with cohorts no older than himself. Finally sensing that the time was right, he spent every *cruzado* he could raise on mercenaries and outfitting his troops. He set sail for Morocco in 1578, appointing his great-uncle, Cardinal Henrique, regent in his absence.

Sebastião was as bad a military leader as he was an administrator, dismissing stratagem and planning as cowardice. He refused to consider the possibility of retreat, and therefore had no plan for it. Outnumbered and outmanoeuvred at the Battle of Alcácer-Quibir, his army of 18,000 men was destroyed. Some 8,000, including Sebastião and most of Portugal's young nobility, were slaughtered. Only 100 or so escaped.

In the wake of this debilitating disaster, the way was open for Spain to step in. From 1578 to 1580, Cardinal Henrique ruled the country, occupied primarily with raising the ruinous ransoms for the captured soldiers of Alcácer-Quibir. In 1580, Felipe II of Spain invaded and within a year was installed as Filipe I of Portugal.

LUÍS DE CAMÕES

Portugal's greatest poet never reaped fame or riches in his lifetime, but his life and his works still entrance the Portuguese today.

Luís Vaz de Camões (1524–80), Portugal's greatest poet, was born poor, and he died poor, but the life he led – of passion and adventure – enthrals the Portuguese almost as much as the epic, eloquent phrases in his works, which many people can quote at length even today.

After attending the University at Coimbra, his prospects were promising. But many twists of fate lay ahead. An affair with one of the queen's ladies-in-waiting caused his banishment to North Africa, where he lost an eye in military service. Returning to Lisbon, Camões was involved in a skirmish that wounded a magistrate. He ended up in prison and then was banished again, in 1553, this time to the colony of Goa in India. It was 1570 before he returned to Lisbon. Having written poetry and plays for many years with some success, he published *Os Lusíadas* in 1572. The poem's worth was recognised immediately, and Camões received a royal pension. His final illness, however, was spent in a public hospital, and he was buried in a common grave.

The title *Os Lusíadas* means "The Sons of Lusus", the mythical founder of Portugal: symbolically, then, it means "the Portuguese". Echoing classical models, the poem chronicled the voyages of Vasco da Gama, before a panorama of strangely mixed Christian and pagan images. *Os Lusíadas* has been hailed throughout Europe (Lope de Vega and Montesquieu were among early admirers), sometimes to the detriment of the rest of Portugal's extensive literature. Under Salazar (see page 68), *Os Lusíadas* became an icon of Portuguese nationalism. Speeches and propaganda were peppered with quotes from it, providing a mythology for imperialism that failed to differentiate between the 16th and 20th centuries.

The 18th-century verse translation by W.J. Mickle, quoted below, though tinged with the lyrical romanticism and chauvinism of that era, captures the proud spirit of the poem from the opening lines:

Arms and the heroes, who from Lisbon's shore,/ Thro' seas where sail was never spread before,/ Beyond where Ceylon lifts her spicy breast,/And waves her woods above the watery waste,/With prowess more than human forc'd their way/ To the fair kingdoms of the rising day.

In the second canto the Moors prepare to attack:

On shore the truthless monarch arms his bands,/ And for the fleet's approach impatient stands:/ That soon as anchor'd in the port they rode/ Brave Gama's decks might reek with Lusian blood:/.

Luís de Camões.

In the world of the Portuguese discoverers, enemy forces take their strength from the netherworld:

As when the whirlwinds, sudden bursting, bear/ Th' autumnal leaves high floating through the air;/ So rose the legions of th' infernal state,/ Dark Fraud, base Art, fierce Rage, and burning Hate:/ Wing'd by the Furies to the Indian strand/ They bend; the Demon leads the dreadful band,/ And in the bosoms of the raging Moors/ All their collected living strength he pours.

At Vasco da Gama's request, his ship's chronicler recounts the "glad assistance" brought by the crusaders who helped take Lisbon from the Moors:

Their vows were holy, and the cause the same,/ To blot from Europe's shores the Moorish name./ In Sancho's cause the gallant navy joins,/ And royal Sylves to their force resigns./ Thus sent by heaven a foreign naval band/ Gave Lisboa's ramparts to the Sire's command.

Engraving of the fall of Lisbon into Spanish rule (1580).

THE CONQUERORS ARE CONQUERED

Portugal was under Spanish rule for 60 years, until a popular uprising against the Habsburgs put the country back in charge of its own destiny.

Throughout the duration of their rule over Portugal, the Spanish Habsburg kings faced many challenges to their authority. Not least among their problems was that King Sebastião kept rising from the grave. After the Portuguese army's massacre at Alcácer-Quibir, Morocco, in 1578 – a devastating blow to national pride - there arose a popular belief, known as *sebastianismo*, that the lost king would rise again. Consequently, a number of false Sebastiãos tried and failed to reclaim the throne.

At the root of the Iberian Union, the conjoined powers of Portugal and Spain that governed the Iberian Peninsula from 1580–1640, was the support it provided for merchants and traders. The Netherlands and France were strongly challenging Portuguese shipping, slicing into vital profits. In any case, there were few options: in 1560 the Casa da India, the national trade corporation, had gone bankrupt and Portugal's treasury was empty.

Antão de Almada, one of the movers and shakers of the Restoration.

> *It was supposed by the bourgeoisie that by combining Spanish and Portuguese interests, the maritime empire could be reclaimed, while the "alliance" would also open up inland trade.*

THE THREE FILIPES

After Alcácer-Quibir, a number of candidates had aspirations to the Portuguese throne. Though the genealogical claim of Felipe II of Spain was more tenuous than those of his competitors, he was the grandson of Manuel I and a far more viable ruler than his rivals. The majority of the populace was opposed to the Spanish king, but the relatively impoverished nobles, clergy and upper bourgeoisie saw that Felipe could provide fiscal and military stability. Ironically, the most powerful group to resist the union was the Spanish ruling classes, who saw the danger of untrammelled Portuguese trading within their traditional markets.

Part of Felipe's appeal was that he promised to maintain Portugal's autonomy: no Spanish representation in Portuguese legislative and judicial bodies; no change in the official language; the overseas empire would still be ruled by Portugal; no grants of Portuguese assets to non-Portuguese; and so on. Felipe took up residence in Lisbon. In 1581 he summoned the *cortes* to declare him King Filipe I.

After the years of mismanaged government, the efficient bureaucracy of the union was a relief. However, with the succession of Felipe II (Felipe III of Spain) in 1598, the Spanish began to press their powers too far. The new king lacked his predecessor's diplomatic savvy, relations between the two countries were bungled, and the Spanish tried to correct their mistakes through force. Resistance grew. Under Filipe III (IV of Spain), who succeeded to the throne in 1619, the union continued to erode. Spain was weakened by the Thirty Years' War with France.

Pedro II, a more effective king than his brother.

Portuguese troops were forced into battle and taxes increased.

The 60 years of union with Spain did nothing to protect Portugal's empire. Between 1620 and 1640, Ormuz, Baia, São Jorge da Mina and many more trade centres fell. In 1630 the Dutch established themselves in Brazil; in 1638 they took Ceylon.

There were still ports and territories controlled by Portuguese traders, but the monopoly of the seas was an era quickly fading from memory. What's more, to a country that had once been intent upon ridding the earth of the last vestige of the "infidels", it was devastating to surrender their missions to the Dutch: purveyors of heretical Protestantism.

For the Portuguese, each of the three Filipes was worse than his predecessor. Filipe II did not even deign to visit the country for years after his coronation. Filipe III systematically breached all the guarantees put in place by his grandfather. The incipient revolution was aided by secret diplomatic agents sent by the French, who were still embroiled with Spain in the Thirty Years' War.

THE BRAGANÇA REGIME

On 1 December 1640, a coup in Lisbon reflected the growing revolutionary fervour. The palace was attacked, and the reigning Spanish governor, the duchess of Mantua, was deposed and arrested, while her strongman, Miguel de Vasconcelos, was defenestrated. Though reluctant to lead the revolt, the Duke of Bragança was declared King João IV. So began Portugal's final royal period: the House of Bragança would hold power until the 20th century.

Most of João IV's 16-year reign was occupied in hapless efforts to form diplomatic ties in Europe. France, England, Holland and the pope all refused to confirm Portuguese independence. Only Spain's preoccupation with other battles, some heroic Portuguese military stands along the frontier, and a well-organised national administration enabled the country to retain its restored independence.

When he ascended the throne in 1656, Afonso VI (João's son), who experienced both physical and mental disability, was still a minor. Later, married off to a French princess, he associated with criminal elements and, worst of all, proved to be impotent, a fact elicited from the public inquiry needed to annul his marriage. He was eventually usurped by his brother, who ruled as Pedro II.

War with Spain waxed and waned from 1640 until 1665. In 1654, a treaty of friendship and cooperation was signed with England: a useful link, but also the first step down a path that guaranteed Portugal's economic subservience to Britain for centuries to come. The alliance was sealed by the marriage of Princess Catherine to the English king, Charles II, in 1662. Included in her dowry gifts were Tangiers and Bombay. In 1661 a treaty was signed with Holland. These moves sparked a new round of battles with Spain. In 1665 a decisive Portuguese

THE CONQUERORS ARE CONQUERED | 61

victory at Montes Claros ended the fighting and three years later, in the Treaty of Lisbon, Spain officially recognised Portugal's independence.

Pedro II became prince regent to his brother in 1668 and ruled from 1673 until 1706. His long reign, although stable, was deeply marked by an unrelenting economic depression. The spice trade had slipped almost entirely out of Portuguese hands, while trade in sugar and slaves went through periods of competition and crisis at a time when Portugal could ill afford such instability.

> Restoration Day on 1 December is still celebrated in Portugal as a national holiday to commemorate the 1640 coup in Lisbon.

On the mainland, olive groves and vineyards offered good profits, but they were largely controlled by English interests. The Treaty of Methuen (1703) established English dominance of the wine industry and served to stifle industrialisation in Portugal. Grain shortages were common throughout the era – perhaps because investment went into vines instead of wheat.

Two of Pedro's finance ministers, the Count of Ericeira and the Marquês of Fronteira, helped plan numerous factories. Glass, textile, iron, tile and pottery industries were all supported by the state in an effort to balance trade deficits.

GOING FOR GOLD

This mercantilist, or export-maximising, approach made some headway, but what finally dispelled the economic gloom was the discovery of gold in Brazil. Even before gold, Brazil had offered a number of valuable commodities: sugar, cotton and tobacco, as well as some spices and dye-stuffs. The husbandry of cattle started slowly, but by the end of the 17th century was providing lucrative exports of meat and leather.

The Jesuit missionaries were extremely influential in Brazil, as both explorers and colonisers. Among other things, they held onto a brazilwood monopoly for over two decades (1625c49). More importantly, they were successful in converting the native populace to Christianity, and in large part preventing their enslavement. But the abundant colonial economy had a great need for enslaved labour, and the Jesuits were pressured to step aside, even though they had the clear support of Rome in the form of a papal bull (1639) that threatened excommunication for the trading of natives.

João V, who succeeded Pedro II in 1706, spent the Brazilian gold with a vengeance. Taking his cue from the French court of Louis XIV, he quickly earned the nickname "The Magnanimous". Palaces, churches and monasteries

A scene in Lisbon harbour during the Great Earthquake of 1755.

were erected, and support was granted to the arts and to education. Along with this extravagance came a certain profligacy. Convents around Lisbon were converted from religious houses into aristocratic brothels. Among the royal constructions were palaces to house João's numerous bastard sons, born of various nuns.

When João died in 1750 he was succeeded by his son José, who proved to be more interested in opera than in matters of state. The full power of the crown was entrusted to a diplomat, Sebastião José de Carvalho e Melo, who eventually earned the title by which he is better known: the Marquês de Pombal.

Enlightened absolutism (unrestrained monarchic power), as typified by the ministry of Pombal, represented both a beginning and an end. The Enlightenment ideal of rationalism meant a leap towards modernity, while the concomitant republican ideal of social equality meant royal absolutism was now on its last legs.

Pombal's insistence on exercising royal prerogative sounded a death knell for the political power of nobles and clergy alike, and allowed the bourgeoisie to take over administrative and economic control. His was an oppressive, dictatorial rule, although he was always careful never to claim any personal power.

THE GREAT EARTHQUAKE

In 1755, on All Saints' Day – just as Mass was beginning – Lisbon was destroyed by a massive earthquake. At least 5,000 people were killed in the initial impact, many while attending morning services. Many more died later. Fallen church candles quickly ignited the wreckage around them. Survivors rushed towards the safety of the Tejo, only to be met by a huge tsunami.

In the subsequent weeks infected wounds, epidemics and famine increased the death toll, which may have been as high as 40,000. The Jesuits tried to fix the blame for what they saw as divine retribution upon Pombal's wayward and "atheistic" policies. He weathered both their criticism and their plot to assassinate him. The Jesuits' power throughout Europe was dissolving, and in 1759 they were officially disbanded and exiled from Portugal.

The catastrophe that shook the country's faith allowed Pombal's policies of secularisation and rational government to take firm hold. He took absolute control, and with the order to "close the ports, bury the dead, feed the living", began reconstruction. José granted his minister emergency powers (which were not rescinded for some 20 years) and Pombal used them to rebuild Lisbon according to a neoclassical plan, both neatly geometric and functionally sound. The social and legal distinction between "Old" and "New" Christians (the latter being Jews who had converted at the end of the 15th century) was abolished. Pombal's economic reforms helped Portugal remain stable when Brazilian gold production waned in the middle of the century and he managed to rebuild Lisbon without depleting the treasury.

As Pombal's sponsor-king, José, neared the end of his reign, the Marquês plotted to force the crown princess Maria to renounce her rights so that her son - another José, and a disciple of Pombal - could continue the policy of despotism. These efforts failed and Maria, a pious but unbalanced woman with no sympathy for Pombal's methods of rule, took over in 1777. She immediately had Pombal tried for crimes against the state and, when convicted, confined him to his estate rather than to prison, out of deference to his age.

The Marquês de Pombal, an enlightened despot.

⊘ POMBAL'S LEGACY

Anyone visiting Lisbon should know a little about the Marquês de Pombal, to better appreciate the city. Under his direction, the whole of the devastated Baixa area was rebuilt in neoclassical style, laid out in an orderly grid system. The upper parts of the city – the Bairro Alto and Alfama – had been spared the worst effects of the tremors. In the centre of the great Praça do Comercio he erected a statue of his king, José, astride his horse. Pombal's own statue was erected much later, on a column in the square that bears his name, and looking out over the new city which, under his guidance, rose like a phoenix from the ashes.

Though she revived religious elements in a government and culture that had become increasingly secular, Maria allowed most of Pombal's essential economic and administrative reforms to stay in place. Her reign was a conservative one, with steady, if slow, economic progress. Both her political and personal health were badly shaken by news of the French Revolution. In 1798, long after her behaviour had become an embarrassment, she was declared insane. Her son João, an awkward, nervous man, took over as regent, becoming king after Maria died in 1816.

THE PENINSULAR WAR

The Portuguese monarchy and nobility feared that the fervour behind the French Revolution of 1789, and, to a lesser extent, the American revolution of the previous decade, might be contagious. They were particularly wary about possible insurgency in Brazil. In 1793, Portugal sent troops to fight revolutionary France, further aligning itself with Britain and against French-controlled Spain. In 1801, Spain invaded in the War of the Oranges. Portugal ceded various political concessions, and lost forever the town of Olivença.

In 1807, Napoleon delivered an ultimatum to Portugal, in which he demanded that Portugal declare war on Britain and close its ports to British shipping. But Portugal could not turn on its long-term allies, and Napoleon was defied. While the royal family speedily sailed to the safety of Brazil, the French General Junot marched into Lisbon. Initially, the Portuguese government offered no resistance.

In July 1808, Britain came galloping to the rescue under the leadership of the master military tactician, Sir Arthur Wellesley (1769–1852), who would later become the Duke of Wellington. The Peninsular War, sometimes called the War of National Liberation, lasted two years, expelling the French but devastating the country. Three waves of attacks were halted by Portuguese victories at Roliça, Vimeiro, Buçaco, and the famous Lines at Torres Vedras. The wars left the country in a rocky state. Since the flight of the royal family, Portugal's capital was effectively located across the ocean in Rio de Janeiro and the nation's general weakness fostered Brazil's claims for autonomy. In 1822 Brazil was declared a kingdom on an equal footing with Portugal.

The regency in Lisbon showed very little political intelligence or common sense, governing with uncoordinated despotism and completely ignoring the burgeoning democratic groundswell. The monarchy's blindness to contemporary political ideas fostered the revolution that would break out in 1820.

The British military occupation, under the leadership of Marshal William Carr Beresford (1768–1854), further undermined Portuguese

British and Portuguese troops commanded by the Duke of Wellington repulse Napoleon's army.

self-determination. British control had been growing throughout the 18th and 19th centuries. In 1810, Portugal was forced to cede to Britain the right to trade directly with Brazil, eliminating its own role as middleman. Portugal was taking on the aspects of a British protectorate, with William Beresford wielding dictatorial control.

THE LIBERAL REVOLUTION

The roots of the liberal uprising of 1820 lay in the French Revolution, its influences disseminated by military and secret societies: especially a Masonic lodge called Sinédrio. A plot against British rule by one of these clandestine groups proved to be a catalyst. A dozen conspirators accused of plotting to assassinate Marshal Beresford in 1817 were summarily tried and executed, a brutal reprisal that heated Portuguese resentment and fostered support for the liberal movement.

In 1820, the Spanish liberals won control of their government, providing further inspiration as well as political support for Portuguese liberal forces. When Beresford left for Brazil on a diplomatic mission to discuss the growing problem, hinqis absence sparked the Portuguese military into revolt. The uprising began in

Citizens rallied in the streets for the liberal revolution of 1820.

Porto, and eventually forced João VI to return from Brazil. By the time he arrived, the new constitutional ideology had gained ground. A constitution was adopted in 1822. The document was ahead of its time, with broad guarantees of individual liberties and no special prerogatives for nobles or clergy. It lasted only two years, but succeeded in ending the Portuguese Inquisition after 285 years.

CONSPIRACY AND CONFUSION

Portugal's profoundly conservative streak made the revolution a simple split between republicans and absolutists. New charters and new efforts to restore full-bodied monarchy kept the country unsettled throughout the first half of the century. In 1824, João VI resisted a conspiracy of royalist extremists led by his own wife Carlotta and his son Miguel.

João's queen was the Spanish princess Carlotta Joaquina, who epitomised the old regime. Her flamboyant leadership of the absolutist cause made her popular, but the failure of her conspiracy to dethrone her husband in favour of her son Miguel – who was then banished to live in Brazil – marked the end of her influence.

The politics of the next 50 years were endlessly complex. In 1826 João VI died, leaving the throne to Pedro, his eldest son, who was still in Brazil. After failing to unite the two kingdoms, Pedro chose to stay in Brazil, abdicating the Portuguese throne to his seven-year-old daughter, Maria. Pedro intended her to marry her uncle, the exiled Miguel, who would rule as regent under a moderate constitution. Miguel had other ideas. Upon his return he abolished the constitution and invoked a counter-revolutionary *cortes* to name him king. There was considerable popular support for these moves, but enough sympathy for constitutional ideas remained for Pedro, who had abdicated power in Brazil, to return and eventually defeat his brother in the Miguelist Wars.

Pedro IV reigned until his death in 1834, when his daughter, then aged 15, finally took the throne as Maria II. She reigned until 1853, during which time the first political parties developed. The liberals, victorious over absolutism, divided into conservatives and progressives. The

⊙ CULTURAL QUESTIONS

The influence of the rest of Europe on Portugal's cultural development in the 19th century was strongly felt. Intellectual conflicts were encapsulated by the "Coimbra question". Two groups of university scholars stood divided: the older group advocated the virtues of the status quo, while the "Generation of 1870", as they became known, called for revision of intellectual and spiritual values. Like their European counterparts, they were rationalist, anti-clerical and anti-monarchist. In their writing could be heard the first strains of emerging socialism. Their daring critiques, however, were suppressed by the government in 1871.

> *Carlotta Joaquina tried her best to make a Versailles of her palace at Queluz, surrounding herself with absolutists and, outrageously, producing children by various lovers.*

Septemberists, named after their revolutionary victory in September 1836, came into power first. They initially restored the constitution of 1822, but then adopted a more moderate one. They were opposed by Chartists who took their stand, and name, from the conservative charter of 1826.

The Chartists came to the fore in 1839, when, supported by the queen and led by António da Costa Cabral, they took power. Costa Cabral's government was authoritarian, and, though it provided stability, became more and more corrupt and autocratic. In 1846 a popular uprising demanded his downfall. Maria II tried to replace him with the equally conservative Duke of Saldanha, a grandson of Pombal, and the country stood on the brink of civil war. English and Spanish intervention prevented mass violence, but resulted in Costa Cabral being returned to power. In 1851 he was (peacefully) ousted for good and Saldanha took his place.

The early period of Saldanha's rule was a period of transformation out of which came the political divisions that would exist throughout the century. Saldanha introduced a compromise that allowed his new party, Regeneração, to encompass both the old Chartists and the moderate progressives. The amendments to the constitution allowed for direct elections and an expanded electorate. A still more radical faction, initially a small group, became known first as the Históricos, and then the Progressistas.

In 1853 Maria II died in childbirth. Her husband, the German duke Ferdinand of Saxe-Coburg-Gotha, ruled as regent until their son, Pedro V, came of age in 1855. Pedro died six years later and was succeeded by his brother, who became Luís I.

LITERARY LUÍS

The best constitutional monarchs are those who avoid politics, and the change from the meddling Maria to the literary Luís was a clear victory for the republican government. Among his other accomplishments, King Luís translated a number of Shakespeare's plays into Portuguese.

Arts and literature were greatly influenced by politics during this period. The energies of both liberal and conservative intellectuals were focused on rebuilding their nation. The best Portuguese prose was in essay form, the best poetry and drama was in satire, and historical writing flourished. Among the celebrated literati of the era were Alexandre Herculano (1810–77), who wrote historical fiction and a monumental history of Portugal; and the brilliantly versatile Almeida Garrett (1799–1854), best known for his drama, but also the author of poetry, novels and essays.

Sphinx sculpture in the Neptune Gardens, Queluz Palàcio, Lisbon.

The reign of Luís lasted until 1889 and was a period of relative peace. Conservatives and liberals alternated in controlling the legislature. Portugal's external affairs were more or less dictated by Britain, their protector under the Congress of Vienna's partitioning of small countries under major powers. But Portugal was dogged in holding on to many of its colonial claims and territories in Africa. The expense of maintaining those colonies was a burden on the rickety national economy, but it helped elevate the country when the holdings finally did pay off during the 20th century.

A sailor of the revolution troops in Necessidades Palace Emmanuel II in 1910.

REVOLUTION AND EVOLUTION

Republicanism failed to restore Portugal to its former glory. Instead, political turmoil followed by a harsh dictatorship hindered growth and modernisation until the 1980s.

The end of the 19th century saw Portugal's finances in complete disarray. The havoc wrought by the Peninsular and Miguelist wars, on top of the loss of Brazil as a colony, was insurmountable. In 1889, Carlos I became king, setting further African colonisation as his primary goal, but his efforts were unsuccessful. In 1892, Portugal declared bankruptcy.

Still dreaming of restoring the empire, Carlos could do little to defuse the growing anti-monarchical sentiment. Socialism and trade unionism were growing influences. The legislative *cortes* had degenerated into a powerless assembly full of obstructive and self-promoting debate. Corruption and inefficiency were rampant.

In 1906, struggling to maintain some form of control, Carlos appointed João Franco as prime minister, endowing him with dictatorial powers. He quickly dissolved the legislature. In 1908 unknown parties, either members of a republican secret society or isolated anti-monarchical fanatics, assassinated Carlos and his son, Luís Filipe, heir to the throne. In the assault on the royal carriage, Manuel, the king's second son, was wounded but survived.

Over the next two years Manuel II tried to save the monarchy, offering various concessions, but the assassination had fortified the republican movement. The long-decrepit House of Bragança finally crumbled to dust.

THE RISE OF REPUBLICANISM

The rising tide of republicanism could not be stopped. The democratic ideal was combined with a nationalistic vision, a shift it was hoped would return Portugal to its long-lost glory. The national anthem adopted in 1910 echoed the theme: "Oh sea heroes, oh noble people... raise

An allegory of the 1908 elections.

again the splendour of Portugal... may Europe claim to all the world that Portugal is not dead!"

The assassination of Carlos sealed the victory of republicanism, but it took time for the various parties and coalitions to sort themselves into a workable government – practically speaking, they never did. Between 1910 and 1926 there were 45 different governments, with most of the changes brought about by military intervention rather than parliamentary procedures. The early leadership pressed their radical anti-Church and social reforms too hard, causing a reaction that revived the influence of the Catholic Church. Labour movements sprang up with the best intentions, but often paralysed industry. First and foremost, the republicans were unable to deliver promised financial reforms and stability, both through their own ineptitude and, later, because of the international depression of the 1920s. It was their economic failure that most significantly eroded their popular support.

Afonso Costa rose to leadership of the republican factions, but the hard stance of his anti-clericalism caused too much ill feeling to allow stability. Coups became standard. General Pimenta de Castro grabbed control briefly, but democratic forces deposed him.

Portugal, initially neutral, joined the Allies under Britain's influence in 1916. The causes behind World War I meant little to the nation but cost thousands of lives, in Europe and Africa, and brought further financial upheaval and political unrest. Sidónio Pais formed a dictatorial government in 1917, but was assassinated in Lisbon the following year. Three years later, António Machado Santos suffered the same fate. In 1926, the democratic government of Bernardino Machado was overthrown by military forces and the constitution suspended. Leadership passed through various hands and finally to General Oscar Carmona. He remained president until 1951, but it was not his leadership but that of his most influential appointee that made stability possible. In 1928, Carmona appointed António de Oliveira Salazar to the post of finance minister, with wide-ranging powers. By 1932, Salazar was effectively prime minister.

General Oscar Carmona, Portugal's president until 1951.

> Censorship was nothing new to a country dominated for so long by the Inquisition. In the 500-year history of publishing in Portugal, little more than 80 years have been free of censorship.

SALAZAR'S NEW STATE

Salazar immediately set about reorganising the country's disastrous financial morass, mostly through the narrow-minded austerity which reflected his own character. Having achieved what no leader had been able to do for a century, Salazar used his political capital to form a dictatorship, taking Mussolini's Italy as his model for national order and discipline.

The "New State", though nominally a corporative economic system under a republican government, was a fascist regime, with the National Union its only political party. It was authoritarian, pro-Catholic and imperialist. A state police organisation, the PIDE, was notorious in its suppression of subversion. A rigid and effective censorship settled like a thick fog over art, literature and free speech. Nothing negative or critical could find its way into print. A formerly lively journalism withered away. In blatant doublespeak, the government often referred to itself as a dictatorship without a dictator.

There was some resistance. In reaction to the powerful militaristic control there were numerous attempted coups and an underground Communist party that grew in power, leading the clandestine opposition. However, Salazar's leadership was never strongly challenged.

Putting self-preservation ahead of ideology, Salazar pretended to adhere to the League of Nations' non-intervention policy during the Spanish Civil War (1936–9) because he could not afford international censure, but actually sent a legion of some 20,000 soldiers to aid General Franco's Nationalist forces. Franco's victory served to validate the authority of Salazar's own regime.

The republican era had seen a minor cultural resurgence, when democratic ideals encouraged efforts at mass education, a proliferation of journalism, and a few writers of modern fiction and poetry. But this was slowed by political upheavals, and effectively quelled by the New State. The greatest writer of the period, the poet Fernando Pessoa (1888–1935), had one major work, *Mensagem*, published in 1934, but it was not until after World War II that most of his works were in print. Few others transcended the romantic nationalism of the era, as formidable barriers to the larger currents of European culture were created. The censorship of the New State slowed original thinking to a trickle, and most of that was devoted to political subversion rather than artistic endeavour.

AFTER WORLD WAR II

During World War II, the New State concentrated on self-preservation. Though Salazar admired Hitler, Portugal's traditional political and economic ties with Britain demanded neutrality, at least. However, Portugal did supply the Axis with much-needed wolfram (the ingredient necessary to alloy tungsten steel), almost until the end of the war. On the other hand, the Allies were granted strategic bases in the Azores. In fact, the war's main effect – though it was not widely advertised – was to replenish Portugal's coffers, as the government did business with both sides.

The defeat of the fascists should have given a signal to Salazar, a warning to mute his totalitarianism, but he was by now firmly entrenched. The changes over the next decade served primarily to protect the dictatorship still further from democratic insurgency.

In the 1950s, opposition to the New State solidified into two blocs. The legal bloc took advantage of the relaxed censorship in the month preceding the 1951 elections (the state's way of giving the impression of some democratic freedom) to run independent candidates. Members of the other, furtive, bloc organised various protest actions and engaged in what propaganda they could. These means kept resistance alive, forcing Salazar's hand and provoking new rounds of repression, deceit and constitutional changes, which eroded both Salazar's authority and popularity.

In 1958, General Humberto Delgado, a disenchanted member of the regime, stood for president, announcing that he would use the constitutional power of that position to dismiss Salazar. Despite mass demonstrations in his support, the official count declared that Admiral Américo Tomás, a Salazar loyalist, had been elected. Afterwards, constitutional decrees were enacted to prevent the repetition of such an event. The president was to be elected not by popular vote, but by an electoral college of the National Assembly, which was Salazar-

General Craveiro Lopes, Portugal's twelfth president (1951–58), before the crowds.

controlled. Delgado was assassinated in 1965 by state police, while attempting to cross the Spanish border back into Portugal.

THE EMPIRE STRIKES BACK

Portugal's entry into the United Nations was prevented by the Soviet bloc, and by opponents of Salazar's imperial colonialism, until 1955. Membership was finally granted not because of any real change, but by a successful diplomatic effort to whitewash his despotism.

Salazar would not change his policies because, despite the increasing cost of maintaining military rule in the colonies, they were very profitable for the homeland. Subsistence crops were increasingly neglected in favour of products like cotton, which fed the mills of Portugal while African citizens went hungry. The policy of *assimilado* – claiming that the goal was to assimilate African cultures into the Portuguese one – allowed Portugal to exploit these "citizens" as free slave labour.

Salazar's imperial intransigence led to serious consequences in the post-war world, where old empires were rapidly crumbling. The violent 1961 Angolan uprising, brutally crushed by the Portuguese, ignited an explosion of African nationalism. Throughout the 1960s, the government became more and more involved in maintaining the colonies, which were renamed "provinces" in a 1951 decree that underscored the insistence on a permanent Portuguese settlement.

As many young men were conscripted for the wars in Africa, popular support waned rapidly. Angola continued to be an economic boon, but the other colonies were a drain.

Salazar trusted ever fewer members of his regime, taking on more direct responsibilities himself for continuing the wars. He also relaxed his policy of fiscal austerity, and increasingly relied on foreign credit to finance the overseas operations.

Salazar reviewing the Portuguese troops in 1940.

THE END OF AN ERA

In 1968, the 79-year-old dictator suffered an incapacitating stroke; the long-awaited succession had arrived. Because Salazar – who was unwilling to face his own mortality – had made no provision for a successor, major upheavals were expected. But the transition to power of "Acting Prime Minister" Marcelo Caetano was relatively smooth. Salazar lived his final years in seclusion and died in 1970.

Caetano, once a protégé of Salazar, had resigned seven years earlier over conflicts with his superior. Called upon to resolve the national crisis, he saw the need for balanced change and stability, but was not bold enough. Many of the gravest injustices of the old regime were righted, but other changes were superficial, and the colonial issue was not confronted. When his early efforts at liberalisation failed to appease opposition unrest, Caetano returned to oppressive hostility.

Discontent among all ranks of the military over the continued ineffective colonial wars led to the formation of the Armed Forces Movement (MFA) in 1973. The following year, General António de Spínola published *Portugal and the Future*, a stinging critique of the current situation, which recommended a military takeover to save the country. The book's messages had been voiced before but never by so powerful a source. Many factors built towards the revolution, but this publication, whose importance Caetano himself said he had profoundly felt, lit the fuse.

BLOODLESS COUP

Two months later, on 25 April 1974, after a handful of premature uprisings, a near-bloodless coup began in Lisbon. Involving General Spínola and his fellow General Costa Gomes, it was conducted by angry "young captains" who commanded the 27 rebel units that seized key points throughout the city. Caetano and other government officials took refuge in the barracks of the National Republican Guard. The formal surrender came after a young officer threatened to crash a tank through the gates. The rebel takeover was quickly accepted throughout the country. The revolution, taking the red carnation as its symbol, sparked nationwide celebration culminating in joyful demonstrations on 1 May.

REVOLUTION AND EVOLUTION | 71

The initial government was a National Salvation group of military men, designed to give way to a constituent assembly as soon as it was practical. A provisional government was soon in place, and negotiations with African liberation movements went ahead. There were divisions about overseas policies, and an odd coup-within-a-coup developed, with Spínola attempting to wrest control from his opponents. It was unsuccessful and liberal forces continued to divest Portugal of its colonies. Guinea-Bissau, Mozambique, the Cape Verde Islands, São Tomé and finally Angola were granted independence. One result of de-colonialisation was a mass return of Portuguese nationals to their homeland – as many as 500,000 people. Angola and Mozambique fell into civil war, while East Timor devoured by Indonesia.

As the economy careered into an abyss, the political pendulum swung the other way, and there was huge social unrest. In 1976 the socialist leader Mário Soares became prime minister, but over the following decade governments frequently came and went. Socialist experiments were attempted as an antidote to years of Salazar. Land reforms were initiated, breaking up *látifundios*, the vast and long-established agricultural estates, particularly in the Alentejo, but these reforms did not prove successful.

In 1982, a long-awaited revision of the new constitution arrived. The democratic alliance and the far right were determined to rid the document of its Marxist taint. They were partially successful, but only after a period of nationwide demonstrations, strikes and resignations. The Council of the Revolution was eliminated, and the hope for a truly classless society remained an unrealised goal.

In the next few years, the country witnessed a shift away from socialism towards capitalism. Although the veteran socialist leader Mário Soares was elected president in 1986 (the first civilian to hold the post in over 60 years) and re-elected by a landslide in 1991, the capitalistic social democrats, under youthful economist Aníbal Cavaco Silva, won an overall majority in July 1987. In 1991, after a campaign based largely on his own forceful personality and his claims that his government had wrought nothing less than an economic miracle, Cavaco Silva won another resounding electoral victory.

JOINING THE EU

Such stability allowed Portugal to emerge from being the most backward economy in Europe to becoming, by the early 1990s, one of the most buoyant. In 1986 it had joined the European Community, and in 1992 took its turn at assuming presidency of the EEC. Among Cavaco Silva's most successful programmes was the re-privatisation of many companies and

General Antonio Spínola exits Queluz Palace after being nominated President of the Republic, 15 May 1974.

⊘ AN UNWILLING RETREAT

Despite international pressure, and increasing agitation within the colonies, Salazar's regime fiercely resisted any incursions on its colonial outposts. In 1961, the territory of São João da Ajuda, a tiny enclave surrounded by the country of Dahomey, consisted only of a decrepit fortress and the governor's estate.

When Dahomey became independent from France, and delivered an ultimatum to Lisbon to return Ajuda, the Portuguese governor was forced to comply, but he waited until the last possible moment to surrender, then spitefully burned down the buildings before departing.

industries nationalised by the Communists after the revolution.

In 1997, the Portuguese economy, then one of the fastest growing in Europe, met the requirements for the country to join the single currency, along with 10 other qualifying European Union states. Major public works projects such as a second bridge over the Tejo in Lisbon had already culminated in the successful hosting of Expo '98, and this, even more than monetary union, was seen by many Portuguese as the final confirmation of their country's arrival as

Ex-Portuguese president José Manuel Barrosso was also a president of the European Commission.

a modern, thriving European economy, poised to meet the challenges of the new millennium.

However, a slowing down of the economy had wrong-footed the socialist government elected in 1995, and in 2002 Durão Barroso became prime minister of a centre-right government. In July 2004, he accepted the post of European Commission president, which he did not relinquish until 2014. Former Lisbon mayor Pedro Santana Lopes became prime minister. In February 2005 a displeased electorate voted in the Socialist Party, now led by little-known José Sócrates, with its first ever overall majority. Restoring balance, the presidential election in January 2006 was won by a familiar social democrat, former prime minister Cavaco Silva. In 2007 the Portuguese experienced their most significant social change in years when they voted to legalise abortion. The same year, Prime Minister Sócrates assumed the EU presidency. In 2009, as leader of the re-elected Socialist Party, he formed a minority government.

Hit by the global recession, Portugal's economic problems were profound. Like Greece, it suffered feeble growth, hampered by debt, low productivity and an ageing population, although its funding requirements were not as severe. In

> *The Portuguese continue to seek their fortunes abroad. Around 2.3 million Portuguese live abroad, nearly three times the number of foreigners living in Portugal. Their remittances make up 1.4 percent of the GDP.*

2010, the government implemented austerity measures in an attempt to reduce the budget deficit, facing the difficult task of meeting the needs of its people while improving its economic outlook. Despite these measures, economic growth fell in the next three years, while unemployment soared to 17.7 percent in early 2013, triggering massive social protests and unrest. Portugal was forced to accept a €78 billion financial bailout from the EU in return for further cuts (the country did not exit the programme until 2014). Eventually, the drastic austerity measures paid off, the budget deficit was more than cut in half (from 11.2 percent in 2010 to 4.4 percent in 2015) and slow recovery began. In 2018 the Portuguese economy grew by 1.7 percent and austerity was eased.

Slowly emerging from the shadow of recession, Portugal received yet another boost of optimism after its national football team won the Euro 2016 in France (beating the hosts in the final), before winning the inaugural UEFA Nations League in 2019.

Of course, the Covid-19 pandemic of 2020–22 had a massive negative impact on tourism and therefore the economy. However, the country has since harnessed the spending power of a new wave of wealthy digital nomads with its D8 visa (for earners of over €3,280 per month).

SALAZAR

António de Oliveira Salazar, who led the country for 40 years, was the dominant figure of 20th-century Portugal.

António de Oliveira Salazar was a country boy, born in 1889, who took the strict conservative values of his father far beyond the small rural world that formed them: ultimately transforming the whole nation into his image of what it should be. As a professor of economics at Coimbra, Salazar was an active polemicist for the right. He made his first political impact as the youthful leader of the Centro Académico da Democracia Cristã (Academic Centre for Christian Democracy), a Catholic intellectual group that opposed the anti-clerical and individualistic philosophy of the republic. He made a brief foray into national politics but only accepted a political position when he could be assured of complete control.

This came in 1928, when the prime minister, General Carmona, offered Salazar the role of finance minister with absolute power over national finance. In 1932, he was appointed president of the Council of Ministers – another name for prime minister. Although there was opposition, dissent, and various plots against his life, Salazar's pervasive influence on Portugal would not truly lift until the April revolution of 1974, six years after a disabling stroke, and four years after his death.

Salazar imposed his own character upon the nation. He was austere, introverted, and seldom travelled outside Portugal. He steered his country through international affairs with as much neutrality as possible. Portugal accepted Salazar's fascism as a kind of defensive posture in the face of the worldwide technological explosion of the 20th century. His conservative and at times reactionary attitudes towards industrialisation, agricultural reform, education and religion kept Portugal apart from the turbulence of the age. His attitude that Portugal was a naturally poor country – good for living in but not for producing anything – was widely held. Catholic cults, like that of Our Lady of Fátima, were encouraged and turned into propaganda.

Salazar also drew upon the romanticised history of Portuguese exploration and trade, inculcating a generation of schoolchildren with the self-aggrandising idea of Portugal's manifest destiny as an empire. The country turned inwards, though still holding on to its colonies for as long as possible, and tried to ignore the changing face of world politics. It was a comforting but debilitating attitude.

Salazar lived quietly, taking modest holidays by the sea or in his beloved Beira countryside. He remained unmarried, though he had a close but apparently celibate relationship with his lifelong housekeeper, Dona Maria de Jesus Caetano.

Salazar in 1958.

On 3 August 1968, in his fortress sanctuary in Estoril, Salazar suffered a stroke that left him an invalid. He left no designated heir, but with surprisingly little turmoil, Marcelo Caetano, a brilliant lecturer but a rather weak politician, was made prime minister. For the remaining two years of Salazar's life, he received few visitors and was given very little public attention. Those close to him chose not to tell him the truth about the succession of Caetano. Instead, they fabricated an image of Portugal still led by the old dictator.

When Dona Maria tried to convince him to retire, he refused and, in a last pathetic boast, claimed that he had no choice but to remain, because there was no one else. He died, aged 81, believing that he was still in control.

The shrine of Fátima draws thousands of pilgrims and worshippers.

Easter procession, Algarve.

SAINTS, MIRACLES AND SHRINES

Religion touches all aspects of Portuguese life. Every town and village has its own saint, which is a cause for celebration at least once a year.

In the middle of the 6th century a young monk named Martin arrived in Mondoñedo, in northwest Spain, where he founded the abbey of Dume. His mission then took him to Braga, the former Roman city that had become the political and religious stronghold of the Suevi, a barbarian tribe that had adopted Arianism, a heretical form of Christianity. Martin, who had been inspired at the shrine of St Martin at Tours, was determined to convert Suevi leaders to true Christianity.

In 559, he converted the Suevi king, Theodomirus. Within a decade, Martin was appointed archbishop of Braga. He found a further challenge, however, among the general population. Nominally Catholics since their conversion under the Roman Empire, the locals had incorporated many non-Christian beliefs and customs into their religion. To Martin, this was unacceptable, and in a written sermon entitled *De Correctione Rusticorum* (On the Correction of Peasants), he called for an end to the use of charms, auguries and divination, the invocation of the devil, and the cults of the dead, fountains and stars.

St Martin did not succeed, nor have 14 centuries of similarly inclined zealots and reformers. Yet, though frowned upon by the orthodox Church, spontaneous, independent Catholicism should not be dismissed as a form of superstition or magic; rather, it is evidence of a vigorous religious tradition.

In the past, when a newborn child proved healthy, it was said that it was conceived when the moon was waxing. The states of the moon were believed to be very influential in the way all living things grow: vegetables, animals and human beings. Similarly, certain fountains were reputed to have particular healing powers. And

Festa das Tochas Flores in the town of Sao Bras de Alportel, Algarve.

> Many unorthodox elements linger to this day as an obstinate strain within Catholic traditions – naturally, there is much wrestling over the issues between the Church hierarchy and the parishes.

under many of these, Moorish princesses were said to be hiding, watching over treasures.

AROUND MIDNIGHT

One of the more dramatic folk practices was the midnight baptism. This developed during the 17th century, and occurred when a pregnant woman was prone to miscarriages or when her previous child was stillborn. The "baptism" used to take place at midnight in the middle of a bridge that divided two municipalities – a powerful spot that is neither one place nor another, at the moment that is neither one day nor the next. Certain bridges, such as the Ponte da Barca in the Minho, were famous for this.

When everything was ready, the child's father and a friend, armed with sticks, used to stand guard at the ends of the bridge. They were there to ward off cats and dogs – potentially witches or the devil in disguise. The first person who passed after the church bells struck midnight was charged with performing the rite. He or she would pour river water over the expectant mother's belly and baptise the child "in the name of the Father, the Son and the Holy Ghost" but the final "Amen" would not be uttered; this would wait until the child was born and could be properly baptised by a priest in church.

Such practices may now be consigned to history, but religious passion still governs behaviour in Portugal, and the church is the central meeting place of the whole parish. At Easter, the cross that represents the resurrection of Christ is taken from the church and carried to all the households. It is kissed as it enters each house, and when it is returned to the church, it is a symbol of the new life shared by the whole community.

Similarly, on All Saints' Day and All Souls' Day (1 and 2 November), the celebrations at the parish cemetery are attended by everyone. Lamps are lit, and tombs are cleaned and decorated with flowers. The whole parish celebrates this strongly felt sense of continuity with the past, praying together for their dead.

Perhaps the strongest evidence that the feeling of community extends beyond this life is the common belief in the "procession of the dead".

Street party during the Festas dos Santos Populares.

Certain people claim that they have the power to hear or see a procession of the ghosts of those parishioners who have recently died. This procession is seen leaving the cemetery, with a coffin in its centre. When it returns, the ghost of the parishioner who will be the next to die will be in the coffin. Thus, it is said, these seers can predict the people who are going to die imminently – but they cannot reveal the names to anybody if they themselves want to remain alive.

PATRON SAINTS

The use of religion to establish a communal identity is most clearly shown by the celebrations for the local patron saint. An organising committee busies itself all year collecting money, planning

SAINTS, MIRACLES AND SHRINES

decorations, and arranging events. The importance of these celebrations is immense, as they represent and solidify local pride. The *festa* is a joyful occasion heralded by firecrackers and by music blaring from loudspeakers placed on the church tower. The pivotal event is the procession after Mass, when the image of the patron saint is carried with great pomp on a brightly decorated stand along a roughly circular path.

After that, the secular celebrations begin. These usually involve dancing to traditional brass bands, folk-dance groups and, nowadays, rock and pop bands as well. A great deal of wine is consumed and the festivities are a popular social focus for young people. Not surprisingly, it is this aspect of the celebration that some priests oppose.

Popular attitudes to saints differ from church doctrine not so much in content as in emphasis. The people place great importance on material benefits and personal, reciprocal relationships with saints. They pray to specific saints for specific problems – St Lawrence if they have a toothache, St Brás if suffering from a sore throat, St Christopher when going on a journey. Our Lady of the Conception, naturally, helps with problems of infertility; the Holy Family is asked to intervene in family problems; and so on. People will also address personal prayers to particular saints' images. If the believer's prayer is answered, this proves that the particular image is a singularly sacred one, a favoured line of communication. In this way shrines develop, whether individual, family, or even national, with images becoming famous for their miraculous powers.

WAX OFFERINGS

When a prayer to St Anthony asks for a specific favour – that a loved one, or even a pig or sheep, recover from a bout of ill health, or an offer of marriage be accepted – a promise is made to give the saint something in return. A wax heart might be given for a successful engagement, or a wax pig if the animal has fully recovered. But if the promise is not fulfilled, punishment may follow.

If you visit churches in northern Portugal, you will often see these *ex voto* offerings hanging on the walls alongside other gifts such as bridal dresses, photographs, written testimonies or braids of women's hair. Shrines of great importance such as Bom Jesus and Sameiro, near Braga, have large displays. At Fátima (see page 80), the best-known shrine in the country, wax gifts accumulate so quickly that special furnaces have been installed to burn them.

> *The notion of the miracle in popular religion is more loosely interpreted than in the Church. Essentially, a miracle is considered to have taken place every time a specific prayer is answered.*

Easter procession in Obidos.

There is also another kind of gift: a personal sacrifice. The church has been strongly critical of this, but until the late 1960s, it was firmly encouraged. If you visit the shrine of São Bento da Porta Aberta (St Benedict of the Open Door) in the beautiful mountain landscape of Gerês near the dam of Caniçada on 13 August, you will find people laboriously circumambulating the church on their knees.

This scene is even more striking because these people are surrounded by others celebrating the day with singing, dancing, eating and drinking. But those on their knees are celebrating, too – because the saint has answered their prayers. You will see the same scene at the Fátima shrine at any time of year.

Another kind of payment to patron saints has all but disappeared, due to strong Church opposition. In the parish of Senhora da Aparecida in Lousada, for example, before the main procession leaves the church, there is another one in which 20 or more open coffins – containing living people, their faces covered with white handkerchiefs – are carried through the streets. Those who ride in the coffins are offering a false burial to the saint who saved them from having to participate in a real one. The occasion, therefore, is a joyful one, although it sounds macabre. There is plenty of light-hearted banter, and the "dead" participants mingle with the other parishioners afterwards, drinking and dancing.

SURVIVING CULTS

The cult of the dead, another morbid religious tradition and one of the targets of St Martin during the 6th century, remains an object of popular fascination in the north. Very occasionally, a body is buried but does not undergo the normal process of decay. Such people are often considered to be saints and there are a number of shrines where the corpses are exposed. The Church nearly always opposes these cults at first, but eventually tolerates them as they grow in popularity: three such shrines are the Infanta Santa Mafalda in Arouca, the São Torcato near Guimarães, and the Santinha de Arcozelo near Porto. Even in an unlikely spot like the small urban cemetery of the elegant Foz neighbourhood in Porto, a shrine to one of these "saints" can be found.

Along rural roads one will frequently find pretty, smaller shrines, but these are intended to protect travellers and are not connected with the cult of the dead. They contain images of Christ or the Virgin or a popular saint. At the base, little moulded flames surround figures that represent the souls of sinners suspended in Purgatory.

COMPROMISE AND COEXISTENCE

Portuguese history is full of examples of the continuing conflict between the spontaneous and all-embracing religiosity of ordinary people, and the more restrictive attitudes of the theologically minded elites – and the ways in which the two have learned to coexist. From the early days of the Western Crusade in the 12th century and the power of military-religious orders like the Knights Templar and the Hospitallers, to the dark days of the Inquisition, religious and secular authorities have vied with each other for power, and used each other to their own advantage. In more recent years, imperialism, as in the colonial era, was seen as a form of religious crusade: each "victory" against native populations along the way was considered a miracle. And Salazar's regime actively encouraged the cult of Our Lady of Fátima, even managing to present Portugal's policy of neutrality during World War II as being based on the soothsayings of the Virgin.

Shrine outside Ferraguda church in the Algarve.

⊙ OUR LADY OF FÁTIMA

Fátima, near the town of Leiria, is one of the largest shrines in Western Europe (see page 226). On 13 May 1917, the Virgin is supposed to have appeared to three children. The event is said to have been repeated on the 13th of the subsequent five months, and each time the Virgin spoke about peace in the world. Fátima became a rallying point for the revival of Catholicism in the 1930s and 1940s.

Today, from May to October the roads around Leiria are lined with pilgrims, many of whom have come great distances on foot to pay the Virgin for her favours. Multiple tour buses run from towns across the region.

The High Cross at Fátima, designed by Robert Schad.

TRAVELLERS' TALES

There were several distinguished names among early visitors to Portugal, and they left with strong and contradictory impressions. Some fell in love with the country, while others were more damning.

English visitors to Portugal long believed themselves to be discoverers of the one exotic land left in well-visited, well-described Europe. In 1845, Dorothy Quillinan, daughter of William Wordsworth, wrote, "There is, I believe, no country in Europe that is less thoroughly familiar to me". A century later, Evelyn Waugh thought it was still a well-kept secret, and wrote: "There is no European capital of antiquity about which one hears so little." But English travellers had been going to Portugal, and writing about it, for some time.

EIGHTEENTH-CENTURY OPINIONS

The most flamboyant of the 18th-century visitors to Portugal was William Beckford, who set up a sumptuous house in Ramalhoa near Sintra in 1787. He inspired Byron's *Childe Harold*, whose first stop on his pilgrimage to Portugal was to wander through Sintra conjuring Beckford's ghost and meditating on the brevity of life and pleasure.

Beckford first visited the peninsula in 1787, shortly after the publication of his Gothic novel *Vathek*. The unorthodox Englishman, who had left England in the wake of a homosexual scandal, caught the fancy of the pious Marquis of Marialva, who hoped to convert him to Catholicism. But Beckford, as we learn from his diary, was desperate not for the salvation of his soul but for an introduction to the court of Queen Maria. England's ambassador Sir Hugh Walpole refused to perform this service for his disgraced countryman. The marquis guaranteed an introduction if Beckford would convert, but the writer had no such intention and he left, petulant and thwarted. By the time he was finally presented at court in 1794, poor Maria had long been insane.

Beckford's *Sketches of Spain and Portugal* give an idiosyncratic, critical but sensitive view

The flamboyant William Beckford.

of Portugal's art, music, nature and society. His is a land of the senses: he describes the *modinha*, a haunting, erotic song, and the luxuriant beauty of the vegetation. His journals provide a brilliant, if haphazard, guide to Portugal's art and climate.

On his first visit to Portugal in 1796, Robert Southey, a Romantic and the future English Poet Laureate, expressed disapproval of the filth of Lisbon, the discomfort of the country inns, and the corruption and superstition of the priests. But on a subsequent visit, four years later, although he still mourned the lack of "genial company", he fell in love with the country, and delighted in the sensual orange groves, long lazy days and lush, fertile fields.

William Mickle, the 18th-century poet and translator of Luís Camões' works, was a great admirer of Portugal's "genial clime" and contrasted the "gloomy mists" of England to the "sun-basked scenes... where orange bowers invite".

LORD BYRON

Lord Byron held strong and divergent opinions on the country – Lisbon he loathed, but other areas charmed him. He wrote to his mother in 1809 (of Lisbon): "except the view from the Tagus, which is beautiful, and some fine churches and convents, it contains little but filthy streets and more filthy inhabitants." But he was far more enamoured of Sintra: "To make amends for this, the village of Cintra [sic], about fifteen miles from the capital, is, perhaps in every respect, the most delightful in Europe; it contains beauties of every description, natural and artificial. Palaces and gardens rising in the midst of rocks, cataracts, and precipices; convents on stupendous heights... It unites in itself all the wildness of the western highlands, with the verdure of the south of France."

Byron's view of Lisbon also resonates in his poetry, where he painted the city as a faithless harlot of a town, a siren who glitters beautifully from the water but who reveals, on closer contact, only filth and treachery:
But whoso entereth within this town,
That, sheening far, celestial seems to be,
Disconsolate will wander up and down,
Mid many things unsightly to strange see;
For hut and palace show like filthily...
Poor paltry slaves! yet born midst noblest scenes.

BORROW'S TRAVELS

The ingratitude of the Portuguese towards the British for their help in expelling Napoleon was a cause of resentment for another Englishman, George Borrow. Travelling in 1835, on a mission for the Bible Society, he complained that the English "who have never been at war with Portugal, who have fought for its independence on land and sea, and always with success, who have forced themselves by a treaty of commerce to drink its coarse and filthy wines... are the most unpopular people who visit Portugal."

Borrow's account of Portugal, although less famous than Byron's stanzas, is an original, entertaining and evocative description. He was a great reporter of human eccentricity, and was also enthusiastic about the beauties of Portugal. Lisbon, he claimed, "is quite as much deserving the attention of the artist as even Rome itself". Sintra, so lavishly praised by Byron, captivated all travellers and was "a mingled scene of fairy beauty, artificial elegance, savage grandeur, domes, turrets, enormous trees, flowers, and waterfalls, such as is met with nowhere else under the sun". It is truly, Borrow wrote, "Portuguese Paradise".

A reminder of Lord Byron's patronage in Sintra.

⊙ SPEAKING TO THE NATIVES

George Borrow was a wonderfully comic traveller, erratic and egotistical. His self-confidence was typified by his belief that after just two weeks he could speak fluent Portuguese. He refused to accept that much of the time people could not understand what he was saying, and his advice to novices speaking a foreign language offered the sort of wrong-headed lesson that some tourists seem to take to heart even today. He confidently made the point: "Those who wish to make themselves understood by a foreigner in his own language should speak with much noise and vociferation, opening their mouths wide."

Portuguese fado singer, Katia Guerreiro, performs at The Bahrain International Music Festival in Manama.

FADO

The Portuguese blues, fado (which comes from the Latin *fatum*, meaning fate), is characterised by elegiac songs about love, loss, the sea, poverty and beauty.

The unique musical tradition of fado has grown out of Portugal's cocktail of culture – a result of the country's early exploration and connections with places overseas. Like the blues, flamenco and tango, it was a music that grew out of hardship and poverty, but became the soundtrack of a nation.

Fado's sad, distinctively Portuguese songs are thought to have developed from the music of the Moors, who influenced the country in many ways, and the Lundum music of the Brazilian slaves, who arrived in Portugal after long sea voyages in the early 19th century. One famous fado song, called *The Black Boat,* talks specifically of a *senzala* (place where the slaves were kept). Many early songs are related to the sea, to faraway lands, and longing for home – subjects unsurprising in such a seafaring nation.

The other major source for the songs is believed to have been the verses of the minstrels and jesters in the middle ages, which share similar themes to those of fado. These included the *cantigas de amigo* (songs about a boyfriend), love songs that are sung solely by women, and satirical songs making jibes about the government and politicians.

Fado seems to have first taken off in the working-class districts of Alfama and Mouraria in Lisbon, and, rapidly gaining in popularity, later spread to the University of Coimbra, where it took on a quite different character. The fado in Coimbra is sung only by men, praising the beauty of women, and often takes the form of serenades.

Fadistas at first came from the working class – this was not the music of the bourgeoisie. Its musicians and singers mixed with the edgier members of society – the criminals and prostitutes. The most famous *fadista* of the 19th

Historic entertainment in a café.

⊘ AMÁLIA RODRIGUES

Portugal's most famous *fadista*, Amália, was born in 1920 into a poor family, and as a child sold fruit on the Lisbon docks. Her remarkable voice was noted by local people, who often asked her to sing for them, and after years of amateur performances she had her first professional engagement aged 19. Her career quickly took off, and she became Portugal's most revered star. Amália appeared in films and became an international icon and a national treasure, continuing to perform in public until 1990. When she died in 1999 there were more than three days' mourning in Alfama. Her house in Lisbon now houses the Museu de Amália Rodrigues.

century, Maria Severa, was a prostitute who sang in her mother's tavern in Alfama. She attracted the attention of the aristocratic Conde di Vimioso with her singing, and they embarked on a scandalous love affair which crossed class barriers in a hitherto unacceptable way.

The Conde's influence saw fado reach the court, but Maria Severa died aged just 26, either from tuberculosis or by suicide. She always sang wrapped in a black shawl, which female fado singers still do today in her memory.

During the mid-20th century, the dictator Salazar (in power from 1932 to 1968) insisted that fado singers become professional and only sing in specially designated fado houses. This was the "golden age" of fado. During this period, famous names included Alfredo Marceneiro and Maria Teresa de Noronha, as well as the guitar players Armandinho and Jaime Santos, but most famous of all was Amália Rodrigues, whose rise to international superstardom saw the status of fado change forever.

THE SINGERS AND THE SONG

The *fadista*, a powerfully voiced singer, is usually backed by a *guitarra* – a twelve-stringed Portuguese guitar with a pear-shaped body rather like an Arabian *oud* – and a classical six-stringed guitar, which is called a *viola* in Portugal. The male fado singer usually wears a black suit; he sings about love affairs, the city, life's misery, bullfighting, politicians, and about the past. The female singer will also wear black, and sings heart-rendingly about love and death, love lost, and tragic romance.

All fado is linked with the concept of *saudade*. This difficult-to-translate term is a kind of nostalgic longing and yearning for something that is lost. It is an emotion that has a peculiar resonance in the Portuguese pysche.

Fado is a performance, and you are expected to be quiet and listen. The fado of Coimbra is usually taken even more seriously than that of Lisbon, which means it is very serious indeed.

For a while after the 1974 Carnation Revolution, fado lost some currency in Portugal, as it was associated with the old regime. However, it crept back, eventually becoming even more widely sung than before. Modern *fadistas* have brought the sound up to date (see page 87).

WHERE TO FIND FADO

There are plenty of places where visitors can experience fado for themselves. It is best to hear

Fado singer, Mariza, performs during a concert in homage to legendary singer Amália.

Late Portuguese fado singer and former judge Fernando Machado Soares.

it sung at its source, in Alfama, Bairro Alto and Mouraria in Lisbon or in Coimbra, although there are fado houses in other towns across Portugal. Finding true, earthy fado has some similarities with seeking out authentic Spanish flamenco. There are smart and formal venues with famous singers, but these tend to work out very expensive when you combine admission charges and the accompanying drinks and meals, and they don't have the same intimate atmosphere.

Alternatively, there are scruffier backstreet bars where the experience feels more spontaneous. These offer *fado vadio* (street fado), which means anyone can stand up and have a go, and some local people come back to do so week after week. The singers might not be of quite the same quality, but the immediacy of the passion and atmosphere may far exceed the more refined version.

> *The Portuguese say that it takes more than a good voice to become a true fadista – it takes soul.*

Singers in the Alfama District.

MODERN FADISTAS

The new wave of *fadistas* is still dominated by women: Mariza, Raquel Tavares, Ana Moura, Katia Guerreiro and Carminho. Of the male new guard, there is Pedro Moutinho, born into a well-known family of *fadistas* in Oeiras. The most natural successor to Amália is Mariza, instantly recognisable with her bleached blonde hair. She was born Marisa dos Reis Nunes in Mozambique (then a Portuguese colony) in 1973, and is of Portuguese-African parentage. At the age of three, the family moved to Mouraria in Lisbon, and she began singing at the age of five in her parents' restaurant. Mariza moved away from fado in her teens, experimenting with other types of music and travelling in Brazil when she was in her twenties, but she came back to fado, and her powerful, theatrical, yet awesomely emotional performances make her a natural star. Her background, with elements of German, Spanish, French, African and Indian ancestry, in some ways represents the story of Portugal, and a particularly emotional song in her repertoire is *Oh Gente da Minha Terra* (Oh People of my Country). Mariza performs in sell-out concerts all over the world, in venues such as the Carnegie Hall in New York and the Royal Festival Hall in London, and has twice received Latin Grammy nominations. In 2010 she returned to her fado roots with a widely acclaimed album, *Fado Tradizional*. Her most recent, *Mariza*, was released in 2018.

Mercado da Ribeira, Lisbon.

PORTUGUESE FOOD

Fresh fish, succulent pork and hearty soups laced with plenty of garlic make Portuguese food stand out from the crowd.

To dine in Portugal is to taste the presence of other countries, other cuisines. It is to conjure up images of empire: Brazil, Angola, Mozambique, Goa and Macau. These and others all "belonged" to Portugal once and, in a manner of speaking, foods from four continents helped to stir the pot.

The period of Portuguese empire when this small nation reached out across the terrifying "Green Sea of Darkness", as the Atlantic was called, has long passed. Yet Portugal, left with only the Azores and Madeira, has preserved the flavours of other cultures in its cooking.

Prince Henry the Navigator, less than 30 years old when he began to promote exploration, was a true scientist in an age of superstition. He ordered his explorers to bring back from new lands not only riches and wild tales, but also fruits, nuts and plants. In 1420 he sent settlers to colonise the newly discovered island of Madeira. With them went plants he believed would thrive in Madeira's volcanic soil and subtropical climate, including grape vines from Crete and sugar cane from Sicily. Even more significant for Portuguese cooking was Vasco da Gama's discovery of the sea route to the East in 1497–8, only five years after Christopher Columbus's discovery of the West Indies.

SPICES OF THE ORIENT

Black pepper was what Vasco da Gama sought, but cinnamon, which he also found in Calcutta, would soon become equally precious to Portuguese cooks. Indeed, one boatload of cinnamon sticks fetched enough money to pay for an entire expedition to India. Cinnamon is perhaps the most beloved spice in Portugal today, certainly for the famous egg sweets (*doces de ovos*, see page 95). Spaniards, on the other hand, prefer vanilla for their puddings and flans. There is a

Portuguese sardines are plump and succulent.

> The Portuguese word for tea – chá – is almost identical to the Cantonese one – ch'a – from which is derived the colloquial English term "char".

good historical reason for this: it was the Spaniards who found Montezuma sipping vanilla-spiked hot chocolate in Mexico and learned the trick of curing vanilla beans, the seed pods of a wild orchid. Perhaps this is why chocolate, too, is more popular in Spain than in Portugal.

The spiciest Portuguese dishes, incidentally, are not found on the mainland but in the Azores and Madeira. These islands were ports of call for the early navigators, who would barter with the native people, offering spices in exchange for fresh fruits, vegetables, meat and the local brew.

NEW FOOD FOR OLD

During Portugal's lavish Age of Empire, its navigators became couriers, bringing New World foods to the Old and vice versa. Mediterranean sugar cane, for example, was cultivated in Brazil. Brazilian pineapples were introduced to the Azores, a colony established under Prince Henry. They still flourish there in hothouses, ripening under wafting wood smoke. Azorean pineapples, chunky, honey-sweet and tender to the core, are teamed today with rosettes of Portugal's mahogany-hued, air-cured *presunto* (prosciutto-like ham) and served as an elegant appetiser in fashionable Lisbon restaurants.

Tiny, incendiary Brazilian chilli peppers took root in Angola, another important Portuguese colony, early on, and became so essential to cooks there that today they're known by a Romanisation of their Swahili name, *piri-piri*. Since Angola ceased to be a Portuguese colony in the mid-1970s, the subsequent influx to Lisbon of thousands of Angolan refugees has meant that *piri-piri* sauce (an oil and vinegar mixture strewn with minced chillies) is as popular a table condiment in mainland Portugal as salt and pepper.

Other exchanges were African coffee, transplanted to Brazil, which today produces about half of the world's supply; Brazilian cashews, which landed in Africa and India; and East Asian tea plants, which were taken to the Azores.

All this transporting of seeds, leaves, barks, roots, stalks and cuttings by Portuguese explorers across oceans and continents dramatically affected Portuguese cooking. New World tomatoes and potatoes came to Portugal about the same time as they did to Spain, in the 16th century. Portuguese cooks might drop a few garlic cloves into the soup or stew along with the tomatoes and potatoes, or tuck in a stick of cinnamon.

A LA PORTUGAISE

It is unlikely that anyone grows nuttier, earthier potatoes today than the Portuguese. Indeed, along the New England coast in the United States, where so many Portuguese families have settled, there is an old saying: "If you want your potatoes to grow, you must speak to them in Portuguese." Tomatoes respond to the Portuguese touch, too, and those harvested in the vast Alentejo province, east of Lisbon, are as juicy, red and tasty as any on Earth.

Francesinha, a traditional Portuguese sandwich

Onions and garlic, indispensable to any respectable Portuguese cook, were probably introduced by the Romans, who are believed to have brought wheat here, too. They aimed to make the Iberian peninsula the granary of Rome. They also probably introduced olives (a major source of income today) and grapes. From shards found in Alentejo, it is known that the Romans were making wine there as early as the 2nd century AD.

The Moors, who occupied a large chunk of Portugal from the early 8th to the mid-13th centuries, enriched the pot even more than the Romans. The southern provinces were the Moorish stronghold – the Algarve and Alentejo, in particular – and many traces of North Africa can still be seen.

It was the Arabs who dug irrigation ditches, who first planted rice (it now grows up and down the west coast), and who also covered the Algarve slopes with almond trees. The Algarve's almonds were ground into paste, sweetened, and shaped into delicate miniature fruits, birds and flowers displaying intricate detail. They are still produced today.

The Moors also introduced figs and apricots to the Algarve, together with the trick of drying them in the sun. They planted groves of lemons and oranges and, as was their custom, they combined fruit with fish and with meat.

It was the Arabs, too, who invented the *cataplana*, a hinged metal pan, a sort of primitive pressure cooker shaped like an oversized clam shell that can be clamped shut and set on a quick fire. The food inside – fish, shellfish, chicken, vegetables or a medley of all – steams to supreme succulence. What goes into a *cataplana* depends on the whim of the cook (and on what is available), but the most famous recipe is *amêijoas na cataplana*, clams tossed with rounds of sausage and cubes of ham in an intensely garlicky tomato sauce. This unlikely pork and shellfish combination was supposedly created at the time of the Inquisition as a test of true Christianity. Pork and shellfish, of course, were forbidden to Jews and Muslims alike.

There is no shortage of examples of Portugal's culinary ingenuity. Thrifty Portuguese cooks with an eye on their wallets made bread a main course by layering yeast dough into a pan with snippets of chicken and sausage and two kinds of ham – a classic from the remote northern Trás-os-Montes which is called *folar*. And when times were particularly hard they would crumble yesterday's bread into shrimp cooking water and come up with the Estremadura favourite known as *açorda de mariscos*.

Less economical but equally inventive is the Serra da Estrela recipe, which involves braising duck with bacon and rice; or smothering red mullet the Setúbal way, with tiny tart oranges; or scrambling flakes of salt cod with eggs and shoestring potatoes (thinly cut and crisply fried), as is done all over the country.

BACALHAU

Dried salt cod, or *bacalhau* (pronounced buckle-yow), is a purely Portuguese invention. António M. Bello, first president of Portugal's gastronomic society, wrote in his *Culinária Portuguesa*, published in Lisbon in 1936, that the Portuguese

> Most supposedly vegetable dishes include meat fat or stock; even a salad is not considered complete without a sprinkling of tuna. Vegetarians may prefer self-catering, shopping at markets for fruit, vegetables and bread.

Shopping at Casa Oriental, Porto.

were fishing Newfoundland's Grand Banks for cod within just a few years of Columbus's discovery of America.

New fishing rules impose restraints and quotas, and cod fishing especially is much altered. Yet Portuguese poems, stories, folk sayings and fado songs still maintain a bittersweet seafaring tradition:

*O waves from the salty sea,
From whence comes your salt?
From the tears shed on the
Beaches of Portugal.*

It was in the 16th century that Portuguese fishermen learned to salt cod at sea to make it last the long voyage home, and to sun-dry it into board-stiff slabs that could be kept for months then soaked in cool water before cooking.

Fish is still sun-dried on racks in the old way on the beach at Nazaré, although much less cod is available now. The Grand Banks have become so over-fished that the Portuguese have taken to importing *bacalhau* from Norway, just to be able to meet their annual demands. This, of course, prices salt cod – once an inexpensive staple of the national diet – beyond the reach of the very people it sustained for centuries.

The best and most famous dishes are *bacalhau à Gomes de sá* (cod cooked in a casserole with thinly sliced potatoes and onions, garnished with hard-boiled eggs and black olives), *bacalhau à brás* and *bacalhau dourado* (two similar recipes composed of scrambled eggs, onions and shoestring potatoes), *bacalhau à Conde de Guarda* (salt cod creamed with mashed potatoes) and *bolinhos de bacalhau* (cod fish balls, a very popular hors d'oeuvre). All these once-humble recipes are served today in the most expensive restaurants. Prepared properly, they are delicious, but if too little care is taken they can be very salty.

Classic cod dish.

⊘ SARDINE SEASON

Nearly as popular as salt cod are the sardines netted off the Atlantic coast. These are what the fishermen of Nazaré go out looking for day after day – although the men are less likely now to wear their traditional tartan, and the flat-bottomed boats have mostly given way to motorised craft. Portuguese sardines are considered the sweetest and fattest in the world, and local women grill them right on the streets, using little terracotta braziers. But you will only see this going on in spring, summer and early autumn: the "sardine season". As every right-minded Portuguese knows, sardines are too bony to eat from November to April.

> Someone once said that the Portuguese live on dreams and subsist on salt cod. They do claim to know 365 ways to prepare it, one for each day of the year.

PORTUGUESE PORK

If salt cod and sardines share top billing as the favourite fish, pork reigns supreme as the king of *carne* (meat). Portuguese pork is incomparably sweet and tender because of the pigs' agreeable diet and life of leisure. In the northerly Trás-os-Montes province, they say that if you want good pork in the autumn you must feed your pigs twice a day in August. Some farmers even go so far as to cook potatoes for their animals.

Small wonder the hams (*presunto* and *fiambre*) and sausages (*salsichas*) are so highly prized here (the best of all are said to come from Chaves). Small wonder, too, that charcuterie figures so prominently in the regional soups and stews. Cooks here will wrap freshly caught brook trout in slices of *presunto*, then bounce them in and out of a skillet so hot the ham is transformed to a crisp, deeply smoky sort of pastry.

But Portugal's most famous pork dish comes from the Alentejo. It is *porco à alentejana*, for which cubes of pork are marinated in a paste of sweet red peppers and garlic, browned in the fruity local olive oil, then covered and braised with baby clams, still in the shell. The clams open slowly under the gentle heat, spilling their briny juices into the ambrosial red mixture. The secret behind achieving the distinctive nut-like flavour of Alentejo pork is that the pigs are turned loose each autumn to forage among the cork oaks. Here they nibble on acorns and wild herbs, as well as the occasional truffle.

Sausage-making is also highly prized in the Alentejo, and this region's garlicky *chouriços*, *linguiças*, *farinheiras* (sausages plumped up with cereal) and chunky, smoky *paios* are without peers. As one of Portugal's food authorities, Maria de Lourdes Modesto writes in *Cozinha Tradicional Portuguesa*, "The grand destiny of the pig in the Alentejo is to become sausage."

Here, every part of the pig is used – ears, snout, tail, feet. At carnival time, the centrepiece of each banquet *festa* is *pezinhos de porco de coentrada*, dainty pigs' feet braised with onions, garlic and fresh coriander.

Another province famous for its pork is the coastal Beira Litoral, particularly the little town of Mealhada, which is not much more than a wide place in the road about 20km (12 miles) north of Coimbra. Here both sides of the highway are lined with restaurants that make suckling pig (*leitão assado*) a speciality. The piglets are rubbed with secret blends of oil and herbs, skewered from head to tail, then spit-roasted over white-hot hardwood coals until their skin

Sausages and chorizo at a Porto market.

is as crisply brittle as an onion's and their milk-white flesh so meltingly tender it falls from the bones at the touch of a fork.

CALDO VERDE

The Portuguese national dish is built neither upon salt cod nor pork. Its key ingredient is cabbage, specifically a richly emerald, tender-leafed variety (*couve galega*). The dish itself is called *caldo verde*, a bracing, jade-green soup which is brimming with potatoes, onions, garlic and filament-thin shreds of green cabbage. Sometimes the soup may be fortified with slices of *chouriço* or *linguiça*, although in the humblest Minho versions (it is here that the recipe originated) it often contains nothing more than water, potatoes, onions, garlic, cabbage and perhaps a tablespoon or two of robust *azeite* (olive oil).

The preparation of *couve galega*, the minutely shredded vegetables that go into the soup, is something passed on from generation to generation in the countryside. The trick is to shred it with the speed of light: the leaves are stacked, perhaps five or six deep, rolled into a fat cigar, then literally shaved as a razor-sharp knife is whisked back and forth across the end of the cabbage roll. The fineness of the cut is what makes a bowl of *caldo verde* resemble molten jade; also, the cabbage is tossed into the pot just minutes before serving, so that its colour intensifies rather than turning to a paler shade.

SOUPS AND STEWS

Next to *caldo verde*, Portugal's most famous soup is probably *açorda à alentejana*, a coriander-strewn, bread-thickened, egg-drop soup seasoned, as someone once remarked, "with enough garlic to blow a safe".

The soups and stews of Portugal – whether they're made of chickpeas and spinach (another Alentejo classic), of tomatoes and eggs (a Madeira speciality), of pumpkins and onions (a Trás-os-Montes staple), or of dried white beans and sausages (the universally beloved *feijoadas*) – are frugal and filling, nourishing and soul-satisfying. To make a meal, all they need for accompaniment are a glass of wine, a chunk of cheese and a crust of bread.

Making bread the traditional way in Estremadura.

⊘ PASTÉIS DE BELÉM

Constant queues testify to the success of Pastéis de Belém in Lisbon. The light-as-air custard tarts on sale here, *pastéis de Belém*, were first created nearby by nuns at the Mosteiro dos Jerónimos, who used the egg whites to starch their habits and so began making the tarts to use up the excess yolks (handily there was a sugar-cane refinery next door). When the liberal revolution in 1820 saw all the convents and monasteries shut down, the monastery began to sell pastries in a bid for survival. Obviously God was on their side: these are some of the finest custard tarts in Portugal, still made to the original secret recipe.

BREAD AND CHEESE

Portugal's simple country breads usually contain only the usual four ingredients – flour milled from hard wheat, water, yeast and salt – but they are kneaded until their dough springs to life. And because they are baked in wood-stoked brick or stone ovens, they have a faintly smoky flavour.

There are fancier breads, to be sure, notably the sweet festival breads, the *pão doce* of Easter and the fruit-studded *bolo rei* of Christmas. There are huskier breads, too, the rough round barley breads and, most famous of all, the *broas* – yeast-raised corn breads of the Minho that are sold by the truckload at the market in the river town of Barcelos.

Cheeses can be bought at country markets everywhere. The queen of them all is the ivory-hued *queijo da serra*, a cheese so strictly demarcated it can be made only from the milk of sheep grazing on the wild mountain herbs of the Serra da Estrela. At the peak of its season – winter – a properly ripened *serra* is as biting, buttery and runny as the finest Brie.

Portugal also produces a number of other delectable cheeses: the nutty, semi-dry *serpa* from the Alentejo town of the same name, which is cured in caves and brushed regularly with paprika-laced olive oil; *beja*, a buttery cheese from Beja, near Serpa; and *azeitão*, lovely little rounds of gold cheese, tangy and creamy, that come from the village of Azeitão on the Arrábida Peninsula just across the Tejo from Lisbon. Finally, there are the *queijos frescos*, snowy, uncured cheeses much like cottage cheese, which calorie-conscious Portuguese sprinkle with cinnamon.

EGG DESSERTS

The Moors are thought to have introduced egg sweets and tarts to Portugal during their 500-year occupation. But it was the 17th- and 18th-century nuns of Portugal who glorified them (see panel on Pastéis de Belém). This is one reason, no doubt, why so many egg desserts bear such names as "bacon from heaven" *(toucinho do céu)*, "nuns' tummies" *(barriga-da-freira)* and "angels' cheeks" *(papos d'anjo)*.

Regardless of their names, what the dozens of different egg sweets have in common is a prodigious use of egg yolk and sugar. Many are flavoured with cinnamon, others with lemon or orange or almonds, and each is shaped in its own traditional way: like little bundles of straw, for example, miniature haystacks, or even lamprey eel. The Portuguese so love this ugly river fish they make golden egg effigies of it for festive occasions.

For dessert, you might encounter sunny little mounds bathed in clear sugar syrup, flans decorated with cinnamon, individual goblets of rice pudding *(arroz doce)* as radiant as molten gold, flat yellow sponge cakes twirled around orange or lemon custard fillings, tiny translucent tarts *(queijadas)* and a poached meringue ring known as *pudim molotov* (one of the few egg desserts that is made out of the whites).

The Portuguese find that nothing complements – or follows – an egg sweet so well as a silky, syrupy wine, usually a vintage port, or a Madeira, but better still will be a good, strong cup of coffee to cut the sweetness.

Freshly baked pastéis de Belém.

COFFEE

Coffee houses are a Portuguese national institution, a gathering place morning, noon and night, where people meet to talk and read newspapers while they drink coffee. This is not surprising in a country whose former colonies – Brazil and Angola – still produce some of the finest coffee beans in the world.

The choice may be a *bica*, a powerful espresso-type brew, or a *café*, which is closer to percolated or filter coffee. Or, you can order *carioca*, which is half *café*, half hot water (it is also the colloquial name for a resident of Rio de Janeiro); it will still be pretty strong and very good indeed. Rossio Square in Lisbon is a great spot to pause for a cup of coffee.

Casks must be tended with skill and care.

WINES OF PORTUGAL

Wine-making is moving into an exciting phase. New favourites are supplementing old reliables, and many smaller *quintas* are producing excellent varieties.

For many years port and Madeira were the only wines that people associated with Portugal. But things are changing: the country's *vinhos verdes* have a well-deserved reputation, and besides classic Bairrada or Dão varieties, wine-lovers can explore the exquisite wines of the Douro, of Tomar in the Ribatejo, and the rich reds of the Alentejo.

PORT WINE

Port wine begins life in the Upper Douro, a demarcated region whose boundaries cling to the banks of the Douro and its tributaries. A wide variety of grapes grow here: preferred reds include Tinta Roriz, Tinta Francesa (a descendant of the French Pinot Noir), Touriga Nacional and Bastardo; among the whites are Malvasia, Esgana Cão and Rabigato.

The regions producing the finest ports presently centre around Pinhão, some 20km (14 miles) east of Régua, and extend to the Spanish border. The famous shipping firms all have their *quintas* (manor houses) in the hills of the Douro. It is here that the fermentation process takes place in autumn, interrupted by the addition of grape brandy, to create the raw, fortified wine. Young port then spends the winter at the *quinta*. In springtime, it is transported to the port lodges (many of which are open to the public) in Vila Nova de Gaia, where it is blended and matured into a variety of styles. It is here that you can learn about and taste the basic differences between ports.

VINTAGE PORT

The most famous and most expensive of the ports is the vintage variety. It is produced from the grapes of a single harvest and is "declared" only in years when the quality is deemed extraordinary. Vintage port is bottled after just

Tawny port is aged in wood for seven years.

> One good place to sample various port wines is at the Port and Douro Wines Institute on the Rua Ferreira Borges in Porto.

two or three years in wood. This is what distinguishes vintage from all other ports: the majority of the ageing process takes place in glass, rather than wood. From a legal standpoint, vintage port must identify itself as such – stating the name of its producer and the year of the vintage – and must carry the governmental seal. For example, the great 1963 vintage must, by law, have been bottled between 1 July 1965 and 30 June 1966.

Vintage port may be drunk 10 years after its vintage date, but most wines hit their stride after about 15–20 years. Classic wines were produced in 1963, 1977 and 1994; 2000, 2003 and 2007 are particularly good years. Taylor, Graham, Croft, Noval and Ferreira are some of the best known among a host of eminent port makers.

CRUSTED PORT

Crusted port differs from vintage port in that its grapes need not come from a single year, or vintage; instead, it is mostly created from two or three different harvests. Crusted port spends extra time in wood, accelerating the maturation process. This extended ageing makes for a lighter-bodied wine. Like vintage port, however, it throws a sediment and needs to be decanted.

LATE-BOTTLED PORT

Late-bottled vintage (LBV) sees even more time in wood – from four to six years. As its name implies, the wine comes from a single year's harvest, but is much lighter in colour than vintage port and need not be decanted. Both the date of the vintage and the date of bottling must appear on the label. When buying, it is worth remembering that shippers generally do not offer late-bottled vintage in the same years as they offer real vintage port.

WOOD PORTS

Wood ports are blended wines – using grapes from several harvests – that are matured in casks until they are ready for drinking. Because they are blended, it is the goal of the shipper to define his style through this wine so that year after year the customer can confidently expect a consistent product. The three main types are ruby, white and tawny.

Ruby is young and hearty and inexpensive. To a port drinker, it is the staple wine, attractive for its full, overt flavour. It is aged for two or three years in cask before bottling. One offshoot of ruby port is called "Vintage Character" port. It will have the same general features but will be of a higher quality, usually older, and more expensive.

White ports are also matured in wood. They can come from either red or white grapes: a clear wine can be obtained from red grapes by separating the juice from the skins during fermentation before the colour has been extracted. Wine-makers have tried to popularise whites by fermenting out the sugar, adding brandy, and marketing them as dry aperitif wines.

Then there is tawny port, a special blend of port wine from different vintages which sees many years in cask. Through the more rapid oxidisation process within the barrel, this wine matures rather more quickly. Tawny port is thus more mellow in style than the "vintage-dated" ports, but it is refined, with a rich tawny colour and fabulously scented bouquet.

Barrels of Colheitas (vintage) port wines.

⊙ CONFUSING COLHEITAS

There is a confusing offshoot of the vintage-dated wines, called "Port of the Vintage" or "Port with Date of Vintage". These wines come from a single year, but will have been aged in wood for no less than seven years. The bottle will often say *Colheitas* (vintage) and give the year; it will show the date of bottling and some indication that the wine has been aged in wood. The house of Nierport has a wonderful stock of these *Colheitas*. They are the first step into tawny ports, but the fact that they are from a single vintage prevents them legally being so titled under the strict regulations on port making and marketing.

Old tawnies are expensive, priced in correlation to the longer ageing period. They should not be confused with the cheap tawny port available abroad, which owes its existence to the demand for a less concentrated but drinkable port wine, which the port shippers have answered by concocting a blend of ruby and white port. The product is a simple wine of pinkish hue, in contrast to the fading russet and complexity of a true tawny. Since the name "tawny" can apply to either wine, the consumer must rely on colour and price to distinguish between the two. Among a wide choice, Ferreira, Noval and Taylor 10-, 20- and 30-year-olds are fine examples of tawny port. Only the "real thing" will reveal why this is the wine which many port houses most prize and which many blenders enjoy as an all-day drink (and have even been seen to add ice cubes to).

VINHO VERDE COUNTRY

The lush, green Minho is the country's oldest and most intensively cultivated wine area, the region of *vinho verde*. The vine seems to be everywhere – along narrow roads, framing houses with pretty bowers called *ramadas*, across new, neat plantations of *cruzetas*, crosses with wire supports a tractor operator can reach.

Not green, as its name suggests, *vinho verde* is made from fully matured grapes from varieties that include Azal, Trajadura, Alvarinho and Loureiro for the whites, and Brancelho, Pedral and Tinto Cão for the reds. The taste is dry, with many subtle shadings; it is light and refreshing, with an alcohol content of only 8 to 11 percent. The fizz – known as *pétillance* to wine connoisseurs, *agulha* to the Portuguese – is not added, but appears naturally during the making.

First, the grapes are fermented to convert their natural sugars into alcohol. Then a secondary fermentation, called the malolactic, takes place. Induced by naturally occurring bacteria, this converts malic acid to lactic; a harsher, rather unpleasant acid into a milder, more palatable one.

While this secondary fermentation is common to wines made in many countries, the *vinhos verdes* are distinguished by their retention of the fermentation's by-product: carbon dioxide. From this comes that characteristic sparkle in the wine, which can vary, depending upon age, technique and storage, from a light tingle on the tongue to a spritely carbonation, the hallmark of *vinhos verdes*.

Notable estate-made *vinhos verdes* come from more than 50 members of the Association of Producers and Bottlers of Vinho Verde, who must produce wine only from their own grapes (not buy them, as bulk producers do). The result is a range of wines produced in small quantities but with individual characteristics.

Much admired among single-estate wines is the Palácio da Brejoeira *vinho verde* produced from a single grape variety, Alvarinho, in Mon-

A vineyard in the Alentejo.

ção. It is also the most expensive. You can, though, taste a good, and cheaper, Alvarinho made by the Adega Cooperativa of Monção.

WINE REGIONS

Truly superb wines, a few eccentric and many sublime, are to be found in Portugal. From the once-cherished Dão area, which in recent years has tumbled from its pedestal, comes Caves São João's good red Porto dos Cavaleiros (its Reserva among the very best Dão wines) or the Sogrape Dão Reserva; and, from Sogrape's technologically advanced winery, the old favourites Grão Vasco and Terras Altas. Bairrada, a small area north of Coimbra, has held its reputation for classic wines, more than 80 percent red, mainly from the Baga grape. The whites include a pleasant *espumante*, or sparkling wine. Good Bairrada wines are made by Sogrape, Messias and Caves Aliança.

For something really special, head for the bizarre and extravagant neo-Manueline Palace Hotel do Buçaco (see page 244), which has a stupendous cellar of its own Buçaco wines, dating from the 1920s.

You can also taste perfectly good Bairrada wines at the cluster of down-to-earth roadside restaurants that can be found in nearby Mealhada, all offering the local speciality, *leitão*, suckling pig.

The Douro is the source of many of Portugal's finest table wines (even in the port region only 40 percent of the grapes go into port). Ferreira, a distinguished port-wine producer, also makes the renowned Barca Velha, probably the finest of all Portugal's red wines. Other Ferreira reds include their Reserva Especial or the more accessible Esteva. Top-ranking Douro wines include those under the Quinta do Cotto label – Grande Escolha is one. As in other areas, Sogrape are conspicuous – Planalto is just one of their good Douro wines. Adriano Ramos Pinto produce the really excellent Duas Quintas red.

LISBON'S WINES

From nearer to Lisbon comes a variety of good wines – the white from Bucelas is a consistent favourite. Pleasant wines, too, come from the Colares area, just beyond Sintra.

To the south of Lisbon two major wineries, confusingly with very similar names, are in Azeitão, near Setúbal (both are open to the public). One, José Maria da Fonseca, makes a very popular red, Periquita, and the excellent dry Branco Seco. If you care for sweet muscatel dessert wines, you might like to try the Moscatel de Setúbal. The second, more modern winery is J.M. Fonseca International, widely known for its very successful Lancer's red, white and rosé, sold in their distinctive clay jars.

Two eminent wines from the Setúbal area are João Pires, and the deep red from the Quinta de Bacalhoa, both developed by the skills of Australian oenologist, Peter Bright, who has lived in Portugal since 1982, and founded the Terras de Alter winery in the Alentejo in 2004.

Wines from Portugal's southernmost province, Algarve, are largely table wines, consumed on the spot, but they should not be dismissed and many are improving.

A range of good-quality wines is made in the eastern Alentejo in such towns as Borba, Reguengos and Vidigueira, which produce a very good white *reserva*. Look, too, for the deep-red and distinctive Esporão. In many good Lisbon restaurants you are very likely to be recommended an Alentejo red, rather than the more usual white, if you choose any variety of *bacalhau* (salt cod).

Gathering grapes for Porto wine during vintage season.

⊘ "GREEN WINE"

No one knows for sure where the eloquent phrase *vinho verde* (green wine) originated. One explanation is that it derived from the Minho region's green landscape, which receives up to 200cm (78ins) of rain a year. Another equally likely explanation is that the name simply refers to the youth or "greenness" of the wine, because it is not allowed to mature in the same way as normal table wines. The fact that *vinho verde* can be either white or red, and called *verde branco* (white) or *verde tinto* (red), introduces an even more colourful note. Whatever the origin of the name, the connotations are the same: a cool, refreshing wine, perfect for summer.

PORT DYNASTIES

In a technological age there are few trades where heritage and family ties are a matter of pride, but port is one of them.

Port has its roots in the wild upper reaches of northern Portugal's Douro Valley, a wine region that has had virtually the same frontiers since the Marquês de Pombal defined them in 1756. At the time, the reforming Pombal, who felt a hearty dislike for the British and their leading role in Portuguese trade, was determined to restrict the hold they had had on the area ever since the Methuen Treaty of 1703 had established their dominance over the industry. In subsequent centuries, port has improved immeasurably in quality and the profits are more evenly spread. But although snobbish exclusivity is long gone, the British are still very much part of the port scene.

The British association with port is long and eventful – although these days the French buy more. British buyers enthusiastically explored the Douro Valley in the 17th century. George Sandeman instructed the Duke of Wellington's troops on the finer points of port. One of the pioneers, cartographer Joseph James Forrester, a Scot, fought tirelessly for high standards and mapped every centimetre of the Douro River. He was made a baron in 1855 for his efforts. It was regarded as a national tragedy when, in May 1862, Forrester's boat overturned and he drowned in the Douro. He was travelling between various wine-growing *quintas*, paying the farmers in gold coins, and it is said that it was his money belt, heavy with gold, that helped to drag him down.

A survivor of the tragedy was another personality in the saga of port: Dona Antónia Adelaide Ferreira, whose vineyards covered huge areas of the Douro.

These and other colourful characters are familiar to everyone in the business. The founders of the port trade are ever-present, their faces and names on labels and wine lodges. Many port brands remain family-run affairs, and some rival companies have inter-family links.

Generations of family firms are at the core of the port business and their names provide lustre to superb wines. But in the nature of business, companies change. The Taylor, Fladgate & Yeatman group, including the much-esteemed Guimaraens, became the Fladgate Partnership. The historic Casa Ferreirinha is owned by multi-armed Sogrape. Cockburn Smithes in 2006 entered the embrace of the renowned family firm of Symington.

The name of Symington has been inescapable since the 1800s. The family owns and manages a distinguished list: Warre's (founded in the 1670s), Silva & Cosens (whose brand is Dow), Quarles Harris, Smith Woodhouse, and Graham's. In the 1990s two

Graham's Port Lodge, Vila Nova de Gaia.

generations and eight members of the Symington family were still involved in management, production, sales and marketing of the fine ports made by these independent companies. The family has, more recently, become prominent in promoting the re-emergence of much underrated Madeira wine.

The wine shippers still meet at lunch on Wednesdays in the Feitoria Inglesa or "English Factory House" in Porto to discuss business and sample a good vintage following the meal.

Efficient modern methods are used in the wine industry these days, but technology blends smoothly with tradition. Even the Symingtons' Gaia offices hold echoes of port's memorable past: they are in Travessa do Barão Forrester, in the very house where Baron Forrester once lived.

📷 FESTIVALS FOR ALL SEASONS

You can't go far in Portugal without stumbling across a festival – colourful occasions that demonstrate a national talent for celebration.

On almost every weekend throughout the year there will be a festival taking place somewhere in Portugal. Saints' days are the biggest single stimulus for holding a *festa*, and every village and town in the country enjoys the protection of a patron saint. *Romarias* are generally more sober affairs with a greater religious dimension. Plenty of these take place too, especially at Easter time.

Good festivals to catch wherever you are in the country include the semi-pagan carnival, the last party before Lent, in February or March; and the solemn celebrations of Semana Santa, the week before Easter, which are particularly awe-inspiring in Braga, in the north. Twice annually (May and October) there is the Fátima Romaria, when thousands of pilgrims pay tribute at the Fátima shrine, founded on the spot where three children are believed to have seen an apparition of the Virgin in 1917.

But Portuguese festivals are not just about religion. In June it's worth going to Lisbon's Festas da Lisboa (www.egeac.pt), with live fado, street parties, music, theatre and more. The Festival MEO Sudoeste (https://festivalsudoeste.com) in August is Portugal's answer to Glastonbury, with lots of international names and a laid-back beach vibe (it takes place in pretty Zambujeira do Mar, in Alentejo). Also in August, you can celebrate the delights of Portuguese shellfish (to a soundtrack of live music) at the Festival do Marisco (www.festivaldomarisco.com) in Olhão.

The annual October pilgrimage to the Fátima Sanctuary.

Colourfully attired women participating in the Flower Festival, in Funchal, which features street dancing and much merry-making.

Braga's festival of Reviver Bracara Augusta.

Regional celebrations

Portugal has many festivals that are unique to a particular region. At Miranda do Douro, Trás-os-Montes, stick dances are performed to the music of bagpipes, cymbals and drums (15 August); in Amarante (early June) young men offer phallus-shaped cakes as tokens of love to the young ladies in celebration of São Gonçalo, the patron saint of love and marriage; at the Festa de São João in Braga, townsfolk bash each other on the heads with squeaky plastic hammers; and in Lisbon street parties celebrate the matchmaking Santo António (June), and men present a sprouting basil plant with a love poem hidden in it to the woman they hope to marry. Others are simpler affairs, where the fringe activities, such as biscuit-eating competitions, are as popular as the main attraction.

Lisbon hosts several lively festivals: one of the biggest is Festas dos Santos Populares in June, which celebrates saints Anthony, John and Peter, and takes place in Alfama. The liveliest night is 12 June, when thousands gather to eat sardines, drink vast amounts of wine and join in the singing and dancing until late.

Festival decorations in Tavira.

Folkloric decorations in Braga.

Medieval festivals inspire re-enactors to dress up in the garb of the times.

Museum of Art, Architecture and Technology (MAAT).

Cathedral Square with Porto Cathedral.

PORTUGUESE ARCHITECTURE

Some of Portugal's finest architecture is found in its religious buildings, but other countries' wealth amassed during the Age of Discoveries also left a legacy of fine palaces.

Portugal's unusual geographical position, cut off from Europe by Spain on one side and facing the Americas on the other, is reflected in its architecture. The country's architects have always looked outside for influence and affirmation, and local traditions have blended harmoniously with imported ideas.

ROMANESQUE

The story of Portuguese architecture really begins in the Romanesque period of the 12th century, when nearly all buildings of any importance were religious ones. This was the time when the kingdom was founded, when Portugal was (largely) reconquered from the Moors, and Christianity was the heartbeat of the nation.

In the north, Romanesque-style churches continued to be built well into the 14th century, when the Gothic style was already spreading throughout the rest of the country. Portuguese Romanesque is an architecture of simple, often dramatically stark forms. The sturdiness of the buildings is frequently explained by the need for fortification against the continued threat of Moorish or Castilian invasion. This fortified appearance is enhanced in the cathedrals of Lisbon and Coimbra by the crenellated facade towers.

Most of these buildings are made of granite. The hardness of this material renders detailed carving impossible, thus favouring a simplicity of form. In areas where the softer limestone abounds, such as the central belt of the country (including Coimbra, Tomar and Lisbon), carved decorations are more common.

These Romanesque churches share a certain robustness; a method of construction based on semicircular arches and barrel vaults; a cruciform plan; and a solid, almost sculptural sense

The Old Cathedral in Coimbra.

> The Romanesque period saw the construction of cathedrals follow the path of reconquest from Braga to Porto, southwards to Coimbra, Lamego, Lisbon and Évora.

of form in the interior which allows for a play of light and shade. This sobriety is accentuated by the paucity of decoration, which is frequently reduced to the capitals of columns and the archivolts surrounding the portals. When the tympana are not bare, the simplified carvings are usually stylised depictions of Christ in Majesty, or the *Agnus Dei* (Lamb of God), or simply of a cross. In some cases, animals and serpents climb the granite columns, as in the Sé Velha (Old Cathedral) of Coimbra or the richly decorated principal portal of the early 13th-century São Salvador, in Bravães in the Minho.

GOTHIC

In France, new methods of construction involving pointed arches and ribbed vaults allowed for lighter, taller architectural forms. As the main weight of the building was now borne outside at fixed points by flying buttresses, the walls could be pierced at frequent intervals. The light filtering into these Gothic interiors became a metaphor for Divine Light, replacing the Romanesque emphasis on Mystery.

The first building in Portugal to use these new construction methods was the majestic church of the abbey of Alcobaça, commissioned by Afonso Henriques. With its great height and elegant, unadorned white interior bathed in a milky light, Alcobaça is one of the most serene and beautiful churches in Portugal. Begun in 1178 and consecrated in 1222, it is almost purely French in inspiration: its plan echoes that of Clairvaux, the seat of the Cistercian Order in Burgundy – a nave and two side aisles of almost the same height, a two-aisled transept, and an apse whose ambulatory fans out into chapels.

The apogee of the national Gothic style came after the Portuguese armies defeated the invading Castilians at the Battle of Aljubarrota. In fulfilment of a religious vow João I commissioned the construction in 1388 of the Dominican Monastery of Santa Maria da Vitória (St Mary of the Victory), better known as Batalha, which simply means battle.

The stylistic influence of Batalha is seen in various churches throughout the country, such as the cathedral at Guarda and the now-ruined Carmo church in Lisbon, which were both begun at the end of the 14th century.

Generally speaking, Portuguese Gothic leaned towards temperance rather than flamboyance, a reflection of the austerity imposed by the mendicant orders and, perhaps, the sombre streak in the national character.

A portal in the lovely Gothic abbey at Alcobaça.

◎ BUILDING BATALHA

Batalha's construction can be divided into three distinct stages.
1. During the first phase (1388–1438) the central nave, with simple ribbing supporting the vault, was built. The Founder's Chapel and the chapterhouse vault have a greater refinement and elegance, influenced by English Gothic. Contact with England was close at this time as João I's wife, Philippa of Lancaster, was the daughter of John of Gaunt.
2. During the second stage, which lasted until 1481, a second cloister was built.
3. The Manueline phase culminated in the Arcade of the Unfinished Chapels and the Royal Cloister.

THE MANUELINE STYLE

The exhilaration generated by Portugal's overseas discoveries had a marked effect on art, architecture and literature. The term "Manueline" was first used in the 19th century to refer to the reign of Manuel I (1495–1521), during which Vasco da Gama reached the coast of India (1498), and Afonso de Albuquerque conquered the Indian city of Goa (1510). The term is now used more often to refer to certain stylistic features predominant during the Avis dynasty (1383–1580), especially in architecture.

Manueline architecture does not have major innovative structural features – the twisted columns, such as those at the Church of Jesus in

Setúbal, perform the same function as do plain ones. Rather, Manueline can be seen as heterogeneous late Gothic, its real innovation lying in its stone decoration, the exuberance of which reflects the optimism and wealth of the period. Inspired by the voyages to the New World, it is ornate and imposing, uniting naturalistic maritime themes with Moorish elements and heraldic motifs: during the reign of Manuel I, the king's own emblems are usually included – as they were in the churches built in the newly discovered overseas territories.

decoration of the church culminates in the famous window, designed with two great ship's masts on either side, covered with carvings, topped, like the southern portal at Jerónimos, by the cross of the Order of Christ.

Manueline architecture also adopted and modified certain Moorish (*morisco*) features. At the Palácio Nacional at Sintra, restored during Manuel's reign, *morisco* features include the use of tiles, merlons, and windows divided in two by columns. Another important *morisco* feature is the horseshoe arch, as in the chapterhouse of

The graceful cloister of Jerónimos Monastery.

The Monastery of Santa Maria de Belém in Lisbon, better known as Jerónimos, is one of the great hall churches of the period – that is, a church whose aisles are as high as its nave. Perhaps the most notable feature of Manueline architecture is the copious carving that surrounds portals and semicircular windows. The imposing southern portal of Jerónimos, together with the window of the chapterhouse at the Convent of Christ in Tomar, well deserve the acclaim they both receive. Construction on the Tomar window began much earlier, in the 12th century, along with the Templar Charola – a chapel with a circular floor plan. During the 16th century, the convent buildings, including four cloisters, were added. The lavish Manueline

the Convent of Lóios in Évora. In Alentejo, many provincial palaces have *morisco* decoration, including latticework ceilings and chimneys.

RENAISSANCE AND MANNERISM

The Renaissance has been described as a narrow bridge crossed the moment it was reached. This was certainly the case in Portugal. In their art and architecture, the Portuguese shied away from Renaissance rationalism, instead inclining towards naturalism or the drama of the Baroque.

The Renaissance in Portugal, then, was best represented by artists from abroad. Foreign sculptors were frequently invited to decorate the portals and facades of Manueline buildings, introducing elements of Renaissance harmony and order within the general flamboyance of the Manueline decorative scheme. The convergence of Manueline and Renaissance influences, and later of Renaissance and Mannerist forms, explains the hybrid style prevalent during this period. Mannerism uses elements of Renaissance classicism but the sense of an ordered, harmonious whole gives way to an exaggeration of these elements.

The Spaniard Diogo de Torralva is thought to have been responsible for one of the finest examples of Renaissance design in the Iberian

Azulejos adorn a facade in Alfama, Lisbon.

peninsula – the Chapel of Nossa Senhora da Conceição (Our Lady of the Conception) in Tomar (c. 1530–40), with its simple exterior and diffusely lit, barrel-vaulted interior. Also in Tomar, Torralva's Great Cloister at the Convent of Christ evokes the balance and harmony of Palladian classicism. Many years after Torralva's death in 1566, this majestic cloister was completed by the prestigious Italian architect Filippo Terzi, a specialist in military architecture who had been invited by Felipe II of Spain (who became king of Portugal in 1581).

BAROQUE

The Baroque is considered to be the stylistic range which, although it uses a basic classical vocabulary, strives for dissolution of form rather than definition. Emphasis is given to motion, to the state of becoming rather than being. This obliteration of clear contours – whether by brushstrokes in painting or as an optical illusion in sculpture and architecture – is further enhanced by a preference for depth over plane. These features all stress the grand, the dynamic and the dramatic.

The first truly Baroque Portuguese church is Santa Engrácia in Lisbon, with its dome and undulating interior walls. This building, begun

> *Painted ceramic tiles called azulejos are a major feature of Portuguese architecture, with their use reaching its apex in the 17th century (for more information, see page 162).*

in 1682, was not completed until 1966. The richness of the coloured marble lining the walls and floor, the dynamic interior space, and the general sumptuousness of the edifice are typical of construction during the reign of João V (1706–50), known as João o Magnânimo.

The wealth from Brazil and the extravagance of João V made the early 18th century a period of great opulence. He was the king who commissioned the Chapel of St John the Baptist at the Church of São Roque in Lisbon. The entire chapel was built in Rome, blessed by the Pope, shipped to Lisbon and reassembled in the church, where it shines with bronzes, mosaics, rare marble and precious stones.

In the north of the country the major centres for the development of the Baroque were Porto and Braga. Here, the influence of the Tuscan architect-decorator Nicolau Nasoni, who came to Portugal in 1725, predominated. He introduced a greater buoyancy and elegance, and rich contrasts of light and shade, and incorporated local characteristics as well. His elliptical-naved Church of Clérigos in Porto had no successor but his secular buildings, such as the Freixo Palace in the same city, with their interplay of whitewash and granite, established a large following.

The gleaming Basilica da Estrêla in Lisbon, dating from the 1780s and commissioned by Maria I, was the last church to be built in the

Baroque Grand Style. By then, architectural styles had moved on and, with the dissolution of the monastic orders in 1834, religious architecture lost its privileged position in Portugal.

ROCOCO

In the rococo style, drama was replaced by fantasy, and an emphasis on flourish, sensuality and ornamentation. The chapel of Santa Madalena in Falperra is a good early example of the style. Rococo was also marked by a growing interest in landscaping. The type of church represented by Bom Jesus in Braga became popular: surrounded by gardens, it sits on the top of a hill and is reached by a sweeping succession of stairways which from a distance seem to cascade downward.

In Lisbon the rococo was more sober than in the north. After the earthquake of 1755, Carlos Mardel designed many of the city's public fountains in a toned-down version of rococo, including those of Rua do Século and Largo da Esperança. Mardel was also responsible for part of the Aguas Livres Aqueduct, which withstood the earthquake, and is still a familiar landmark.

NEOCLASSICISM

Although it took place at much the same time, the Pombaline style of the reconstruction of Lisbon (see page 112) is closer in many respects to classical models than to the rococo constructions in the north. The neoclassical style proper, with its emphasis on Greco-Roman colonnades and porticoes, was introduced to Lisbon in the last decade of the 18th century. It received court approval when used for the Royal Palace of Ajuda (begun in 1802 and never completed), after a fire destroyed the wooden building that had been the temporary royal residence since the earthquake.

After this, perhaps the only noteworthy public building to be built in Lisbon in the first half of the 19th century was the Theatre of Dona Maria II (1843), with its white Greco-Roman facade. The dissolution of the monasteries had a negative effect on the development of public buildings, as well as on religious architecture.

The middle-class ambience of Porto proved fertile ground for conservative neoclassicism. It was favoured by the English community connected with the port industry, perhaps because of affinities with the work of Scottish architect Robert Adam (1728–92). British consul Sir John Whitehead commissioned the Feitoria Inglesa in Porto and the Hospital of Santo António, perhaps the finest neoclassical buildings in the country.

ROMANTICISM

If neoclassical art and architecture represented an escape from the turmoils of the present into a restrained, harmonious classical ideal, another form of escapism was an important ingredient of Romanticism. It was typified by

Church by Bom Jesus, Braga.

flights into medievalism and orientalism, or into altered states of dreams and madness.

The most extraordinary architectural manifestation of this was the Pena Palace in Sintra (commissioned around 1840 by Prince Ferdinand of Saxe-Coburg-Gotha, the consort of Maria II). The building is a strange mix of medieval and oriental forms, including Manueline, Moorish, Renaissance and Baroque, and incorporating parts of the site's original structure – a 16th-century monastery. The result is a pastiche of English Gothic revivalism.

MODERN STYLES

One of the best examples of Portuguese architecture from the first half of the 20th century is the Art Deco Casa Serralves in Porto (now a museum), but there are also many gorgeous Art Nouveau cafés in Lisbon and Porto. Under Salazar, the fashion was for brutalist Soviet-style blocks, with exceptions such as the pared-down aesthetic of the Gulbenkian Museum. More recently, Porto architects such as Fernando Távora and Alvaro Siza Viera have established solid reputations: the rebuilding of the Chiado district after Lisbon's 1988 fire was entrusted to the latter, who also designed Porto's beautiful Museu de Arte Contemporânea (see page 264).

The postmodernist work of Tomás Taveira is also notable in Lisbon, particularly his office towers at the Amoreiras (see page 155). In addition, Expo '98 was a launching pad not only for some stunning modern pavilions, the Gare do Oriente railway station, and Europe's longest bridge, the Ponte Vasco da Gama (see page 144), but also a clear, uncluttered building style across Portugal. A prime example is Rem Koolhaas' Casa da Música in Porto, which mixes minimalist Modernism with traditional elements, such as *azulejos*. Close to Obídos,

Lisbon's triumphal arch.

Portugal has modern landmarks, too, such as the mosque in Lisbon's Avenidas Novas.

ⓞ POMBAL'S PROJECT

The reconstruction of Baixa, the lower city of Lisbon, which the Marquês de Pombal embarked on after the devastating earthquake of 1755, was the most ambitious urban planning scheme ever seen in Europe, and serves as the statesman's lasting memorial. "Pombaline Lisbon", as it is known, is built on a grid system, with clean, uncluttered lines. The area is epitomised by the Praça do Comércio, the huge square bounded on three sides by neoclassical arcades. In the centre stands a large equestrian statue to José I, erected in 1755. The majestic triumphal arch, however, was not completed until the 1870s, long after Pombal's death.

the spectacular Bom Sucesso development is a collection of villas and leisure facilities designed by star architects including Alvaro Siza Viera.

The most breathtaking new addition to the contemporary architecture landscape is the Museu do Côa, in the Douro, a monolithic triangular block, all concrete walls and sharp angles, designed by Porto architects Pedro Tiago Pimentel and Camilo Rebelo. Meanwhile in Lisbon, the wave-like Museum of Art, Architecture and Technology (MAAT), designed by the British architect Amanda Levete, as well as the ultramodern headquarters of the Energias de Portugal (EDP) company, offer a glimpse into the city's future.

Sumptuous carvings at Lisbon's Estação do Rossio train station.

PORTUGUESE ART THROUGH THE AGES

From rock engravings to neoclassicism and Modernist masterpieces, the country's museums, galleries and churches cover the artistic spectrum.

Portugal has a rich collection of artworks spanning the centuries, from prehistory to modern times. In terms of masterpieces from more recent times, the 15th century was the first great age of Portuguese painting. Almost no works from the 12th to the 14th centuries have survived, although frescoes were certainly painted in churches. One interesting, rare example of an early 15th-century fresco is a surviving fragment from a secular painting – the allegory of justice entitled *O Bom e o Mau Juiz* (The Good and the Bad Judge), in a Gothic house in the town of Monsaráz.

The most notable surviving religious fresco of the same period is the *Senhora da Rosa* in the sumptuous church of São Francisco in Porto. It has been attributed to an Italian painter, António Florentino, who, it is thought, may also have painted the portrait of João I now at the Museu Nacional de Arte Antiga in Lisbon.

Detail from Nuno Gonçalves' The Adoration of St Vincent polyptych, showing Henry the Navigator and the future João II.

> Portugal is also home to Europe's largest collection of outdoor palaeolithic rock art, discovered only in the 1990s, and now in a protected site close to Museu do Côa in the Douro (see page 273).

By far the most brilliant contribution to painting during this period was the introduction of Flemish-influenced painted altarpieces called retables (*retábulos* in Portuguese). In 1428, the Flemish master Jan van Eyck was invited to the court of João I to paint a portrait of the Infanta Dona Isabel, future wife of Philip the Good (Philippe le Bon, 1396–1467), Duke of Burgundy. The Netherlands were, at the time, under the control of the dukes of Burgundy, who were renowned for their excellent taste in art. When the Flemish artists turned from illumination to the painting of altarpieces, they added to their own love of realistic detail the Burgundian passion for gemlike decoration.

THE POLYPTYCH OF ST VINCENT

The most outstanding *retábulo* of the 15th-century Portuguese School is the polyptych of St Vincent attributed to Nuno Gonçalves, in Lisbon's Museu Nacional de Arte Antiga. The mystery that enshrouds this work has increased its aura. The panels were lost for centuries, and there are conflicting accounts of their reappearance at the end of the 19th century. No sooner were they cleaned and hung publicly than an angry controversy arose as to the identity of their creator as well as of the figures depicted. The drama was tragically heightened when one eminent scholar died by suicide after a dispute concerning two documents that radically altered the direction of the research. The documents were later proved false.

The theme of the polyptych has also given rise to dispute. Some see in it the veneration of the Infante Santo Fernando, uncle of Afonso V, who

Another detail from the polyptych, showing St Vincent and the members of the Regnant House.

died at the hands of the Moors. But nowadays it is generally thought to represent the adoration of St Vincent, patron saint of the kingdom and of the city of Lisbon. The important point of departure was the identification of the Infante Henrique (Henry the Navigator) to the left of the saint in the third panel from the left.

The panels, from left to right, are known as the Panel of the Monks (of the Cistercian Order), the Fishermen, the Infante, the Archbishop, the Calvary and finally, the Relic Panel.

The real genius and originality of the work lie in the exquisiteness of the portraiture and the masterful attention to realistic, pyschologically-influenced detail. It appears to be the visual representation of King Afonso's dreams of conquest and of the magical world of Prince Henry's navigations, blessed by the patron saint of the kingdom.

THE FLEMISH INFLUENCE

During the reign of João II (1481–95), when voyages of discovery occupied the energies of the nation, there was a lull in painting activity. However, with the discovery of the sea route to India and consequent prosperity, painted *retábulos* again became a dominant form of expression. At the end of the 15th century, Portugal was one of the largest importers of Flemish paintings. Many of the altarpieces in Portuguese churches were Flemish, and some can still be seen today, such as the *Fons Vitae* at the Misericórdia church in Porto.

Nevertheless, Portuguese painting maintained local features, giving rise to the "Luso-Flemish" style. Manueline painting evolved during the reign of Manuel I (1495–1521), although the style is more closely associated with architecture (see page 108). It has been characterised by features such as monumentality, a fine sense of portraiture, brilliant gem-like colours, a growing interest in the naturalistic depiction of both architectural and landscape backgrounds, and an increasing preoccupation with expressive detail. Sculpture exploded in a frenzy of detail during this period, celebrating the sea and covering buildings in a barnacle-like frenzy of exuberant detail.

During this period painting was not the expression of an individual sensibility, but more often the collaborative effort of a master and his

⊘ PEDRO AND INÊS'S TOMBS

While little surviving painting predates the 15th century, some lovely pieces of sculpture do. The crowning glory of 14th-century funerary sculpture is the tombs of King Pedro and his lover, Inês de Castro at Alcobaça (see page 43 for their dramatic story).

The sarcophogi do justice to the tale: the sculptor is unknown and the influences are hybrid, but the naturalistic detail and rich symbolism are unsurpassed. Inês, surrounded by angels, is crowned queen in death as she never was in life. Pedro's tomb displays a superb rosette, believed to symbolise a wheel of fortune representing life's vicissitudes.

assistants. Attribution, then, is extremely difficult, and often paintings are known as the products of particular workshops rather than artists. The two principal workshops were those of Jorge Afonso in Lisbon and of Vasco Fernandes in Viseu.

Afonso was appointed royal painter in 1508: documents identify various projects with which he and his workshop were involved, but none shows his direct responsibility, although he is believed to have painted some of the panels in the rotunda of the Convento de Cristo in Tomar.

for the altarpiece originally in Lamego Cathedral (now in the Museu Regional in that town), dated 1506–11, as well as the one in the Viseu Cathedral of a slightly earlier date.

The pronounced stylistic differences between the two works confused scholars for some time, but it is now assumed that Flemish assistants at Lamego account for the differences. The panels for the chapels of Viseu Cathedral, of which those of the Calvary and St Peter are the most renowned, are also attributed to Grão Vasco, but these date from his mature phase (1530–42).

Detail from the sepulchre of Inês de Castro.

> The altarpiece and the panels for the chapels in Viseu Cathedral, painted by Grão Vasco, are now in the museum that bears his name.

GRÃO VASCO

Vasco Fernandes, better known as Grão (the Great) Vasco, is undoubtedly the most celebrated regional Manueline painter. For many years, the myth of Grão Vasco obscured his real work in a plethora of attributions – he was thought to be the author of Gothic and Renaissance paintings, although a single lifetime would not have sufficed for so large an output. But he was responsible

Noteworthy for their emotional strength and drama, these works are also characterised by a denser application of paint than that used by the Flemish masters. Furthermore, the faces of the Portuguese works tend to be less stylised, more expressive, and, it would seem, often drawn from specific local models, just as the landscape backgrounds are drawn from the Beja region rather than being imaginary or purely symbolic.

THE 16TH AND 17TH CENTURIES

As in architecture, the Renaissance or "rebirth" of art based on classical models was resisted by Portuguese artists and mainly represented by those from abroad. Mannerism employed many elements of Renaissance classicism, but the sense of an ordered, harmonious whole gives way to an exaggeration of those defining elements. The most characteristic feature of this style is a certain elongation, together with unexpected highlighting of seemingly incidental sections of a work.

The 17th century saw the flourishing of portrait painting in Portugal as elsewhere in Europe. Perhaps the most celebrated portraitist of the period was Domingos Vieira (1600–78), known as "the Dark" to distinguish him from his contemporary Domingos Vieira Serrão. His nickname stemmed from his predilection, in works such as the portrait of Isabel de Moura (in the Museu Nacional de Arte Antiga in Lisbon), to make dramatic contrasts between deep, velvety backgrounds and the rich, creamy whites of ruffs and headgear.

NEOCLASSICISM

During the 18th century, two outstanding painters emerged: Francisco Vieira, known as Vieira Portuense (1765–1805), and Domingos António Sequeira (1768–1837). The two met in Rome, which was the essential location for any serious artist. Vieira Portuense also spent some time in London, where the classicising Roman influence was tempered by that of Sir Joshua Reynolds (1723–92).

The work of Sequeira is a study in the transition from neoclassicism to Romanticism, a rare example of a single life encapsulating two eras. He was nominated court painter in 1802 by João VI, and was commissioned to provide paintings for the rebuilt Ajuda Palace. Political turbulence forced Sequeira to emigrate to France, and then to Italy, where he died.

His work can be divided into three stages: the first, largely academic and neoclassical in inspiration, corresponds to the first period he spent in Rome, and to his work as a court painter. The second stage (1807–23), which includes the *Alegoria de Junot* (in the Soares dos Reis Museum, Porto), is stylistically freer and more individualistic, with Goyaesque contrasts of dark and light. The final phase of Sequeira's work corresponds to his visits to Paris and Rome. These late works show great painterliness and luminosity. The four cartoons for paintings in the Palmela collections are now in the Museu Nacional de Arte Antiga in Lisbon.

ROMANTICISM

Romanticism was a form of escapism into medieval, oriental and mystical realms. Heroic, religious and ceremonial works gave way to more intimate and personal pieces. The mid-19th

King Sebastian, by Cristovão de Morais.

A detail from Calvário by Gregório Lopes.

century also coincided with the rise of the middle class. Courtly art had breathed its last. The liberal revolutions questioned the long-upheld notion of history as the unfolding of a predetermined order, in favour of a relativism which heralded modern times. Similarly, the idea that art expresses timelessly valid principles gradually gave way to the subjectivist and individualist notions which continue to hold sway in art today. Sequeira represented the mystical, religious side of early Romanticism. With his death, the movement in Portugal underwent a change: nature became the new religion. The humbling of man before the larger, inscrutable forces of nature was already a contemporaneous theme elsewhere. Lisbon-born Tomás José da Anunciação (1818–79) became the foremost romantic landscapist of his generation, along with Luís Cristino da Silva (1829–77).

Not surprisingly, portraiture not only became the art form of the bourgeoisie *par excellence*, but it also gave increasing emphasis to the sitter's inner life. In Miguel Lupi's *Sousa Martins' Mother*, painted in 1878 and now in the Museu Nacional de Arte Contemporânea in Lisbon, the illumination of the hands and face—the most expressive parts of the body—conveys a sense of pensive dignity.

At the end of the 19th century, Romanticism began to give way to naturalism in both landscapes and portraits – although the difference between the two styles was largely one of emphasis, and António Silva Porto and José Malhoa were the foremost naturalist painters. But in stark contrast to their luminous outdoor scenes, Columbano Bordalo Pinheiro (1857–1929) continued in the tradition of studio painting. Columbano, as he is known, is considered the Grand Master of Portuguese 19th-century art. He studied under Miguel Lupi at the Academy of Fine Arts (founded

Admiring a painting in Lisbon's Fado Museum.

An early nineteenth-century portrait of entrepreneur Joaquim Pedro Quintela by Domingos António Sequeira.

⊘ PAULA REGO

Paula Rego's art calls to mind grotesque fairy tales, psychoanalytic images, and the mysteries of childhood. Her paintings present a kind of magical realism that is uniquely recognisable, presenting a narrative and providing unsettling, intriguing subjects, such as apparently dysfunctional family relationships. Rego was born in Portugal, and grew up there during the Salazar years, but was later sent to a finishing school in England, then went on to study at the Slade. Despite having lived in London since 1976, where her work is widely exhibited, in her paintings she always seems to return to the place of her childhood.

in 1836), and then spent three years in Paris. His brother, Rafael Bordalo Pinheiro, was perhaps even more popular in his day. A celebrated ceramicist, he was also known for his biting political caricatures.

MODERNISM

The artistic ferment that gripped much of Europe and America in the first decades of the 20th century arrived late, or in a very diluted form, in Portugal. The political turmoil that ended the monarchy in 1910 did not provide a propitious context for an artistic revolution, and there was then a window of only some 20 years before Salazar's authoritarian regime closed the door to all external cultural influences.

But some ideas took root. In 1911, the Museu Nacional de Arte Contemporânea was founded in Lisbon, and the first Salon of Humorists represented a move away from conventional salon painting. One of the most daring and interesting of this generation of painters was the Cubist Amadeo Souza-Cardoso, whose premature death in 1918 was a great loss. Many of his works are now in the Centro de Arte Moderno at the Fundaçao Calouste Gulbenkian in Lisbon, and some can be seen in a museum in his home town of Amarante. Another star was José Almada Negreiros (1893–1970), one of the most charismatic and energetic cultural figures in Portugal. His early caricatures drew the attention of the poet Fernando Pessoa, who became his friend, and whose posthumously painted portrait now hangs in the poet's old home. One of Negreiros' most important commissions was for the frescoes at the port of Lisbon, in 1943–8.

The military regime, initiated in 1926 and led by António de Oliveira Salazar from 1932–68, prevented contact with outside stimulus, so all the artistic and intellectual exchange necessary to keep the arts alive had to be clandestine during these years. The return to democracy in 1974 (six years after Salazar's death) breathed new energy into the arts and an outburst of fervent activity echoed the sense of exhilaration after long years of repression and censorship.

Among contemporary artists, Paula Rego is one of the brightest stars. Others include Helen Almeida, the conceptual artist daughter of Portuguese sculptor Leopoldo de Almeida (whose works include Lisbon's Monument to the Discoveries); Joana Vasconcelos, who transforms decontextualised everyday objects into sculptures, installations and performances; and Adriana Molder, known for her stark portraits inspired by film and literature.

Internationally renowned contemporary artist, Paula Rego.

POUSADAS AND MANOR HOUSES

Pousadas and manor houses offer something different from ordinary hotels. Above all, they give visitors a chance to experience local life and colour, usually in extremely comfortable surroundings.

Converted castles, palaces, monasteries, *quintas*, manor houses, water mills: there is no other country in Europe that offers good-quality accommodation in such variety. If taking a stroll around the castle walls before retiring to a grand bedroom once used by royalty, or waking to the tinkling sound of a stream beneath a miller's cottage sounds appealing, Portugal could be for you.

POUSADAS

Portugal's *pousadas* are rich in character and promise a memorable stay. They are nationwide establishments, now under the management of the Pestana hotel group. Usually they are historic buildings, national monuments or notable regional houses, and are found in both urban and rural areas throughout the country.

Architecturally and historically fascinating, *pousadas* have earned a reputation for quality and service. Lofty rooms and heavy stone walls do not always lend themselves to luxury – in fact, some are extremely simple – but the style of decor is always sympathetic to the character of the building. Some *pousadas* also provide air conditioning and a swimming pool. They pride themselves, too, on the high standard of their restaurants, which are open to non-residents, and serve dishes based on regional recipes. A relaxed and distinctly Portuguese ambience is perhaps the one thing that they all have in common. There is now a choice of around 35 *pousadas*, although many offer only a limited number of rooms, some as few as six.

For travellers in the lush green northwestern corner of Portugal, there is an especially good choice. To mention just a few: in the medieval town of Valença do Minho you will find the **Pousada de Valença do Minho, São Teotónio**. It sits on

An elegant corridor in the Pousada dos Lóios, in Évora.

a high point inside the ancient walled city with a spectacular view of the Rio Minho across to Spain and the Galician mountains. It is also perfectly located for walks through the winding city streets.

Further east is the **Pousada do Gerês-Canicada, São Bento**, a chalet-style building on a hill just south of the Parque Nacional Peneda-Gerês. Its floor-to-ceiling windows overlook the Caniçada Dam and a forest. It has its own pool and tennis court.

CASTLES

If you fancy staying in a castle, try the **Pousada do Castelo de Óbidos**, in the delightful old walled town of Óbidos, north of Lisbon. Built into a section of the 12th-century castle, the *pousada* is very small, with only eight rooms, and very popular, so advance reservations are essential. Castelo **Palmela**, with 26 rooms, is another castle *pousada* that is much in demand. Originally a fortress, it became a monastery in the 15th century and was severely damaged in the 1755 earthquake. Now the refectory is the dining room and the cloisters are used on festive occasions for gala dinners.

MANOR HOUSES

The manor house scheme, to which numerous gracious old houses belong, began in the north of the country. The scheme, run by Turihab and called Solares de Portugal, was created to conserve some of the country's most beautiful manor houses and palaces. The owners of these magnificent homes can no longer afford the maintenance and have opened them up to tourists, who are quite often treated as guests of the family. The term "manor houses" has broadened to encompass an extremely wide range of accommodation, which is available throughout the country. Privately owned manor houses are also known as *solares*. Stately manor houses, elegant country homes, farmhouses and rustic cottages are all included in this one general description. They are often listed under three categories:

Casas Antigas: elegant manor houses or estates originating from the 17th and 18th centuries. Furnished according to the period, they are sometimes full of antiques and artworks.

Quintas and Herdades: both are agricultural farms, but a *quinta* differs in being a walled estate. Although mostly located in rural settings, some are handily situated for towns.

Casas Rústicas: usually located in the heart of villages or on farms, and often quite isolated. Their architecture has a rustic feel, but they maintain a good level of comfort and amenities.

The Pousada Palacio de Estoi.

⊘ WHERE TO BOOK

Although reservations can be made directly, there is a central agency in Lisbon that handles bookings for all *pousadas*. There is no minimum-stay requirement. Contact Pousadas de Portugal, Rua Soares de Passos 3, Alto de Santo Amaro, 2300-314 Lisbon; tel: 218 442 001; www.pousadas.pt. For Turihab properties contact Praça da República, 4990-062 Ponte de Lima; tel: 258 741 672; www.turihab.pt or www.solaresdeportugal.pt. Several other agencies handle bookings for manor houses, including Manor Houses of Portugal, Rua Ricardo Marques 41, 4900-008 Viana do Castelo; tel: 258 835 065; www.manorhouses.com.

Piodao, a traditional shale village in the mountains of Coimbra.

Beach and cliffs near Lagos on the Algarve.

NATURAL PORTUGAL

This is a land where complex forces of nature have created diverse environments and, with them, the opportunity for a variety of different lifestyles.

For a country no more than 565km (350 miles) long and 220km (137 miles) wide, at best, and edged by the Atlantic Ocean, Portugal enjoys a surprising diversity of topography, geography and climate. Half a day's journey in almost any direction leads through climatic zones, from wet to dry, hot to cool, through mountains to plains, from rich pastures to poor, from large estates to small farms, and from affluence to poverty. Adaptation, community by community and region by region, to the heterogeneous forces of nature has fashioned a country set apart from its neighbours and unique in Europe.

CLIMATE

Portugal is the mixing pot for three powerful climatic systems. It is attacked from the west by moist westerlies from the Atlantic, carrying rain deep into the country. These are arrested by a dry continental climate giving hot dry summers and cold dry winters in the interior. From the south a Mediterranean climate invades, bringing similar hot dry summers but cooler, moist winters.

The high landmass of Serra da Estrela acts as a fulcrum point for all these different climates. Descend from the mountain at any point and you will find different characteristics on the other side. Rain patterns vary from north to south, with the north receiving the highest rainfall, especially between November and March. Summer conditions are not too dissimilar, with all regions generally enjoying high temperatures tempered in coastal regions by Atlantic influences. Inland regions, particularly in the port-wine areas and Alentejo, suffer very high temperatures in summer. One of the most useful indicators of a Mediterranean climate is the olive tree. This grows happily throughout most of Portugal with the exception of the mountainous regions. However, only Algarve enjoys anything approaching a truly Mediterranean-type climate and this has allowed its development as a year-round destination for holiday-makers. Even Algarve is not immune from Atlantic westerlies which sometimes bring spells of wet weather in winter.

Portugal has an abundance of olive groves.

> Portugal is home to one of Europe's largest artificial lakes, formed by stemming the Guadiana river with the Alqueva dam, at a cost of $1.7bn (see page 210 for details).

MOUNTAIN LIFE

Rolling granite mountains, safe refuges in ancient times, dominate the north. Many settlements from those early days remain even today. Here residents eke out an existence in a harsh environment using tools (adapted for their own needs) which have hardly changed over the centuries.

Although most of the mountain areas are lightly populated, there is an area of near-wilderness tucked away on the northern border of the country. Recognised as a sanctuary for wildlife and valued for the traditional way of life that persists in the villages on the fringes, the Parque Nacional Peneda-Gerês area, covering 720 sq km (278 sq miles), was opened in 1971. It is the country's only *national* park although other areas of natural beauty have been designated *natural* parks and are also protected, but by less stringent regulations.

Most of the highest peaks in the northern mountains lie within the park. Many of these exceed 1,300 metres (4,265ft), with Nervosa reaching a height of 1,545 metres (5,070ft). But although this region is the most mountainous in

Waterfall in the Peneda-Gerês National Park.

⊘ THE STORY OF MAIZE

The introduction of maize in the 16th century proved a lifeline for the people of the hill villages, for here was a crop they could adapt to their own situation. Land around the villages was pressed into use for maize and animals were moved to still higher pastures for the summer. More changes were demanded to store the crop and grind the corn. This resulted in granite-built stores perched on mushroom-shaped legs, *espigueiros*, as seen at Soajo. Water provided the power for grinding the corn. Water mills, again built of granite, were erected in profusion, often with the water of a single stream powering a succession of mills.

the country, it is not home to the highest peak of all. This distinction is reserved for the Serra da Estrela (Mountain of the Stars), an isolated, majestic mountain range in the centre of the country, which rises from the plains of Alentejo. Here, Torre, at 1,993 metres (6,539ft), marks the summit of continental Portugal.

GEOLOGY

Considering its size, Portugal has remarkably diverse geology. Ancient crystalline rocks of granite and gneiss predominate in the mountainous regions, often presenting a landscape of grey rounded hills and steep valleys. For many inhabitants, it is the only natural building material available and they have perfected the tools and ways to work this material to an art form. Granite is a hard material but it has just enough malleability to make it workable. The evidence is all around, especially in the north. Farms, churches, water mills and fencing posts are all solidly constructed from granite.

The likes of limestone and marble can be found in the central region, especially near Évora, where it is mined commercially, and near Coimbra. The latter is particularly valued by sculptors, who have used it extensively over time. There is another significant limestone region, which is now protected as the Parque Natural das Serras de Aire e Candeeiros (see page 227) – an area riddled with deep caves, several of them open to the public.

Mértola in Alentejo developed as a port under the Romans, to ship ores down the Guadiana from nearby São Domingos, and there are significant remains of the port area to be seen.

The Romans were overwhelmed by the beauty of the Rio Lima in the north. This, for them, was the Lethe, the mythical River of Forgetfulness. This meandering river has created a fertile valley as beautiful as any you'll see in Portugal, where productive farming has been practiced for centuries. In modern times, the Rio Douro has played a significant role in the development of

The Douro River plays a major part in Porto's port industry.

the port-wine trade. Good roads now penetrate the area but at the height of the port trade, all the wine had to be shipped down this difficult and dangerous river.

Perhaps the largest remaining river community is Lisbon itself, on the shores of the Rio Tejo (Tagus). The mouth of the Tejo proved a natural harbour offering safe anchorage to early traders. The prosperity of Lisbon has barely faltered throughout the ages.

RIVER COMMUNITIES

Many of the rivers arising in the mountainous interior on the western side of the Iberian peninsula flow to the Atlantic through Portugal. In fact, only one, the Mondego, is truly Portuguese, rising in the region of Serra da Estrela and flowing into the sea at Coimbra. Some of these rivers were once navigable, allowing boats access deep into the countryside. Early settlers were not slow to use the Rio Guadiana in this way to penetrate inland in search of metal ores.

COASTAL LIFE

With 832km (516 miles) of coastline, it is not surprising that the Portuguese are people of the sea. Fishing has sustained them over the centuries, providing an industry which has grown large, especially through cod fishing, yet also remained a small local activity. The coast is still littered with villages that rely heavily on reaping the sea's harvest, and especially on the sardine, which keeps many small fishermen in business. Tuna fishing is another sector that grew to massive proportions. Shoals of tuna migrate along the southern shoreline towards spawning grounds in the Mediterranean. Floating traps were used to catch the fish and fishermen were on hand to complete the job, but over-fishing led to a decline in numbers and the industry collapsed.

flora responds with equal diversity. Many species simply reflect the climatic influence of the region. Certain erica heaths, green lavender *(Lavendula viridis)*, and ulex species (gorse) typify western Atlantic plants and are found almost exclusively in the far west of the country. They can coexist with Mediterranean cistus species. Algarve offers the best display of Mediterranean flora, including wild orchids, like the bumblebee orchid *(Ophrys bombyliflora)* and the yellow bee orchid *(Ophrys lutea)*.

Narcissus is associated with the Iberian peninsula and many are endemic, although some are

Cork bark drying in the sun.

Fish (there is reckoned to be more than 200 species off these shores) is not the only commercial product. Algarve has produced salt from ancient times; the Romans salted fish here to export back to Rome, and there are still saltpans in operation. Seaweed for fertiliser is now less of an industry at Aveiro than it once was. Here, specially shaped boats, *moliceiros*, were used to collect seaweed from the extensive system of lagoons in the area.

The magnificent beaches adorning much of the coastline are now the basis for another important industry: tourism.

FLORA

With so many different habitats, climates and microclimates in this hugely diverse country, the

⊙ THE CORK INDUSTRY

About half the cork in the world comes from Alentejo. The cultivation of cork is not for the impatient: there's a wait of 25 years before the first crop is stripped from the trunk, and a further decade before the next harvest. Cork is a labour-intensive industry, as machines cannot duplicate the expertise of the men who strip bark from the trees, although the punching out of corks and stoppers is increasingly mechanised. Although plastic corks and screwtops are becoming popular for wine bottling, the cork industry is successfully fighting back, thanks in part to the perception of real cork as more of a prestige product in emerging wine markets like China.

found throughout the Mediterranean. Portugal has its fair share, from the diminutive jonquil, *Narcissus gaditanus*, to more popular garden species like *N. bulbocodium* and *N. triandrus*.

FAUNA

Wild boars are one of the largest mammals roaming in Portugal. Their foraging marks can be seen in many parts of the country, from the golf courses of Algarve – much to the fury of the green keepers – to the inland forests. Boar hunting is a form of tourism Alentejo is keen to develop. The best wildlife sanctuary is the Parque Nacional Peneda-Gerês in the north (see page 286). Brown bears have not been seen for centuries but there are still some wolves, and plenty of beech martens, deer, badgers and otters.

Birdlife is particularly rich in some areas, especially around the saltpans in Algarve, where some 300 species have been recorded. Around Lisbon 200 sq km (77 sq miles) of the Tejo estuary are protected as one of the most important wetland areas in Europe. The west coast estuaries and wetlands are situated on some of the major migratory routes, so spring and autumn are particularly rewarding for ornithologists. Sadly, in some areas years of uncontrolled hunting have significantly reduced wildlife.

TREES OF LIFE

Forestry in Portugal is big business, with over one-third of the country, some 3 million hectares (7.5 million acres), under forest. Pine, said to be of use from cradle to grave, is used to produce timber for furniture and construction as well as resin for pitch and turpentine. Pine accounts for around 40 percent of the country's wooded land. Pulp, used to manufacture paper and cardboard, is economically the most important woodland product. The Australian eucalyptus was introduced in 1856 for the paper industry, but its future is now in the balance. Environmentalists and farmers both oppose further plantations on the grounds of its destructive influence. Not only are eucalyptus rapacious in their demand for water, but they provide poor natural habitats and their litter is so slow to decompose that it further inhibits naturally occurring cycles within the soil.

The almond and the carob are indigenous to Algarve, the latter bearing long wizened beans that yield a fine variety of oil.

One major problem is forest fires, which cause widespread devastation annually, ruining huge tracts of forest land. The most recent ravaged the Algarve and Madeira in 2016, causing several fatalities, displacing families and consuming vast areas of forest.

Beach flora.

Colourful, detailed apartment building façade in Lisbon.

National Palace of Pena, Sintra.

Tavira, a picturesque town along the south coast of Portugal.

Capela das Malheiras chapel, Viana do Castelo.

INTRODUCTION

A detailed guide to the entire country, with principal sites clearly cross-referenced by number to the maps.

Bite-size sweets, or doces.

There isn't a wrong way to explore Portugal – except to make too many plans in advance. Train services here are efficient and the buses adequate, and slow travel has a charm of its own, but a car will allow you flexibility and make it easier to access the more remote places.

The roads are good and a motorway links Lisbon with Porto in the north, two hours' drive away, and goes on to Galicia in Spain. The roads south from Lisbon cross the Tejo and head for Alentejo and Algarve. Away from the national highways, east–west motorways help you leap distances but north–south roads tend to be narrower and more winding.

Lisbon and its environs are the best starting point for a first taste of Portugal. From there, if the weather is fine, you may want simply to head south, to the glorious beaches of Algarve. After relaxing for a few days, you could start exploring the countryside. Meander through the expanse of Alentejo, which largely consists of spectacular plains, with the entrancing ancient town of Évora in their midst.

Cutting back towards the Atlantic, still heading north, is the old university town of Coimbra and the surrounding sights. Look in on some of the traditional fishing communities along the coast: to the north is Porto on the Rio Douro and the wine districts of Douro and Minho. Here, world-famous port, delicious *vinhos verdes* and other wines are produced.

Belém's Aviation Memorial.

The far interior north of Portugal is called Trás-os-Montes, a remote and hauntingly beautiful area. South of here, and still ruggedly hilly, is the Beira Alta; below that, the plains of Alentejo creep up into the province of Beira Baixa. And if you have time to visit Madeira and the Azores, you will discover lush, mountainous islands, rich in dramatic landscapes and subtropical flora.

140

Climbing the hills of Lisbon on the Elevador da Bica funicular railway.

LISBON

A dramatically beautiful city of colourful, charismatic winding streets, rich history and vibrant culture, Lisbon blends old-world charm with an increasingly hip persona.

Lisbon (Lisboa) is a bewitching city. It is remarkably picturesque, draped across its seven hills and overlooking the wide blue expanse of the River Tagus (Tejo), with wonderful *miradouros* (viewpoints). It is not only a cultural feast, with more than 30 museums, but has a thriving nightlife, with the charismatic districts of Alfama and Bairro Alto coming alive after dark; buzzing restaurants, fado houses, and bars and clubs are all available to keep you going until daylight if you are so inclined.

Long somewhat overlooked as a European capital, Lisbon has been experiencing a revival of interest in recent years. It remains one of the cheapest capitals in Western Europe and is increasingly popular with creative sorts, drawn by the city's great weather and youthful energy. With hostels and glamorous hotels sprouting up, and cruise ships mooring up daily, there has never been a better time to discover all that Lisbon has to offer.

A flavour of Lisbon's attractions can be sampled in a crowded one-day visit, but that is barely enough to scratch the surface of the city's complexities. Three days allows time to absorb the atmosphere, though city lovers will probably find even a week too short. Lisbon's climate of hot summers and mild winters makes it an ideal place to visit for most of the year, although spring and autumn are good times to enjoy the city at its best.

Many of the highlights of a visit to Lisbon are conveniently concentrated in a few main areas in the heart of the city, centred around the Baixa, with a significant cluster out along the riverside at Belém. Baixa is the hub of the city centre, watched over by Castelo São Jorge, below which cling the narrow streets and alleys of Alfama. To the west lies the hill of Bairro Alto, entered through the Chiado area. North, beyond Rossio, the main thoroughfare, Avenida

Main attractions
Sé
Castelo de São Jorge
Museu Nacional do Azulejo
Elevador de Santa Justa
Igreja São Roque
Museu Nacional de Arte Antiga
Mosteiro dos Jerónimos
MAAT
Museu Calouste Gulbenkian

Maps on pages 146, 140

Café life, commemorated.

Flower shop near Rossio Square.

View of Alfama from Largo das Portas do Sol.

da Liberdade, leads to Praça Marquês de Pombal and Parque Eduardo VII. East is the newer neighbourhood of Parque das Nações, with many pleasures of its own to offer.

BUILDING BRIDGES

Most architecture in the city is post-1755, after the great earthquake, except for Alfama and Belém, which escaped virtually unscathed. There has been an upsurge in the restoration of old buildings in recent years and many dilapidated palaces and mansions have been tastefully renovated, becoming elegant restaurants, fashionable boutiques, art galleries and even nightclubs. Crumbling houses in the old quarters have also been restored and are hugely popular as Airbnb offerings, and in outlying neighbourhoods there are new hotels, plus vast and popular shopping malls, office complexes, cinemas and museums.

Visitors usually arrive by air and enter the city from the northeast, but a spectacular entrance is over the Ponte 25 de Abril from the south. The **Pilar 7 Bridge Experience** (daily 10am–8pm, until 6pm in winter) allows visitors to take an elevator to a glass-bottomed viewing platform on the side of the bridge. A second bridge, Ponte Vasco da Gama, further up the river, was built for Expo '98 beside what is now the Parque das Nações.

A TOUCH OF HISTORY

The mythical founding of the city on seven hills is attributed to Ulysses (Odysseus) and his encounter with the nymph Calypso. Left behind when he departed, the heartbroken nymph turned herself into a snake whose coils became the seven hills. In reality, there has been a settlement on the site at least since prehistoric times. Its advantageous geographical position caught the attention of Phoenician traders in search of safe anchorage who developed a port, Alis Ubbo (Serene Port), around 1200 BC. The Greeks, then the Carthaginians, subsequently laid claim to the site. In 205 BC Olisipo (as it was then known) was incorporated into the Roman province of Lusitania. Julius Caesar elevated the status of the city to a *municipium* in 60 BC and renamed it Felicitas Julia. What little remains of the Roman occupation today is from this period of relative prosperity and growth. As the Roman Empire crumbled, the city was left unprotected and vulnerable to attacks by a succession of barbaric Germanic tribes.

After the arrival of the Moors in the 8th century, the city enjoyed 400 years of stability and increasing prosperity, which came to an end in 1147, when the first king of the newly formed nation of Portugal, Dom Afonso Henriques, captured Lisbon. Around 1260 the Moors were finally vanquished and the capital moved here from Coimbra. A university was established in 1290 by King Dinis but transferred to Coimbra in 1308. A power struggle between the Church and the Crown over the next 200 years saw the university shunted between the two cities. In the end, Coimbra won that particular battle and Lisbon was left without a university until 1911.

The dawn of the "Age of Discoveries" at the end of the 15th century turned Lisbon into an important trading centre. Wealth from the opening up of the sea route to India by Vasco da Gama flowed into the country and the city entered a golden age that lasted for a century. A 60-year period of Spanish rule then saw a decline in fortunes, and for a while after the Spanish were ousted Lisbon suffered economically as maritime trade declined. The discovery of gold in Brazil ensured a return to former prosperity but most of this fortune was squandered by Dom João V on lavish building projects that were destroyed in the massive earthquake of 1755. The Marquês de Pombal was on hand to oversee the rebuilding of the city (see page 62).

Since then, Lisbon has witnessed the end of the monarchy, gunned down in its main square, and endured a long period of dictatorship under Salazar, which kept the city free of modern development. Today, its charms are being discovered by a raft of new visitors; indeed, since the world financial downturn began in 2008, Lisbon has been the fastest-growing city destination in southern Europe.

> **Tip**
>
> Walking is the best way to see the city, but there is a good transport system of trams *(eléctricos)*, buses, taxis, lifts *(elevadores)* and the metro. You can buy a 24-hour pass (€6.60), that covers buses, trams, funiculars and the metro, or invest in a Navegante card (€0.50), which you charge up as you go; a single metro journey costs €1.65.

The vast Praça do Comércio.

BAIXA AND THE CITY CENTRE

Baixa (the lower quarter) covers the level area in between the hills of Alfama and Bairro Alto. It slopes gently to the banks of the Rio Tejo (Tagus) from Rossio and down through Pombal's famous grid system of streets. City life centres around the vast expanse of the **Praça do Comércio** ❶ by the riverside. The earlier name of the square, Terreiro do Paço, is still used and dates back to the time before the earthquake when the 16th-century royal palace stood on the site. Behind the elegant Pombaline neoclassical arcades are municipal and judicial offices, and on the northwest side of the square is the city tourist office, **Ask Me Lisboa** (www.visitlisboa.com). You can also visit the new Lisboa Story Centre (www.lisboastorycentre.pt here, a playful audiovisual exhibition that vividly immerses the visitor in the city's history, and includes a dramatic cinematic recreation of the 1755 earthquake. Lisbon's former Stock Exchange is to the east. In splendid isolation in the middle of the square stands a bronze statue of the ruler at the time of the earthquake, Dom José I, which gave rise to the English name of Black Horse Square. The riverside serves as a quay for ferry boats along the Tagus and across to the *Outra Banda*, the communities on the southern shore of the river. Completely overshadowing the delicacy of the arcaded buildings is the impressive triumphal **Arco Rua Augusta**. The arch is a late 19th-century addition to the square. Near here, the former colonial bank headquarters has been turned into the colossal eight-storey **MUDE (Museu do Design e da Moda)** ❷ (Rua Augusta 24; www.mude.pt).

A short walk along the road, from the northeast corner of the square, is the notable Manueline doorway of the church of **Nossa Senhora da Conceição Velha** ❸. Further along, the unusual pyramidal stone facade of the 16th-century **Casa dos Bicos** ❹ (House of the Pointed Stones) seems almost modernistic. There is a clear distinction between the lower storeys, which survived the 1755 earthquake, and the top two storeys, which were faithfully reproduced

Walking down Rua Augusta.

The neo-Manueline Rossio Station.

ⓘ MUDE

MUDE (Museu do Design e da Moda; www.mude.pt) means "change" in Portuguese. This fantastic museum combines Lisbon's former Design Museum – perhaps the world's best collection of modern design – with works from the priceless collection of art mogul Francisco Capelo. The Design Museum collection is a roll call of modern design classics, featuring furniture and household objects by anyone who's anyone in design: Charles Eames, Frank Gehry, Verner Panton, Philippe Starck, and many more. Ex-stockbroker Capelo's contribution is a breathtaking collection of fashion, which includes 1,200 couture pieces.

from old engravings during the 1980s. Now it houses the headquarters of the **José Saramago Foundation** (www.josesaramago.org), a private cultural institution dedicated to the life and work of José Saramago, Portugal's first Literature Nobel Prize winner. It's also a branch of the Museu de Lisboa (see page 161) with a permanent archaeological exhibition presenting parts of the Roman city wall of Olisipo. A short distance further along the road lies the little-noticed 13th-century fountain **Chafariz do Rei**, once the major source of the city's water supply.

Leaving the square from the northwest corner you pass the spot where, in 1908, Carlos I and his heir, Luís Felipe, were assassinated. Close by is the **Praça do Municipio** ❺, with an 18th-century *pelourinho* (pillory) and the **Câmara Municipal** (Town Hall; www.cm-lisboa.pt), where Portugal was declared a republic in 1910. Further west, trains arrive from Estoril and Cascais at the Cais do Sodré railway station close to the city's main market, **Time Out Mercado da Ribeira** ❻ (www.timeoutmarket.com/lisboa). Opened in 2014, Time Out Mercado da Ribeira has become a foodies' paradise with dozens of food stalls representing the best restaurants in Lisbon. Tasting menus are great value and the place has already become a favourite meeting point for Lisboans and tourists alike. This colourful place is also a traditional market, selling an amazing array of fresh produce, including fish landed at the nearby Ribeira dock.

Back in the Praça do Comércio, make a grand entrance through the Arco Rua Augusta into the neat grid of streets which form the main area of Baixa, the lower town. Pedestrianised Rua Augusta provides plenty of diversions along the way as it sweeps up towards Rossio. Shops are definitely the main attraction but, at busy times, street entertainers and balloon sellers lend a carnival atmosphere and pavement cafés bring a relaxed but buzzy feel to the scene. At one time, the streets of the grid represented various crafts, hence names such as Rua da Prata (silver), Rua do Ouro (gold) and

The grand artifice of the Teatro Nacional in Lisbon.

Rua dos Franqueiros (haberdashers). Today, many of these streets are home to banks and offices as well as shops.

Rua Augusta opens into **Praça Dom Pedro IV** ❼, better known by its common name of **Rossio**, and the focus of major city events for 500 years, until the 18th century. This was where citizens gathered to enjoy carnivals and bullfights or to witness public executions, particularly the autos-da-fe of the Inquisition. Now, cafés, flower sellers, shops, kiosks and traffic create a swirl of activity and colour in a square, which is a great place for a coffee or early evening drink, at rooftop bars such as the eponymous Rossio.

At the northern end of the square, the **Teatro Nacional** (Dona Maria II Theatre; www.tndm.pt/en), built in the 1840s, overlooks the two fountains brought from Paris in 1890, which flank the statue of Dom Pedro IV. They are rather more authentic than the statue, which is a cobbled version of a statue of Emperor Maximilian of Mexico. A ship carrying it from Marseilles to Mexico docked in Lisbon just as news came of the emperor's assassination. Pressed for cash, the city council snapped it up as the bargain of the day and attempted some remodelling in the hope that no one would notice.

Paço dos Condes de Almada (Palace of the Counts of Almada), just to the east of the theatre, is where the *Restauradores* (Restorers) conspired in 1640 to wrest power back from the occupying Spaniards. The Igreja de São Domingos nearby oversaw the sentencing of victims of the Inquisition, who had been tried in the palace that once stood on the Teatro Nacional site. South of the church the **Praça da Figueira** (Fig Tree Square), with its statue of João I, has a quieter ambience.

To the northwest of Rossio is the **Estação do Rossio** (Rossio Station), with its lovely neo-Manueline facade. Trains from Sintra arrive on the fourth floor, at the level of Bairro Alto (the upper part of town), from where an escalator takes passengers down to Baixa level. They emerge not far from **Praça dos Restauradores** ❽, named in honour of the Restorers. Until 1821,

St Anthony is the unofficial patron saint of Lisbon.

The cannons and view from Castelo São Jorge.

> **Tip**
>
> Head to Rua dos Bacalhoeiros in Alfama, to find a wonderful shop full of stuck-in-time design, the Conserveira de Lisboa (www.conserveiradelisboa.pt), which specialises in canned fish.

access to the square was closed off to keep out the rabble inhabiting Rossio Square and thereby create a peaceful haven for the gentry. After that it was opened up to the general public and used for celebrations and dances.

EAST TO ALFAMA

Alfama is the oldest part of the city, and clings tenaciously around the feet of the Castelo de São Jorge. The steep, narrow streets and alleys of this old Moorish quarter spill down to the riverside, and a succession of conquerors over the millennia has left vestiges of their occupation. A tapestry of life unfolds around every corner: drink it all in, but keep a tight hold on your valuables. The area really comes alive on 12 and 13 June for the feast of St Anthony of Padua (1195–1231), the unofficial patron saint of Lisbon, who was born in the area (he acquired his title after a sojourn in Italy).

Head up from Baixa past the Igreja de Madalena, dating from the late 18th century but preserving a Manueline porch from an earlier church. On the left, as the Romanesque facade of the Sé comes into view, is the small church of **Santo António da Sé**, built on the alleged site of St Anthony's birthplace. The history of the saint and his relations with the city are presented in a branch of the Museu de Lisboa (see page 161) next to the church.

SEEING THE SÉ

Dom Afonso Henriques, the first king of Portugal, ordered the **Sé** ❾ (Cathedral; free) to be built soon after banishing the Moors from Lisbon. The first incumbent was an Englishman, Gilbert of Hastings, who fared rather better than the 14th-century Bishop Martinho Anes, who was flung from the north tower for harbouring Spanish sympathies. Today the cathedral's fortress-like facade stands testament to the turbulent times in which it was constructed. There has been much restoration over the centuries but the two original crenellated towers, softened by the large rose window in between, remain the most striking feature.

Inside, the barrel-vaulted ceiling leads to a low lantern, and to the left, on entry, is the baptismal font where St Anthony was christened in 1195. Further along, in the first chapel on the left, is a beautifully detailed crèche (nativity scene) by the sculptor Joaquim Machado de Castro. The chancel is 18th century and the ambulatory was remodelled in the 14th century. In the third chapel from the south side of the ambulatory are the tombs of Lopo Fernandes Pacheco and his wife. He was a companion in arms to Afonso IV (1325–57), and responsible for much of the cathedral's remodelling during those years.

In the **cloisters,** excavations in what were once the gardens have revealed vestiges of Moorish buildings overlaying Roman remains – beneath those, there is evidence of an Iron Age settlement. This part of the cathedral has recently undergone extensive renovation works.

In the sacristy is the cathedral **treasury** (Mon–Sat 10am–5pm) where

The Museu Escola de Artes Decorativas.

numerous sacred objects are on view. Of most importance is the casket containing the remains of St Vincent, the official patron saint of Lisbon, which were brought here by the order of Afonso Henriques from Sagres in Algarve. Legend relates how ravens accompanied the boat that carried his remains from Spain and again on the journey from Algarve to Lisbon. To this day, the raven is a feature of Lisbon's coat of arms. Discounted tickets are available which give you access to both the cloisters and the treasury.

Still heading uphill, you will reach the **Miradouro de Santa Luzia** which is a good vantage point to look down over Alfama. The church of the same name is decorated externally with some interesting *azulejo* panels, one showing the heroic soldier Martim Moniz, who died keeping the city gate open – an act that enabled Afonso Henriques to capture Lisbon.

A little further up is **Largas das Portas do Sol** ❿ (Sun Gate), where one of the original city gates once stood. A statue of St Vincent looks out over the city from this popular viewpoint. Terrace cafés provide an excuse to linger, and the 17th-century palace of the counts of Azurara, now the **Museu Escola de Artes Decorativas** ⓫ (Museum of Decorative Arts; www.fress.pt), is certainly worth a visit. The museum is a showcase for the work of Portugal's master craftsmen.

THE CASTELO DE SÃO JORGE

Perhaps the most beautiful view of the city is from the ramparts of **Castelo de São Jorge** ⓬ (www.castelodesaojorge.pt), which crowns the first hill east of the city centre. If you want to take the hard work out of the climb up to the castle, you could take a taxi or catch the No. 28 Graça tram to Portas do Sol, then visit the Sé and surrounding sites on the walk down. The castle can be seen from nearly anywhere in Lisbon, serving as a romantic reminder of the capital's ancient roots. Many of the castle walls and towers are from the Moorish stronghold, although there were earlier fortifications on this site.

The knife grinder is a familiar figure in the streets of Lisbon, as in any Portuguese town.

Iconic No. 28 Graça tram with equally iconic Lisbon Cathedral behind.

After the Portuguese drove out the Moors in 1147, the residence of the Moorish governor, Paço de Alcáçova, became the royal palace of Dom Dinis (1279–1325). It remained a royal residence until Dom Manuel (1495–1521) decided to build a more comfortable abode down by the river. Except for a short period when Dom Sebastião preferred the military fortification of the castle to the graceful splendour of the palace, it served its time as a barracks and prison until 1939, when it was freed from any official duties.

All that is left now are walls, 10 towers and the remnants of the palace, but shaded gardens, fountains, cafés and a restaurant, presided over by a statue of Afonso Henriques, make it an ideal spot to escape the heat of summer. The *miradouro* (lookout spot) provides a marvellous panorama of the city, and from here it is possible to pick out many of the city's landmarks. Further good viewpoints lie to the north at the Baroque **Igreja de Nossa Senhora da Graça** ⓭ and, beyond that, the even higher Senhora do Monte.

Back down the hill, the **Museu do Fado** (Largo do Chafariz de Dentro; www.museudofado.pt tracks the development of Portugal's *saudade*-charged musical soul.

OUTSIDE THE CITY WALLS

A short walk from the castle leads to the **Igreja de São Vicente de Fora** ⓮ (www.patriarcado-lisboa.pt). *De fora* ('out') describes the church's position outside the city walls. It was built on the site of a 12th-century monastery dedicated to St Vincent to commemorate the battle fought by the crusaders to capture Lisbon. The white limestone building, with short twin towers, was designed by Italian architect Filippo Terzi; construction began in 1582, and took more than 40 years.

Of more interest than the church interior are the cloisters (daily), which are covered with 18th-century *azulejos* depicting La Fontaine's *Fables*. The former refectory, off the cloisters, has served as the Pantheon of the Royal House of Bragança since the mid-19th century. Portuguese kings, queens,

The Aqueduto das Aguas Livres.

princes and princesses, the earliest being João IV (who died in 1656), are entombed here.

A flea market, **Feira da Ladra** ⓯ – literally, the Thieves' Market – takes place on Tuesday and Saturday from dawn to dusk in the Campo de Santa Clara. You must cross this square to reach the Baroque **Igreja de Santa Engrácia** ⓰, now the **Panteão Nacional** (National Pantheon; www.panteaonacional.gov.pt), containing monuments to many of Portugal's non-royal heroes. Work on this church started in 1682 but was not completed until 1966, giving rise to the Portuguese idiom for a project that is never finished: *"obras* [works] *de Santa Engrácia"*. Although the building is in the compact, satisfying shape of a Greek cross, with a central dome, the stamp of Salazar on its eventual completion has left it a somewhat sterile monument.

Back down towards the riverside, opposite **Estação Santa Apolónia**, the station for international arrivals, is the **Museu Militar** ⓱ (www.visitlisboa.com/en/places/national-military-museum). This museum charts Portugal's military history in paintings and extensive collections of armour and weapons in a building which was, until 1851, the national arsenal.

Head eastward, along the coastal route, paralleling the railway lines, then turn left up Calçada dos Barbadinhos to the **Museu da Agua da EPAL** ⓲ (Water Museum; www.epal.pt). Named after the engineer of the Aqueduto das Aguas Livres (see page 155), it was the first steam pumping station of its kind in Portugal. The building, in a surprisingly tranquil oasis, records the history of Lisbon's water supply from Roman times and includes the story of the aqueduct.

Further east stands the tile museum, the **Museu Nacional do Azulejo** ⓳ (www.visitlisboa.com/en/places/national-tile-museum). Again, the easiest route runs parallel to the railway track, but you may find it worth taking a taxi. The building was originally part of the Convento da Madre de Deus, founded in 1509 by the widow of João II, Dona Leonor of Lancaster. All that remains of the original exterior is the Manueline doorway, but the 18th-century interior of the main church

The Santa Justa Elevator.

Tip

As of September 2024, Lisbon authorities have increased the tourist tax to €4 (added to the accommodation bill) for the first seven days of a stay in the city. There are also plans for an additional 'arrival tax' to be charged at airports and other ports of entry.

provides the perfect foil for the national collection of *azulejos*, in a breathtaking combination of gilded woodwork, blue-and-white Dutch *azulejos* and superbly painted walls and ceilings. One of the most outstanding tile scenes is a 1730 panorama of Lisbon, some 37 metres (120ft) long. Besides tiles and architecture, there are paintings to admire, a bookshop in which to browse, and a very pleasant café-restaurant.

Heading east out of the city, 5km (3 miles) upriver, beside the Oriente Metro station, is the **Parque das Nações** (www.portaldasnacoes.pt), the Expo '98 site, stretching along 2km (1.25 miles) of waterfront. Its attractions include one of the largest sealife centres in Europe, the **Oceanário de Lisboa** (www.oceanario.pt), the huge Atlantic Pavilion, the Camões Theatre, a waterside cable-car ride, the **Pavilhão do Conhecimento** (www.pavconhecimento.pt) interactive science museum (lots of fun for children), and the **Vasco da Gama Tower**, which has a viewing platform with amazing views, and also houses a luxury hotel.

Looking up at the Elevador de Santa Justa.

THROUGH BAIRRO ALTO

Bairro Alto (the upper quarter) rises to the west of Baixa. This area is renowned for its shops and restaurants. Shoppers can approach via the fashionable **Chiado** district, looking in at the popular French-owned FNAC department store, built after the 1988 Chiado fire; or have a great coffee in A Brasileira in Rua Garrett, a café favoured by generations of artists and politicians, now rather more by tourists.

The walkway into the Chiado from the top of Raoul Mesnier de Ponsard's **Elevador de Santa Justa** ❷⓿ is accessible, and you can take the lift to the top of the tower to the café and viewing platform (www.carris.pt/viaje/carreiras/54e-elevador-santa-justa/).

The walkway, alongside the roofless **Convento do Carmo** ❷❶, used to connect the lift with the Largo do Carmo and entrance to the **Museu Arqueológico do Carmo** (www.museuarqueologicodocarmo.pt).

This remarkable ruin is one of Lisbon's most poignant sights. It was built by Nuno Alvares Pereira, João I's young general at the Battle of Aljubarrota (1385), who spent the last eight years of his life here. Left unrestored after the 1755 earthquake, the remains of the nave give the most eloquent reminder of that tumultuous event.

Gothic arches soar skywards over a grassy nave, a venue for occasional concerts, while the part that survived serves as an archaeological museum with some curious tombs and an eclectic mixture of exhibits from as far afield as South America and England. In summer, the museum is used as one of the venues for the Lisbon Music Fest (www.lisbonmusicfest.com).

From the convent, turn right on Rua Garrett, then left on Rua Serpa Pinto, to reach Lisbon's opera house, the **Teatro de São Carlos** ❷❷ (http://tnsc.pt). La Scala in Milan and the San Carlos theatre in Naples were the inspiration behind the theatre's construction in 1792, and the Italian influence is obvious.

A short walk to the northwest, along Rua Nova da Trindade, brings you to **Igreja São Roque** ㉓ (St Rock Church). Behind an unremarkable post-1755 facade lies an opulent interior.

The ceiling has been painted to give a beautiful trompe l'oeil effect, and the eight chapels are all individual works of art. There are notable *azulejos* by Francisco de Matos and an excellent canvas, *Vision of St Rock,* painted by Gaspar Dias around 1584.

The main draw is the **Capela de São João Baptista**, said to be the costliest chapel in the world and commissioned in 1742 by João V. Luigi Vanvitelli and Niccolo Salvi designed and built it in Rome, where it was blessed by the Pope, then dismantled and transported to Lisbon. Gold, silver and bronze decorate the extravagant confection of lapis lazuli, alabaster, marble and ivory, central to which is a mosaic of St John. Adjoining the church is the **Museu de São Roque** (https://museusaoroque.scml.pt/en/museum-church), a small but impressive collection of vestments and ecclesiastical furnishings in rich Baroque designs.

NORTH AND WEST OF BAIRRO ALTO

The Portuguese delight in gardens, so naturally Lisbon is laced with green spaces. Perhaps the finest of them all is the **Jardim Botânico** ㉔ (www.museus.ulisboa.pt), to the north of the Praça do Príncipe Real, one of the richest such gardens in Europe.

Created in 1873, it has a magnificent wall of 100-year-old palm trees, banana trees, bamboo and water lilies, and many tropical plants.

Northwest, up the Rua das Amoreiras, beyond Largo do Rato, is a large, simple building, the **Mãe d'Agua das Amoreiras** ㉕, which once stored the city's water supply, brought in along the **Aqueduto das Aguas Livres**.

South from Amoreiras (head down Rua Ferreira Borges into Domingo Sequeira) are the attractive Jardim da Estréla and the splendid late

The tram is the most pleasant way to get around in Lisbon – No. 28 from Chiado to the castle has the most scenic route.

The atmospheric ruins of the Convento do Carmo.

18th-century **Basílica da Estrela** ㉖, with its great dome and multi-hued marble interior. Close by is the little English Church of St George, and the adjacent **Cemitério dos Ingleses** (English Cemetery) where Henry Fielding (1707–54), the author of *Tom Jones*, was buried, after a trip to the warmer climes of Lisbon failed to cure his gout or asthma.

Special permission is required to visit nearby **Palácio de São Bento** ㉗ (east along Calçada da Estréla), now the Portuguese Houses of Parliament (www.parlamento.pt, open to the public last Sat of the month with tours from 3pm, reservation required; free). Originally built as a monastery, the palace was transformed into the parliament building at the end of the 19th century and was renovated in 1935.

On the docks at Alcântara, the **Museu do Oriente** (Doca de Alcântara; www.museudooriente.pt, housed in a former fish warehouse, has an interesting collection which examines Portugal's historical connections with Asia. The restored LxFactory (http://lxfactory.com), once a textiles plant, is now a trendy collection of over 50 shops, restaurants, cafés and bars.

Down by the river is the **Museu Nacional de Arte Antiga** ㉘ (Museum of Ancient Art; www.museudearteantiga.pt). This, one of Lisbon's most important museums, is located in a fine 17th-century palace (property of the Counts of Alvor), with a tasteful modern extension. The term "ancient" may be misleading, as most of the exhibits are only a few centuries old, but there are fine displays of 16th-century porcelain, purloined by Portuguese sailors from India, Japan and Macau, as well as some impressive displays of furniture, sculpture and glass.

Perhaps of most interest, the museum's galleries also hold a wide selection of paintings by Nuno Gonçalves and other artists of the 15th–16th-century Portuguese School (see page 114), as well as works by Hieronymus Bosch, Brueghel the Younger, Hans Memling, Giambattista Tiepolo, José de Ribera and other great masters of the art.

Interior of Museu de Arte Sacra.

The Basílica da Estrela.

BELÉM

In a green spacious zone by the river, on the western side of town beyond the **Ponte 25 de Abril** ㉙ and the restaurants and nightclubs around the renovated dock at **Alcântara**, a number of monumental buildings stand as testimony to Portugal's maritime past, coexisting with the modern architecture of new cultural centres. Belém means Bethlehem, and reflects the country's involvement with the crusades.

It is here that you will find arguably Lisbon's most glorious monument, the **Mosteiro dos Jerónimos** ㉚ (www.mosteirojeronimos.pt), built to honour Vasco da Gama and his successful journey to India in 1498, and now a UNESCO World Heritage Site. This vast, opulent limestone building, a masterpiece of Manueline (or late Gothic) architecture (see page 108), took 70 years to complete.

The main body of the church is breathtakingly high-ceilinged and elegant. Ribbed vaulting, supported by polygonal columns, becomes an eye-catching star-shaped feature where the transepts cross, and elephant-supported tombs are a reminder of India. The delicacy of the sculpting makes the double-storey cloisters well worth a visit.

Built on the western side of the monastery, in the latter part of the 19th century, is a wing that houses the **Museu Nacional de Arqueologia** ㉛ (National Museum of Archaeology), with an interesting collection of folk art dating from the Stone and Bronze ages. Part of the same wing, the **Museu da Marinha** ㉜ (Maritime Museum;) tells the story of Portugal's seafaring discoveries, with grand royal barges and fishing vessels on display in a separate building.

The **Planetário Calouste Gulbenkian** ㉝ (Planetarium) behind it gives regular presentations, three or four times a day, mainly in Portuguese, but with some shows in other languages. Both the museum and the planetarium form part of the **Centro de Conhecimento do Mar** (Maritime Knowledge Center; http://ccm.marinha.pt), which

> **Fact**
>
> The towerblock Amoreiras Shopping Centre (www.amoreiras.com; daily 10am–11pm) is a popular destination in Lisbon, centrally located and with more than 300 shops covering every category from haute couture to pet supplies. There are also numerous food outlets, a play centre, cinemas, post office and a church.

Guarding the Palácio de São Bento.

KIOSK CAFÉS

Try retro Portuguese drinks at Lisbon's ultra-cool, renovated kiosks. These were operational originally in the 19th century, but had gradually closed down, only to be reopened, complete with vintage-style tipples and snacks in 2004. The lovely, ornate wrought-iron, circular kiosks are to be found in central locations such as Camões Square, Jardim do Principe Real and Praça das Flores. They serve fizzy drinks and beer alongside traditional drinks such as *orchata* (a chilled almond concoction), lemonade, iced tea, port wine, and old-fashioned recipes, such as sweet, refreshing *capilé*, made with spleenwort (a type of fern) and orange blossom. They also serve traditional Portuguese snacks, such as cod-fish or olive sandwiches.

PLACES

> **Tip**
>
> The giant Centro Comercial Colombo (open daily 8.30am–midnight) – with more than 360 shops, including a hypermarket – is opposite the Benfica Football Stadium (Estadio da Luz; www.slbenfica.pt; guided tours daily 10am–7pm), the site of the 2004 Euro final. Travel to Colegio Militar Metro.

also includes an archive, a library, an aquarium and a frigate.

Nearby stands the huge **Centro Cultural de Belém** ❸❹ (www.ccb.pt); exhibitions and events here are usually excellent. It also contains the ultra-minimalist **Museu Colecção Berardo** (www.ccb.pt/macccb), which contains a dazzling array of modern art, with works by Picasso, Magritte, Warhol, Bacon, Pollock and many more, along with sculpture, photography and installations.

On the bank of the Rio Tejo, on the far side of the broad Avenida da India and a small park, stands the **Torre de Belém** ❸❺, on the site where Vasco da Gama and other navigators set out on their explorations. This exquisite little 16th-century fortress is another fine example of the Manueline style, with its richly carved niches, towers and shields bearing the Templar cross. One of the most popular tourist attractions in Lisbon, there is usually a long queue to enter and hoards of visitors crowd around in the middle of the day. The nearby striking modern building, featuring circular holes that allow for river views beyond the tower, is home to the biomedical research foundation, Champalimaud Centre for the Unknown.

On the waterfront a short distance away, you can't miss the impressive **Padrão dos Descobrimentos** ❸❻ (Monument of the Discoveries; www.padraodosdescobrimentos.pt). Erected in 1960, the monument is a stylised caravel, with Prince Henry the Navigator at the fore gazing seawards and other leading figures of the age behind him.

East of the monument, on the Calçada da Ajuda, rises the ornate rose-coloured **Palácio de Belém** which once served as a royal retreat but is now the official residence of the president of the Republic (www.museu.presidencia.pt; guided tours Sat 10.30am–4.30pm). Adjacent, in what was once the royal riding school, is the **Museu Nacional dos Coches** ❸❼ (Coach Museum; https://lisbonticketing.com/products/national-coach-museum-museu-dos-coches-entry-ticket), which houses one of the finest collections of coaches

The doorway to the Mosteiro dos Jerónimos.

in Europe. A new museum building, designed by the Pritzker Prize-winning Brazilian architect, Paulo Mendes da Rocha, was inaugurated in 2015. Both parts of the museum are linked.

The newest addition to the riverside is the ultramodern, wave-like building of the **Museum of Art, Architecture and Technology** ❸ (MAAT; www.maat.pt) designed by British architect Amanda Levete. It presents exhibitions by contemporary artists, architects and thinkers, and the treasures of the EDP Foundation's Art Collection. The museum also includes the complex of the Tejo Power Station with fine examples of industrial architecture from the beginning of the last century, plus the interesting Electricity Museum (Museu da Electricidade). The impressive MAAT footbridge, connecting the museum roof to the Largo Marquês de Angeja, opened in 2018.

Up the hill to the side of the palace is the magnificent **Palácio Nacional da Ajuda** ❸ (www.palacioajuda.gov.pt), built after the great earthquake as a royal palace but never completed. It is now used for exhibitions and concerts, and numerous rooms are open to the public.

THE NORTHERN HILLS

Travelling northeast and crossing the Avenida da Ponte again (all but the most hardy will do this by public transport or taxi), you will find that the **Parque Eduardo VII** ❹ provides an immediate escape from the clamour of the city and offers magnificent views back down to the Tejo. The park was named to mark the state visit of King Edward VII of England in 1903, which was the first he made to a foreign country after his coronation. In the top left-hand corner of the park, but reached from Rua Castilho, are two greenhouses, the **Estufa Quente** (Hot House), originally built to house exotic orchids, and the better-known **Estufa Fria** (Cold House).

At the southeast corner of the park is the **Praça Marquês de Pombal** ❹, or the Rotunda, as it is more commonly known. From his lofty perch in the centre, a statue of the Marquês looks out over the city he rebuilt. From here,

The Museu Calouste Gulbenkian is surrounded by a sculpture park.

The manicured gardens of Parque Eduardo VII.

the **Avenida da Liberdade** sweeps southwards, linking the Rotunda with the Baixa area. The *avenida* was developed as a dual carriageway in 1879 and became the epitome of style, with palm trees and water features lining the route. It's now the best place in Lisbon to shop for big name labels, such as Gucci and Prada. The little **Parque Mayer**, about two-thirds of the way down, is an enclave of restaurants and theatres, the latter specialising in popular comedy known as *revistas*, satirical variety shows commenting on current political events (https://teatro-mariavitoria.bol.pt/Comprar/Bilhetes/Lista).

A colourful kiosk on the Avenida da Liberdade.

GULBENKIAN'S LEGACY

Instead of returning to Baixa, leave the Parque Eduardo VII by the northern exit and walk northeast for a short way to a large landscaped complex containing the **Museu Calouste Gulbenkian** ㊷ (Avenida de Berna 45; http://gulbenkian.pt). The Calouste Gulbenkian Foundation was set up by the Turkish-Armenian oil magnate, who was born in Istanbul in 1869 and became very attached to Portugal having sought refuge here after being harassed and hounded by the Allies in World War II. The foundation is the most important funding source for the arts in the country, and there are Gulbenkian libraries and museums throughout the country. When Calouste Gulbenkian died in 1955, his collection, one of the richest private collections in the world, was bequeathed to the nation.

The museum's contents include displays of Middle Eastern and Islamic art, Chinese porcelain, Japanese prints and gold and silver Greek coins. Among magnificent exhibits from the West are paintings by 17th-century masters like Rubens and Rembrandt, and by Impressionists such as Renoir, Manet and Monet. There are also rich Italian tapestries, and a whole room dedicated to the Art Nouveau creations of René Lalique.

A pleasant walk through the park-like complex leads to the **Centro de Arte Moderna** (http://gulbenkian.pt), which displays the work of 20th-century Portuguese artists, including

The bullring at Campo Pequeno.

Paula Rego (see page 119) and a collection of 20th-century British art.

For a rather different form of entertainment, you can take the Metro one stop northwest to the zoo, or **Jardim Zoológico de Lisboa** ㊷ (www.zoo.pt), which is set in the attractive Parque das Laranjeiras (Orange Tree Park).

Just southwest of the zoo, on the edge of the Parque Florestal de Monsanto, you will find an unexpected gem in the form of the glorious, pink-washed **Palácio dos Marquêses de Fronteira** ㊹ (www.fronteira-alorna.pt; guided tours June–Sept Mon–Sat 10.30am, 11.30am, noon, Oct–May 11am and noon; free), built as a hunting villa for the first Marquês de Fronteira in 1640. The house and beautiful formal gardens are decorated with some unusual and captivating *azulejos*.

CAMPO GRANDE: NORTH AND SOUTH

On Campo Grande you will find the group of pleasant modern buildings that make up the **Cidade Universitária** ㊺ (University), although the nearby **Arquivo Nacional da Torre do Tombo** ㊻ (http://antt.dglab.gov.pt), a fort-like building that holds the national archives, is architecturally more striking. In an 18th-century palace at the end of Campo Grande is the main site of the **Museu de Lisboa** ㊼ (Lisbon Museum; www.museudelisboa.pt), with an interesting collection of archaeological pieces and engravings that trace the history of the city, housed in the charming Palácio Pimenta. The other sites of the museum are at Casa dos Bicos, Teatro Romano (Roman Theatre), Torreão Poente in the Praça de Comércio, and Santo Antonio.

Heading south along Avenida da República, the large 19th-century bullring, **Campo Pequeno**, is hard to miss, and is not a bad place to witness one of Portugal's relatively animal-friendly bullfights (www.campopequeno.com).

If you head north from Campo Grande up Avenida Padre Cruz, you will reach **Parque do Monteiro-Mor**. Located in old manor houses in these gardens is the **Museu do Trajo e da Moda** (Costume and Fashion Museum; www.facebook.com/MuseuNacionaldoTraje).

Sculpture in the park of the Gulbenkian complex.

Long legs at the Jardim Zoológico de Lisboa.

AZULEJOS: A NATIONAL EMBLEM

Brightening up everything from cathedral cupolas to beer houses, *azulejos* are an integral part of Portugal's architectural heritage.

The Portuguese have had a lasting love affair with *azulejos* – painted ceramic tiles – ever since they first set eyes on those imported from Seville in the 15th century. *Azulejos* are not unique to Portugal, but they have become almost a national emblem.

Local production of tiles began soon after the arrival of the geometric Sevillian prototypes. Early ones, used mostly in church interiors, were mainly in shades of blue, with patterns established during the course of firing by separating the colours using rivulets of linseed oil or ridges of clay. Quality improved with the introduction of the Italian *majolica* technique, in which the tile was covered with white enamel onto which paint could be applied directly. This greater freedom permitted more artistic expression. Tapestry designs based on Moorish patterns began to appear, founded on a module of four tiles in blue, yellow, green and white.

The next leap was the introduction of tin-glazing techniques used in the production of Delftware from Holland. It dominated tile production for a period, but by the mid-18th century there was a return to polychrome tiles. During the rebuilding of Lisbon after the great earthquake of 1755, the demand for tiles escalated. They were used for internal and external decoration in every aspect of architecture: churches, private homes, public buildings and even on park benches. New factories opened to supply the demand but, inevitably, artistic standards fell and many tiles had to be imported. The best place to trace the development of the tiles is in the Museu Nacional do Azulejo, in Lisbon (see page 153).

Azulejo tiles are employed for useful purposes as well as decorative ones.

Tiles along the Miradouro Santa Luzia in Lisbon.

Lisbon's Igreja de São Vincente de For cloisters are covered with 18th-century azulejos depicting La Fontaine's Fables.

The 17th-century Palácio dos Marquêses de Fronteira in Lisbon is decorated with unusual azulejos.

Masterpieces of decorative art

Towards the end of the 17th century, tile painting became a recognised art form in Portugal. One of the earliest masters to find fame in this field was António de Oliveira Bernardes. Together with his son, Policarpo, he set up a school of painters in Lisbon which rapidly became influential. Many beautiful works produced by this school in the first half of the 18th century found their way into churches, monasteries and palaces.

The interior of the Capela de São Lourenço in Algarve is covered with *azulejos* depicting the life of the saint; many believe it to be the work of Policarpo. Art historians also greatly admire the work of Policarpo in Setúbal's São Filipe chapel.

Restoring the historic azulejo tiles is skilled and demanding work, especially since the tiles are considered part of the country's heritage.

A letter box set into a wall in Obidos is tiled with a floral motif. Once azulejos were no longer confined to churches and palaces, they cropped up everywhere.

Used tiles can be found for sale at Feira da Ladra, Lisbon's legendary flea market, displaying secular motifs as well as sacred designs.

The centre of Cascais.

ESTORIL AND CASCAIS

Close to Lisbon, these neighbouring resorts are well connected to the city, convenient for exploring as far north as Sintra, and also a delight for windsurfers and golfers.

Handily located for **Lisbon** ①, south-facing Estoril and Cascais are the most significant coastal resorts outside Algarve, although neither is especially large. They grew to prominence as a playground for Lisboetas, but modern times have witnessed a role reversal: these resorts and their environs are now home for wealthy commuters to Lisbon, and are the preferred places to stay for many visitors who like a tranquil base from which to explore the capital.

WEST ALONG THE COAST

The train offers the quickest and most convenient way of travelling the 29km (18-mile) distance between Cascais, Estoril and Lisbon. It arrives in Cais do Sodré station on the west side of the city, close to the riverside, where the green (verde) Metro line begins. Some of the mainline trains also stop at Belém, which is convenient for visiting one of the capital's most interesting areas (see page 157). The train service between Lisbon and Estoril and Cascais is frequent, and the journey only takes about 40 minutes.

Driving, you can take the inland A5 route, which is faster, or the slower but more scenic *Marginal* (N6) route along the riverside out of Lisbon, which leads through Belém to the elegant hillside neighbourhood of Restelo, the location of many embassies and diplomatic residences. **Algés** is the first town outside the city limits.

A string of small riverside towns follows. **Dafundo** has several splendid old mansions standing in rather sad contrast alongside dilapidated rent-controlled housing. It also has the **Aquário Vasco da Gama** (https://ccm.marinha.pt/pt/aquariovgama), a fascinating world of sea turtles, eels, barnacles and all kinds of fish; it has been open since 1898, although it is now rather eclipsed by the Oceanarium in the Parque das Nacões. **Cruz Quebrada** is the site of

◎ **Main attractions**
Aquário Vasco da Gama
Casa das Histórias Paula Rego
Boca do Inferno
Praia do Guincho

Map on page 166

Stone pier along Estoril's sandy Tamariz beach.

Casino Estoril was the inspiration for Ian Fleming's 007 novel, 'Casino Royale'.

the **Estádio Nacional** soccer stadium, while **Caxias** is known for its flower-decked villas, 18th-century gazebos and an infamous coastal prison-fort. In **Oeiras** you will find a fine 18th-century Baroque church, a lovely park, modern apartment blocks and an austere 16th-century fort and vintage car museum.

Just beyond lies the 17th-century fortress of **São Julião da Barra**, marking the point where the Tejo meets the Atlantic. **Carcavelos** has several moderate hotels and a broad sandy beach.

ELEGANT ESTORIL

And so to **Estoril** ❷, the first point of what has frequently been referred to as the Golden Triangle, and which includes Cascais and Sintra. A flowering, palm-lined, pastel-coloured resort, it first gained fame at the turn of the 20th century for its therapeutic spring waters. During World War II, Estoril became well known as the low-key haunt of international spies. Later, this corner of the Atlantic, with its mild weather and gracious lifestyle, became a home from home for dispossessed European royalty and for refugees fleeing the political upheavals after the war. Among the Triangle's illustrious residents were former kings Simeon of Bulgaria and Umberto of Italy, and Bolivia's ex-leader, Antenor Patiño.

With changing times, local aristocrats are selling or renting out their villas. More and more Portuguese and foreigners come to the Triangle to live,

ESTORIL AND CASCAIS

retire or keep summer homes. Estoril now has the atmosphere of a rather staid, if attractive, resort – a kind of up-market, rather more glitzy version of Eastbourne.

Estoril's fine sandy **Tamariz** beach is attractively set with a touch of the picturesque, added by a castellated private house surrounded by palms at the eastern end. This Atlantic location been awarded a Blue Flag for cleanliness, as have Duquesa and Conceição nearby.

The **casino** (www.casino-estoril.pt) in the heart of the town is a low, white modern building with immaculately kept gardens. In order to gamble here, you need to show a passport, driver's licence or identity card to get in, and the minimum age limit is 18. Some people come to the casino just to see the show, usually a colourful international extravaganza, but it's fun to keep an eye on the betting. As in all crowded venues, keep your valuables hidden. There is alsoan art gallery, a cinema and several bars, clubs and restaurants.

FESTIVALS AND RALLIES

The **Estoril Music Festival** (www.festori-lisbon.com) takes place in July. Concerts and recitals are held in Estoril Cathedral, Cascais Cidadela (fort) and other impressive settings. The **International Handicrafts Fair** (**FIARTIL**; https://fialisboa.fil.pt/home-2-2/) has become a major production, lasting throughout the months of July and August. Located near the casino, the fair features arts and crafts, food, wine, and folk music performances from all over the country.

There is a lot to do in the way of sports in the Triangle. The **Autódromo do Estoril** ❸ (www.circuito-estoril.pt), the automobile race track located inland on the road to Sintra, used to draw large crowds for the Grand Prix Formula One races but the track fails to meet current safety requirements for Formula One racing. However, it still hosts regular events including the popular Estoril Classics (www.estorilclassics.pt).

Mild winters and summers tempered by cool westerlies provide ideal weather conditions for golf all year round. There are several courses on the north side of

> **Fact**
> Estoril and Cascais are joined by a pedestrianised promenade along the beach, which makes for a delightful stroll. The walk takes about half an hour without stops, but there are plenty of snack bars and restaurants along the way.

Golfing in Oitavos.

GOLF IN THE GOLDEN TRIANGLE

The Estoril Golf Club's course, on the outskirts of town, is one of the loveliest in Europe. It was laid out by McKenzie Ross on a hillside dotted with pine and eucalyptus groves. The smaller 9-hole Estoril-Sol Golf Course is located in a pine wood at Linhó near Sintra. Overlooking the Atlantic coast just west of Cascais is the Quinta da Marinha hotel and golf club. Designed by Robert Trent Jones, this attractive course, in a private 110-hectare (270-acre) estate, weaves through umbrella pines, water features and wind-blown sand dunes. Quinta da Beloura, designed by William Roquemore and opened in 1993, lies beneath the hills of Serra de Sintra. Six lakes provide golfers with plenty of watery challenges.

Penha Longa, built with Japanese finance, is more than a golf course; it is a country club with a whole range of sporting activities, and includes a five-star hotel. The 18-hole and 9-hole courses designed by Robert Trent Jones II embrace natural woodland and rocky outcrops. The complex is located between Serra de Sintra and the Atlantic. The Praia d'El Rey lies about an hour's drive from Lisbon on the A8 motorway. It is a Championship Links course right by the sea; here too there is luxury accommodation, tennis and other activities on offer, and a spa.

the Tejo and four within easy reach on the south. **Penha Longa Resort** ❹ (www.penhalonga.com) is one of the best.

CASCAIS: RESORT OF KINGS

Once a royal resort, the attractive little town of **Cascais** ❺ is much livelier than its more sedate neighbour, although it still retains the laid-back atmosphere of a wealthy seaside suburb. In 1870, King Luís I established his summer residence in the 17th-century citadel on the Bay of Cascais. Before that, it was known only as a fishing port. Local people claim that it was a fisherman from Cascais, Afonso Sanches, who actually discovered America in 1482, and Christopher Columbus merely repeated the trip 10 years later and got all the glory. In 1580, the Duke of Alba attacked Cascais when Spain was laying claim to Portugal, and in 1589 the English arrived here to retaliate for the Spanish Armada's 1588 foray. The fishing port still remains, with the comings and goings of the colourful fishing boats in the bay, the noisy nightly auction at the central fish market, and good shopping and restaurants.

Around the port has grown a resort with all the vibrancy that Estoril lacks, and yet it has managed to avoid spilling beyond its original boundaries. Pedestrianised streets are paved with traditional black-and-white *calçada* blocks, re-creating dynamic wave patterns – you will spot the same paving in former Portuguese colonies such as Macau. A busy Wednesday market, where you can buy fresh fruit and vegetables as well as handicrafts, is repeated on a smaller scale on Saturday morning.

There are several old churches and chapels in Cascais, including the 17th-century **Nossa Senhora da Assunção** with its plain facade, lovely tiles and marble nave. It contains several paintings by the 17th-century artist, Josefa de Obidos.

On the outskirts of town, in an exotic garden, is the **Museu-Biblioteca Condes de Castro Guimarães** (https://bairrodosmuseus.cascais.pt). Housed in a candyfloss-pale, fairy-tale mansion – the former residence of the Conde de Castro Guimarães, who donated it to the people of Cascais on his death

Kayaks for rent on Praia dos Pescadores near Cascais.

The cliffs of Boca do Inferno.

in 1927 – this museum displays 17th-century Portuguese silver, tiles and furniture, and some good 19th-century paintings, as well as prehistoric finds.

The **Museu do Mar Dom Carlos** (www.cm-cascais.pt/museumar; free) is the best place to get a glimpse of the community's past. It tells the lives of the fishermen and has many photographs of King Carlos, a keen oceanographer, who started the bathing season with his arrival here each September during the 1890s. The penultimate king of Portugal, Carlos was assassinated in Lisbon in 1908.

Dedicated to the renowned Portuguese artist Paula Rego, the **Casa das Histórias Paula Rego** (bairrodosmuseus.cascais.pt) has a fine collection of her paintings, drawings and etchings, plus a nice café. The museum resembles two red pyramids and was designed by the famous Portuguese architect Eduardo Souto de Moura, co-author of the Serpentine Gallery in London.

There are also opportunities for horse riding around Cascais, at the Centro Hípico da Quinta de Marinha (www.quintadamarinhahipico.com), inland from the beach at Guincho (see page 169).

Close to Cascais, the clifftop Casa da Guia has incredible views, some excellent restaurants, shops and more.

THE BEACHES

The main beaches lie between Cascais and Estoril; there is a small beach to the west, **Praia de Santa Marta**, but it is barely big enough for a game of volleyball. Take a short walk beyond, along the main road, and you will come to the **Boca do Inferno** (Mouth of Hell), a narrow inlet with arches and caverns. Waves crash into the inlet with some ferocity, especially when the Atlantic swell is running high; this scene was the subject of *A Sea Cave Near Lisbon* (1896), the first film to feature a cave.

Beyond here lies the rocky Atlantic coast. Lisboetas flock here at weekends to enjoy seafood lunches. Some also come to swim at the broad, clean beach of **Praia do Guincho** ❻, where the waves can be wild and the undertow fierce; needless to say, it is a popular spot for windsurfers.

Bustling town above the popular Praia dos Pescadores.

Admiring the view from the Palácio Nacional da Pena.

SINTRA

Known by the Romans as the Mountains of the Moon, the Serra da Sintra holds a delightful confection of palaces and monuments, along with some splendid beaches.

Main attractions
Palácio Nacional de Queluz
Palácio Nacional de Sintra
Palácio Nacional da Pena
Convento dos Capuchos
Quinta da Regaleira
Mafra

Maps on pages 166, 172

With its lush forests and gentle surrounding plains, beautiful, fantastical Sintra has long been a favourite summer resort for Portuguese and foreign visitors. The area, a mix of lush wooded hills and extraordinary pleasure palaces, was declared a World Heritage Site by UNESCO in 1995. Lord Byron was enamoured of Sintra and likened it to "Elysium's gates". In *Childe Harold,* he wrote: "Lo! Cintra's glorious Eden intervenes in variegated maze of mount and glen."

Some 32km (20 miles) to the northwest of Lisbon, Sintra is another world, with its own climate – a clash of warm southerlies and moist westerlies over the Serra da Sintra. The most practical way to travel is by train from Rossio station. Trains to Sintra run regularly, taking 40 minutes and stopping at Queluz-Belas, for the palace, after 20 minutes. If you drive, try to avoid rush hour. The road to Sintra from Lisbon starts at the Praça Marquês de Pombal and is well marked. Avenida Duarte Pacheco runs into the *auto-estrada* or super highway that leads out of town, past the Aqueduto das Aguas Livres, up the hill through Parque de Monsanto, turning right to join the highway to Sintra.

QUELUZ PALACE

A slight detour to visit **Queluz** ❼ is worthwhile. The town has become a rather drab Lisbon dormitory, but its rose-coloured palace is anything but. The **palácio** (Queluz Palace; www.parquesdesintra.pt) was built as a simple manor for King Pedro II in the mid-1600s and was enlarged when the court moved there. Most of the palace, including its magnificent facade, is Baroque, but the courtyard and formal gardens were modelled after Versailles. In summer, concerts are sometimes held in the Music Room. At other times, the public may visit the lavishly decorated Throne Room with its fine painted wood ceiling, the Hall of Mirrors, the Ambassador's

Ceremonial façade at Queluz Palace.

Making use of the high winds.

The Palácio Nacional at Sintra, with its distinctive chimney cones.

Room, and others. The kitchen, with a stone chimney and copperware, has been turned into a luxury restaurant, **Cozinha Velha**. The palace and gardens are a spectacular stage for **Noites de Queluz**, enchanting musical recreations of 18th-century court life. The Alter Real horses of Escola Portuguesa de Arte Equestre (http://arteequestre.pt), with the riders in full courtly regalia, also perform outside the palace (see full programme on website).

SINTRA VILA

Back on the main road, continue along rolling hills past modest whitewashed villages and rich *quintas* (manors) to arrive at the Serra de Sintra. At the base of the mountain lies the village of **São Pedro de Sintra**, where, on the second and fourth Sunday of each month, a wonderful country fair and flea and book market takes place. São Pedro is also known for its popular tavernas, with spicy sausages, hearty codfish and heady wines. The road now climbs slightly and curves around the mountain to reach **Sintra Vila** Ⓑ, the historic centre of Sintra, where you will find the tourist office, off Praça de República. The road to the left, Rua Gil Vicente, leads down to **Museu Ferreira de Castro** Ⓐ (https://cm-sintra.pt/atualdade/cultura/museus-municipais-de-sintra/museu-ferreira-de-castro), dedicated to the works of the great Portuguese novelist Ferreira de Castro (1898–1974). A little further on is **Lawrence's Hotel** Ⓑ, formerly Estalagem dos Cavaleiros, where Lord Byron stayed in 1809, and now restored as an inn under its original name (www.lawrenceshotel.com).

The centrepiece of Sintra is the royal palace, the Paço Real, now called the **Palácio Nacional de Sintra** Ⓒ (www.parquesdesintra.pt; daily 9.30am–7pm), parts of which date from the 14th century. Broad stairs lead up to the stately building with Gothic arches, Moorish windows and two extraordinary chimney cones above enormous kitchens. Of special interest are the Sala dos Brasões, with remarkable ceiling panels painted in 1515, which show the coat of arms of 71 Portuguese noble families (that of the Távoras was removed after the conspiracy against King José in 1758); the Sala dos Arabes, with marble fountain and 15th-century Moorish tiles; the Sala dos Cisnes, an enormous reception hall with swans painted on the panelled ceiling; and the Sala das Pegas, its ceiling covered with magpies brandishing banners reading "Por Bem". It is said that when Queen Philippa caught João I dallying with a lady-in-waiting he claimed it was an innocent kiss. "Por Bem", he said, which loosely translated means: "It's all for the best". Philippa's response is not recorded.

THE OTHER SINTRA

Estefânia, the third district of Sintra, is where you go to catch the train or a local bus to Lisbon. Walking in that direction from the historic centre, you will reach the **News Museum** D (www.newsmuseum.pt/en), which opened in 2016 and is dedicated to news, media and communications. Subsequently, you will reach the **Casa Museu Anjos Teixeira** E (www.cm-sintra.pt/museu-anjos-teixeira), which houses an important collection of sculptures.

Shortly after this, on the left and before the bus and railway stations, is Sintra's handsome Town Hall. It has a square castellated tower with a steeple in an exuberant Gothic style. Housed in a grand building, in Avenida Heliodoro Salgado, is the **Museu das Artes de Sintra** F (MU.SA; www.cm-sintra.pt/musa-museu-das-artes-de-sintra), containing works by Hockney, Lichtenstein and many other 20th-century artists.

MOUNTAIN RETREATS

Sintra's other palace-museum, the **Palácio Nacional da Pena** G (www.parquesdesintra.pt), dominates the town from the top of the mountain. The road winds up steep rocky slopes through thick woods to the castle, built on the site of a 16th-century monastery: you can walk up, drive or take a quaint bus.

Across the way, reached by the bus to Palácio Nacional da Pena, are the ruins of another mountain-top castle, the **Castelo dos Mouros** H (www.parquesdesintra.pt), dating from about the 11th century. The fortifications visible along the mountain ridge were restored in

> **Tip**
> If you don't wish to walk the 1.5km from Sintra station to the main historic town centre or up the hill to the palace, you can take the no. 434 bus.

HOTCH-POTCH PALACE

The Palácio Nacional da Pena is entered through **Parque da Pena,** where there are lakes with black swans, myriad flora and tiled fountains. Some think the palace is better viewed from afar. Close at hand, the castle is an architectural potpourri: Arabic minarets, Gothic towers, Renaissance cupolas, Manueline windows. But its interior of cosy domesticity is appealing, with rooms furnished as they would have been around the start of the 20th century. It was commissioned by Prince Ferdinand of Saxe-Coburg-Gotha, husband of Queen Maria II, and built by German architect Baron von Eschwege around 1840. At the entrance to the castle a tunnel leads to the ruins of the original monastery. The old chapel walls are decorated with fine 17th-century tiles and there is a splendid altar of alabaster and black marble.

A winged sculpture.

Tile detail on an outside wall at the Quinta de Monserrate.

The great library at Mafra.

the middle of the 19th century. To the southwest rises the highest peak, **Cruz Alta**, at 540 metres (1,772ft), marked by a stone cross. The mountainside is a luxuriant mass – subtropical plants, mossy boulders, giant ferns, walnut, chestnut and pine trees, and rhododendron bushes. One of the strangest sights on the mountain is the **Convento dos Capuchos** (www.parquesdesintra.pt), a 16th-century monastery built entirely of rocks and cork. Some say the monks lined their cells with cork to obtain absolute silence, but there is little noise here other than bird sounds. More likely, the cork helped insulate them from the long bitter winters.

PALATIAL ACCOMMODATION

On the outskirts of Sintra Vila (on the way to Colares) stands the **Palácio de Seteais**, an obscure name said to mean "the seven sighs". This was where the Convention of Sintra was signed in 1809, after the defeat of Napoleon by British and Portuguese forces. It is said that the terms of the treaty upset the Portuguese so much that the palace became known for their sighs of despair. Seteais was restored and turned into a luxury hotel in 1955 (www.tivolihotels.com) and should be visited, if only for tea or a drink. The elegant rooms contain crystal chandeliers, wall hangings, murals and antique furnishings. From the gardens you have a magnificent view of the surrounding countryside.

Almost opposite is the remarkable **Quinta da Regaleira**, built at the close of the 19th century as an assembly of Gothic, Manueline and Renaissance styles that would be out of place anywhere but here. This is one of Sintra's most spectacular sights, with magical gardens filled with follies, which culminate in the initiation well, reached via a mysterious descending spiral staircase.

Nearby is the **Palácio de Monserrate** (www.parquesdesintra.pt), a strange Moorish-type villa built in the 19th century. The exotic garden (daily 9.30am–8pm) and greenhouse are worth seeing for the trees and plants from all over the world: palms, bamboos, cedars, magnolias, cork oaks, pines and giant ferns. Once part of the Monserrate gardens,

SINTRA | 175

the **Quinta de São Thiago** (www.quintadesaothiago.com) is a 16th-century manor with a fine chapel, splendid kitchen, cell-like bedrooms, gardens, and its own swimming pool. You can also stay in the nearby **Quinta da Capela** (www.quintadacapelaeventos.com).

COASTAL EXCURSIONS

For a delightful excursion, the road to **Colares** leads through vineyards, whitewashed hamlets and stone walls to the sea. En route you could visit the **Adega Regional** ❾ (www.arcolares.com; free), a traditional winery. Colares grapes grow in sandy soil in a humid maritime climate. The wines are dark ruby and very smooth.

Cabo da Roca ❿ is a wild desolate cape, the westernmost point of continental Europe, and visitors receive a certificate to mark their visit. Heading north, there are several beaches frequented mainly by the Portuguese: broad, sandy **Praia Grande** ⓫ and **Praia das Maçãs** ⓬. The attractive fishing village of **Azenhas do Mar** ⓭ has a natural rock swimming pool.

MAGNIFICENT MAFRA

Heading north towards the coast you reach **Ericeira** ⓮, a beach resort and fishing village. From here, an easy 10km (6-mile) drive inland takes you to **Mafra** ⓯, a name shared by a modest village and a vast palace-convent (www.visitlisboa.com/en/places/national-palace-of-mafra) that rises like a mirage across the plain. The complex of buildings, almost, making these talented men masters to local apprentices. The most famous teacher was Joaquim Machado de Castro, who also worked on Lisbon's Basílica.

The limestone facade is 220 metres (720ft) long. At its centre is the **church**, with two tall towers and an Italianate portico. The interior is decorated with the finest Portuguese marble, while the 14 large statues of saints in the vestibule were carved from Carrara marble by Italian sculptors. Most impressive is the **library**, full of Baroque magnificence and light. Among its 35,000 volumes are first editions of *Os Lusíadas* by Camões. Other areas open to the public include the hospital, the pharmacy, the audience room and the chapterhouse.

> **◉ Fact**
>
> Mafra is the site of the church of Santo André. Pedro Hispano was priest here before he was elected Pope John XXI in 1276 – the only Portuguese pope in the history of the Vatican. His time as pope was brief: less than a year after his election he was killed by a collapsed ceiling in the papal palace.

Palácio Nacional da Pena.

Cristo Rei monument.

SETÚBAL AND THE ARRÁBIDA PENINSULA

A mixture of industrial sprawl, nature reserves, ancient sites and huge sandy beaches, the Arrábida peninsula is little known to visitors but home to many Lisboetas.

Main attractions
Cristo Rei
Costa da Caparica
Igreja de Jesus
Parque Natural da Arrábida
José Maria da Fonseca Winery

Lisboetas call it *Outra Banda*, or the other shore: meaning the southern bank of the Tejo, long neglected because of the inconvenience of getting there. This changed after 1966 with the completion of what was then Europe's longest suspension bridge, the Ponte 25 de Abril, and an even longer bridge, the Vasco da Gama, in 1998.

The region between the Tejo and Sado rivers, known as the Arrábida peninsula, has been developed rapidly and not always wisely. Directly across the Tejo is the unassuming ferry-boat port of **Cacilhas** ⓰. Its main charm is a string of riverfront fish restaurants with grand views of Lisbon. Some might be interested in visiting the **Fragata Dom Fernando II e Glória** (http://ccm.marinha.pt), a 19th-century, 50-gun frigate of the Portuguese navy, now part of the marine museum (see page 157). About 5km (3 miles) west of Ponte 25 de Abril is Trafaria; the whole town was burned to the ground on the orders of Pombal in 1777 as punishment for resisting press gangs, but was later rebuilt.

Most visitors tend to drive through the neighbouring industrial town of Almada without stopping, except those who want to see the **Cristo Rei monument** ⓱ (Christ the King). A lift takes you to the top of the 82-metre (276ft) pedestal – so high it seems to dwarf the 28-metre (91ft) figure on top – for a magnificent view of Lisbon.

Most people avoid the *Outra Banda* dormitory district by taking the A2 highway directly from the bridge. After a few kilometres, a turn-off leads to **Costa da Caparica** ⓲ (see page 179).

ON TO PALMELA
Continuing south on the highway, the road marked **Palmela** ⓳ leads to a small town with a great medieval castle. This has been restored and converted into the luxury *pousada* **Castelo**

Map on page 166

Ponte 25 de Abril.

Palmela (www.pousadas.pt) with a lounge in the cloisters and an elegant dining room in the old refectory. The church is a beautiful Romanesque structure, its walls covered with 18th-century tiles.

Built by the Moors, the castle was reconstructed in 1147 as a monastery and the seat of the Knights of the Order of St James. In 1484, the bishop of Évora was imprisoned in the dungeon for his role in the conspiracy against João II. He died a few days later, probably poisoned. The castle was badly damaged by the 1755 earthquake, but was rebuilt and monks remained there until the abolition of religious orders in 1834.

Just outside Setúbal rises another great castle, **Forte de São Filipe**, with a magnificent view of the Sado estuary. Felipe II of Spain ordered its construction in 1590, to keep a watch over the area – Portugal was under Spanish rule at the time. The chapel is decorated with tiles that recount the life of the king's namesake, St Philip, signed by the master painter Policarpo de Oliveira Bernardes and dated 1736.

Palmela's castle-pousada.

SETÚBAL AND THE TRÓIA PENINSULA

According to local legend, **Setúbal** [20] was founded by Tubal, the son of Cain. It is said that the Phoenicians and Greeks, finding the climate and soil similar to those of their homelands, planted vineyards here. Setúbal is known to have been an important fishing port since Roman times. Today it is an industrial town: a centre of shipbuilding, fish-canning, and the production of fertilisers, cement, salt and muscatel wine.

Setúbal's pride is the recently renovated **Igreja de Jesus**, a spectacular monument dating back to 1491. The church was designed by Diogo Boytac, one of the founding fathers of the Manueline style of architecture. The narrow building has a high arched ceiling supported by six great stone pillars that look like coils of rope; its apse is etched with stone and lined with tiles, and the pebbled, multicoloured Arrábida marble gives it a distinctive appearance. There are also lovely tiled panels along the walls. The cloister houses a museum, the **Museu de Setúbal** (https://visitsetubal.com/en/convento-de-jesus-museu-de-setubal), which contains religious art from the 15th to the 17th centuries.

Nearby is the **Praça do Bocage**, with palm trees and a statue honouring one of Setúbal's illustrious sons, the 18th-century sonneteer Manuel Barbosa du Bocage. Off the square stands the church of **São Julião** with a handsome Manueline doorway, built in 1513. The inside walls are decorated with 18th-century tiles showing fishing scenes and depicting the life of the saint.

Also of interest is the **Museu de Arqueologia e Etnografia** (http://maeds.amrs.pt; free) with models depicting the main industries: fishing, farming and textiles.

Setúbal's harbour is fascinating, especially in the early morning, when brightly painted trawlers arrive loaded with fish, and fishermen mend nets and work on their boats. Best of all is the lively fish auction.

Setúbal is the main point of departure for the peninsula of **Tróia** ㉑, a long, narrow spit jutting out into the Sado estuary. Ferry boats make the 20-minute crossing frequently in season.

On the northern end of the peninsula there are apartment blocks, houses and a glamorous new resort. The Tróia Golf Club (www.troiagolf.com) has an 18-hole course designed by Robert Trent Jones.

On the southern end of the peninsula, however, there are still many kilometres of pine forest and glorious empty beaches and dunes. Tróia was once thought to be the site of the Roman town of **Cetóbriga** ㉒, destroyed by a tidal wave in the 5th century, though this theory has since been abandoned by most scholars. Still, substantial **Roman ruins** have been found here, including fish salting tanks; it's thought that this complex was once the biggest in the western Roman Empire for the production of *garum*, a fermented fish sauce. The remains of tombs and baths are also visible. Underwater, you may see the walls of Roman houses.

Cooling fountains at the Praça do Bocage.

Costa da Caparica is a popular spot for surfers.

⊙ COSTA DA CAPARICA

South of Lisbon is the city's playground: 8km (5 miles) of broad, sandy Atlantic beaches lined by acacia and eucalyptus trees, moderately priced hotels and cheerful fish restaurants. This popular stretch is cleaner than the Estoril/Cascais coast, and the currents are safer than those of the Atlantic north of the Tejo. The farther south you go, the less built-up the coastline becomes, lined with shady pine forests and dotted with ramshackle little cafés. Nude bathing is popular at the southern end.

There are regular buses from Lisbon to Costa da Caparica town (www.tsuldotejo.pt), or you can take the ferry to Cacilhas (from where there are buses to the town) from Cais do Sodré in Lisbon.

> **Tip**
>
> From Cetóbriga you could choose to return to Setúbal via Alcácar do Sal, a drive of some 120km (75 miles), though of course it is much quicker to take the inexpensive car ferry from Tróia; the downside is you may have to wait in a long queue in peak season.

SERRA DA ARRÁBIDA

A delightful excursion from Setúbal goes west through the **Parque Natural da Arrábida**, along the ridge of the Serra da Arrábida, which rises to 600 metres (2,000ft). As you leave the city, the only sight that mars the natural beauty of the coast is the cement factory, usually spitting black smoke. A road descends to **Portinho da Arrábida** ㉓, a popular bathing beach with transparent waters, white sand and the splendid **Gruta da Santa Margarida**. Hans Christian Andersen, who visited the region in 1834, marvelled in his diaries at this cave, with its imposing stalactites. But it was the poet and historian of the Peninsular War, Robert Southey (1774–1843), who consecrated Arrábida for English readers, calling it "a glorious spot". Of swimming at the base of the mountain, he writes: "I have no idea of sublimity exceeding it". Today, scuba diving is also popular here.

Regaining the ridge, continue along the skyline drive. The next turn-off leads to **Sesimbra** ㉔, a fine resort with a nearby port and a long fishing tradition. The **castle** (www.visitsesimbra.pt/en/to-visit/20/sesimbra-castle; free) above the village, although known as Moorish, has been entirely rebuilt since the time of the Moors. Afonso Henriques captured it in 1165, but the Moors utterly razed the structure in 1191. King Dinis almost certainly helped with the rebuilding, and King João IV enlarged, enhanced and repaired it in the 17th century. Inside the walls are ruins of a Romanesque church.

João IV also ordered the fort of São Teodosio to be built, to protect the port from pirates. A newer fort, the Nova Fortaleza on the seafront, now occupied by the police station, is at the heart of the town. Small bars and restaurants fill the streets around it and they are always full of appreciative customers at weekends. Swordfish is the local speciality.

Going westward about 11km (7 miles) the road ends at **Cabo Espichel** ㉕. This promontory, and the shrine of **Nossa Senhora do Cabo** (www.visitportugal.com/en/content/

Sesimbra.

santuario-de-nossa-senhora-do-cabo-espichel), used to be an important pilgrimage site, as shown by the long rows of dilapidated pilgrims' quarters on either side of the church. There is still a fishermen's festival here each October, and on the edge of the high cliff is the small fishermen's chapel of Senhor de Bomfim, with a breathtaking view; the cliffs are wonderful for walking.

Vila Nogueira de Azeitão The road back to Lisbon goes through **Vila Nogueira de Azeitão** ㉖, sometimes simply called Azeitão, which means "large olive tree". In the centre of this attractive village is the stately Palácio Távora, where the Duke of Aveiro and his friends are said to have plotted to overthrow King José. They were burned at the stake in Belém in 1759. Lovely Baroque fountains border the town's main street. The Igreja São Lourenço has been restored and has beautiful 18th-century altars, paintings and tile panels.

The Azeitão fair (Mercado Mensal de Azeitão), once held in the central square on the first Sunday of the month, became so popular that it caused havoc and had to be moved to the outskirts of town. Less picturesque now, it is still a major attraction, offering everything from shoes and pottery to furniture, plus a large section devoted to livestock. In the village is the original **José Maria da Fonseca Winery** ㉗ (tel: 212 197 500; www.jmf.pt), founded in 1834. The old family residence, which now houses a small museum, stands nearby. The winery still produces one of Portugal's best red table wines, the soft, rich Periquita, as well as Setúbal's popular muscatel wines.

Not far from town stands one of the oldest inhabited manor houses in the country, the **Quinta da Bacalhoa**, built in 1480. It had fallen into ruin and was restored by an American woman from Connecticut, Mrs Herbert Scoville, who bought it in 1936. The **gardens** are admirable, with their clipped boxwood hedges in geometric design, orange and lemon groves, and a pavilion features beautiful tile panels. One of these tile scenes, showing Susanna and the Elders, is dated 1565, and is said to be the earliest known dated panel in Portugal. The beautiful estate is now owned by the renowned Bacalhoa winery, and may be visited on a pre-booked guided tour with tasting (tel: 212 198 067; www.bacalhoa.pt; Mon–Sat 10am–6pm). Now owned by a gold-mining magnate, it is one of the largest wineries in this part of Portugal.

Another attractive manor house, the **Quinta das Torres** (https://quintadecatralvos.pt/outros-espacos-e-quintas/quinta-das-torres-de-azeitao), stands just outside the neighbouring village of **Vila Fresca de Azeitão**. This 16th-century *quinta*, decorated with tile panels and set in a romantic garden, has been converted into a cosy inn and restaurant. In the village, there is yet another lovely church, São Simão, with more ancient tiled walls and polychrome panels.

The small town of Vila Nogueira de Azeitão.

Festival decorations in Tavira.

ALGARVE

Moorish arches drenched in sunshine and spectacular coves of golden sand: the Algarve offers a touch of the exotic that attracts visitors by the million.

Main attractions
Parque Natural da Ria Formosa
Ilha de Tavira
Praia da Rocha
Fortaleza de Sagres
Serra de Monchique
Castelo de Silves
Loulé market

Map on page 184

If one region of Portugal stands alone, it is the Algarve. Its history under long Moorish control, its climate – more typically Mediterranean – and its abundance of fine sandy beaches endow Algarve with a character so different that it could easily be taken as a separate country. In the minds of many visitors, it is.

Separated from the rest of Portugal by rolling hills, Algarve – the southernmost province – seduced the ancient Phoenicians with its abundance of sardines and tuna, which they salt-cured for export almost 3,000 years ago. Four centuries later, around 600 BC, the Carthaginians and Celts arrived, followed in turn by the Romans, who adopted the Phoenician practice of curing and exporting fish: the precursor of Portugal's large sardine-tinning industry. They also built roads, bridges and spas, such as that in Milreu.

But Algarve really blossomed under Moorish rule, which began in the early 8th century. The province's name comes from the Moorish *Al-Gharb*, meaning "The West". The Moorish period was one of vibrant culture and great scientific advances. Moorish poets sang of the beauty of Silves, its principal city, while the more practical settlers introduced orange crops and perfected the technique of extracting olive oil, still an important Portuguese product. The blossoming almond trees in January and February are one of the most beautiful sights of Algarve thanks, according to folklore, to the passion a Moorish king once felt for a northern princess.

Legend has it that the princess, pining for the snows of her homeland, slowly began to waste away. Distraught, the king ordered thousands of almond trees to be planted across the region, then one February morning carried her to the window where she saw swirling white "snowflakes" carpeting the

Praia da Rocha.

ground – the white almond blossoms. She quickly recuperated, and the two lived happily ever after.

MOORISH LEGACY

King Afonso Henriques led the Portuguese conquest southwards in the 12th century. Later his son, Sancho I, with the help of a band of crusaders, was to spearhead the siege of Silves and its estimated population of 20,000 people. It took 49 days before the Moors of Silves were forced to surrender. But in 1192 they reconquered the city and remained there for another 47 years. It was Sancho II, supported by military-religious orders under Paio Peres Correia, who finally crushed them. The last major city to fall was Faro, in January 1249.

The Arabic influence is visible even today: in many of the town names, in words beginning with the "al" prefix, in the so-called "North African blue" used for trimming the whitewashed houses, in the roof terraces used for the drying of fruit, and in the white-domed buildings still popular in many towns. Algarvian sweets made of figs, almonds, eggs and sugar called *morgados* or *Dom Rodrigos* are yet another reminder of the area's ancient heritage.

For centuries almond, fig, olive and carob trees represented a major part of Algarve's agriculture, as they are suited to dry inland areas. The carob, whose beans are now fed to cattle but which also produce a variety of oils, are said to have sustained the Duke of Wellington's cavalry during the Peninsular War. Thanks to the gentle climate, Algarve also produces pears, apples, quinces, loquats, damask plums, pomegranates, tomatoes, melons, strawberries, avocados and grapes.

REGIONAL SPECIALITIES

Wine critics regard all Algarve wines as undistinguished, and even in quite modest restaurants the house wine is usually from the better Alentejo range, or perhaps from even further to the north. But many local wines are quite palatable and should not be written off completely.

You will find good beer, the preference of most young Algarvios, widely available. Older men passing the time in tavernas and *tascas* drink *medronho*, a clear firewater with the kick of a mule, distilled from the fruit of the strawberry tree, *Arbutus unedo*. Another individual drink in Algarve is *Brandymel*, a type of honey brandy.

The pleasant market town of Loulé (see page 197), with its central tree-shaded walkway, is the crafts centre of Algarve, but local handicrafts are widely sold everywhere. Among them are baskets, hats, mats and hampers of rush or straw, which are made by local women who pick and dry the esparto grass in spring, then shred it into thin strips before they weave and plait it. You will see mats of grass, and of cotton and wool (although some of those on sale come from Alentejo). Cane basketry is almost always the work of men in the eastern towns of Odeleite, Alcoutim and Castro Marim. Despite the modern prevalence of cardboard boxes, baskets are still used to carry eggs, to display golden smoked sardines, and as fish traps.

Lagos, Loulé and Tavira – as well as numerous stores along the main N125 highway – are good places to find pottery, from big pitchers, plant pots, hand-painted plates and tiles, to the distinctive, lace-like chimney tops that embellish Algarve's skyline. You will find a considerable range of copper pots and bowls – one such shop is on a street corner beside the market in Loulé. If you walk down the avenue you will see – and hear – coppersmiths at work in tiny workshops.

Woodwork is also a regional craft, from spoons made in Aljezur to the brightly coloured mule-drawn carts you still see on the roads. Handmade lace is a skill that is being kept alive in such places as Azinhal. Up in the hills of Monchique (where a small craft shop has grown to an extensive display) you will find wooden furniture and woollen weaves.

KEY ROUTES AND PLACES

The southern coastline, so richly endowed with golden sandy beaches in spectacular settings, is the region's prime asset. At the onset of mass tourism in the 1960s it attracted

Faro, the capital city of the Algarve region, is a popular destination.

Ilha de Tavira rescue equipment.

developers, and much of the central region, around Albufeira, is now well developed. Those looking for smaller, quieter coastal resorts can still find them by travelling out to the west beyond Lagos and, to a lesser extent, east of Faro. Inland Algarve has its share of pretty villages and remains largely unspoilt countryside, although it is rapidly becoming the preferred area for expatriate settlers.

Driving around Algarve is not difficult. The N125 travels the length of the coast, while the A22 motorway (tolls payable) shadows it just inland. It is possible to drive from Spain in the east to Sagres in the west in a little over two hours.

FARO: THE HUB OF ALGARVE

The roots of **Faro** ❶, the capital of Algarve, are ancient but not well documented, although it is certain that it was used by Greeks and Romans as a trading post before it became a flourishing Moorish town. Largely devastated by the 1755 earthquake, the city now has an architectural hotchpotch of styles and eras.

The centre of Faro is walkable, its character changing as you wander through streets of tiny houses, 19th-century mansions, modern villas and shops. It's a bustling capital and has considerable charm. The main pedestrianised street, Rua de Santo António, is in the middle of the Moorish quarter (Mouraria), which lies between the old city (Vila-Adentro) and the 19th-century Bairro Ribeirinho, all of which lead from the port.

On the south side of the little harbour, through the 18th-century Arco da Vila that penetrates the old city walls, lies a peaceful and historic inner town, the Vila Adentro. At its centre is the Renaissance **Sé** (Cathedral; http://turismo.diocese-algarve.pt with its 13th-century tower. Eighteenth-century polychrome tiles are an impressive feature in its chapels as well as in the body of the church. The red chinoiserie organ is also 18th century, and the choir stalls are a notable trophy from Silves Cathedral, installed when the seat of the diocese was moved to Faro in the 16th century.

Evening scenes in Albufeira.

In the square behind the cathedral a former convent with strikingly beautiful Renaissance cloisters is now the **Museu Municipal** (www.cm-faro.pt/pt/menu/1802/museu-municipal-de-faro.aspx), with a selection of Roman mosaics and stonework from Faro and from the important Roman site at Milreu (see page 197).

On Praça da Liberdade, the **Museu Regional do Algarve** displays some interesting relics of Algarve peasant life.

Beside the harbour, in the Port Authority building in the Bairro Ribeirinho, the **Museu Marítimo** (Maritime Museum; https://museusdoalgarve.wordpress.com) is worth a visit to see the broad range of Algarve fishing methods. Among the exhibits are model boats and a vivid depiction of the old way of trapping tuna in the bloody "bullfight of the sea".

Faro's most bizarre and macabre sight is the **Capela dos Ossos** (Chapel of Bones, reached through the Baroque Igreja do Carmo with its impressive facade and twin towers. The little chapel was built in 1816, its walls entirely covered with bones and skulls (allegedly 1,245 of them) from the church cemetery. Some find this grim display of mortality less depressing than the high-rises that contrast with the church's fine facade.

LIGHTHOUSE AND LAGOON

Faro is protected on the seaward side by a huge lagoon dotted with sandbanks, with the airport on the western edge. Some of the sandbanks are large, especially the outer barrier islands, and the southernmost point is marked by the Cabo de Santa Maria lighthouse (*faro* means lighthouse in Portuguese).

The sand spit that starts near the airport and extends out as a long crescent, Ilha de Faro, can be reached by car and is the location of **Praia de Faro** ❷, a sandy resort much loved by the local people. Ilha da Culatra is the only other inhabited sand spit and can only be reached by ferry from Olhão (timetables at www.olhaocubista.pt/horariobarcos.htm) or Faro. The whole of this natural lagoon and the adjacent area, stretching some 50km (30 miles) from Ancão in the west to Cacela in the east, has been protected since 1987 as the **Parque Natural da Ria Formosa** ❸ (see tip for visitor centre details). This lagoon system provides 90 percent of Portugal's harvest of clams and oysters. It is also an important bird sanctuary, especially for waders such as egrets and oystercatchers, and some rare species, including the purple gallinule.

EAST OF FARO

Travelling eastwards out of Faro takes you to the busy 17th-century town of **Olhão** ❹, built in the Moorish style, with a large fishing port. On the seafront by the leisure boats' pontoons are the town's modern (1998) market halls. Arrive at the fish market early and be prepared to use your elbows to reach

> **Tip**
>
> Get a taste of the Parque Natural da Ria Formosa at the park headquarters (Centro de Educação Ambiental de Marim) at Quelfes, 3km (2 miles) east of Olhão. The park combines lagoons, marsh and islands and is great for birdwatching, as well as for spotting other rare creatures such as the European chameleon.

The exterior of Faro's Igreja do Carmo.

Fishing boats prepare in the early morning in the port town of Tavira.

Tavira garden.

the slithery hills of fish that the women hawk at the tops of their voices, poking them to prove their freshness. The best buys are gilt-head bream *(dourada)*, bass *(robalo)* and sole *(linguado)*. The other halls sell fruit and vegetables.

If you are not catching the ferry out to beautiful Culatra beach, move on to **Fuzeta**, where there is a sandy beach and a boat that can take you out to uninhabited **Ilha da Armona** (summer ferries also run here from Olhão; www.olhaocubista.pt/horariobarcos.htm) for a spot of sunbathing.

Almost next door to Fuzeta is Pedras del Rei, the starting point for an exciting little journey by train over to the beach of **Barril** ❺ on the Tavira sandbank, the Ilha de Tavira. There is a footpath by the track, should the train be full.

A café or restaurant along the broad palm-lined promenade of **Santa Luzia**, a colourful fishing village overlooking the lagoon, is the place to sit and watch the fishermen stacking up encrusted octopus pots *(alcatruzes)* after removing their catch.

TEMPTING TAVIRA

One of the larger towns on the eastern side, **Tavira** ❻ is a delightful spot that has avoided the excesses of development and lost none of its grace. It elegantly borders both sides of the Rio Sequa, which becomes the Gilão as it slides under the seven-arched Roman-style bridge, the Ponte Romana, towards the sea. With its estuary and outlying island, Tavira flourished in the 16th century. But trade dwindled as the fish disappeared, and this lovely town, composed of narrow streets, pastel-coloured patricians' houses, miniature towers, domes, unusual four-sided roofs and minarets, today leads a quieter life.

There are more than two dozen churches and chapels in Tavira, of which the most interesting are the **Igreja da Misericórdia**, built in 1541 but remodelled after the 1755 earthquake, with some lovely *azulejo* decorations; and the church of **Santa Maria**, rebuilt on the site of the town's old mosque. Many of the churches are closed, but information about access to the major ones, as well as maps of the area, is available from the tourist office, to be found up the steps from the town hall in the main square (Rua da Galeria, 9).

A short ferry journey from the town will take you to the long white beaches of **Ilha de Tavira**, an unspoilt paradise.

Atmospheric fortified hamlets where time appears to stand still are not what you expect to find along the southern coast of Algarve, but there is one at **Cacela Velha** ❼. It has a miniature 18th-century fortress and a gleaming white church. The whole village clings tightly to a perch looking over a lagoon.

The border with Spain is reached at the Rio Guadiana. Facing Spain is **Vila Real de Santo António** ❽, its grid of geometric streets bearing the stamp of the Marquês de Pombal – the man who was responsible for redesigning old Lisbon in the 18th century. Pombal intended this town to be a model administrative, industrial and fishing centre – he founded the Royal Fisheries Company here – but he lost favour with the court and his plans never really took off. All the same, fishing remains an important activity.

Just west of Vila Real is the largest touristic development this side of Faro, **Monte Gordo**. The clutch of high-rise buildings lining broad tree-lined streets and overlooking a vast flat beach as yet remains fairly compact.

MOORS, MINES AND MARSHLANDS

Further inland along the Guadiana lies the architecturally appealing **Castro Marim** ❾. This little town is also one of the oldest and historically most important areas of Algarve. Once a major Phoenician settlement, it also played host to the Greeks and Carthaginians before the Moors and Romans invaded. Portugal's kings later used it as a natural point from which to fight the infidels to the east.

The huge castle, built by King Afonso III after he dispelled the Moors in 1249, is still standing, overlooking the surrounding valley. In 1319, it was the first headquarters of the Order of Christ. The fort on the hill opposite dates from 1641.

Surrounding the town is the Castro Marim fen or marsh, wetland home of

Stone pavement mosaic in Faro.

Castro Marim.

⊘ ILHA DE TAVIRA

Tavira Island is a well-kept Algarve secret – a long, thin slick of land just off the coast, accessible via boat from Tavira. It is 11km (6 miles) long and 150 metres–1km (165yds–0.5 miles) wide, and is lined by some of the region's loveliest beaches, with powder-soft sand lapped by Mediterranean waters. It is part of the Natural Reserve of Ria Formosa, and so retains its unspoilt beauty. There is a campsite here and several cafés, but that's about it.

The most popular beach on the island is Praia do Barril. To the east of it, the island narrows into a thin sandy strip no more than 50 metres/55yds wide, which is the site of the beautiful and aptly named Praia da Terra Estreita (Narrow Land Beach), also known as Praia de Santa Luzia.

> **Fact**
>
> Algarve has many spectacular beaches but Praia da Marinha, south of Porches, is one of the most photogenic, its red sandstone cliffs eroded into arches and stacks. For a large expanse of sand backed by colourful cliffs, try Falésia just west of Quarteira.

many migratory birds including storks, cranes and flamingos, and a hundred different species of plant life. An area of 2,000 hectares (5,000 acres) is now protected as the **Reserva Natural do Sapal** ❿ (https://cm-castromarim.pt/site/conteudo/reserva-natural-do-sapal-de-cmvrsa/m2).

Among the least-travelled routes in Algarve is the peaceful road along the Rio Guadiana. It is a soothing meander through golden, furze-covered hills dotted with cork, olive and fig trees. (Road numbers are N122 and 1063 for the riverside drive.) **Alcoutim** ⓫ is the northernmost Algarve town, and here it often seems as if time has stood still. Sunning dogs in the only square in town have priority, so you will have to park around them.

From the promenade that extends along the edge of the Guadiana River you can see the nearby Spanish town of **Sanlucar de Guadiana** reflected in the slow-moving water. Signs to the "castle" are a little misleading, as they lead to an empty shell of walls – but the view from here is worth the short walk.

An inland return route will take you through **Martim Longo** ⓬, near the former open-air copper mine at Vaqueiros. Martim Longo is a peaceful town home to traditional blacksmiths, puppet-making workshops and the lovely whitewashed, red-roofed Igreja Matriz, which is home to 16th-century Manueline windows. Continue through Cachopo to reach Faro.

WEST OF FARO

The coastal route out to the west heads towards the main area of tourist development and to some of the most picturesque beaches. First stop outside Faro is at **São Lourenço** ⓭ for the small 18th-century church of the same name. Inside it is tiled, from top to bottom, in beautiful blue *azulejos* (ceramic tiles) depicting the life and martyrdom of São Lourenço himself.

Nearly all the well-known golf courses, more than 30 of them, lie west of Faro, each one an exclusive development with luxury accommodation. Among them are Quinta do Lago, Vale do Lobo, which has a famous 16th hole

Albufeira beach rock formations.

across a coastal ravine, and Vila Sol at **Vilamoura** ⓴. They take up a huge area on the edge of the Ria Formosa reserve, presenting a neat face of colourful flowerbeds and well-manicured lawns.

Just to the west of Vilamoura is the small resort and fishing village of **Olhos d'Agua**. The bonus here is that it is too small to attract the large tour operators. Tucked into a small cleft, the fishing village is as picturesque as any in Algarve, with sculptured rock stacks decorating the beach.

ALBUFEIRA

Once a small fishing village favoured by the Romans and the Moors, **Albufeira** ⓯ today is enduringly pretty, while overwhelmingly touristy – rather like the Algarve version of the Costa del Sol in Spain – yet has retained its character slightly better than some other Algarve resorts. It has lively nightlife, scores of noisy bars, plenty of restaurants ranging from pizza joints to those serving more typical regional fare, and late-night dancing. The steep streets descending into the old part of town are still very attractive, as are the rock-protected beaches where the fishermen keep their boats, traditionally painted with large eyes to ward off evil, as well as with stars and animals.

There is a bustling fish market near the Pescadores (fishermen's) beach and a fruit, meat and vegetable market in the main square. Although development has been intense in this region, the coast westwards is a delightful symphony of eroded cliffs, stacks, gullies, grottoes and arches reaching a crescendo at Lagos. It is still possible to follow your nose and divert off to quiet beaches.

Whichever route you take towards the west, it is likely you will end up in **Alcantarilha** ⓰. It's worth a stop here if only to look in on the parish church, and especially the Capela de Ossos around the corner, which is packed with a chilling array of skulls. For family fun, visit nearby **Aqualand** (www.aqualand.pt; advance tickets can be purchased online), a large water park, with chutes and slides aplenty.

The beach at Albufeira.

A street corner in Lagos.

The lighthouse guards the coast at Cape São Vincente.

Alternatively, try **Zoomarine** (www.zoomarine.pt) in Guia. The park promotes environmental awareness and offersopportunities to interact with the dolphins. Head south from here into **Armação de Pêra** ⑰. This mundane resort is rescued by an attractive promenade and beach, and it is a good place to eat fish.

All the grandeur and cragginess return to the coastline here and it is quite a descent to reach the beach at **Rocha da Pena**. Sitting on a bluff between two sandy coves is the simple white church of **Nossa Senhora da Rocha** ⑱, dedicated to fishermen. Inland from here is **Porches**, which is famous for its painted pottery.

At the next roundabout on the N125 is **Lagoa**, increasingly commercial and with a lively morning market. This is also where farmers bring their grapes to the central cooperative wine cellar. A left turn at this roundabout leads down to Carvoeiro, a craggy coastline of isolated beaches, like that of Algar Seco. **Praia de Carvoeiro**, which is a lively tourist spot itself, has a pleasant little beach framed by cliffs studded with villas.

Portimão ⑲ (once a Roman harbour, Portus Magnus) lies west of Carvoeiro. An important fishing port, it is also one of the best shopping towns on the coast. Built on the west bank of the Arade estuary, Portimão is famous for its grilled sardines – have lunch beside the river to try some – and for its pastry shops. Facing it is the pretty fishing village of **Ferragudo** ⑳, with cobbled streets, pavement cafés and a good fish market. Close by is ocean-fronted **Praia da Rocha** ㉑, which has a superb, much-photographed beach characterised by strange towering rock formations standing in the blue-green sea. The beach's most recent attraction is the **Ocean Revival Underwater Park** (www.wildsea.eu/portugal/algarve/portimao/wreck-dive-the-fantastic-ocean-revival-park.html). One of the largest artificial reefs in the world, this makes an excellent destination for divers who can explore four sunken warships and observe the marine life. The town itself, however, is a bit of a concrete jungle, although it does have all the facilities that visitors could ask for.

LAGOS

Moving west from here you will come to **Lagos** ㉒, with a fine maritime tradition and a safe harbour beside a river estuary. Founded by the Carthaginians, it was taken by the Romans in the 5th century BC, when it was called *Lacobriga* (Fortified Lake). The Moors took it over in the 8th century and renamed it *Zawaia* (Lake). The city finally fell to the Portuguese during the reign of Afonso III. In 1434 Gil Eanes left from Lagos and became the first sea captain to round Cape Bojador, off northwest Africa, south of the Canary Islands – which was then the limit of the known world.

Most of Lagos was rebuilt in the 18th century, but some evidence of its darker past still stands in the columns and semicircular arches of Portugal's first slave market in the **Praça da República**. Nearby stands a statue of Henry the Navigator, who sent ships from here off into the unknown. Note, too, the modern monument by João Cutileiro recording King Sebastião's departure to the disastrous battle of Alcácer-Quibir in 1578.

A walk through the city's attractive streets will lead you to the **Igreja de Santo António;** on the outside a sober-looking church, but inside an extraordinarily beautiful example of gilded carving. The nave has an impressive painted wooden barrel vault and Baroque paintings on the walls.

The church can only be visited through the **Museu de Lagos** (https://museu.cm-lagos.pt), which has a delightful collection of exhibits on local life in Algarve. Its eclectic collection of local finds, dating from the Bronze Age and Roman times, is layered over with fascinating glimpses of local life, and though the layout may at first seem old-fashioned, it is one of the most intriguing museums in the country.

Lagos has several pretty coves and beaches, especially **Praia Dona Ana**. Don't miss the rock formations at **Ponta da Piedade** ㉓. From the foot of the cliffs you might also hire a boat from a local fisherman to explore the grottoes, with their cathedral-like natural skylights.

Beyond Lagos lie three relatively unspoilt fishing villages, each of a different character and each worth a visit. **Luz** ㉔ is the first of these, and perhaps the most developed, and is followed by **Burgau** and **Salema**. The countryside changes drastically, particularly after Salema, to a rockier and more undulating landscape. The trees look smaller and squatter, permanently bent by the unrelenting wind.

Improved roads make driving in this area easier than it once was, but the new road actually bypasses the Knights Templar church of **Nossa Senhora de Guadalupe** ㉕, (Hermitage of Our Lady of Guadalupe), where Henry the Navigator is said to have worshipped. It is easier to spot it when travelling west and to visit it on the return.

> **Fact**
> It was to Sagres that seafarers returned in 1419 with the news that they had discovered an uninhabited island they called Porto Santo, which was later found to be part of the Madeiran archipelago.

Fisherman Beach.

> **Fact**
>
> The eucalyptus trees which now grow in profusion in the Serra de Monchique smell lovely but are unpopular with environmentalists since they are bad for the soil and highly flammable.

SAGRES

Sagres ㉖ is a small fishing town, with Baleeira Bay as its port. The attraction to visitors is **Fortaleza de Sagres**, the fortress at **Ponta de Sagres**, used by Henry the Navigator early in the 15th century. He invited the most renowned cartographers, astronomers and mariners of his day to work here, and thus formed a fund of knowledge unsurpassed at the time, although modern historians believe he did not found a formal School of Navigation. Nothing that Prince Henry built is left, so it is hard to be sure. But you can see clues – notably a huge, 43-metre (140ft) compass rose on the stone ground of the fortress. There is a modern exhibition hall and tourist facilities in the fort, and a 1km (0.5-mile) walk along the top of the cliff.

All that remains now is to continue driving through this windswept terrain passing the small Fortaleza de Beliche, now a small *pousada* and restaurant, to reach **Cabo de São Vicente** ㉗, known to ancient mariners as *O Fim do Mundo*, the End of the World. From within the walls enclosing the lighthouse you can look down upon St Vincent's rocky throne.

Legend has it that in medieval times Christian followers of the martyred St Vincent defied the Moors and buried his body on the cape, with a shrine to honour him. Sacred ravens were said to have maintained vigil over the spot and over the ship that carried the bones of the saint to Lisbon. Here, even on a calm day, waves crash against the cliffs with spray-tossing violence. In spring, the smell of the sea competes with the scent of cistus, the rock rose bush whose perfumed leaves were once supposedly used by the Egyptians for embalming.

THE WILD WEST COAST

Algarve's west coast is virtually a continuous vista of cliff and sand, frequently pounded by a restless ocean and almost constantly under surf and spray. Although there are endless beaches, there are few towns of significance. **Odeceixe**, the most northerly town on this stretch of Algarvian coastline, is a small Moorish-style,

The Serra de Monchique.

ALGARVE | 195

windmill-topped village. A road follows the river for 3km (2 miles) to a beautiful sandy beach beneath towering cliffs at Praia de Odeceixe.

The most popular west-coast circuit starts from Cabo de São Vicente and continues north through the vast, dune-backed Carrapateira to the attractive village of **Aljezur** ㉘. The 10th-century castle was the last to be taken from the Moors. Directly to the west are the great sweeps of the **Monte Clérigo** and **Arrifana** beaches, the best on this coast. Heading inland from Aljezur towards Monchique leads back into the heart of Algarve.

MOUNTAINS AND SPRINGS

Towering above rolling hills, the granite mountains of **Serra de Monchique** attract streams of visitors to enjoy the views from the summit. In spring, Monchique is covered in flowering mimosa, and wild flowers bloom in the valleys between the Fóia and Picota peaks. **Fóia** ㉙ is the highest point of Algarve, reaching 902 metres (2,960ft) above sea level. It is easily accessible along a winding road lined with cheerful restaurants selling roast chicken. The summit is heavily forested with transmitter aerials and the promised views are revealed only on clear days. Picota (774 metres/2,539ft) presents a different challenge and can be reached only on foot.

The town of Monchique is rather disappointing if you merely drive through it, but park the car and walk the steep streets and you get a better feel for the place. Worth visiting is **Caldas de Monchique** ㉚ (http://monchiquetermalresort.com), off to the right heading south, hidden in a deep valley and surrounded by chestnut, cork, pine, orange and eucalyptus trees. The spa has been in use since Roman times and the waters are believed to cure a number of ailments, from convulsions to rheumatism. The springs pour out an estimated 20 million litres (4 million gallons) of water a year.

RURAL VILLAGES

Descending from the heights, but away from the coastal tourist zone, a more

Fresh lemons grow in groves.

A bridge leads to the town of Silves in Algarve.

A bronze statue of King Don Sancho in Silves.

The interiors of Palácio dos Condes de Carvalha.

rural lifestyle is found in the towns and villages. Here, locals have managed to shrug off the effects of regular visitors and continue their traditional ways. One of the most interesting places is **Silves** ㉛, between Albufeira and Portimão. Silves was already populated by the 4th century BC and reached its greatest splendour under the Moors, who made it the capital of Algarve.

In its glory days Silves was the home of some of the greatest Arab poets. They recorded its ruin when the city fell to Portugal's King Sancho I in 1189: "Silves, my Silves, once you were a paradise. But tyrants turned you into the blaze of hell. They were wrong not to fear God's punishment. But Allah leaves no deed unheeded," wrote one. Two years later the Moors occupied Silves again, before it was finally reconquered by the Portuguese.

Yemenite Arabs built the walled city, but the **castle** (www.cm-silves.pt/) – atop a Roman citadel, itself built on Neolithic foundations – and the defensive towers were rebuilt in the later Almohad period (12th–13th centuries) and heavily restored in modern times. The Moorish castle and the Christian cathedral dominate the city, the dark-red sandstone contrasting with the soft pinks and faded blues of the older surrounding houses. A sense of history still permeates Silves and the castle.

The Moorish cistern to the north once supplied the city's water, and is architecturally similar to 13th-century cisterns found in Palestine and in Cáceres, Spain. Built by both the Romans and the Moors, the advanced irrigation system transformed Algarve into the garden of Portugal.

The **Sé** (Cathedral) is 13th-century Gothic, restored in the 14th century and almost destroyed by the earthquake of 1755. Its apse is decorated with square arches, pyramidal battlements and fanciful gargoyles. The inner chapel of João de Rego dates from the 1400s. Various tombs here are said to be those of crusaders who helped capture Silves from the Moors in 1244. Here, too, for four years lay the remains of João II, who died in nearby Alvor in 1495, aged 40 – from dropsy according to some doctors, from poisoning according to others.

FROM ALTE TO ESTÓI

Northeast of Albufeira on the N124 is **Alte** ㉜, a graceful village lying at the foot of hills and huddled around its parish church. Nossa Senhora da Assunção dates from the 16th century and has magnificent 18th-century tile panels. The tiles in the chapel of Nossa Senhora de Lurdes, among the best in Algarve, are of 16th-century Sevillian origin. Alte is a typical village of the province with its simple houses, delicate white-laced chimneys, and timeless serenity.

A nearby stream has transformed the area into an oasis amid the region's arid landscape. It's a lush garden of oleanders, fig and loquat trees and rose bushes. The blue-and-white tile panels at Fonte Santa (Holy Fountain)

ALGARVE

are inscribed with verses by a local poet, Cândido Guerreiro. This area is perfect for picnics, or a walk up the Pena hill where you can visit the **Buraco dos Mouros** (Moors' Cave). Further up the mountain is the **Rocha dos Soidos**, a cave filled with stalactite and stalagmite formations.

Heading back towards Faro you reach **Loulé** ㉝, a small town whose old quarter – Almedina – is a maze of narrow streets, reminiscent of a North African casbah. The interior of the chapel of Nossa Senhora da Conceição (near the tourist office) is tiled with attractive 17th-century *azulejos*, and the Igreja da Misericordia has a fine Manueline doorway.

One of Loulé's greatest attractions is the Saturday **market**, held in the onion-domed market halls, selling food of every kind, from home-grown fruit to live chickens. It draws visitors in from all over the Algarve. Loulé also has an extremely lively carnival in February, one of the best in the country.

Take a very slight detour east before you reach Faro and you will come to **Estói** ㉞, a pleasant village with a fine parish church, but best known for its 18th-century **Palácio Estoi** which has been turned into a luxurious *pousada* (www.pousadas.pt). The highly ornamental gardens of this "Queluz of the South", with their statues and rococo fountains, and a splendid tiled staircase, are well worth seeing.

The town has a huge market – more of a country fair, held on the second Sunday of the month. It is a lively affair where you can buy a horse, sell a few sheep, stock up on fruit and vegetables or just buy sugared cakes to eat as you mingle with the crowds.

VILLA ROMANA DE MILREU

Close by is the Roman **Villa Romana de Milreu** ㉟ (https://bilheteira.patrimoniocultural.gov.pt/pt/monument/35), a site discovered in the late 1800s. There are some lovely mosaics here, the remains of thermal baths, and a well-preserved villa dating from the 2nd century. The largest structure, a temple, was consecrated as a Visigothic basilica in the 3rd century.

The Cathedral in Silves was formerly a mosque.

ⓞ ALGARVE ON A PLATE

Heaps of crustaceans, and other seafood, fresh-from-the-sea fish, eel and octopus are major elements of Algarve's culinary specialities, but it is also a region that is rich in fresh fruit and vegetables, ripened in the baking sunshine of the south. A much-loved dish is *amêijoas na cataplana*, clams cooked in a copper pan of Arab origin, but other delights include slow-grilled sardines, sea bream or red mullet, razor clams or octopus, squid cooked in its ink, and bean stew with whelks. The rolling wooded hills of the interior mean that game and pork dishes are on the menu too. You can also discern the Arabic influence on cuisine here, particularly through the local sweets, usually created using nuts and dried fruits from Algarve's orchards.

View from the castle over Castelo de Vide.

ÉVORA AND ALENTEJO

The Romans left more than a few footprints here, and there are historic towns and castles around almost every corner, while Alentejo boasts some of the country's grandest landscapes.

Main attractions
Templo Romano, Évora
Sé, Évora
Évoramonte
Paço Ducal, Vila Viçosa
Monsaraz
Marvão
Vila Nova de Milfontes
Mértola

Maps on pages 200, 203

Alentejo, literally "beyond the Tejo" (the River Tagus), has a distinctive character and beauty unlike that of any other Portuguese province. Its vast plains, coloured burnt ochre in summer, are freckled with cork oaks and olive trees, which provide the only shade for the small flocks of sheep and herds of black pigs.

Nicknamed *terra do pão* (land of bread) because it is covered with field upon field of wheat and oats, Alentejo also supports acres of grape vines, tomatoes, sunflowers and other crops.

The largest and flattest of the Portuguese provinces, about the size of Belgium, Alentejo occupies one-third of Portugal's total area yet has only six percent of its population. It stretches from the west coast east to the Spanish border and separates Ribatejo and Beira Baixa in the central regions from Algarve in the south. The open countryside is punctuated by picturesque whitewashed towns and villages, many built on the low hills that dot the horizon.

Alentejo is rich in handicrafts. Rustic pottery with naive, colourful designs can be found everywhere. In addition, certain towns specialise in particular crafts or products: hand-stitched rugs come from Arraiolos, loom-woven carpets from Reguengos, cheese from Serpa, tapestries from Portalegre, and sugar plums from Elvas.

GETTING AROUND ALENTEJO

Geographically the province is split into two regions, Upper *(Alto)* and Lower *(Baixo)* Alentejo. Évora is the capital of the former and Beja of the latter. To the east are two low mountain ranges, the *serras* of São Mamede and Ossa. Some of the towns in these ranges, particularly Marvão, have breathtaking, even precipitous, settings. Portugal's third-longest river, the Guadiana, flows through the province and in places forms the border between Portugal and Spain. This is by no means

Painted chairs for sale in Alentejo.

the only waterway, however. The region is crisscrossed by a network of small rivers and dams.

Roads that connect the towns are excellent. Most of the traffic is local and slow moving. You will need to equip yourself with a reliable road map or GPS; signposting is limited, and without a map you could drive many kilometres before discovering you have taken a wrong turn.

The Portuguese in general are not renowned for their tidiness, but the Alentejanos are the exception. The towns are litter-free and there is always a *dona de casa* in view whitewashing her already pristine home. Cool and simple is the theme for Alentejo architecture: low, single-storey buildings are painted white to deflect the sun's glare, and given a traditional blue or yellow skirting. Large domed chimneys indicate chilly winters. This practical style is followed from the humblest cottage to the large hacienda-style homes of the wealthy landowners; ornate and impressive architecture is reserved for cathedrals and churches.

Inland, Alentejo's temperature in the summer can reach inferno level. What little wind there is blows hot and dry from the continental landmass – no cooling sea breezes here. Temperatures can drop dramatically in winter, resulting in bitterly cold nights.

ALENTEJO'S HISTORY

Alentejo is steeped in history, which goes back to the days of Roman colonisation. Later, it was the seat of the great landed estates *(latifundia)* of the Portuguese nobility and home to former kings. Even as late as 1828, Évora – the capital of the Alto Alentejo – was considered the second major Portuguese city, an honour that was first bestowed on it by King João I (1385–1433).

Estremoz, whose ancient castle has been converted into a comfortable *pousada* (www.pousadas.pt), was a nerve centre of medieval Portugal. Vila Viçosa was the seat of the dukes of Bragança, whose royal dynasty began in 1640 with the coronation of João IV and ended in 1910 with the fall of the monarchy.

POLITICS, PASTIMES AND POPULAR SONG

Modern Alentejo is a far cry from the days of aristocratic domination, although farming techniques in the smallholdings have changed little. The greatest change is political: after the restoration of democracy in 1974 Alentejo became the heartland of Portuguese Communism. Many of the great estates – so vast that they included villages, schools and even small hospitals – were taken over by the farm workers during the revolution. Some of the landowning families were forcibly ejected, but the majority were absentee landlords anyway, living in properties nearer Lisbon or Porto. There is now a new landowning generation with a modern approach to agriculture and skilled at effective farm management.

> **Fact**
> To find out about the Rota dos Vinhos do Alentejo (www.vinhosdoalentejo.pt), visit the Alentejo Wine Route Support Office, at 88 Rua Cinco de Outubro in Évora. There is a tasting room here as well, where you can acquaint yourself with the region's different grape varieties.

Heading home from market.

> **Tip**
>
> Visit Arraiolos, 20km (12 miles) north of Évora, to see women at work on the town's famous hand-stitched carpets, based on Persian ones introduced in the 13th century. You can buy your own sample, large or small, to take home, and there's a fine pousada nearby if you want to stay over.

Farming is the pulse of Alentejo, and the lives of its people revolve around the seasons. Aside from Évora the towns are small and the population is scattered in hamlets linked to farms. Secondary schools are restricted to the larger towns; in the more remote areas the general practice among young people is to leave school early to work in the fields, or, as in so many rural regions, to head to the cities.

One of the main pastimes for rural folk is hunting birds, small prey or wild boar (today heavily controlled). During the season (roughly October to February) you will often see men out with their shotguns, pouches and a pack of dogs.

Singing and dancing are popular across the length and breadth of Portugal, and Alentejo does its share. Here, the folk songs are the domain of the men. These songs are slow, rather melancholic, but of a completely different style from the haunting fado that is heard elsewhere. A slow tempo is set by the stamping of the men's feet as they sing in chorus, swaying to the rhythm by the time they reach the end of the song. A performance is well worth listening to; ask at an Alentejo tourist office about where to hear these songs, known as *ceifeiros*.

Évora, the capital of the Alto Alentejo, is the largest and the most important of all Alentejana towns. It is a superb city, full of fascinating sights, all of which are in a good state of preservation. Fortunately, they are likely to remain so, as the entire city has been proclaimed a World Heritage Site by UNESCO.

It takes about two and a half hours to drive from Lisbon to Évora, and a tour could comfortably be managed as a day trip. But that would be a pity, as it would not leave time to see the lovely towns and villages along the way. To base yourself in Évora is easy; there are plenty of small guesthouses and hotels.

THE ROUTE FROM LISBON

To reach Évora from Lisbon, cross the Tagus via the Ponte 25 de Abril and head south and east, bypassing Setúbal on the A6 (IP7). You will not need a welcome billboard to tell you when you reach the Alentejo; suddenly you will find yourself at the edge of the rolling plains. Look for the jumbled twigs on top of high chimneys and buildings – homes to the storks that flourish in the province. As you drive further inland you will also notice the waning breeze and the gradual increase in temperature.

Short detours off the main road lead to small Alentejo towns. **Pegões**, rather dry and dusty, is typical. Further along, **Vendas Novas** is shady and neat with an air of affluence.

Montemor-o-Novo ❶ can be seen from quite a long way off, its ruined medieval castle crowning its low *monte* (hill). The castle ramparts are thought to date from Roman times. The town is divided into the upper old town and lower new town. As you might expect,

Lights decorate the Évora streetscape for Festa de São João.

the old town is more interesting. It was here that St John of God (São João de Deus) was born in 1495. He was baptised in the parish church, of which only the granite Manueline portal is still intact. In the square outside the church is a statue commemorating the saint, a Franciscan monk of great charity and humility. Although it does not have the population to support them, the town has five churches, three convents and two monasteries.

ÉVORA: ALENTEJO'S CITY

As you enter **Évora** ❷ on the main Lisbon road, there is a small tourist office just before the Roman walls, where you can pick up a street map marked with suggested walks that take in the most important sights. The best place to park is outside the walls, then walk to **Praça do Giraldo** Ⓐ at the centre of the city where the main tourist office is located (www.cm-evora.pt). This large square is arcaded on two sides and has a 16th-century church and fountain at the top. From here you can explore the inner city with ease.

The city's history can be traced back to the earliest civilisations on the Iberian peninsula. Évora derives its name from *Ebora Cerealis*, which dates from the Luso-Celtic colonisation. The Romans later fortified the city, renamed it *Liberalitas Julia*, and elevated it to the status of *municipium*, which gave it the right to mint its own currency. Its prosperity declined under the Visigoths, but was rekindled under Moorish rule (711–1165). Much of the architecture, with arched, twisting alleyways and tiled patios, reflects the Moorish presence. Évora was liberated from the Moors by a Christian knight, Geraldo Sem-Pavor (the Fearless), in 1165, in the name of Afonso Henriques I, Portugal's first king.

For the next 400 years Évora enjoyed great importance and wealth. It was the preferred residence of the kings of the Burgundy and Avis dynasties, and the courts attracted famous artists, dramatists, humanists and academics. Great churches, monasteries, houses and convents were also built. The splendour peaked in 1559,

Évora's Água de Prata Aqueduct was built in 1531–1537 by King João III and designed by the architect Francisco de Arruda, who previously built the Belém Tower.

Convent in Évora's historical centre.

The ruins of a Roman temple – the Temple of Diana – at Évora.

when Henrique, the last of the Avis kings (and also Archbishop of Évora), founded a Jesuit university. In 1580, following the annexation of Portugal by Spain, Évora's glory waned. The Castilians paid little attention to it, except as an agricultural and trading centre, and even after Portuguese independence was restored in 1640 it did not regain its former brilliance.

ROMAN REMAINS

The oldest sight in Évora is the **Templo Romano** B (Temple of Diana), at the top of the lanes opposite the tourist office in Praça do Giraldo. It dates from the 2nd or 3rd century AD and is presumed to have been built as a place of imperial worship. The Corinthian columns are granite, their bases and capitals hewn from local marble. The facade and mosaic floor have disappeared completely, but the six rear columns and the four at either side are still intact. The temple was converted into a fortress during the Middle Ages, then used as a slaughterhouse until 1870; an inelegant role but one that nevertheless saved the temple from being torn down.

From a good viewpoint in the shady garden just across from the rear of the temple, you can look down over the lower town and across the plains: the tiny village of Evoramonte is just visible to the northeast. To the right of the temple is the **Convento dos Lóios** C and the adjacent church of **São João Evangelista.** The convent buildings have been converted into an elegant *pousada* (www.pousadas.pt), but the church is open to the public. Founded in 1485, its style is Romano-Gothic, although all but the doorway in the facade was remodelled after the 1755 earthquake. The nave has an ornate vaulted ceiling and walls lined with beautiful tiles depicting the life of St Laurence Justinian, archbishop of Venice, dated 1771 and signed by António de Oliveira Bernardes. The sacristy and wax room behind the altar contain paintings and part of the Roman wall, and beneath the nave you can see an ossuary and Moorish cistern. The church is privately owned, as is the neighbouring palace of the dukes of

Cadaval, a wonderful building sometimes open for exhibitions (www.palacio-cadaval.com).

THE CATHEDRAL

The nearby **Sé** D (Cathedral; www.evoracathedral.com) is a rather austere building. Its granite, Romano-Gothic-style facade was built in the 12th century, while its main portal and the two grand conical towers – unusual in that they are asymmetric, with one tower adorned with glittering blue tiles – were added in the 16th century. Before going inside, take a close look at the main entrance, which is decorated with magnificent 14th-century sculptures of the Apostles. With three naves stretching for 70 metres (230ft), the cathedral has the most capacious interior in Portugal, and the vast broken barrel-vaulted ceiling is quite stunning.

Once you have seen the cathedral, it is worth paying the nominal sum to see the cloisters, choir stalls and **Museu de Arte Sacra**. The latter, in the treasury within one of the towers, contains a beautiful collection of ecclesiastical gold, silver and bejewelled plates, ornaments, chalices and crosses. The Renaissance-style choir stalls, tucked high in the gallery, are fashioned with a delightful series of wooden carvings with motifs both sacred and secular. From the choir stalls you get a good bird's-eye view of the cathedral. The marble cloisters are 14th-century Gothic, large and imposing, more likely to inspire awe than meditative contemplation.

Next door to the cathedral is the **Museu Nacional Frei Manuel do Cenáculo** E (www.cm-evora.pt/locais/museu-nacional-frei-manuel-do-cenaculo), which has works by Josefa de Óbidos (1630–84), one of a small number of women painters of the time.

MORE ÉVORA LANDMARKS

At the old **Jesuit University** F (Universidade; www.uevora.pt), some elegant and graceful cloisters are visible. You have to follow a short road down to the east of the city to reach it. The marble of the broad cloisters seems to have aged not at all since the 16th century,

> **Tip**
>
> If you're visiting Évora during the summer and want to cool off, go to one of the open-air municipal swimming pools (www.cm-evora.pt) on the edge of town. Although well patronised because they are inexpensive, they are spotlessly clean, with plenty of lawn on which to stretch out and dry off.

The macabre Capela dos Ossos.

Tranquil street, Évora.

Carvings on the Cathedral in Évora.

and there remains still the peaceful atmosphere prized by the serious academic.

The classroom entrances at the far end of the cloister gallery are decorated with *azulejos* representing each of the subjects taught. If you take a slow walk back up the hill and head for the Igreja São Francisco, you will pass by another church, the **Misericórdia** ⓖ, noted for its 18th-century tiled panels and Baroque relief work. Behind it is the Casa Soure, a 15th-century Manueline house that was formerly part of the Palace of the Infante Dom Luís.

As you walk along, have a good look at the houses. Nearly all of them have attractive narrow wrought-iron balconies at the base of tall rectangular windows. An odd tradition in Évora, as elsewhere in Portugal, is that visiting dignitaries are welcomed by a display of brightly coloured bedspreads hung from the balconies.

When you reach the Misericórdia church, take a brief detour to **Largo das Portas de Moura** ⓗ. The gates mark the fortified northern entrance to the city, which was the limit of construction and safety in medieval times. This picturesque square is dominated by a Renaissance fountain, which dates from 1556.

Heading west along the Rua Miguel Bombarda, keep an eye out for the church of **Nossa Senhora da Graça** ⓘ (Our Lady of Grace), just off the Rua Miguel Bombarda. Built in granite, it is a far cry from the austerity of the cathedral. A later church (16th-century), its influence is strongly Italian Renaissance. Note the four huge figures supporting globes which represent the children of grace.

The most interesting thing about the **Igreja de São Francisco** ⓙ (https://igrejadesaofrancisco.pt) is the **Capela dos Ossos**, but the chapterhouse is worth seeing too. It is lined with *azulejos* depicting scenes from the Passion and contains an *altar dos promessas* (altar of promises) on which are laid ex votos; wax effigies of various parts of the body given in thanks for cures. The church also has an interesting Manueline porch.

ⓞ A MOTHER'S CURSE

The church of São Francisco (see above), dating from the late 15th or early 16th century, has a remarkable chapel: the *Capela dos Ossos*. This bizarre and macabre room is entirely lined and decorated with the bones of some 5,000 people. It was created in the 16th century by Franciscan monks, when a large number of monastic cemeteries in the town were occupying valuable land. The skulls and bones have not merely been stored here in a random fashion; a lot of creative thought has gone into their placement. At the entrance you will see the inviting (albeit creepy) inscription: *"Nós ossos qui estamos, pelos vossos esperamos"* – "We bones lie here waiting for yours."

Most gruesome of all are the corpses of a man and a small child hanging at the far end of the chapel. These centuries-old bodies are said to be the victims of the curse of a dying wife and mother. Her father and son were supposed to have made her life a misery and their ill treatment eventually killed her. On her death bed she cursed them, swearing that their flesh would never fall from their bones. The corpses are far from fleshy, but there is plenty of leathery substance still attached.

Braids of human hair dating from the 19th century are hung at the entrance of the chapel – votive offerings placed there by young brides.

Évora's public gardens – the **Jardim Público** – near the church provide a very pleasant walk; if you're lucky you may catch the band playing on the park's old-fashioned wrought-iron bandstand. The delightful **Palácio de Dom Manuel** Ⓚ (1495–1521), or what remains of it, stands in the park. It has paired windows in horseshoe arches, typical of the style that gained its name from Dom Manuel. The palace itself is not open to the public.

If you're not intent on going inside Évora's monuments, a night stroll reveals its exterior architecture handsomely. Nearly all the monuments are floodlit until midnight, and the winding narrow streets are extremely inviting on a balmy evening.

During the last week of June, Évora is filled with visitors who come to enjoy the annual **Feira de São João**. This huge fair fills the grounds opposite the public gardens. There's a local handicraft market, an agricultural hall, a display of local light industry and the general hotchpotch of open-air stalls, as well as folk singing and dancing, and typical local food served by restaurants.

ÉVORAMONTE AND ESTREMOZ

Alentejo has a number of megalithic monuments scattered across its plains, and some of the most important are just outside Évora (the tourist office will give you a map). The best preserved and most significant stone circle, or cromlech, on the Iberian peninsula is 12km (7 miles) west of the city. Close to the hill of Herdade dos Almendres, the **Cromeleque do Almendres** ❸ has 95 standing stones.

Near to the agricultural department of the University of Évora in Valverde, just southwest of Évora, is the largest dolmen on the peninsula. The **Zambujeiro Dolmen** stands some 5-metres (17ft) high with a 3-metre (10ft) diameter and dates from about 3000 BC.

On the road from Évora to Estremoz lies **Évoramonte** ❹, a village at the foot of a 16th-century castle. It was here that the convention ending Portugal's civil war was signed on 26 May 1834. A

Estremoz is famous for its pottery, which is on sale in shops all over town, and also at the Saturday market in Rossio, the main square of the lower town.

Évoramonte Castle boasts fantastic views.

Old-fashioned street light in Estremoz.

Terracotta-tiled view of Estremoz, Alentejo region.

commemorative plaque is placed over the house where the historic event took place. **Évoramonte Castle** perches high on a hill and offers remarkable views, well worth the clamber up to the top. Built in Italian Renaissance style with added Manueline knots, it grew out of a Roman fort.

ESTREMOZ: STEEPED IN HISTORY

About 22km (14 miles) northeast, in the centre of the marble-quarrying region, lies the lovely town of **Estremoz** ⑤. Although much smaller than Évora, it has some fascinating monuments, and a pinky glow courtesy of the local marble from which many buildings are constructed. The old part of town, crowned by a castle now converted into a *pousada* (www.pousadas.pt), was founded by King Afonso III in 1258, but is most often associated with King Dinis, whose residence it was in the 14th century. His wife, the saintly Queen Isabel of Aragon, is honoured by a statue in the main square, and a chapel dedicated to her can be seen in one of the castle towers (ask at the *pousada*).

The chapel is at the top of a narrow staircase; small and highly decorated, it is where Isabel is said to have died, although some say that she died in the nearby King's Audience Chamber. The chapel walls are adorned with 18th-century *azulejos* and paintings depicting scenes from the queen's life. Behind the altar is a tiny plain room bearing a smaller altar, on which the Estremoz faithful have placed their *ex votos*, or offerings.

The most impressive part of the castle is the wonderful 13th-century keep, which is entered via the *pousada*. To get to the top you need to be fairly fit – or make a slow and steady ascent. The second floor has an octagonal room with trefoil windows. From the top platform there is a breathtaking view. The red rooftops contrast beautifully with the whitewashed houses and the green plains beyond, many of which are planted with rows of olive trees.

Across the square from the *pousada* is King Dinis' palace. It must once have been a beautiful place, but all that remains standing after a gunpowder explosion in the palace arsenal in 1698 is the Gothic colonnade and star-vaulted **Audience Chamber**. It is used nowadays for exhibitions of work by local artists.

Having survived the narrow roads and hairpin bends on the drive up to the castle, the descent seems easy. The upper town is connected to the lower by 14th-century ramparts and modern buildings; the wrought-iron balconies are decorated with coloured tiles.

Estremoz is known for the small clay figures known as *bonecas*, which can be seen in the little municipal museum in Largo Dom Dinis.

If you like Portuguese wines then you may be familiar with the name Borba, where a cooperative produces a good red wine. The ancient village of **Borba** (about 11km/6 miles from Estremoz), which is said to date back to the Gauls and Celts, does not have much to show except for a splendid fountain, the Fonte das Bicas, built in 1781 from local white marble.

VILA VIÇOSA: THE BRAGANÇAS' BASE

Down the road from Borba is **Vila Viçosa** ❻, the seat of the dukes of Bragança, an entire town built of shimmering white marble. Because the surrounding area is pocked by marble quarries, the usually expensive stone is in abundance. It is a place completely different in style from the Moorish-influenced towns perched on the hilltops. It is cool and shady, its large main square (Praça da República) is filled with orange trees, and elsewhere there are lemon trees and lots of flowers everywhere. Viçosa means lush, and its luxuriant boulevards are a pleasure to walk along.

Vila Viçosa is best known for the **Paço Ducal** (the Ducal Palace of the Braganças), a three-storey building with a long facade, which is open to the public for guided tours. Its furniture, paintings and tapestries are very fine, and well worth seeing. The palace also contains an excellent collection of 17th- to 19th-century coaches.

The palace overlooks a square in which stands a bronze statue of João

Alentejo is full of unexpected buildings such as this chapel transformed from what was once a mosque.

The overgrown castle ruins at Vila Viçosa.

IV, the first king of the Bragança dynasty. To the north of the square is a striking gateway, the Manueline **Porta do Nó** (Knot Gate), a stone archway that appears to be roped together, and is part of the 16th-century town walls.

FROM ELVAS TO MONSARAZ

Heading east for about 28km (17 miles) from Estremoz, along the main road to the Spanish border, you will come to the strongly fortified town of **Elvas** ❼. Founded by the Romans, it was long occupied by the Moors and finally liberated from them in 1230 – about 100 years later than Lisbon.

The town was of great strategic importance during the wars of independence in the mid-1600s.

The fortress of **Santa Luzia,** south of town, was built by a German, Count Lippe, for the purpose of repelling the Spanish. The older castle above the town was originally a Roman fortress, rebuilt by the Moors and enlarged in the 15th century.

If you walk around the ramparts that once encircled the town you can't fail to be impressed by the effective engineering. The town itself is very attractive, from the triangular "square" of Santa Clara, with its 16th-century marble pillory, to the main Praça da República, with geometric mosaic paving.

The **Aqueduto da Amoreira** ❽, just outside the town, was designed by a great 15th-century architect, Francisco de Arruda. Its 8km (5-mile) length and 843 arches took nearly 200 years to complete. The cost was borne by the people of Elvas under a special tax named the *Real de Agua*.

Handwoven rugs used to be manufactured throughout Alentejo, but nowadays the small town of **Reguengos** ❾ is the only place where they are still made, in a factory that has been using the same looms for the past 150 years (Fábrica Alentejana de Lanifícios; www.fabricaal.com/en).

To reach it, return to Borba then travel south for about 60km (38 miles). Reguengos is a nucleus of megalithic stones and dolmens, found at several sites near the town, and is known for its wine.

The medieval arches of Monsaraz.

ⓞ ALQUEVA DAM

The Alqueva dam on the Guadiana River, close to the Spanish border, is one of Europe's largest artificial lakes, with a surface area of 250 sq km (96 sq miles). The idea was first mooted in 1957 under Salazar, but the controversial project stalled and was only completed in 2006. A Roman fort was encased in concrete before being submerged, and the village of Aldeia da Luz, which lay in the flood zone, was moved stone by stone and rebuilt. The commendable purpose of the dam project was to irrigate farmland, produce hydroelectric power, and provide a huge reservoir, but dams are rarely constructed without some destruction, and here the tragedy was that waters submerged 160 rocks covered with Stone Age drawings and flooded the habitats of rare flora and fauna.

About 16km (10 miles) northeast of Reguengos is the delightful walled town of **Monsaraz** ⑩, so small it can easily be explored on foot – leave your car at the gate. It was fortified by the Knights Templar when the Moors were the enemy. In time, Reguengos became more influential and Monsaraz less so, which helped it become the relaxed and peaceful village it is today. Its main street, Rua Direita, is all 16th- and 17th-century architecture, yet the town maintains a medieval atmosphere. In one Gothic house is a famous 15th-century fresco, an allegory on justice: *O Bom e o Mau Juiz* (The Good and the Bad Judge). From the ramparts there are great views over to the Alqueva dam.

PORTALEGRE

The lush countryside that surrounds **Portalegre** ⑪ is rather different from that in the low-lying lands. This area is in the foothills of the **Serra de São Mamede**, and the cooler and slightly more humid climate makes the landscape much greener. To get there, return to Estremoz and take the N18/E802 north – half of the route is now the IP2.

Quite a large town by Alentejo standards, Portalegre is unusual in that it is not built on top of a hill, but on the site of an ancient ruined settlement called Amaya. In the mid-13th century, King Afonso III issued instructions that a new city was to be built. He called it Portus Alacer: Portus for the customs gate which was to process Spanish trade, and Alacer (*álacre* means merry) because of its pleasing setting. King Dinis ensured that the town was fortified in 1290 (although only a few of the ruined fortifications can be seen today) and João III gave it the status of a city in 1550.

The lofty 16th-century interior of the **Sé** (Cathedral) is late-Renaissance in style. The side altars have fine wooden *retábulos* and 16th- and 17th-century paintings in the Italian style. The sacristy contains lovely blue-and-white *azulejo* panels from the 18th century, depicting the life of the Virgin Mary and the Flight to Egypt. The cathedral's

Marvão Castle offers spectacular views towards the Serra de São Mamede.

Elvas Castle, Alcáçova.

Carrying greenery in the Jewish Quarter of Castelo de Vide.

The white houses of Marvão.

facade is also 18th century, and is dominated by marble columns, granite pilasters and wrought-iron balconies.

Portalegre's affluence began in the 16th century, when its tapestries were in great demand. Continued prosperity followed in the next century with the establishment of silk mills. One tapestry workshop remains, the **Fábrica Real de Tapeçarias** (www.mtportalegre.pt), in the former Jesuit Monastery in Rua Fernandes, where looms are still worked by hand. Examples of the town's handiwork can be seen in the **Museu da Tapeçaria de Portalegre Guy Fino** (), housed in an 18th-century mansion in Rua da Figueira.

Portalegre was home to one of Portugal's major writers: poet, dramatist and novelist José Régio (1901–69). His house has been opened as a museum. Of particular interest is his collection of regional folk art and religious works. Also of note is the 17th-century Yellow Palace, where the 19th-century radical reformer Mouzinho da Silveira lived. The ornate ironwork here is quite remarkable.

SPECTACULAR MARVÃO

Marvão ⓬ is one of the most spectacular sights of Alentejo. About 25km (15 miles) north of Portalegre, it is a medieval fortified town perched on one of the São Mamede peaks. Its altitude (862 metres/2,830ft) affords it an uninterrupted view across the Spanish frontier. The precipitous drop on one side made it inaccessible to invaders and an ideal defensive barrier.

At this height the land is barren and craggy. The seemingly impenetrable castle was built in the 13th century from the local grey granite. Clinging to the foot of the castle is the tiny village, just a few twisting alleyways flanked by red-roofed whitewashed houses. Close to the church of Espírito Santo, on the street of the same name, is a Baroque granite fountain. On the same street is the sober-looking Governor's House, its only decoration two magnificent 17th-century wrought-iron balconies.

On the road to Castelo de Vide are the ruins of the Roman settlement of **Medóbriga**. Many artefacts discovered here are now in Lisbon.

CASTELO DE VIDE: FORT AND SPA

Completing the triangle of noteworthy upper Alentejo towns is **Castelo de Vide** ⓯, a delightful town built in the shadow of an elongated medieval castle situated on the summit of a foothill on the northern *serra*. The town was originally a Roman settlement. Alongside it ran the major Roman road that traversed the Iberian peninsula. The settlement was sacked by the Vandals at the beginning of the 4th century, occupied by the Moors during their domination of the southern part of the peninsula, and eventually fortified by the victorious Portuguese in 1180.

Castelo de Vide is a spa town. You can drink its curative waters from plastic bottles, which are sold in the supermarkets, or sip from one of the numerous fountains located in and around the town. Perhaps its prettiest outlet is the quadrangled, covered fountain (Fonte da Vila), set in the small square below the Jewish Quarter. The Baroque fountain has a pyramid roof supported by six marble columns. The central urn is carved with figures of boys, and the water spills from four spouts.

As in nearly all fortified Alentejo towns, Castelo de Vide has two very distinct faces. The first is the older one, situated next to the castle, and the most interesting and picturesque part of it is the medieval **Judiaria** (Jewish Quarter). This host of back alleys, cobbled streets and whitewashed houses is liberally splashed with green, as potted plants sprout their tendrils from every available niche, windowsill and step.

Notice the doors: this section of Castelo de Vide has the best-preserved stone Gothic doorways in Portugal. It also has the oldest synagogue, dating from the 13th century (daily 9.30am–1pm, 2.30–6pm). The majority of the inhabitants of the neighbourhood appear to be elderly people who sit in the doorways of their homes calmly watching the world go by.

Further down the hill is the newer part of town: essentially 17th- and 18th-century buildings with wider,

> **Fact**
>
> Flor da Rosa used to be a thriving pottery centre. The trade has dwindled in recent years, but pots are still made in the traditional way, and you may be able to see the craftsmen at work. Once fired, the finished pieces are known for their strong heat resistance. Unfired pots and pitchers are used to keep water cool.

The Fonte Da Vila, a 16th-century fountain in the historic town of Castelo de Vide.

Alentejo produces some fine wines. Its reds are full-bodied and mature well in the bottle.

Landscape of Castelo de Vide village, north of Alentejo region.

less steep streets, more space, more order and more elegance. On the main square, **Praça Dom Pedro V**, stand the grandiose 18th-century parish church and the old town hall, **Paços de Concelho**, remarkable for its huge 18th-century wrought-iron gate securing the main entrance.

Near the town you will find still more megalithic stones, including the 7-metre (22ft) Menhir da Meada. These *pedras talhas* seem to be everywhere, standing in fields, in open scrubland or in villages, inscrutable and ageless.

PORTALEGRE'S NEIGHBOURS

Nisa ⓮ is a small, rather rambling town northwest of Castelo de Vide. It has the mandatory medieval castle, walls and an unusual squat, round-towered chapel. Homemade cheese is Nisa's speciality.

Some 24km (15 miles) south of Nisa on the road back to Estremoz is **Flor da Rosa**, where you may be able to buy local pots. But the most interesting place to see is the Convento de Flor da Rosa, dating from 1356 and founded by the Order of Knights Hospitallers of St John. An eclectic building, with a solid Gothic cloister, it was in use as a monastery right up until the end of the 19th century, and is now a *pousada*, Mosteiro do Crato (www.pousadas.pt).

Two royal marriages took place in **Crato** ⓯, a couple of kilometres down the road. The first was that of Manuel I, who married Leonor of Spain in 1518 (his third marriage); the second was seven years later when King João III married Catarina of Spain. The main square is dominated by a splendid 15th-century stone veranda, the **Varanda do Grão-Prior**, which is all that survives of the priors' residence.

Some 13km (8 miles) further south, in countryside filled with olive groves, is **Alter do Chão** ⓰, a medieval town with equine traditions. It is from here that the Alter Real horse, closely related to the Lusitano breed, takes its name. The state-owned **Alter Stud Farm** (Coudelariade de Alter; www.alterreal.pt; tours Tue–Sun 11am, 3pm) was founded in 1748 by José I (as he became two years later). Based on

Andalusian stock, the animals thrived until the Napoleonic Wars when the best of them were stolen and the royal stables abolished. Happily, the breed, which excels in dressage, has been revived to a highly respected standard.

UNSPOILED BEACHES

If you like unspoiled cliffs and beaches, quiet roads and villages, then you will delight in the Alentejo coast, although more and more tourists are discovering it. It borders the open Atlantic and the ocean is therefore much rougher than on the south coast. There are plenty of sheltered bays for swimming, although the water is chilly.

Alentejo's coast is not renowned for its nightlife. Bars, discos and fancy restaurants hardly exist; nor do large hotels, except at Vila Nova de Milfontes. There are campsites, however, and all the villages have at least one *pensão*. You'd better bring along your phrase book, or download Portuguese on your Google Translate app; where tourists are relatively few, so are local people who speak English.

Most people approach the coast from Lisbon, from where access is easy thanks to the extended motorway network. Heading south, the IP8 branches southwest just before Grândola to **Santiago do Cacém** ⓱, crowned by a castle built by the Knights Templar, which gives good views over the town and coast.

Anyone interested in all things Roman should consider making a trip to nearby **Miróbriga** ⓲ (Tue–Sun 9am–12.30pm, 2–5.30pm). This Iron Age and Roman site is quite extensive and has been well excavated. There is also an interesting little Museu Municipal nearby, located in a former prison.

Now it's just a short hop to Alentejo's largest coastal town, **Sines** ⓳, which is famous for being the birthplace of Vasco da Gama in 1460. It's not what you would call a beauty spot. The old part and the harbour are still picturesque, but the nearby oil refinery and power station are hard to ignore.

Leaving Sines to the south, you can clear your lungs at the village of **Porto Covo** ⓴. Though development has begun at the back of the village, it remains an intimate place, with cobbled streets swept scrupulously clean. The main square, grandly named Largo Marquês de Pombal, is very small, bordered by houses and the tiny parish church. A few small trees and plentiful benches surround the square. Down by the sea you can find shops, cafés and restaurants. Nearby secluded coves are easy to walk to.

Just off the coast of Porto Corvo is the fortified **Ilha do Pessegeiro** (Peach Tree Island), which in bygone days provided protection from raids by Dutch and Algerian pirates.

Returning to the main road, some 15km (9 miles) south of Porto Corvo is the small town of Cercal, beyond which you reach **Vila Nova de Milfontes** ㉑, the loveliest and most popular of Alentejo's resorts. The only time it gets really busy is in high summer

The hotel Flor da Rosa, Crato.

Pousada de São Francisco, Beja.

Vila Nova de Milfontes.

when many Alentejanos and Lisboetas come for their annual holiday at the large campsite. There are a few bars, some seafood restaurants and a range of accommodation. One of the attractions here is the lovely **Castelo de Milfontes**, converted from an ivy-clad fortress – drawbridge and all – which overlooks the estuary of the River Mira.

The river estuary provides long golden beaches and a calm sea. Park out at the headland overlooking the ocean, and you can turn back to see the town to your left, the winding river and the hills beyond – all very idyllic. If you are planning a day or two on this coast, then this is the place to stay. In early August it hosts the four-day Festival do Sudoeste (https://festivalsudoeste.com), which could be described as Portugal's Glastonbury and attracts top names.

Almograve and Zambujeira do Mar offer more stunning, often deserted beaches and some fine clifftop viewpoints across the basalt cliffs to the sea. Of the two very small villages, Almograve is by far the nicer. Between these two beaches is another, Cabo do Girão, but it is naval property and access is prohibited.

SOUTHERN ALENTEJO

You may well choose to start an exploration of the Lower Alentejo from a base in Lisbon, but you could also start here by going inland to the pretty town of **Odemira** ㉒, set on the banks of the Rio Mira, after which it is named. It is full of flowers and trees, so green that you are apt to forget that it is in Alentejo at all. Nearby is **Barragem de Santa Clara** ㉓, a huge dam on the Mira, where water sports are popular.

Ourique ㉔ is an agricultural town north of the dam. In its surrounding fields (Campo do Ourique), fruit, olives and cork trees grow. These fields, however, have seen far more than mere farming in their time. In the nearby hamlet of **Atalaia**, archaeologists have excavated an extraordinary Bronze Age burial mound. And it was on the site of a battle called Ourique in 1139 (which may or may not have been here) that a fateful encounter was fought between the Portuguese and the Moors. Afonso

Henriques had just become the first king of Portugal, and the victory on this battlefield strengthened his determination to expel the Moors from all Portuguese soil, giving a tremendous boost to the flagging morale of his battle-weary forces.

BEJA

The capital of Lower Alentejo, **Beja** 25, is the hottest town in Portugal during the height of summer. It is a three-hour drive from Lisbon and an hour or so from Évora, or, if you are following the route from Ourique, it is about 60km (38 miles) on the IP2 (the old N123) or the N391.

A town existed on the present-day site as early as 48 BC, and when Julius Caesar made peace with the Lusitanians the settlement was named after this event, Pax Julia. During the 400-year Moorish occupation the name was adulterated to Baju, then Baja, until it finally became Beja.

It is now a fairly prosperous town, its income derived from the production of olive oil and wheat. A long-term German Air Force base here, dating from the 1960s, was turned over to the Portuguese in 1990. Beja is not a beautiful town, but it does have some interesting sights.

One of them is the 15th-century **Convento da Conceição**, a fine example of the transition between Gothic and Manueline architecture. The Baroque chapel is lined with carved, gilded woodwork. The chapterhouse, which leads to the cloisters, is tiled with superb Hispano-Arabic *azulejos* dating back to the 1500s. Their quality is rivalled only by those to be found in the Royal Palace at Sintra.

Legend has it that in the 17th century a nun at the convent fell in love with a French soldier, and when he returned to France she wrote him a number of love letters that were later published in Paris, becoming something of a literary sensation.

Dissolved in 1834, the convent building also houses a notable **Museu Regional** (www.museuregionaldebeja.pt).

The small and modest Santo Amaro is the oldest church in Beja. It is

Fact

José Maria Eça de Queiroz, a diplomat and a graduate of Coimbra University, wrote passionate, biting novels that attacked the upper-class mores of his day. He spent 15 years in England, which he detested, but while there wrote some of his famous works, including *Os Maias* (The Maias).

Odemira, set on the banks of the Mira.

Quiet street in Serpa.

Pork stew with clams.

thought to date back to the 7th century and is a rare example of Visigothic architecture. The Misericórdia church in the Praça da República is also worth a look. Beja's 13th-century **castle** still stands, and its castellated walls run around the town perimeter. The tall keep contains a military museum, and a narrow balcony on each side from which you can enjoy a remarkable view across the plains.

Driving in to **Serpa** ㉖ (about 30km/ 18 miles east of Beja) is – as with so many small Alentejo towns – like driving into a time warp. The castle and fortified walls were built at the command of King Dinis. A significant difference here from other 13th-century walls is that these have an aqueduct built into them. The church of Santo António, originally built in 1463, is worth seeing for its cloister and azulejo tiles depicting the life of St Francis.

A well-preserved gateway is the **Portas de Beja**; the gates, along with the rest of the walls, were almost sold by the town council in the latter half of the 19th century. Cooler heads prevailed and the walls were saved, although a great part of them had been destroyed in 1707 when the Duke of Ossuna and his army occupied the town during the War of the Spanish Succession.

There are several churches worth seeing (notably the 13th-century Santa Maria), as well as the delightfully cool and elegant palace belonging to the counts of Ficalho, the **Paço dos Condes de Ficalho**. It was built in the 16th century and has a majestic staircase and lovely tiles. The present lady of the house, Condessa de Ficalho Dona Maria das Dores, is the granddaughter of José Maria Eça de Queiroz (1845–1900), one of Portugal's great 19th-century novelists.

The Rio Guadiana is considered the most peaceful of Portugal's three big rivers (the others being the Tagus and Douro), but an exception is at **Pulo do Lobo** (Wolf's Leap) between Serpa and Mértola. This is a stretch of high and wild rapids, which can be reached by road and is worth a visit if you are in the area – you will probably find you are the only tourist there.

⊘ FOOD AND DRINK

Alentejo's culinary specialities should not be missed. Try *sopa Alentejana* – a filling soup of bread, with lots of fresh coriander (a herb used a great deal in Alentejo cooking), garlic and poached eggs. One of the classic meat dishes is *carne de porco à Alentejana* – chunks of pork seasoned in wine, coriander and onions and served with clams. Two much heavier but delicious stewed dishes are *ensopada de cabrito* – goat boiled with potatoes and bread until the meat is just about falling off the bone – and *favada de caça*, a game stew of hare, rabbit, and partridge or pigeon, with broad beans. The best Alentejo cheese comes from Serpa. Made from sheep and goat's milk, it has a creamy texture and a strong, slightly piquant flavour. Évora has its own goat's cheese, which is hard, salty and slightly acid. It is preserved in jars filled with olive oil.

Alentejo is a *região demarcada* – a demarcated wine region. Most towns have their own cooperative winery from which you can buy stocks at rock-bottom prices, and most restaurants have a low-priced cooperative house wine. In Lisbon, Alentejo reds are often drunk with *bacalhau*, instead of the more usual white. Try the reds from the Reguengos cooperative or those from Borba (see page 209), and white wines from the Vidigueira cooperative (https://adegavidigueira.pt/en).

MÉRTOLA

Mértola ㉗, an ancient fortified town set in the confluence between the Guadiana and the Oeiras rivers, is one of Alentejo's hidden gems. To get here from Serpa you can either take a secondary road to the south, or return to Beja, then take the main road south and turn off to the left. Whichever way you approach, the sight of the town's strongly built walls crowned by a sturdy **castle** (www.museudemertola.pt) is as impressive as it is unexpected.

Mértola has a long history, reaching back to Roman times. For five centuries under the Romans it was an important port on the then navigable Guadiana for exporting mineral ores from the nearby Minas de São Domingos, near the Spanish border. Its importance continued under the Visigoths, whose handiwork can be seen in the castle tower, and later the Moors. Twice in the 11th and 12th centuries it was capital of a kingdom which included Beja. With the growth of agricultural produce in the region Mértola was active in exporting grain to North Africa. When the river eventually silted up, the town slipped quietly into oblivion.

Leave plenty of time to explore the astonishing remains of the Roman port, the parish church, the castle and several museums (a single ticket covers all the sites), as well as the **Igreja Matriz**. Outwardly a Christian church, this pristine white building was originally a mosque, one of the few in Portugal to have survived virtually intact.

The exhibition of Islamic pottery in the **Museu de Mértola Cláudio Torres** (http://museus.cm-mertola.pt) is not enormous, but it is the finest in Portugal; and the **Casa Romana** (www.museudemertola.pt/nucleos-exposicao/casa-romana) is very sophisticated. The town hall here burned down some years ago, and during the clearing-up operation the remains of a Roman villa were discovered. After finishing an excavation, the town hall was rebuilt and the Roman remains turned into a basement museum. The display allows visitors to walk through the foundations of the villa, which is brought to life with a small collection of artefacts.

Sunset on the Senhora da Guadalupe chapel, Serpa.

A church in Beja.

PRESERVING ARTS AND CRAFTS

Local customs form a thread of continuity in rural Portugal, and none is stronger than the craft skills that are found throughout the country.

Portugal is a land rich in tradition, and in rural areas the skills and artistry of local craftspeople have been passed from generation to generation. Most skills are specific to one locality: pottery is perhaps the only national craft – although with important variations in design and decoration. Craft work is a significant cottage industry, but there is a danger of skills dying out, especially in regions with few visitors. To prevent this, EU funding has been channelled towards promoting the work of artisans to save skills, create employment and retain life in dying villages.

There are plenty of craft shops in the large towns, but the real joy is to stop in tiny villages and discover the spinning and weaving cooperatives formed by women, as in Mértola. See bobbin lacework, watch ceramics in the making, buy jute dolls, and marvel at the basket creations made from leaves of the dwarf fan palm.

The products of some regions have gained national importance. Arraiolos in Alentejo has a centuries-old tradition of rug- and carpet-making which has grown into a major industry; and the hand-embroidered bedspreads of Castelo Branco, which have been made since the 17th century, are also popular throughout Portugal and now in demand by tourists.

You will see distinctive hand-painted furniture throughout the Alentejo. Estremoz sells little figurines in its weekend market; Caldas da Rainha is known for its ceramics; while Peniche, also in Estremadura, is famous for lace.

Painted clogs in Viana do Castelo.

Clay-thrown, handpainted olive dishes, often embellished with the name of the locality, come with a separate nook for discarded olive pits.

Brightly coloured traditional costume.

The ubiquitous Galo de Barcelos.

The galo de Barcelos

There is no escape from the Barcelos cockerel. Its fame arises from a legend (as colourful as the little figure itself), which has been embroidered and enlarged with every telling. The central theme relates the story of a murder committed in the northern town of Barcelos many centuries ago. A certain Galician pilgrim came under suspicion as the perpetrator, and no matter how strongly he protested, his pleas of innocence fell on deaf ears, and he was sentenced to death.

Before his execution he was granted a last wish: to make a final plea before the judge, who, in the midst of entertaining guests to dinner, agreed to see him. In desperation, the condemned man pointed to the roast fowl on the dinner table and cried, "As surely as I stand innocent, so will that cock crow." Miraculously, the rooster obliged. The judge forfeited his dinner, and the pilgrim's life was saved.

Ceramic figures of the Barcelos cock are on sale everywhere. The symbol now also adorns everything from T-shirts to tea towels, and finds a place in most visitors' luggage.

Vila Real pottery is distinctively black and is made by covering pots with soil and ash to exclude oxygen and burning brushwood over them.

Handmade dolls in Marafona.

A skilful resident of Obidos makes lace to sell at a local market.

Alcobaça Abbey.

ESTREMADURA AND RIBATEJO

Although ribboned with silver sand, the coast is not the major attraction in this region. It is inland that you will find some of the country's finest and best-loved monuments.

The region north of Lisbon reaching up towards Coimbra has not managed to establish itself as a major travel destination, in spite of its many attractions. Bordered by an endless ribbon of silvery sand, the Costa de Prata (Silver Coast), Nazaré apart, still only has small resorts. Most of the region's attractions, the monasteries at Alcobaça, Batalha and Tomar, the religious sanctuary at Fátima and the spectacular deep caves in the limestone *serras*, are inland.

With its points of interest fairly widespread, it is an area tailor-made for a rambling tour. Allow around three days to take in most of the major sites and longer if you want to savour everything the region offers. The circular route described here goes anticlockwise from Lisbon up to Batalha and back.

NORTH FROM LISBON

The quickest ways to escape Lisbon are either by the A1 or the A8 heading north. Alternatively, for a slower but more interesting journey, cross the Rio Tejo on the Ponte Vasco da Gama and take the road on the eastern side of the river. The A1 will take you to the modest town of **Vila Franca de Xira**, the centre of Portuguese bullfighting. Every July and October the town comes alive with the bullfighting festival, known as the Festas do Colete Encarnado (Festival of the Red Waistcoat) after the costumes of the *campinos*, traditional herdsmen.

Santarém ❶ is the central town of Ribatejo. It was named after Santa Iria, a young nun who was accused of being unchaste and martyred in 653 near Tomar. Her body, thrown into the river, washed ashore here. A riverbank shrine has a statue whose feet act as a sacred gauge to the water level – if they are touched by floods, even Lisbon is in danger.

Among several fine churches, the Romanesque-Gothic church of **São**

Main attractions
Castelo de Almourol
Convento do Cristo, Tomar
Fátima
Mosteiro de Santa Maria da Vitória, Batalha
Cistercian Abbey, Alcobaça
Óbidos
Ilha Berlenga

Map on page 224

Festa dos Tabuleiros in Tomar.

Preparations behind the bullring – traditional or outdated?

João de Alporão contains a beautifully carved tomb of Duarte, a son of Pedro I who died in battle in 1458. It contains just one of Duarte's teeth, the sole relic that was delivered to his wife.

In northeastern Santarém is the church of **Santa Clara** (free), originally part of a 13th-century convent, containing the elaborate tomb of Dona Leonor, daughter of Afonso III. The church of **Nossa Senhora da Graça** (free), a Gothic structure with a beautiful nave, holds several tombs, among them that of Pedro Alvares Cabral, coloniser of Brazil.

In **Alpiarça,** across the river, look for the 19th-century architectural gem of the **Casa dos Patudos** (http://casadospatudos.blogspot.pt), today a wonderfully eclectic museum containing paintings by Portuguese artists including acclaimed naturalist painter Silva Porto, ceramics and more.

A diversion to **Abrantes** ❷ is worthwhile, if only to see the nearby Castelo de Almourol, romantically located on an island in the middle of the Tejo. The road on the east side of the river offers the most interesting route. Abrantes itself has little to offer visitors except perhaps for the castle of **Santa Maria do Castelo** and the local church, Igreja de Santa Maria do Castelo. Here, in 2014, renovation works uncovered frescoes from the end of 15th century and the beginning of the 16th century underneath the *azulejos*.

Turn back along the north bank just before Tancos and look for the sign to **Castelo de Almourol** ❸. It crowns a rocky island in the river, but there are ferries (Mar–Oct 10am–1pm, 2.30–7pm, Nov–Feb until 5pm) that will take visitors across for €4. A trip around the island will cost more.

The Romans recognised the importance of the site on this key communication route and built a castle, although there may have been an earlier settlement. Later, the castle was occupied by the Visigoths, the Moors and finally the Christians. Afonso Henriques entrusted it to the Knights Templar in 1147 for help in fighting the Moors. The Grand Master Gualdim Pais rebuilt the castle leaving an inscription over the door, and it remained garrisoned for a time. When the Moors were expelled from Portugal the strategic importance of the castle declined and it eventually fell into disuse. It takes only a few minutes to wander around the walls of the fortress.

TOMAR

From the castle it is a fairly short run north to **Tomar** ❹, a delightful town with a host of good points: a setting on the banks of the Rio Nabão; the splendid Convento do Cristo, which is a UNESCO World Heritage Site; and medieval streets paved with stone and fancifully patterned with exuberant flowers. With its pleasing ambience and rich culture, its ancient legends and appealing daily life, Tomar is a town in which to linger and explore for a couple of days.

Tomar was the headquarters of the Knights Templar in Portugal, an order that was formed in 1119, during the crusades. The order spread quickly throughout Europe, gaining extraordinary wealth. It also made powerful enemies, and in the early 1300s, amid accusations of heresy and foul practices, and finally the suppression of the order altogether, the Knights took refuge in Tomar, where Grand Master Gualdim Pais had built a castle back in 1162. They re-emerged in 1320, resurrected as the Order of Christ, whose proud symbol, the Cross of Christ, became the banner of the Age of Discoveries.

In Tomar they left behind the marvellous ruins of the old castle and, within its walls, the still-intact church and cloisters. The **castle** (www.conventocristo.pt) is set on a hill above the city, a 10-minute walk away, and commands a view over the rooftops of the old town.

MONASTERY AND SYNAGOGUE

The **Convento do Cristo** (www.conventocristo.pt) is a maze of staircases and passages, nooks and crannies. The seven cloisters (just four are open to the public) have been added at irregular angles and over several centuries, and even the beautiful main entrance is oddly tucked into a corner. The original Templar church is on the right, just inside the entrance. Begun in 1162, the sixteen-sided temple was modelled on Jerusalem's Church of the Holy Sepulchre. Here, the knights would hear services while seated on their horses, and pray for victory in battle.

The chapterhouse and Coro Alto, added much later, provide a sharp contrast to the original temple, as does the adjoining 16th-century cloister with 17th-century tiles where some of the tombs of the knights are found. From here there is access to the upper level and then into the other cloisters. From the terrace of the small Claustro de Santa Bárbara, there is a view of the amazing, ornate Manueline window, structured around two deep relief carvings of ships' masts, knots, cork, coral and seaweed. The whole is topped by a shield, crown and cross, symbol of the union of church and king.

The Convento do Cristo was built by the Knights Templar in around 1160.

The Convento do Cristo was built as part of a defensive system against the Moorish invaders.

> **⊙ Fact**
>
> The Virgin revealed three "secrets" to Lucia. The first two were messages of peace, but it was not till June 2000 that the Vatican revealed the third, which prophesied the assassination attempt on Pope John Paul II on 13 May 1981; at the time the Pope declared that Our Lady of Fátima had helped him survive.

From the opposite side of the building you can see the castle yard where the knights trained their horses and spent their off-duty hours.

Also on this side lies an unfinished chapel: bad luck during construction persuaded the superstitious knights to abandon it.

Tomar's synagogue in Rua Joaquim Jacinto is now a museum (www.center-ofportugal.com/es/poi/sinagoga-de-tomar; free). Although a high percentage of Portuguese people have Jewish ancestry, and Tomar was once the home of a thriving Jewish community, there are very few Jewish people left.

When King Manuel I married Isabella of Castile in 1497, a condition of the marriage contract was the expulsion of the Jews. They were allowed to remain if they converted, although laws governing fair treatment were not closely monitored.

Later, the Inquisition legitimised brutal discrimination against them. The synagogue/museum is simple and moving, decorated with gifts from all over the world.

Fátima statuary.

OTHER TOMAR SIGHTS

The church of **São João Baptista** has a dark wood ceiling and a sombre atmosphere. Sixteenth-century wood-panel paintings on the walls depict scenes such as the Last Supper and Salome with the head of John the Baptist. On the left is a delicately carved pulpit.

Standing alone on the edge of town, **Santa Maria dos Olivais** is a simple church dating from the 12th century and containing many Templar tombs. The town's tourist office is on Avenida Dr Cândido Madureira, near the road to the castle.

En route from Tomar to Fátima, it is well worth a stop at **Ourém** ❺, or more specifically at Ourém Velha, the fortified site on top of an easily defended hill. The history of the castle is known only from the time it was recovered from the Moors in 1148 by King Afonso Henriques. Little was attempted in the way of restoration until King Dinis (1279–1325) arrived on the scene. He rebuilt this as he did many other castles in Portugal.

THE LOURDES OF PORTUGAL

Fátima ❻, some 12km (8 miles) from Ourém, is not a place for non-believers, and there is even a notice to advise you of this. It is a place for pilgrims – of which there are up to 2 million a year. On 13 May 1917, three shepherd children had a vision of the Virgin here. Thereafter, she appeared before the children and, on one occasion, as a shining light to the townspeople who gathered with them on the 13th of the subsequent months (see page 80). The two younger children died shortly after the apparitions, but the older, Lucia de Jesus Santos, lived well into her eighties in a convent near Coimbra (she died in 2005). The processions that take place on the anniversaries of the visions – 13 May and 13 October – draw thousands of people from around the world.

ESTREMADURA AND RIBATEJO

Surrounded by acres of car parks is the vast white **basilica** (www.fatima.pt), consecrated in 1953. In front of it is a huge esplanade large enough to hold 100,000 worshippers, and the **Chapel of Apparitions** (daily 24hr), which Our Lady of the Rosaries ordered to be built in her sixth and final appearance on this spot. Inside the basilica lie the tombs of the two visionary children who died, Jacinta and Francisco Marto. Close by is a church, congress and study centre dedicated to Pope John Paul II (same hours as basilica).

CASTLES AND CAVES

West of Fátima, along scenic well-paved roads, lies the pleasant town of **Porto de Mós** ❼, worth a brief stop even if only to look at the **castle** (https://visite.portodemos.pt), capped with green cones and standing on a hill. The castle has a fairly long pedigree and still contains some original Roman stonework. As with Ourém castle, King Afonso Henriques recovered it from the Moors in 1148. After several restorations, it remained in military use at least until the Battle of Aljubarrota in 1385, when João I is said to have rested his troops here before the fight. Afterwards the king rewarded his captain, Nuno Alvares Pereira, with the gift of this fortress for leading his troops so bravely. It was his grandson, Afonso, a cultured and much-travelled man, who endeavoured to convert the castle into a palace and disguise the strong military lines.

As a change from monuments, a diversion into the **Parque Natural das Serras de Aire e Candeeiros** ❽ offers fine limestone scenery and a chance to visit Portugal's largest caves. Take the N243 towards Torres Novas to find **Grutas Mira de Aire** (www.grutasmiradaire.com), **Grutas de Santo António** (www.grutassantoantonio.com) and **Grutas de Alvados** (www.grutasalvados.com). The latter two lie on a spur off the main road. All three are different enough to be worth visiting. If you only have time for one, then perhaps Grutas Mira de Aire is the best choice. The caves are reached down more than 600 steps through well-illuminated caverns with imaginative and descriptive names, to the underground river. Fortunately, there is a lift for the return to the surface.

BATALHA: AN ESSENTIAL STOP

Batalha ❾ is one of Portugal's most beautiful monuments, and another UNESCO World Heritage Site. The origins of **Mosteiro de Santa Maria da Vitória** (www.mosteirobatalha.pt), to use its full name, lie in Portugal's struggle for independence from Castile. One of the decisive battles for independence was fought at Aljubarrota, not far from Batalha. The Castilian king, Juan, who based his claim to the throne on his marriage to a Portuguese princess, invaded Portugal in 1385. The 20-year-old Dom João, Master of the Order of Avis and illegitimate son of Pedro I, promised to raise a monastery to the Virgin Mary if the Portuguese won.

The Basilica of Our Lady of the Rosary was built to commemorate the events of 1917, when three peasant children claimed to have seen the "Virgin of the Rosary".

Fátima, a place for pilgrims.

The exterior of Batalha Abbey.

The main entrance to Alcobaça Abbey.

With his young general, Nuno Alvares Pereira, João defeated the Castilians, and became João I. The monastery was constructed between 1388 and 1533.

On the other side of the building you may enter the **Claustro Real** (Royal Cloister). Arches filled with Manueline ornamentation surround a pretty courtyard and are patterned with intricate designs. The chapterhouse is the first room off the cloister. It has an unusual and beautiful ceiling and its window is filled with a stained-glass Christ on the Cross, remarkably rich in colour. This chamber holds the tombs of two unknown soldiers, whose remains were returned to Portugal from France and Africa after World War I, a war that claimed 8,145 Portuguese soldiers' lives. The sculpture of "Christ of the Trenches" was given by the French Government, and a photograph of its extraordinary discovery on the battlefields of Flanders can be seen in the refectory opposite, where there is a small World War I museum.

To reach the **Capelas Imperfeitas** (Unfinished Chapels), go outside the monastery. This octagonal structure is attached to the outside wall and its open roof is very striking. Ordered by King Duarte I to house the tombs of himself and his family, the chapel was begun in the 1430s but construction was never finished – no one is quite certain why. The shell contains simple chapels in each of seven walls. The chapel opposite the door holds the tomb of the king and Leonor, his wife. The eighth wall is a massive door of limestone, with endless layers of beautifully detailed ornamentation in carved Manueline style.

ALCOBAÇA

Twelve km (8 miles) south of Batalha is the town of **Alcobaça** ⑩, named after two rivers, the Alcoa and the Baça. At its heart is the magnificent **Cistercian Abbey** (www.mosteiroalcobaca.pt), yet another UNESCO World Heritage Site. The first king of Portugal, Afonso Henriques, founded it to commemorate the capture of Santarém from the Moors. He laid the foundation stone himself in 1148.

The abbey's Cistercian monks were energetically productive. Numbering, it is said, 999 ("one less than a thousand" according to records), they diligently tilled the land around the abbey, planting vegetables and fruit. In Sebastião I's reign, the exceedingly wealthy and powerful Santa Maria Abbey, as it is also known, was declared by the Pope the seat of the entire Cistercian order. The monks here were particularly known for their lively spirits and lavish hospitality. They ran a school, perhaps the first public school in Portugal, and a sanctuary and hospice as well. In 1810, however, the abbey was sacked by French troops. In the liberal revolution of 1834, when all religious orders were expelled from Portugal, the abbey was again pillaged.

The long Baroque facade, added in the 18th century, has twin towers in the centre, below which are a Gothic doorway and rose window surviving from the original facade. Directly inside the serene and austere church, the largest in Portugal, three tall aisles and plain walls emphasise the clean lines. In the transepts are the two well-known and richly carved tombs of Pedro I and Inês de Castro (see page 43). Off the south transept are several other royal tombs, including those of Afonso II and Afonso III, and a sadly mutilated 17th-century terracotta of the Death of St Bernard. To the east of the ambulatory there are two fine Manueline doorways that were designed by João de Castilho.

An entrance in the north wall of the church leads to the 14th-century **Claustro de Silencio** (Cloister of Silence). Several rooms branch off the cloister, including the chapterhouse and a dormitory. There is a kitchen, with an enormous central chimney and a remarkable basin through which a rivulet runs: it supposedly provided the monks with a constant supply of fresh fish. Next door is the refectory, with steps built into one wall leading to a pulpit. To the left of the entrance is the **Sala dos Reis**, with statues of many of the kings of Portugal, probably carved by monks themselves. The panel in the same room, which tells the history of Alcobaça Abbey, is a rare example of a manuscript *azulejo* panel.

A characteristically graceful vaulted dome inside the monastery at Batalha.

Portugal's largest cave in Parque Natural de Serras de Aire e Candeeiros.

Alcobaça today is the centre of a porcelain and pottery industry. There are numerous shops around the central square, and some factories welcome visitors.

THE SILVER COAST

From Alcobaça, it is a relatively short drive out to the coast to reach the fishing port **Nazaré** ⓫, which nestles along a sweeping bay. In summer, thousands of holiday-makers pack the beach in rows of peaked, brightly striped canvas tents that create a striking image.

Nazaré, named after a statue of the Virgin that a 4th-century monk brought to the town from Nazareth, lives literally on two levels. In the lower part of town, small, white-walled fishermen's cottages line the narrow alleyways. High above on the cliff that towers 109 metres (360ft) over the old town is the quarter known as **Sítio**. Reached by a funicular that climbs the tallest cliffside in Portugal, Sítio is dominated by a large square, and on its edge a tiny chapel, built to commemorate a miracle in 1182, when the Virgin saved the local lord by stopping his horse plunging off the cliff as he pursued a deer.

The 17th-century **Nossa Senhora da Nazaré** on the other side of the square is the focus of festivities during the second week of September that include processions and bullfights in the Sítio bullring. The steep, narrow pathway and steps from the lighthouse west of the church afford stirring views of Atlantic breakers.

The abundance of tourists vitiates some of Nazaré's charm, but it also assures that visitors are well catered for. Pleasant seafood restaurants and small hotels line the sandy bay; esplanade cafés, bars and souvenir shops abound. But the life of the hardy fishermen goes on.

Because they had no natural harbour, the fishermen used to launch their boats from the beach. They managed this by pushing their craft down log rollers into the sea then clambering aboard and rowing furiously till they overrode the incoming breakers. When they arrived home again, the boats were winched ashore by oxen

The arches of Alcobaça Abbey.

The medieval market of Óbidos.

and later by tractors. The building of a modern anchorage to the south of the beach has relieved the Nazaré fishermen of this arduous task.

The Nazaré fisherfolk's traditional dress is today seen more in souvenir shops than on the street. Some women still wear coloured petticoats under a wide black or coloured skirt and cover their heads with a black scarf; the men still favour woollen shirts in traditional plaids, but few wear the distinctive black stocking bonnets.

CALM WATERS AND A WALLED TOWN

The road south out of Nazaré leads first past the new fishing harbour and then down the coast to **São Martinho do Porto** ⑫. Here a huge encircling sandbank creates a virtual lagoon, although there is a small opening to the sea. These calm, shallow waters are readily warmed by the sun but, with only a limited exchange of water, the risk of pollution in the bay is high. Moving south again, the road sweeps grandly by the university town of **Caldas de Rainha** (Queen's Spa) – where there is a regular morning fruit market and the charming Museu de Cerâmica (http://museudaceramica.blogspot.com), which contains local and international ceramics dating from the 17th century. The road then continues on to Óbidos.

A picture-postcard view of town walls crowned by a castle announces **Óbidos** ⑬. The old walled town, its streets tumbling with bougainvillea, presents a well-groomed appearance to the steady influx of day-trippers. The pretty town retains some authenticity, as no new building has been permitted, and only the existing structures within the walls can be used as tea shops, residences and gift shops. Everything in the narrow jumbled streets is painted white, with blue or yellow trimmings, and there are some colourful window boxes.

The town has a long history: it was occupied by the Moors before falling into Christian hands. King Dinis, the indefatigable castle-builder, tidied it up and restored the **castelo** early in the 14th century. Damaged in the

Mending nets, a task that stays unchanged.

Powerful waves rock the shore at Costa de Prata.

PLACES

> **Fact**
>
> Between Óbidos and Peniche some delightful coastal scenery and excellent restaurants make it worth taking a short detour to Baleal, a tiny island joined to the mainland by a causeway. For golfers, the Praia d'El Rey course (www.praia-del-rey.com) offers a splendid challenge.

great earthquake of 1755, the castle was subsequently restored and has been converted into a delightful *pousada* (www.pousadas.pt). It is the place where everyone wants to stay, and gets booked up well in advance.

Apart from wandering around unprotected town walls and enjoying the ambience of the town, there is little to see in the way of monuments. The 17th-century **Igreja de Santa Maria** (1634–84) dominating the market square attracts the most attention, chiefly for the religious paintings by Josefa de Óbidos, the female artist born in the town in the 17th century.

BACK TO THE COAST

Like many of Portugal's coastal towns, **Peniche** ⓮ has no natural harbour, only a bay sheltered by the rocky promontory of **Cabo Carvoeiro**, the second most westerly point in Europe. A sea wall has been built to protect the bay. Peniche is a town of around 27,000 people. Here, the spare white houses cling to the slopes for shelter from the sweeping northwesterly winds. Too stark and exposed for tourism to have taken hold, the town typifies life in Portuguese fishing communities.

The **Fortaleza** physically dominates the town. The veteran leader of Portugal's Communist Party, Alvaro Cunhal, escaped from this notorious prison in 1960 by embarking on a daring descent down the cliffs to a waiting boat that reportedly took him to a Soviet-bloc submarine. In 2019, the building re-opened as the **Museu Nacional Resistência e Liberdade** (National Museum of Resistance and Freedom), dedicated to the overthrow of the Estado Novo regime (www.museunacionalresistencialiberdade-peniche.gov.pt/en).

You can get a powerful sense of the Atlantic swell that is the fisherman's constant companion by taking the ferry from Peniche out to **Ilha Berlenga** ⓯, 7km (4 miles) offshore. The ferry runs from June to September and the journey takes an hour.

The return to Lisbon is best made via the highway from Óbidos, entering Lisbon via the IC2.

Santa Maria church, Óbidos.

> **ILHA BERLENGA**
>
> It's an adventure to discover Portugal's beautiful Ilha Berlenga, a rocky chunk of island that looks as if part of the Hebrides drifted out into the Atlantic. Visiting the island, once out of the shelter of the peninsula, powerful currents rock the boat with unexpected force, but the destination is worth the discomfort: the only buildings are a 17th-century fortress (now converted to an inn), a lighthouse and a few fishermen's cottages.
>
> The entire island has been designated a national bird sanctuary, and seagulls and eider ducks are everywhere. Officials patrol the makeshift paths to ensure that visitors do not disturb the birds. The greatest excitement lies in taking a trip around the reefs, caves and smaller islands, past a breathtaking sea tunnel called the Furado Grande.

Fort of St John the Baptist in Berlenga island.

The University of Coimbra.

COIMBRA

Coimbra grows old but never grows up. University freshers arrive each year to revitalise traditions and pour their souls into fado. For visitors it is a great mix of history and youthful exuberance.

Perched on a hill overlooking the Rio Mondego, **Coimbra** ❶ is surrounded by breathtakingly beautiful countryside. The city itself is a mixture of ancient and new, green and urban. The tourist office in the centre of the lower town, in the Praça da República, will provide you with a good map of the city.

The university is the most stalwart guardian of Coimbra's rich history. Students clad in black capes, the traditional academic dress, resemble oversized bats as they flit around town.

The hems of the capes are often ripped, a declaration – at times – of romantic heartache, as part of the tradition of "traje rasgado" (torn outfit). But these capes have only come back into style relatively recently, as for a time they were associated with Salazar's New State, and therefore not worn in the years after the 1974 revolution.

In May each year, the university celebrates the *Queima das Fitas*, the "burning of the ribbons", when graduating students burn the ribbons they have been wearing, the colour of which signifies their faculty – yellow for medicine, for example. The celebrations last a week, and their grand finale is a long drunken parade.

Another Coimbra tradition is fado, a more serious cousin of the Lisbon variety. The sombre Coimbra fado theoretically requires you to clear your throat in approval after a rendition, and not applaud. It is performed only by men, often cloak-wrapped graduates of the university.

The country's third-largest city, Coimbra lies at the centre of an agricultural region and has a large market. The students are not the only ones in black: it is the traditional dress of many of the rural women who come into town as well. Coimbra also has a considerable manufacturing industry.

Main attractions
Biblioteca Joanina
Museu da Ciência
Museu Machado de Castro
Sé Velha
Mosteiro de Santa Cruz
Jardim da Manga

Maps on pages 236, 244

Scientific decorations at the University of Coimbra.

A decorative doorway in Coimbra.

THE CITY'S HISTORY

Coimbra traces its roots to the Roman municipality of *Aeminium*. It gained in importance when the nearby city of Conímbriga (see page 243) proved vulnerable to invasion.

Convulsions in the empire and various attacks brought an end to Roman rule in the city. The Moors took over in 711, ushering in 300 years of Islamic rule, with a few interruptions.

One such occurred in 878 when Afonso III of Asturias and León captured the city. Coimbra was not permanently retaken by Christian forces until 1064. It then became a base for the reconquest, and the city was walled. From 1139 to 1385 Coimbra was the capital of Portugal.

The 12th century was an age of considerable progress for Coimbra – including the construction, which began in 1131, of the city's most important monastery, Santa Cruz, still standing today. A lively commercial centre, the city included both Jewish and Moorish quarters. Division was not only by religion, but also by class. Nobles and clergy lived inside the walls in the upper town, while merchants and craft workers lived outside in what is today known as the Baixa, the lower area, down by the river, and heart of the modern town.

The university, founded in 1290 in Lisbon, moved to Coimbra in 1308, only to return to Lisbon nearly 70 years later. It was not until 1537 that the university settled permanently in Coimbra. A few years later, it moved to its present site at the top of the hill.

Most areas of interest are easily reached on foot. There is also a handy elevator which rises from Avenida Sá da Bandeira to Rua Padre António Vieira. Don't try to drive within the city. The old city and the university crown Coimbra's central hill, and the Baixa, which is the main shopping and eating district, lies at the foot of the hill along the Rio Mondego.

Linking the two banks of the river, too, is a hi-tech footbridge with bright zigzag railings. There are plenty of picturesque riverside restaurants at which to take it all in.

THE OLD CITY AND UNIVERSITY

Once enclosed within walls, the old city is a tangle of narrow streets and alleys, lined by ancient buildings and filled with squares and patios. The university buildings are a compelling mix of styles, from the odd Baroque **Torre**, a clocktower, to bleakly Salazarist faculty blocks. The modern centre of the university is the statue of King Dinis, its founder, on the site of an earlier castle in **Largo Don Dinis** Ⓐ, also home to the **Museu Académico** (https://visit.uc.pt/pt/space-list/museu_academico), where the displays include historic university capes and posters. Nearby stand the buildings that house the faculties of science and technology, medicine and letters and the New Library.

Of more historical interest than these stolidly functional buildings is the Pátio das Escolas (Patio of the Schools), within the **Universidade Velha** Ⓑ, the Old University. To enter the patio, pass through the 17th-century Porta Férrea, a large portal decorated in the Mannerist style, to a large, dusty courtyard that is used for parking. Here are some of the oldest and stateliest buildings of the university. The figure of João III, who installed the university in Coimbra, still reigns from the centre of the patio. Behind him, there is a magnificent view of the river.

The building in the furthest corner from the Porta Férrea is the **Biblioteca Joanina** (https://visit.uc.pt/pt/space-list/joanina), among the world's most resplendent Baroque libraries. The three sumptuous 18th-century rooms were built during the reign of João V, whose portrait hangs at the far end. Bookcases, adorned in gilded wood and oriental motifs, reach gracefully to an upper galleried level; even the ladders are intricately decorated. Note the fine frescoes on the ceilings. More than 300,000 books fill the cases and are still consulted by scholars.

Next door is the **Capela de São Miguel** (St Michael's Chapel), begun in 1517, and remodelled in the 17th and 18th centuries. The chapel is notable for its carpet-style tiles, the painted ceilings, the altar and the Baroque

> ### ⓘ Fact
> Trains from Lisbon (Oriente) take 1.5–2 hours and stop at Coimbra B station 3km (2 miles) north of the centre, where passengers take a linking train to Coimbra A, the delightful little station in the middle of town. You don't need a separate ticket.

A mosaic welcomes you to the university at Coimbra.

ⓘ MUSEU DA CIÊNCIA

Several small university museums were merged to form the impressive **Museu da Ciência** Ⓒ (Science Museum; www.museu-daciencia.org), located in Largo Marquês de Pombal. One of Europe's most important science collections, this award-winning museum has some 250,000 objects on display. Categories include botany, mineralogy, geology, palaeontology, astronomy and medicine, with information provided in both English and Portuguese.

This museum is a great choice for families as there are plenty of child-friendly interactive displays, including the key "Secrets of Light and Matter", and some fascinating visual exhibits, such as a bed of flowers seen from the perspective of a bug-eyed insect.

organ. Beside the chapel is a small museum of sacred art.

The arcaded building to the right of the Porta Férrea on the Via Latina houses the **Sala dos Capelos** (https://visit.uc.pt/pt/space-list/Sala_Capelos), where degrees are conferred and academic ceremonies take place. Portraits of Portugal's kings hang from its walls. Other rooms that you may enter are the rectory and, right by the bell tower, the **Sala do Exame Privado**, the Private Exam Room.

OLD AND NEW CATHEDRALS

A short walk down from the university takes you to the **Sé Nova** D (New Cathedral), whose sand-coloured facade presides over a rather uninteresting square. Built for the Jesuits in 1554, it became a cathedral in 1772. Inside, the altar and much else is of lavishly gilded wood. Many of the paintings around the altar are copies of works by Italian masters.

The **Museu Machado de Castro** E www.cm-coimbra.pt/areas/visitar/conhecer-coimbra/museus/museu-nacional-machado-de-castro) is housed in the old Episcopal palace and the neighbouring 12th-century church of São João de Almedina. Constructed over the city's Roman forum and *cryptoporticus* (underground galleries), the palace was the residence of Coimbra's early bishops. The museum is named after Portugal's greatest sculptor, Joaquim Machado de Castro (1732–1822), who was born in Coimbra. It holds an extensive and varied collection of medieval sculpture, as well as superb later pieces.

The **Sé Velha** F (Old Cathedral), renovated in the 20th century, was built between 1162 and 1184. It served as a cathedral until 1772, when the episcopal see was moved to the Sé Nova. The fortress-like exterior is relieved by an arched door with an arched window directly above. The intricate Gothic altar within is of gilded wood, created by two Flemish masters in the 15th and 16th centuries. Sancho I was crowned king here in 1185, and João I in 1385. There are several tombs in the cathedral, including those of the 13th-century Bishop Dom Egas Fafe (to the left of the altar) and Dona Vetaça, a Byzantine princess who was a governess in the Coimbra court in the 14th century. Construction of the early Gothic cloister began in 1218.

Work on the **Colégio de Santo Agostinho**, on Rua Colégio Novo, was started in 1593. The ecclesiastical scholars and monks who first occupied it would probably be astonished by its present-day purpose, for this pleasant building, lined with pretty *azulejos*, is now home to the university's Psychology Department.

Nearby, on Rua Sobre-Ripas, the medieval **Torre de Anto** G (Anthony's Tower) was once part of the 12th-century city walls. Much later it was the home of the poet António Nobre (1867–1900), including during his days as an undergraduate student.

The **Casa de Sobre-Ripas** H, on the same street, is an aristocratic 16th-century mansion. Note the archetypal

The Old Cathedral of Coimbra, built in the 12th century.

Manueline door and window, but don't bother knocking: it is the Faculty of Archaeology, and not open to the public. Here, it is believed, Maria Teles was murdered by her husband João (eldest son of the tragic Inês de Castro) who had been convinced by the jealous Queen Leonor Teles that his wife – the queen's sister – was unfaithful to him.

The **Arco de Almedina**, an entrance to the old city just off Rua Ferreira Borges, was also part of the medieval walls that encircle the old town hill. Housed in the tower here is the **Núcleo da Cidade Muralhada** ❶, a model display of the town with its original town plan and defensive towers, plus details of its history. Head upstairs for superb views and to spy down through the holes carved into the stone floor. In times of war or invasion, boiling oil was poured through these holes to thwart potential aggressors.

BAIXA COIMBRA

The Baixa is the busy shopping district, and Rua Ferreira Borges, with many fashionable shops, is the busy, principal street. Although this district lay outside the walls of the old city, it dates back to almost the same time.

The **Mosteiro de Santa Cruz** ❶ (https://igrejascruz.webnode.pt; free) in Praça 8 de Maio (a continuation of Rua Ferreira Borges) was founded in 1131 by the St Augustine fathers. In the 14th century a grim scene was enacted when Dom Pedro had the body of his murdered lover exhumed, crowned and propped on a throne here, forcing his courtiers to pay homage to her corpse and kiss her decomposing hand. The facade and portal of the church date from the 16th century. Inside, the small church is light and spacious. Eighteenth-century *azulejos* adorn the walls: the right side depicts the life of St Augustine of Hippo; on the left, scenes relate to the Holy Cross.

Another striking work by a major 16th-century artist is the exquisite pulpit on the left-hand wall, by sculptor Nicolau Chanterène. The **sacristy** contains several interesting paintings including *The Pentecost* by the 16th-century Grão Vasco, a silverwork collection, and some clerical vestments. You can see the tombs of the first two kings of Portugal, Afonso Henriques and Sancho I, ensconced in regal monuments. The chapterhouse and the lovely Cloister of Silence may also be visited.

Behind the church of Santa Cruz lies the **Jardim da Manga** (Garden of the Sleeve), so named because Dom João III reputedly drew this oddity of a garden on his sleeve – although the design has also been attributed to João de Ruão, a French sculptor working in Portugal in the 16th century. Curiously modernistic, this monumental garden was completed in 1535, and intended as a representation of the fountain of life. Beside the church is an atmospheric café in an ecclesiastic setting that was clearly part of the church.

If you wander down Rua da Sofia, which turns off 16th-century Praça

Museu Machado de Castro.

> **Tip**
>
> To find the boisterous student nightlife, head for the restaurants around Rua la Sota, one street back from the river in Baixa Coimbra. And try the *chanfana* – goat stewed in wine – a dish from the Beira Litoral, to the north.

8 de Maio, you may be struck by the fact that it is extraordinarily wide for a street of that period. It was the original base for several colleges of the university before they were moved to new homes.

Praça do Comércio, off Rua Ferreira Borges, is an oddly shaped square lined with 17th- and 18th-century buildings. At the north end stands the sturdy **Igreja de Santiago** Ⓚ, a church dating from the end of the 12th century. The capitals are decorated with animal and bird motifs. At the square's south end is the **Igreja de São Bartolomeu** Ⓛ, built in the 18th century.

SANTA CLARA

The Santa Clara section of town lies across the river. **Mosteiro Santa Clara-a-Nova** Ⓜ (New Santa Clara Monastery; https://rainhasantaisabel.org) is worth a visit if only for the view over Coimbra. Inside is the tomb of Queen Isabel, who was canonised in 1625 and became the city's patron saint. Closer to the river, too close for its own comfort in fact, is **Santa Clara-a-Velha**, the old Santa Clara Monastery. This 12th-century edifice is simpler and more lovely than its replacement, for which it was abandoned in 1677. Waterlogged for centuries, it has been successfully restored.

Nearby **Quinta da Lágrimas** is where Inês de Castro is believed to have been murdered (see page 43). The family home is now a luxurious hotel and the grounds contain the **Fonte das Lágrimas**, the spring which is said to have risen on the spot where the luckless Inês cried for the last time and met her violent end.

To the east of the city, the **Mosteiro Celas** is notable for its cloister, and the pretty church of **Santo António dos Olivais** was once an old Franciscan convent.

SHOPS, PARKS AND BOATS

The lanes of the Baixa have some delightfully old-fashioned shops. The covered market on **Rua Olimpio Nicolau** is open daily.

Coimbra has numerous parks: the **Jardim Botânico** (www.uc.pt/jardimbotanico; free except for greenhouses), on Alameda Dr Júlio Henriques, next to the 16th-century Aqueduto de São Sebastião, is a lovely garden, laid out in the 18th century.

The **Portugal dos Pequenitos** (www.portugaldospequenitos.pt) is an outdoor theme park displaying small-scale reproductions of traditional Portuguese houses and monuments, which children love to clamber over and explore.

Other parks are **Santa Cruz**, off Praça da República, and **Choupal**, west of the city – a larger green space that is good for walks and bicycle rides. Tiny **Penedo da Saudade** has a nice view.

If you want some physical exercise, and a complete change from historical monuments, there are canoes and pedalos for hire on the river. Basófias (www.basofias.pt) offer daily (except Mondays) river cruises lasting an hour.

Exploring Portugal dos Pequenitos.

A stroll in the Jardim Botânico.

Praça da República, Aveiro.

SIDE TRIPS FROM COIMBRA

Within easy reach of Coimbra you will find gleaming lagoons, colourful fishing villages, exotic forests, and the most extensive Roman ruins in the country.

Main attractions
Conímbriga
Serra do Buçaco
Aveiro
Vista Alegre
Praia de Mira
Figueira da Foz

Map on page 244

Coimbra ① might be the main focus of interest in this vicinity, but there are plenty of opportunities for short excursions to other noteworthy places. The countryside towards the coast is especially bucolic with an old-fashioned rural way of life. The coast also offers plenty to see, especially Aveiro with its canals and lagoons. Castles and palaces feature too, as well as Roman ruins.

CONÍMBRIGA

Portugal's largest excavated Roman ruins are at **Conímbriga** ② (www.conimbriga.pt), 15km (9 miles) south of Coimbra, near the town of Condeixa; the drive is easy, and there is a bus service. The site is complemented by the **Museu Monográfico de Conímbriga**, one of the country's finest museums.

As you enter the site, you are walking down the road that gave Conímbriga its original importance: the highway from Olisipo to Bracara Augusta. In front of you is an enormous wall. Passing through the main entrance and continuing along the path to the right, you will come to the arch of the aqueduct (rebuilt), parts of the aqueduct itself, and the remains of several buildings that were possibly small shops.

The building known as Cantaber's House stretches to the south. The house is full of ornamental fountains and pools, but more interesting are the baths, which lie at the extreme south end. They are easily recognisable by their hexagonal and round shapes, and by the piped heating system (that great Roman innovation), visible through the stone grid covering the floors. Around the other side of the wall you can see more baths: public ones. For Romans, bathing was an important daily ritual, and the bathroom was also a place to discuss politics. Beyond the baths is an area of marvellously patterned mosaics; some are covered to protect them from the elements. The museum

A Roman mosaic, Conímbriga.

Fact

After taking a bath, the Romans would cover themselves with olive oil and then scrape their skins clean with a curved blade called a strigil. Those who could afford it would bring a slave along to perform this service for them.

is small but carefully designed. A long case displays ceramics, jewellery, and artefacts relating to weaving, agriculture, lighting, writing and hygiene. There are also statues and a model of the forum and temple.

SERRA DO BUÇACO

Northeast of Coimbra lies the **Serra do Buçaco** ❸ (Buçaco Forest), a darkly haunting area which for centuries has been protected, enabling 700 varieties of native and exotic trees to flourish. Benedictine monks established a hermitage here in the 6th century. The Carmelites, who built a monastery in 1628, began cultivation of the forest, planting species brought back from sea voyages, including Himalayan pines, monkey puzzles, Japanese camphor trees, huge Lebanese cedars, and ginkgoes. In 1643 the pope threatened to excommunicate anyone harming the trees.

A royal hunting lodge was built in neo-Manueline style at the end of the 19th century, next to what remained of the convent. The Italian architect Luigi Manini, somehow managed to inject his own interpretation of Romantic Revivalism into the construction and the intended modest hunting lodge turned into a sumptuous palace. After the fall of the monarchy in 1910, it became the spectacular and luxurious **Palace Hotel do Buçaco** (where you may still, at a price, lodge in the suite of the last king, Manuel II). A

SIDE TRIPS FROM COIMBRA

small church, the cloister, and several monks' cells remain from the monastery. It was in one of these cells that the Duke of Wellington spent the night before the Battle of Buçaco on 27 September 1810. His victory in this battle was the first serious setback suffered by Napoleon's army, as the French attempted for the third time to conquer Portugal. The victory is still celebrated annually on the anniversary, with a re-enactment of the battle, in full period costume.

A high-quality wine is produced on the estate and is available in the restaurant. If you are keen to try it, book yourself in for lunch at the hotel and enjoy a real treat (www.bussacopalace.com).

Downhill from Buçaco is the village of **Luso** ❹, renowned as a spa for the water that flows freely from fountains and which is available bottled throughout Portugal. A common sight here is of local people overburdened with an assortment of plastic water bottles jostling to fill them at Fonte de São João (St John's Fountain).

The N1/IP2 north towards Aveiro leads through the heart of the Barraida wine country. A slight diversion into **Curia** ❺ allows the opportunity of picking up a special map of the region from the *Turismo*. Armed with this, you can find your way to the local winery at Sangalhos, Caves Aliança (www.bacalhoa.pt), where you can taste wine or visit the fabulous museum in its cellars, which displays beautiful artefacts variously collected or stolen by José Berardo, one of Portugal's richest men. The collection includes 1,500-year-old phallic symbols from Niger and a fine collection of fossils and ethnographical items.

TO THE COAST AND AVEIRO

Aveiro ❻ has been described as the Venice of Portugal. The comparison, although exaggerated, stems from the canals that traverse the city and the boats that ply them. The canal system is modest, however: there is only one main canal, with two smaller ones along the edges of town. But they are linked with the *ria*, the lagoon that extends

Entrance to Serra do Buçaco.

Details from Hotel Buçaco Palace.

◉ CONIMBRIGA'S PAST

Conímbriga was probably settled as early as the Iron Age (800–500 BC), and it was not until the latter part of the 2nd century BC that the Romans arrived. Conímbriga profited from its location by the Roman road between Olisipo (Lisbon) and Bracara Augusta (now Braga), and around AD 70 was designated a municipium.

Conímbriga's prosperity was not to last. Crises in the empire and Barbarian incursions prompted the construction of the defensive wall, still prominent today, but despite this, in 464 the Suevi successfully attacked the city. Conímbriga continued to be inhabited, but lost to neighbouring Aeminium (Coimbra) its status as an important centre.

Only part of the estimated 13-hectare (32-acre) site has been excavated.

Visitors will find it hard to forget that Luso is a spa town.

Colourful moliceiros take to the water in Aveiro.

47km (29 miles) just inland of the Atlantic and is fringed by dunes and long sandy beaches. Known to the Romans as Talabriga, Aveiro once lay directly on the ocean, but over the centuries a strip of sediment has built up, creating the *ria* but blocking ships and trade.

The lagoon plays a significant part in Aveiro's economic importance as an expanding port for fishing fleets and industrial cargoes. Other important local industries include wood, cork, and ceramics from nearby Vista Alegre. Next to the canals are large saltpans, another local resource. Once the lagoon was famous for brightly painted *moliceiros*, the boats with large, graceful prows that were widely used to gather *moliço* (seaweed) for fertiliser, and which today are used for transporting tourists.

Aveiro was a small settlement during the Middle Ages. It was designated a town in the 1200s, and in 1418 was encircled by fortified walls, at the suggestion of Infante Prince Pedro after whom the city park is named. Shortly after this, Aveiro was granted the concession of a town fair; the March Fair continues to this day with local produce on display.

The 16th century was a time of growth and expansion for the town. With dredged access to the sea and to the interior, Aveiro became a trade centre from which products of the entire Beira region were exported. In 1575, a violent storm shifted the sandbanks in the lagoon, blocking the canal from the sea. The inevitable decline in Aveiro's importance encouraged emigration, which caused a dramatic decrease in population (to about one-third). In 1808, another storm reopened the sea passage, but it was not until the last half of the 19th century that Aveiro's fortunes picked up.

EXPLORING AVEIRO

Aveiro makes a good base for a trip on the *ria* or to nearby beaches, but the city is worth exploring as well. The best way to get around Aveiro is to pick up a free bicycle between 10am and 7pm from a BUGA park, under a local scheme to encourage cycling in the town. Aveiro is divided in two by the principal canal. The southern part is where the aristocracy once lived; the northern half is the old fishermen's section.

The southern half centres around the **Praça da República**. In the simple square, the nicest building is the solid and rather prim town hall. On the east side of the square, the 16th- and 17th-century **Misericórdia** church has a lovely Renaissance portal and 19th-century tiles on its facade. In a square further south the 17th-century **Carmelite Convent** once housed the barefoot Carmelite order, who embraced a simpler way of life, focusing on solitude. Note the paintings on the ceiling, which depict the life of St Teresa of Avila.

The town's **Museu de Aveiro** (www.cm-aveiro.pt/visitantes/museus-de-aveiro/museu-de-aveiro-santa-joana) is housed in the 15th-century **Convento de Jesus**. The convent has some fine 17th-century paintings and its church is effusively gilded. Arching over the choir are lovely hand-painted ceilings, and off the choir is a chapel with beautiful tiles. Just outside is the tomb of Santa Joana Princesa, daughter of Afonso V and patron of the city, who lived in the convent for 14 years until her death in 1489. Intricately carved in coloured marble and delicate inlays, with statues supporting and crowning it, the tomb took 12 years to construct.

The **São Domingos Cathedral** is near the museum. Its Baroque facade has twisted columns and sculpted figures of Faith, Hope and Charity. Inside, an enormous skylight over the altar lends the church an airiness that many Baroque churches lack. The huge blue altar rises strikingly in the all-white interior. The tomb of Catarina de Ataíde is here, a woman honoured, under the name Natércia, by the poet Luís Camões in his sonnets. The church was founded in 1423 and remodelled during the 16th and 17th centuries.

To the east of the centre lies a beautiful train station (Estação de Aveiro). The facade of the old building is elegantly decorated with blue tiles showing portraits and scenes from everyday life.

Several blocks away is the refreshing **Parque Dom Infante Pedro**, in the grounds of the old Franciscan Monastery. Colourful flowers, lush trees, fountains, and a small lake where you can hire paddle boats make this a nice spot for a break.

THE OLD QUARTER

North of the canal lies the fishermen's section, where narrow houses support facades that sometimes rise beyond roof levels. The arches and curves on these false fronts are reminiscent of the fishing boats and their curved prows. The fish market, where the catch is sold each morning, is in this area. There is also the white, oddly shaped chapel of **São Gonçalinho** and the church of **São Gonçalo**. Inside this 17th- and 18th-century building gleam a gilt altar and newly placed tiles.

The beautiful *ria* is a prime reason for coming to Aveiro. You can tour its length

Public art in Aveiro.

> **Tip**
>
> Several companies run boat trips on the ria, including Aveiro Emotions (www.aveiroemotions.com) and Ecoria (www.ecoria.pt). You can usually choose between a traditional moliceiro and a modern panoramic boat; either way, trips typically last around an hour, longer if a meal is included.

by boat, car or bus, although boat is by far the most rewarding. The lagoon and its subsidiary canals extend as far south as Mira and as far north as Ovar. There is a fair range of hotels in the area and many campsites. You will see traditional colourful *moliceiros* (the annual regatta is in July), shorelines dotted with saltpans, forests and villages, glorious sea birds plummeting into the water, and the sandbar that blocks the city's access to the sea. A road bridge takes you over the mouth of the estuary to **Costa Nova**, where there are brightly coloured traditional houses and excellent fish restaurants. Just 3km (2 miles) north of here, **Praia da Barra** is home to the Iberian peninsula's tallest lighthouse and (together with Costa Nova) is famed for its great surfing conditions. For information on the town, head to the tourist office, in an Art Nouveau building at Rua João Mendonça 8.

Continuing north, São Jacinto is a bustling port and part of the **Reserva Natural das Dunas de São Jacinto** (www.icnf.pt), an inviting little nature reserve with ponds and trails, which is famed for its birdlife. Visitor numbers are limited, so it is advisable to reserve online in advance.

AROUND AVEIRO

From Aveiro a good road leads south to Figueira da Foz and back to Coimbra along the riverside. Fairly soon after leaving Aveiro, past Ilhavo, divert right to the **Vista Alegre Factory** ❼ for its porcelain (http://vistaalegre.com). Famous throughout Portugal, it started production in 1842 and is still run by the same family. There is also a shop on site.

Mira lies close to the road a little further south. Keep going through the town and head for **Praia de Mira** ❽ on the coast. This is the most southerly point of the lagoon and canal system that surrounds Aveiro. Candy-striped beach huts add a jaunty air to the resort, but the main attraction is the inland lagoon, where there is safe boating and where picnickers enjoy shade from the surrounding pine trees.

Heading south, dip into the attractive quieter beach at **Praia de Quiaios**, situated just 10km (6 miles) north of the major holiday resort of **Figueira da Foz** ❾; the latter is favoured by both Portuguese and Spanish visitors. Turn a blind eye to the high-rise blocks and look at the broad expanse of beach and the cheerfully coloured beach huts, again in delightful candy stripes.

There is a fast road along the north side of the river to **Montemor-o-Velho**, dominated by a 14th-century castle on a prominent mound. Like many in Portugal, it was held by the Moors before being taken by the Christians. Within the walls are gardens, the ruins of a 16th-century Manueline palace and the restored **Igreja de Santa Maria da Alcáçova**, built around the time the castle was restored. In August, the castle is the evocative setting for Festival Forte, an electronic music festival. To enjoy a rural atmosphere on the return to Coimbra, take the road from here along the south side of the river.

The striped houses of the Costa Nova.

A tribute to the fishermen of Figueira da Foz.

A shrine high in the mountains.

BEIRA ALTA AND BEIRA BAIXA

This is a region of extreme contrasts, incorporating the Serra da Estréla (the highest mountain range in Portugal), areas of sheep and cattle grazing, and sturdy castles.

Main attractions
Viseu
Termas de São Pedro do Sul
Santar
Castelo Branco
Palácio Episcopal
Monsanto

Map on page 252

The provinces of Beira Alta and Beira Baixa, the Upper and Lower Beiras, constitute a large rural section of eastern Portugal – a modest and hardy geographical region in a country that is among the poorest in western Europe. However, it is rich historically, marked over centuries by the invasion routes of both Spaniards and Moors, in many defensive castles and remnants of fortresses.

The area has its natural attractions as well: the dramatic mountains of the Serra da Estréla and the stark plains and plateaux of the Baixa are some of the most beautiful natural landmarks in Portugal.

The region is bounded by the Spanish frontier to the east, the Rio Douro to the north, and the Tejo (Tagus) to the south. The western boundary is a ragged line 60km (38 miles) east of Porto.

BEIRA ALTA

Guarda ① is the principal city and administrative capital of the Beira Alta's eastern district. The charter of Guarda was granted by Sancho I, Portugal's second king, in 1199, although the city had been established by 80 BC when it had a role in the attempted secession from Rome.

Roman ruins can be found just outside town, near the Romanesque chapel of Póvoa de Mileu, notable itself for a small rose window and nicely carved capitals. Three town gates from the 12th- and 13th-century castle and town walls still stand: the Torre de Ferreiros (Blacksmiths' Tower), the Porta da Estréla (Star Gate), and the Porta do Rei (King's Gate), along with the castle keep. From the top there is a magnificent view of the mountains, and the broad plains to the north.

The **Sé** (Cathedral) was built of granite cut from the surrounding area. Work started in 1390 and was not completed until 1540, so that there

Beira Alta farmer on his way home.

252 | **PLACES**

Portugal has about 15 varieties of cheese, most made with goat's or sheep's milk.

were many Renaissance and Baroque elements added to the original Gothic. Diogo Boytac (1460–1528) worked on the cathedral, which bears some resemblance to Batalha.

The exterior has flying buttresses and fanciful gargoyles. Inside, the 16th-century stone *retábulo*, later highlighted with gilt, represents scenes from the life of Christ; the stone carving is the work of João de Ruão, also known as Jean de Rouen (1500–80). A beautiful Renaissance doorway, off the north aisle, leads to the Capela dos Pinas, which contains the late Gothic tomb of a bishop.

The town museum, in a 17th-century seminary, has archaeological finds and a range of paintings, while a large park by the station includes an excellent, modern children's playground.

Guarda has been dubbed the city of four Fs – *fria, farta, forte e feia*, which means: cold, plentiful, strong and ugly. The predominance of heavy grey granite may be ugly to some, but the old parts of the city are pleasant. "Strong" in this context alludes to Guarda's history as a defence point against the Moors and Castile. "Plentiful" refers, no doubt, to the rich land surrounding the town, noted particularly for its sheep farming.

Cold it certainly is, in winter: situated some 1,066 metres (3,500ft) above sea level, Guarda is Portugal's highest city – high enough for frost and snow in winter.

AROUND GUARDA

Northwest of Guarda is the quintessential fortress village of **Trancoso**, a delightful tangle of cobbled lanes surrounded by 13th-century walls. Don't miss the castle with its unusual Moorish tower and the medieval *juderia* (Jewish district). South of Guarda lie two handsome castle towns: on the main road to Castelo Branco is **Belmonte** ❷, birthplace of Alvares Cabral, who discovered Brazil, and home to the **Museu Judaico de Belmonte** (https://cm-belmonte.pt/diretorio/museu-judaico), portraying the fascinating history of Judaism in the town, and how it continued in secret some 500 years after the Inquisition. Just south of here is **Sortelha** ❸, a tiny village with a castle surrounded by rocky crags, within a "magic ring" of stone. Ancient civilisations may have shaped some of the rocks, and they certainly mined in the area – there are entrances to mines that have been closed for centuries.

Stretching southwest is the **Serra da Estréla**, the highest mountains in the country and the source of Portugal's most highly rated *serra* cheese, whose production is centred on Covilhã. The highest point of continental Portugal is **Torre** ❹, at nearly 2,000 metres (6,500ft). Nearby is a pilgrimage site, a statue of the Virgin carved into the rock, to which the faithful journey on the second Sunday of August. There are also a couple of gift shops and an overpriced restaurant.

The Serra offers skiing in winter and pleasant walking (or driving) with grand views in all directions. The prime winter resort is **Covilhã** ❺, southeast of Torre. It is too low to receive much snow itself, but it is a short drive to the ski area at **Penhas da Saúde** ❻.

VISEU: HUB OF BEIRA ALTA

The western district of Beira Alta is governed by the city of **Viseu** ❼, about halfway between Guarda and Aveiro. In the 2nd century BC the Romans built a fortified settlement here, and some of their road system can still be seen, along with a number of Latin-inscribed stones.

A thorn in the side of the colonisers was a rebel Lusitanian named Viriathus, who harassed Roman legions until he was finally betrayed and killed. A monument to him lies at the edge of a park – the Cova do Viriato – on the site of a Lusitanian and Roman military encampment. Here, you can still see the old earthworks once used by the Romans. Viseu was made a bishopric during the 6th century AD, the time of the Suevian-Visigothic kingdom, and a record still exists: a signature of the Bishop of Viseu, dated AD 569.

The city suffered alternating invasions of Moors and Christians from the 8th to the 11th centuries. Fernando the Great of Castile and León captured it for the Christians in 1057. Teresa, mother of the first king of Portugal, granted the city its first charter in 1123. From the 14th to the 16th centuries, building in Viseu seems to have been concentrated in the upper part of

> **◎ Fact**
>
> The information offices for the Parque Natural da Estréla in Guarda, Seia, Gouveia, and Manteigas have details of hiking routes with places to stay.

The exquisite vaulting in Viseu's cathedral.

town. About this time an active Jewish colony evolved here. In 1411 the Infante Dom Henrique (Prince Henry the Navigator) became Duke of Viseu, and towards the end of that century the town walls were completed. But the surrounding area was becoming a centre of vigorous agricultural activity, and by the 16th century the walled area was becoming depleted.

Perhaps this was fortunate, because over the next two centuries much of this space was filled with a lavish assortment of Baroque churches, chapels, mansions and fountains. Today the architectural richness lends a dignified air to the enclosed city.

PURE BAROQUE

A city highlight is the 13th-century **Sé** (Cathedral; Mon–Fri 8am–noon, 2–7pm, from 9am Sat–Sun; free). The ribbed vaulting is beautifully carved to look like knotted cables, and the ceiling of the sacristy is extravagantly painted with animals and plants. The twin-towered **Igreja da Misericórdia** across the square is whitewashed granite and pure Baroque. You should also save some time for the **Museu Grão Vasco** (www.museunacionalgraovasco.gov.pt), in the old Bishop's Palace in the same square. Many of the works represent the fine school of Portuguese primitive painting that flourished here in the 16th century, and of which Grão Vasco Fernandes (see page 116) was the acknowledged master.

The **Feira de São Mateus** (http://feirasaomateus.pt), held annually from mid-August to mid-September, is a major event in Viseu, with music, food and fireworks. A Tuesday market is held year-round. Viseu is well known for its lace, carpets and black pottery.

AROUND VISEU

Northwest of Viseu is the small town of São Pedro do Sul and, some 4km (2.5 miles) southwest, the **Termas de São Pedro do Sul** ❽ (www.termas-spsul.com), which are probably the oldest as well as the best known and most frequented hot springs in the country. Sinus problems, rheumatism, hangovers or a foul temper – the springs are said to be a cure for all

A cloudless day in Santar.

ailments. There are other delightful villages in the area, too. Just south of São Pedro do Sul is **Vouzela** 9, with a lovely 13th-century church, and close by is the village of **Cambra**, clustered around the remnants of its castle.

South of Viseu, just off the secondary road to Nelas, **Santar** 10 is a little gem of a place, once known as the Court of the Beiras. Due south is **Oliveira do Hospital** 11, a small town that once belonged to the Hospitallers. As a mark of this, tombs of the Ferreiros in the parish church (the Igreja Matriz) are crowned by a carving of an equestrian knight on the wall above.

Southwest (continue down the main road in the direction of Coimbra), in the village of **Lourosa** 12, is the ancient church of São Pedro. Spain's King Ordoño II ordered its construction in 911; it has a central nave, horseshoe arches, Moorish windows and Visigothic decoration.

BEIRA BAIXA

Travelling south now towards the Beira Baixa, you come to the Rio Zêzere, which roughly divides Beira Alta from Beira Baixa. The river flows most swiftly from early April to late June. A good place for water sports is the **Barragem de Castelo do Bode**, a dam that blocks the flow of the River Zêzere to form a long, many-armed lake that runs south into the province of Ribatejo. (The most direct route is to take the IC3/N110, then turn left about 8km/5 miles south of Tomar.) Both the river and the lake have fine fishing, with canoeing, waterskiing and windsurfing available in places.

The Rio Tejo marks the southern limit of Beira Baixa. Upstream the Tejo crosses into Spain. On both sides of the border is desolate scrub country. The gorge formed by the river is steep-sided and virtually inaccessible for vehicles other than four-wheel-drives. Along much of the Portuguese side of the river runs an ancient Roman road, which was originally the route from Vila Velha de Rodão to the Spanish town of Santiago de Alcántara. Water now conceals large chunks of the work, but where the road rises above the surface

> **Tip**
> The scenic 49km (30-mile) Ecopista do Dão (www.ecopista-portugal.com) cycle route links Viseu with Santa Comba Dão. It is advisable to start the trip from the latter as the ride is much easier.

Castelo Branco became a city in 1771.

Looking out over Castelo Branco from the old battlements.

Giant boulder at Monsanto.

you will see that instead of building the road with flat stones, the entire way is paved with local slate stood on edge, its upper surfaces rutted by centuries of cart traffic.

CASTELO BRANCO

The capital of Beira Baixa is **Castelo Branco** ⑬, which stands at the junction of the IP2/E802 and the N112. It is an ancient city whose origins, like those of so many communities in Portugal, are lost in time. Its "modern" history dates back to 1182, when it and the surrounding area were given as a gift to the Knights Templar by Dom Fernão Sanches. It received a charter in 1213 and became a city in 1771, in the reign of José I.

The battlements of the "white castle" that gave the city its name provide a fine view, though the castle itself is in ruins. The old town is delightful, with narrow winding streets. Points of interest include two churches, São Miguel and Misericórdia Velha, the latter a 16th-century structure with a notable doorway; and **Praça Velha**, also called Praça de Camões – a fine medieval square near the ancient municipal library.

The most important thing to see in Castelo Branco is the splendid **Palácio Episcopal**, built on the orders of the Bishop of Guarda, in 1596. It served as the winter residence of the bishops of the diocese. It now houses the **Museu Francisco Tavares Proença Júnior**, which displays archaeological and regional items, but is most interesting for its large collection of *colchas*, the beautiful hand-embroidered bedspreads for which the town is famous.

In 1725, Bishop João de Mendonça commissioned a **garden** to be laid out beside Castelo Branco's Palácio Episcopal. Although relatively small, it is considered one of Portugal's finest formal gardens, and is an extraordinary sight, with a multitude of statues, fountains and pools.

The statues have been placed in homage to just about everybody and everything the bishops thought important: the kings of Portugal, of course; the saints, Apostles and evangelists, along with the virtues; and the seasons of the year, the signs of the zodiac and the elements of the firmament. There were even more statues, but the invading French armies of 1807 carted off the best. The plinths have been left standing in their places, in many cases with the name of the missing item clearly engraved.

MONSANTO

From Castelo Branco it is easy to get to the small village of **Idanha-a-Velha** ⑭, northeast of the city. This was an episcopal see until 1199, when the see was moved to Guarda. There remains a strange, ancient basilica with dozens of Roman inscriptions inside. It is said that Wamba, the king of the Visigoths, was born here.

A Roman bridge in the village is still in use, and various coins, pottery and bones have been found.

Nearby is the granite village of **Monsanto** ⓯, once declared "the most typical Portuguese village", with many of its houses tucked between giant boulders. Built around and atop a steep rocky mass in a broad valley some 50km (30 miles) northeast of Castelo Branco, Monsanto sits in the middle of a major invasion route. Its intriguing castle commands a superlative view in every direction. It is thought that this *monte* has been fortified since Neolithic times, and the castle is so well integrated into the natural rock it looks as if it grew here.

Some say it was during the Roman invasion in the 2nd century BC, others claim it was some 1,400 years later during a Moorish invasion, that the people of Monsanto, under a long siege and nearly out of food, fooled their attackers by killing a calf, filling its belly with rice, and hurling it off the ramparts. The attackers were so impressed with the evidence of ample supplies that they packed up and left. One of the biggest feast days is on 3 May, when young villagers toss down pitchers filled with flowers from the battlements, symbolically re-enacting the event. Much of the castle was destroyed at the beginning of the 19th century. One Christmas Eve there was a tremendous thunderstorm, and a bolt of lightning hit the gunpowder magazine. The gunpowder exploded, and the irons flew from the hearth and struck dead the governor, an unpopular figure who that year had forbidden the traditional burning of a tree trunk in front of the parish church. Divine retribution, the people of the village believed.

The folk music of the Monsanto area is charming if strange. Half chanted, half sung, there is nothing quite like it elsewhere in the country. Its rhythm is beaten out with the assistance of a square tambourine known as an *adufe*.

The great Idanha plain stretches south from here, beyond Castelo Branco, where there are large areas of pine and eucalyptus. It is a vast area of cattle-raising country: bitterly cold in winter, scorching hot in the summer months, it is not a region that is much visited by tourists.

Idanha-a-Velha is one of the oldest towns in Portugal, but has a very small population.

A Roman settlement was recorded at Idanha-a-Velha in the first century.

⊙ COLCHAS

If you have been impressed by the beautiful linen bedspreads you saw in the museum, or those being made in the attached embroidery school, you might be inspired to buy a modern version to take home with you. Since the 17th century it has been the custom for brides-to-be to hand-embroider their wedding bedspreads. From this practice and skill, a cottage industry was born. Traditionally the spreads were white, but in recent years, they have become available in interwoven colours. Earlier patterns were geometric, echoing Persian carpets, but other decorative themes have become popular as well, including those showing flowers and birds. The intricate work involved means that a single item can take up to a year to complete, and prices are accordingly high.

A cobbled street in Porto.

PORTO

An evocative city on the Rio Douro, Porto's charms lie in its timeworn sun-baked buildings, vibrant riverfront cafés and ancient cobbled backstreets. The flipside is a thriving commercial centre and a lucrative port wine trade.

Porto ❶ is the commercial centre of northern Portugal, a fascinating city with a long and colourful history that is reflected in its culture, lifestyle and architecture. In many ways, Porto is a northern European city, with granite church towers, stolid dark buildings, and hidden Baroque treasures. But there is a real southern European feel here as well, particularly around the Ribeira *bairro*, where the narrow backstreets -hung with washing and studded with dusty, old-fashioned shops - have a hint of Naples about them.

Posed majestically on the rocky cliffs overlooking the Rio Douro, Porto is linked by six bridges to Vila Nova de Gaia, where most of the port wine lodges are located, fronted by their moored *barcos rabelos* (see page 265). These days, large ships dock at the seaport of Leixões, but coal barges, fishing trawlers and other small vessels still sail up the river, and a river trip is a great way to see the city. The climate in town is temperate, and the Portuenses, as the inhabitants are called, are traditionally industrious – as reflected in the well-known Portuguese saying: "Coimbra studies, Braga prays, Lisbon shows off and Porto works."

In Roman times, the twin cities at the mouth of the Douro were known as Portus on the right bank and Cale on the left. During the Moorish occupation, the entire region between the Minho and Douro rivers was called Portucale. When Afonso Henriques founded the new kingdom in 1143, he took the name of his home province and called it Portucalia.

Porto prospered from the seafaring exploits of the golden epoch of discoveries. Its shipyards, adapting Douro river *caravelas*, produced caravels that sailed around the world. Prince Henry the Navigator, who initiated and inspired Portuguese exploration, was born here.

Main attractions
Casa do Infante
Centro Português de Fotografia
Rua Santa Catarina
Port Wine Museum
Casa da Música
Port wine lodges

Maps on pages 260, 268

Driving over Dom Luís Bridge.

Café Majestic along Rua Santa Catarina.

THE WINE TRADE

In the 17th and 18th centuries, the wines of the Upper Douro were robust table reds. Then, in 1820, a "climatic accident" occurred, with warm weather producing unusually sweet grapes with a resulting sweet tipple: particularly appreciated by the British. In the following years, the wine companies added *aguardente*, or brandy, to stop the fermentation and fix the sugar content. This was the beginning of the sweet fortified wine so famed today. England's long connection with the city they called Oporto had been developing with the wine trade (see page 97). The Methuen Treaty of 1703 opened English markets to Portuguese wines, and the English shippers of Porto became increasingly rich and powerful. In 1727 they established a Shippers' Association, which regulated the trade and controlled prices paid to Portuguese growers. Thirty years later, to combat the English monopoly, the Marquês de Pombal founded the Alto Douro Wine Company. Today the business is organised and controlled by the city-based Port and Douro Wines Institute.

Porto is an energetic and lively commercial city with an individual taste in food and drink. Regional specialities include roast pork, fresh salmon, lamprey, trout and tripe. Some of the best and most popular bars and restaurants are by the river around Cais de Ribeira and in Vila Nova de Gaia opposite. You may hear the mournful style of music known as fado in a few restaurants, such as Mal Cozinhado at Rua Outerinho 13, while those seeking more vigorous nightlife should head for the Foz de Duoro district 4km (2 miles) downstream by the sea.

THE OLD CITY

The heart of the city is the **Praça da Liberdade** Ⓐ, with its central equestrian statue of Pedro IV. On the north side of the square is the broad Avenida dos Aliados, its bright flowerbeds covering part of the city's Metro, which opened in 2002. The avenue leads uphill to the **Câmara Municipal** Ⓑ (Town Hall) and the modern statue of Almeida Garrett (1799–1854), liberal poet and novelist, and native son of Porto.

To the southeast of Praça da Liberdade lies the Praça da Almeida Garrett, where the railway station, the **Estação São Bento** C, has a fine entrance hall decorated with traditional *azulejos* depicting historical scenes. From here you can catch a train for a journey along the Rio Douro to Pocinho.

Heading south, you'll arrive at the 12th-century **Sé** D (Catherdral; charge) was signed with England. The Gothic cloister is decorated with fine tiles, while the gilded wood. Just below, in the Medieval Tower, is a tourist office offering tours of the city and river (https://visitporto.travel). There is a good choice of options to suit various time frames and budgets; particularly the river trips, which start from a 50-minute cruise of the six bridges for €15.

Nearby on Pena Ventosa, the site of an ancient citadel, is the impressive 18th-century **Paço Episcopal** E (Episcopal Palace). Just beyond is the **Casa Museu de Guerra Junqueiro** F, in the house of the highly regarded poet of that name, who died in 1923. His memorabilia and furnishings are on display.

Across the avenue stands the 15th-century **Igreja Santa Clara** G (€4 entry), next to one of the best-preserved sections of the old city wall. Santa Clara has been rebuilt several times but is noted for its splendid gilded wood choir stalls and altars. Sacheverell Sitwell wrote: "After it, every other building in Porto, even São Francisco, is drab and dull."

To the west, the **Igreja São Lourenço** H (charge), better known as Igreja dos Grilos (after the nickname for the Jesuit saints that once lodged there), was built in 1570 and is one of the earliest examples of Portuguese Baroque design.

THE WESTERN SIDE

At the end of Rua Infante Dom Henrique stands a bastion of English life in Porto, the **Feitoria Inglesa** I (English Factory House; free). Here, the old British port-wine shippers do their business, play billiards or cards, read English newspapers and enjoy English food, as they have for the past 200 years. While visits are usually only possible on invitation, the Feitoria opens

Praça da Liberdade is considered the centre of Porto.

Azulejos adorning the walls of the Railway Station.

The well-known Sandeman silhouette is hard to avoid in Porto.

Colourful laundry on the line.

the doors to its ballroom, libraries and drawing rooms as part of the yearly Open House Porto festival.

Around the corner, on Rua da Alfândega, stands the much-restored **Casa do Infante** ❶ (charge, free on Sundays), where Prince Henry the Navigator was born in 1394. For a time it served as the customs house; it is now a museum with three floors of exhibits relating to the history of Porto's trade and industry. Also on display are the Roman foundations and mosaics discovered during excavation.

Going by the Praça do Infante Dom Henrique, you reach the **Igreja São Francisco** ❶, founded by King Sancho II in 1233 and rebuilt in the 14th century. The interior glitters in Baroque splendour with gilded columns, arches and statues. On the site of a convent, which burnt down in 1832, is the **Palácio da Bolsa** ❶ (Stock Exchange; guided tours 9am–6.30pm; charge), noted for its opulent reception hall. Up the hill is the **Instituto dos Vinhos do Douro e Porto** ❶ (Port and Douro Wines Institute), the government agency established in 1932 to control the quality of port. Tastings and tours are on offer, and there's also a wine shop.

Following the Rua Belmonte past old homes with balconies and tiled walls, you arrive at the church of **São João Novo** ❶ (free), built in 1539.

The road leads to the **Centro Português de Fotografia** ❶ (free), housed in a former prison and mainly showcasing the work of Scottish-born photographer Frederick William Flower (1815–89), who lived in Porto for most of his life.

Just beyond is the singular 18th-century **Torre dos Clérigos** ❶ (https://torredosclerigos.pt), the tallest granite tower in Portugal. This was designed, along with its church, by Nicolau Nasoni, who was also architect of the fine Baroque Solar de Mateus near Vila Real. Unless you really have no head for heights, it is worth climbing the 225 or so steps for the view over the city. Just north of the tower lies the main **university** building, a handsome granite structure built in 1807 as the Polytechnical Academy. Across the Praça do Lisboa on Rua das Carmelitas, the **Lello** library and bookshop should not be missed. Dating from 1906, the art nouveau building features a winding wooden staircase, bright red steps and a striking stained-glass ceiling. Rumour has it this arresting interior was an inspiration to J. K. Rowling, who frequented the shop during her time living in Porto.

East of São Bento railway station lies the busy square of **Praça da Batalha** ❶, with a statue of Pedro V in the middle, and the imposing 18th-century church of São Idelfonso with a facade of bright blue-and-white tiles. The main shopping street is **Rua Santa Catarina**, where bargains may be found in a variety of goods, from shoes to pottery. On the same street at no.112 is **Café Majestic**, famous not only for its excellent coffee but also for its beautiful interior: decorated in marble and wood and decked out with impressive mirrors, cherubs and chandeliers. It is still visited by the local elite. Rua das Flores is the spot for finding the best gold and silver shops.

CAIS DA RIBEIRA

Take the steep roads down to the river, and you will find yourself drawn to the **Cais da Ribeira** ®, one of the liveliest parts of the city and a UNESCO World Heritage Site. Many small shops and restaurants are built right into what remains of the old city wall, some showing watermarks around 2 metres (6ft) from the floor where the river has burst its banks. During the day you can take a river trip from here, and in the evening its restaurants brim with customers. Ten minutes' walk downriver brings you to the *electrico* stop, a tram that goes out to Castelo de Queijo on the coast.

The splendid steel arch further upriver is a railway bridge, **Ponte de Dona Maria Pia**, built in 1876 to plans by Alexandre Gustave Eiffel and only recently put out of use by the new Ponte São João. In the centre of Porto is the handsome **Ponte Dom Luís I** ⓢ, built in 1886, which provides splendid views. This two-storey iron bridge has two decks, the lower of which is restricted to public transport, taxis, pedestrians and cyclists, and leads directly to port cellars in Vila Nova de Gaia (see page 264).

OUTSIDE THE OLD TOWN

On the western side of the city, in the old royal Palácio dos Carrancas, is the **Museu Nacional Soares dos Reis** ⓣ, named after a 19th-century sculptor. It has a fine collection of archaeological artefacts, religious art, regional costumes, ceramics and contemporary paintings, as well as sculpture. Paintings by Grão Vasco are on display, among them pictures of St Catherine and St Lucy.

On the western side of the Jardim do Palácio de Cristal (entered from Rua Entre Quintas) is the intriguing **Museu Romântico** Ⓤ (€2.20 entry, free on weekends), which recreates and evokes the life of the Portuguese 19th-century bourgeoisie. It's located in the Quinta da

Porto is often called the invincible city, because of its resistance against Napoleon during the Peninsular War.

Casa da Música is the major concert space in Portugal.

> **Fact**
>
> On the Festa de São João (23–24 June), festivities take place near the Ponte Dom Luís I. There is a regatta of the port-wine boats, with singing, dancing around bonfires and feasting on roast kid and grilled sardines – and a tradition of hitting each other over the head with plastic hammers.

Macieirinha, where King Carlo Alberto died in exile in 1843 after abdicating the throne of Sardinia. The mansion is set in a rose garden and contains most of its original furnishings.

North of here, via Rua de Don Pedro V, is the splendid **Casa da Música**. Designed by top Dutch architect Rem Koolhaas, this ultra-modern geometric building has an extraordinary interior space. Regular concerts are staged here, ranging from fado to classical music, but the building may also be visited and appreciated for its innovative architecture and interior design.

To the northwest, in Boavista, is the Art Deco **Casa de Serralves**, set in an attractive 18-hectare (44-acre) estate. The mansion holds a wide and eclectic range of temporary modern art exhibitions. In the grounds also lies the stunning **Museu de Arte Contemporânea** (hours as above), designed by Porto architect Alvaro Siza Vieira, which has both permanent and temporary exhibitions. As well as a large, light exhibition space, the building comprises an auditorium, a restaurant and a library.

PORT WINE LODGES

Porto is best known for being the home of port. A drink which has made something of a comeback in recent years, it's shedding its previous stuffy image as primarily a gentleman's after-dinner drink to be enjoyed with a fat cigar.

Vila Nova de Gaia, across the Ponte Dom Luís I, is an industrial zone with ceramic, glass, soap and other factories. But above all, Gaia is the true seat of the port wine industry, where most warehouses or lodges are to be found. There are about 80 port wine lodges here: many of the larger ones welcome weekday visitors to tour the installations and, better still, taste their wines (which most visitors will then purchase). Most prominent is Sandeman, whose distinctive silhouette, designed in 1928, rises definitively against the skyline.

Another good choice is British-owned **Taylor's** (http://taylor.pt). The port wine lodges line the waterfront and fly their flags from *barcos rabelos* moored alongside.

In spring, the new wine is brought down from the Upper Douro by truck, and is then left to mature in 530-litre (140-gallon) oak casks, or pipes. Here the blending takes place, with wines from different vineyards and different years blended to produce a distinctive aroma, taste and colour before the wine is bottled and again left to mature.

In the evening, many people cross the bridge to eat and enjoy a great view of the city opposite. Apart from traditional restaurants, at the far end of the quay there is a wide choice of places to eat and drink in the modern riverside Cais de Gaia complex, with terraces and river views.

For unrivalled panoramas of the city and the river, take the **Gaia Cable Car** (www.gaiacablecar.com), which links Gaia riverside promenade with the Jardim do Morro (upper station). A single adult ticket currently costs €7 (€10 return).

The azulejos-rich exterior of Igreja do Carmo, a Carmelite church.

BARCOS RABELOS

> The *barcos rabelos* have become a symbol of port wine, the product with whose destiny they have been entwined for hundreds of years.

On his return to Lisbon after discovering the sea route to India in 1498, Vasco da Gama proclaimed *"Somos a gente do mar"* (We are the people of the sea). Using small, light, high-prowed caravel sailing ships based on an ancient Mediterranean design, 15th- and 16th-century Portuguese explorers voyaged the world and Portugal became the greatest maritime nation on earth. Of course, the nation was largely responsible for initiating the trans-Atlantic slave trade, forcibly displacing African men, women and children to work on plantations across Brazil and the Caribbean.

By the late 16th century, Portugal had lost its monopoly on the slave trade thanks to fierce Dutch, French, Spanish and British competition. As Portugal retreated into centuries of introspection, the boat-building techniques and traditions left by ancient mariners were retained.

VIKING INFLUENCES

In traditional *barco rabelo* building the hull's shell is laid first, then the ribs are placed. This is the Nordic "clinker-building" method, which may be a direct Viking legacy; a comparison between the bare hull of a *rabelo* and that of a reconstructed longboat in Oslo's Viking Museum shows striking similarities. Other features of the *rabelo's* design evolved in the 17th century, the nascent period of the trade in port wine. Ever since then, the grapes for port have been grown in the upper reaches of the Douro Valley, from where the wine is transported to Vila Nova de Gaia for shipment abroad. The adapted indigenous boats of the Douro were constructed in large numbers and put to this use on the treacherous river, stacked with casks of wine. Flat bottoms were needed to shoot the rapids, negotiate the shallows, and achieve high loading ratios. A tall platform at the stern gave the helmsman a clear view over the rows of casks, and a huge steering oar, or *espadela* – effectively a rudder – was needed to change course rapidly. This also had to be capable of being levered out of the water to avoid smashing boats in the rapids and rocky shallows. Intrepid boatmen slept and ate on board, suspending cauldrons from a beam to boil their *bacalhau* (dried cod).

The damming of the Douro for hydroelectric power brought an end to the *rabelo's* interdependence with the port trade. But although port now makes the journey from the Upper Douro by road, the *rabelo* has proved an irrepressible symbol of the product. Boats are still constructed, at great expense, to compete in the annual race of *rabelos* owned by the port-shipping firms. The enthusiastically contested regatta is held on 24 June, the festival of São João (Porto's patron saint), when the city erupts in revelry. Boats set off from the mouth of the Douro.

The set of rules ensuring that the *rabelos* are constructed precisely according to the specifications evolved during their heyday is taken very seriously. The craft have to be built in yards along the Douro, with the hull constructed from maritime pine, and laid down by the "clinker-building" technique. The largest *rabelos* are around 24 metres (80ft) long by 5.5 metres (18ft) wide with 80 sq metres (860 sq ft) of sail billowing in the wind, and need at least a dozen crew members to operate. Payloads are up to 65 casks, each holding 522 litres (138 gallons) of port.

The regatta proves that the boats are more than advertisements for their owners' wares.

Boats along the Douro river.

The city of Amarante, on the Rio Tâmega.

THE DOURO VALLEY

Renowned worldwide for the wine it produces, the Douro Valley is graced by centuries-old vineyards growing on steeply terraced hillsides.

The history of port wine has endowed the Douro region with romance and respect. Douro means "of gold" and the river, gleaming at sunset, does resemble a twisting golden chain as it winds through the narrow valley between the steep hills and terraced vineyards. The countryside is exceptionally beautiful, particularly in spring and autumn, and is enhanced by the neat rows of vines which furnish the hillsides.

Although the Douro stretches from Spain to the Atlantic at Porto, only the inland part of the valley, the Alto Douro, is recognised for growing the grapes used for port wine. The demarcated region starts some 100km (60 miles) upstream from Porto at Barqueiros, just before Régua, and follows the river all the way to Spain. Some of the tributaries of the Douro – the Corgo, Torto, Pinhão and Tua – are included in the area. It was Portugal's authoritarian Marquês de Pombal who staked out the Douro in 1756, making it the first officially designated wine-producing region in the world. Subsequent legislation designated the Upper Douro as the port wine region.

Characteristically, the schistose soils are stony and impoverished and the climate extreme. Summers are very hot and dry, and made hotter by the direct rays of the sun reflected on the crystalline rock; winters are cold and wet. The large lumps of surface schist act as storage heaters, absorbing the sun's heat in the day and releasing it throughout the night. The slopes nearest to the river grow the finest grapes and this land is thus highly prized.

CHOOSING A BASE

Peso da Régua (see page 270) is the capital of the Douro Valley, with an office of the Port Wine Institute; it is also the headquarters of the port-growers' association, which grades and

Main attractions
Amarante
Quinta da Aveleda
Lamego
Parque Arqueológico do Vale Côa
Mateus
Vila Real

Map on page 268

Amarante's historic bridge.

PLACES

> **Tip**
> Cycling and walking enthusiasts can take on the scenic 9.3km (5.8-mile) Tâmega Line Ecotrack which runs on the abandoned railway line between Amarante and Chapa stations, very close to the Tâmega River.

certifies the wine travelling to Porto. The smaller town of Pinhão 25km (15 miles) further upstream is regarded as the centre of the wine industry, and this is where all the famous names have their farms. It is a handy place to stay, although it is hardly bristling with hotels.

Taylor's (a distinguished port house) have restored and extended a *quinta* on the banks of the Douro, now the Vintage House Hotel, providing quality accommodation. The area has a number of restored houses and farms that are part of the manor house system (see page 121), some of them in very fine locations.

Casa de Casal de Loivos, above Pinhão, has a fine overview of the Douro or, if you prefer to bury yourself in the country, Casa da Lavada, a restored 14th-century fortified manor house, provides modern comforts. It is high in the mountains of the Serra do Marão, in a village where visitors are still a curiosity. Traditional hotels are found in the surrounding towns of Amarante, Vila Real or Lamego. **Porto** ❶ is a good base for organised trips into the surrounding area. Coach trips are well advertised but it is easy enough to catch a train from São Bento station on the Douro line. The end of the line is Pocinho, not too far from the Spanish border. There are branch lines to Amarante, Vila Real and Mirandela.

The river is now navigable for much of its length and boat trips up the river are a regular feature and a pleasant way to see the countryside. One option is to go by boat as far as Pinhão and return by train.

UPRIVER FROM PORTO

There is little to detain the motorist between Porto and Amarante so the fast A4 is the best way to travel. It speeds up what would otherwise be a very slow journey through *vinho verde*-growing countryside. The main area for *vinho verde* lies to the north in Costa Verde and Minho.

Amarante ❷, on the banks of the Rio Tâmega, is delightful, at least in the old part of town. Geese paddle contentedly among punts and trailing willow trees on the river, while afternoon tea-takers look on from overhanging wooden balconies. Dominant in the town is the three-arched **Ponte de São Gonçalo**, built in 1790. It became a battleground in the Peninsular War in 1809 when General Silveira, supported by Marshal Beresford's troops, successfully fought off the French.

The bridge leads to the **Igreja e Mosteirode São Gonçalo** (daily 9am–5pm; free), named after the local patron saint and protector of marriages.

Amarante's association with fertility rites reaches back into the mists of time, and some claim the town's name is derived from *amar*, meaning "to love". These ancient beliefs have empowered São Gonçalo, beatified in 1561, to assist believers in everything pertaining to love and marriage. He is honoured every June by a festival which, as you may imagine, is a particularly raucous occasion, with the local men out in the streets offering distinctly phallic-shaped cakes to any women prepared to accept them.

The convent, however, is much more sombre. It was begun in 1540 but not completed until 1620. Inside is the tomb of São Gonçalo, who died in about 1260, and some lush gilded carved woodwork. Anyone aspiring to love and marriage need only touch the effigy of the saint to be blessed within the year. Sadly, the limestone figure is now quite worn in places.

Above the rear cloister is the **Museu Amadeo de Souza-Cardoso** (www.amadeosouza-cardoso.pt; June–Sept Tue–Sun 10am–12.30pm, 2–6pm, Oct–May Tue–Sun 9.30am–12.30pm, 2–5.30pm; €4 entry), which has some superb contemporary and Modernist Portuguese paintings – Souza-Cardoso was a Cubist artist who came from Amarante.

Nearby is the **Quinta da Aveleda** (https://fareharbor.com/embeds/book/quintadaaveleda; visits upon prior booking only), seat of one of Portugal's main wine empires and a leading exporter of the country's famous *vinho verde*. A visit to the *quinta* includes a tour of the beautiful gardens, as well as the bottling plant. At the wine lodge you can

> **Fact**
> Boat trips on the river are privately run and therefore not promoted through tourist offices. Trips last from a few hours to a few days, and most hotels and quintas will tell you what's on offer.

THE DOURO VALLEY | 269

> **Tip**
>
> The best time to visit the Douro Valley is during the *vindima*, in September, when the grapes are being collected. Some vineyards give tourists the chance to participate in the grape harvest, joining in with the picking and then trampling the fruit barefoot in the pressing basins to release the juice.

taste two different types of *vinho verde*, accompanied by local cheese, and buy a bottle or a case from the old distillery, which has now been converted to a store.

Beyond Amarante the road turns abruptly south to twist and climb through the Serra do Marão. *Vinho verde* vines climb the trees here and huge granite tors stand in the summit region. Beyond is a descent to the small village of **Mesão Frio** ③, and a sweeping view of the Upper Douro winding peacefully through the gorges of the wine country.

The road follows the river's north bank, passing through the small spa town of **Caldas de Moledo** before reaching **Régua** ④ (its full name is Peso da Régua), a busy river port and the headquarters of the **Casa do Douro**, an organisation that has a great deal of power in the regulation of wine production. Located in a converted manor house close to the waterfront, the nearby **Museo do Douro** (www.museudodouro.pt; daily Mar–Oct 10am–6pm; Nov–Feb until 5.30pm; €7 entry) offers an excellent introduction to this UNESCO heritage region, its culture and people. The museum comprises an exhibition area, a documentation centre, an archive, a library, and a reading room, as well as a restaurant, a shop and a wine bar where you can taste some of the best Douro wines. In this area lie some of the oldest British and Portuguese estates, and information about them can be had from both the Casa do Douro and the tourist office near the market. Here the road crosses the Douro and runs along the picturesque southern bank.

SOUTH OF THE RIVER

Before following the south bank towards Pinhão, there is a worthwhile diversion to **Lamego** ⑤, which is a city of historical importance. The Lusitanians arose in revolt against the occupying Romans, refusing to pay the heavy taxation, so the Romans burned the town to the ground. Fernando of León and Castile took the city, aided by the legendary El Cid, and allowed the Muslim *wali* to continue to govern

Nossa Senhora dos Remédios church.

> **PILGRIMAGE CHURCH**
>
> Atop Lamego's other hill is the visually striking church of **Nossa Senhora dos Remédios,** crowning a vast stairway reminiscent of Braga's Bom Jesus. The first chapel was founded by the Bishop of Lamego in 1361, and dedicated to St Stephen. In 1564, it was pulled down, and a new one built. From that time, there has been a steady stream of the faithful seeking cures. The first week in September is the time of the major pilgrimage, and there is a jolly accompanying festival which seems to have little to do with healing or piety. The present sanctuary was started in 1750, and was consecrated 11 years later – but the magnificent Baroque-style staircase leading up to it, begun in the 19th century, was completed only in the 1960s. Fountains, statues and pavilions decorate each level.

Lamego, as long as he converted and paid tribute to the king. But the city's most significant moment in Portugal's history was in 1143, when the *cortes* (representatives of the realm) met for the very first time. At this meeting, the nobles declared Afonso Henriques to be Afonso I, the first king of Portugal.

Lamego's 12th-century castle, on one of the city's two hills, preserves a fine 13th-century keep, with windows that were added later and a very old and unusual vaulted cistern. The cistern is possibly Moorish, with monograms of master masons.

The **Sé** (Cathedral; daily 8am–12.30pm, 2.30–7pm), a Gothic structure, was built by Afonso Henriques in 1129. Only the Romanesque tower is left from the original building. The city museum, housed in the 18th-century Bishop's Palace, has a collection that includes Flemish tapestries dating from the 16th century and works by Grão Vasco.

Just outside Lamego (start on the Tarouca road), in the valley of the Rio Balsemão, is the tiny **São Pedro de Balsemão** ❻, a Visigothic church believed to be the oldest in Portugal, with parts of the structure dating back as far as the 6th century.

Following the south bank of the Douro towards Pinhão is a rewarding drive; you can enjoy the flowing lines of vineyards patterning the hillsides, broken only by signs displaying such well-known names as Sandeman, Barros and Quinta Dona Matilde.

Pinhão ❼, on the north side of the river, seems an unlikely town to lie at the heart of the wine region. It is worth a stop at the railway station to see the *azulejo* panels depicting scenes of the Rio Douro or to taste some wine in the barrel-shaped café by the river. The tourist office (57 Rua António Manuel Saraiva; tel: 254 731 059) has information about the wine estates in the region. For more insight, the **Quinta Nova Nossa Senhora do Carmo**, a hotel and winery that also contains a museum offering guided tours, boasts a collection of old tools used for wine production and plenty of information on the traditional techniques of winemaking. Tasting of some local wines is included in the ticket price.

A SCENIC CIRCULAR TOUR

A tasty sampler of typical Douro scenery and traditional villages can be enjoyed on a short circular tour from Pinhão, taking around half a day. It starts on the south side of the river, along the road climbing the hillside to **São João da Pasqueira** ❽. This village has some fine 18th-century houses mixed with surprisingly modern properties.

Follow left-turns signposted Barragem de Valeira to drive through dilapidated, overgrown vineyards ravaged by the Phylloxera scourge in the 19th century and never replanted. Watch out on the descent towards the *barragem* (reservoir) for the pointed hill, **São Salvador do Mundo** ❾, which is littered with churches and chapels.

Tall, colourful houses in the town of Lamego.

Azulejos (tile painting) in Nossa Senhora dos Remédios, Lamego.

> **Tip**
>
> For an innovative blend of traditional dishes and nouvelle cuisine, head to Cêpa Torta restaurant in Alijó (www.facebook.com/restaurante.cepatorta).

Around where the **Barragem de Valeira** ❿ now stands is where Baron Forrester, the 19th-century English pioneer, lost his life in 1861: in those days the river here tumbled over dangerous rapids. Born in Hull in 1809, Joseph James Forrester came out to Portugal as a young man to work for his uncle in Porto. He was fascinated by the wine industry and spent many years boating up and down the river making a detailed map. His widely acclaimed work won him his title in 1855, the first foreigner to earn such an honour. It was the river that eventually claimed his life at the age of 51. He was out boating with Antónia Adelaide Ferreira and others when they ran into trouble at the Cachão de Valeira rapids. The boat capsized and Baron Forrester drowned; dragged down, it is said, by the weight of his money belt. Antónia Adelaide Ferreira survived, helped by the buoyancy of her crinoline dress.

Cross the *barragem* to regain the north shore and zigzag up the hillside towards Linhares. Vineyards make striking patterns and create the scenery for much of the way towards Tua and Alijó. **Alijó** ⓫ is one of the bigger towns in the area and is the location of a *pousada* named after Baron Forrester. The route back heads through Favaios to Pinhão.

ROCK ART

Winding eastwards from Pinhão through **São João da Pasqueira** and along the hill contours, past quaint churches and villages, you will come to Vila Nova de Foz Côa and the valley of the Rio Côa. Work in the 1990s to build a dam in this remote region uncovered a remarkable collection of rock engravings.

In 1996 the Portuguese Government declared the Côa Valley protected as the **Parque Arqueológico do Vale Côa** ⓬ (www.arte-coa.pt; tel: 279 768 260; Mar–May daily 9am–5.30pm, June–Sept until 7pm, Oct–Feb Tue–Sun 9am–5.30pm; visits must be reserved in advance). In 1998, the park, which has the largest area of palaeolithic engravings in Europe, was declared a UNESCO World Heritage Site.

Historical re-enactors dress up for a medieval festival in Lamego.

At present, only three rock-art sites in the valley can be visited, not by individuals, but on a guided tour with a vehicle. These are at Penascosa, Ribeira de Piscos, Canada do Inferno and Fariseu (seasonal). The tours all last around 90 minutes. Tours to Canada do Inferno start from the Museu do Côa; tours to Ribeira de Piscos start from the visitor centre at **Muxagata** ⓭; while tours to Penascosa leave from the reception centre in **Castelo Melhor** ⓮.

The stunning Museu do Côa (same hours as the park) stands in the middle of nowhere like an installation in the landscape. The museum houses cutting-edge displays on the rock art, as well as temporary exhibitions, and has a restaurant with wonderful views over the park.

NORTH TO VILA REAL

Going from Pinhão to the north leads to **Sabrosa** ⓯, the birthplace of Fernão de Magalhães, known in English as Ferdinand Magellan, the man who led the first circumnavigation of the world between 1519 and 1522 under the Spanish flag. Just before Constantim, look out on the right for a diversion to the sanctuary of **Panóias** ⓰ where there is a field with a series of enormous carved stones, believed to have been used as altars for human sacrifice. Inscriptions in Latin invoke the ancient god Serapis, known to both Greek and Egyptian mythology.

Beyond Constantim but before Vila Real is the village and fantastical palace of **Mateus** ⓱ (www.casademateus.com; daily 9am–6pm) with its celebrated gardens. It was built by Nicolau Nasoni in 1739–43 for António José Botelho Mourão. Today, an illustration of the palace graces the distinctive label of the popular rosé wine from this area, even though there is no formal connection.

Mateus Rosé is still Portugal's best-selling wine export, with distribution in more than 150 countries. The exquisite building, with its striking Baroque facade, double stairway and huge coat of arms, frequently hosts musical events.

Azulejo is a tin-glazed, ceramic tilework that has become a hallmark of Portugal.

Vineyards along the Douro River.

> **Fact**
>
> Pressure to stop the flooding of the Côa Valley included a rap song recorded by high-school students from Vila Nova de Foz Côa, with the line "Petroglyphs can't swim". Although the dam project was abandoned in 1995, many carvings had already been submerged by the construction of the Pocinho dam in 1982.

VILA REAL

An ancient settlement in the Terra de Panóias, **Vila Real** ⑱ was founded and renamed by King Dinis in 1289. Its name, "royal town", is appropriate, as Vila Real once had more noble families than any city other than the capital. Walking through ancient streets, you will see many residences marked, often above the main entrance, with the original owners' coats of arms. As likely as not, descendants of the family will still be living there.

The 19th-century writer Camilo Castelo Branco lived in Vila Real and wrote many of his most enduring works using the town as a backdrop.

Vila Real became a city proper only in 1925, but the importance of the region dates from 1768, when the vineyards were developed commercially: the area has good red and white wines, but it is the rosé that is best known – especially Mateus. Now a lively bustling industrial centre, Vila Real is one of the largest towns in the region.

The **Sé** (Cathedral) was originally the church of a Dominican convent. Although much of the present building dates from the 14th century, Romanesque columns still remain from an earlier structure. The oldest church is the ancient **Capela de São Nicolau**, on a promontory of high land behind the municipal hall, overlooking the valley of the Rio Corgo. Another church of note is **São Pedro**, whose Baroque touches were completed by Nicolau Nasoni (1691–1773), the Tuscan-born architect who designed the manor house in Mateus. Among fine houses dating from the 15th–18th centuries is the **Casa de Diogo Cão**, an Italian Renaissance-style building that was the birthplace of Cão, the navigator who discovered the mouth of the River Congo in 1482.

As far as local crafts are concerned, the Vila Real region is noted for the black pottery of Bisalhães and the woollen goods of Caldas do Alvão and Marão. The **Jardim Botânico da UTAD** (http://jb.utad.pt; Mon–Sat 9am–6pm) is one of the largest botanical gardens in Europe, and offers a relaxing walk for those who prefer natural gems.

Steam train chugging along over the Douro Valley.

Selling baked goods at the market in Amarante.

PORT WINE, THE DOURO'S TREASURE

The story of port wine is one of triumph over adversity. From bare, inhospitable terrain came an extraordinary wine that is famed the world over.

Upstream from Porto lies the country's most inhospitable region. Dry and stony, with barely a covering of dusty soil and with excessively high summer temperatures, combined with months of drought, the Upper Douro seems an unlikely area to have emerged as a global producer of world-famous port wine.

Covering a vast area of some 243,000 hectares (600,000 acres) with around 15 percent covered by vines, the history of port production has its roots in a modest cottage industry where the discerning locals were producing exceptionally high-quality wine for their own use. Exploiting the region to produce wine in commercial quantities was beset by huge problems, but it seemed that every disadvantage, every deterrent, contributed to its success. The soil, or rather the lack of it, was just one. Vines planted into the schist (rock) sent their roots searching deep down through the cracks and crevices to find water. The vast root system that developed allowed the plants to survive burning summers without irrigation, thus yielding grapes high in sugar.

The pre-dammed Rio Douro, steep banked and virtually unnavigable, was another apparent drawback that proved essential to the region's success, for without it there would have been no means of exporting the wine. Grapes harvested at the steep higher levels were transported to the split-level factories below, and the resulting wine was then lowered to the river for transport on the distinctive flat-bottomed *barcos rabelos*.

More than 80 varieties of grape have been used in port wine but modern plantings are limited to about six varieties.

Teams, mainly of women, spread along the rows and sweep systematically across the vineyard; strong young men carry away the baskets. The close-packed vineyards create geometric green patterns on the hillsides, transforming the rolling landscapes of this region.

In the Douro region, there are still port producers who crush their grapes by the traditional method: by foot.

Enjoying a glass.

Bringing in the harvest

The Upper Douro is a pleasure to visit at any point during the summer, but harvest time is the most rewarding. The harvest *(vindima)* usually starts towards the end of September – the exact date being dictated by the conditions of any particular year – and by this time temperatures have cooled to a pleasant heat.

In spite of recent mechanisation, grape picking is still largely done by hand. Extended families of itinerant workers from surrounding villages often return year after year to the same farms to bring in the harvest. Traditionally, men and women adopt different roles in the field, but they all come together at meal times. Lunch is almost party time: the estate owners provide an abundant meal and the pickers relax and enjoy it.

When the mood is right, and with a contented team of workers, the sound of singing can be heard emanating from the vine terraces. It is a time of great celebration, of relief that the crop has survived the vagaries of the weather and of thanksgiving for a harvest, even in years when it is not at its most bountiful.

Port casks.

The flat-bottomed rabelos, designed to suit the shallow waters of the Douro, carry the port barrels downriver.

Grapes from an Alentejo vineyard.

Bom Jesus do Monte Monastery, Braga.

COSTA VERDE AND THE MINHO

Verdant and lush, this is a land of vineyards, tranquil riverside towns, busy markets, and a great European wilderness: the Peneda-Gerês National Park.

The Minho region north of Porto is often described as Costa Verde, or the Green Coast, a reference to the vineyards and lush green of its well-watered landscape. In reality it is a much larger area than just the coast. It extends northwards to the Rio Minho, the boundary with Spain, eastwards to include the Parque Nacional da Peneda-Gerês and south to encompass Braga and Guimarães. It is a region of great natural beauty, especially the verdant Lima Valley and the wild and mountainous Peneda-Gerês, where farming techniques and lifestyles pass from generation to generation with relatively little change.

Grapes are grown everywhere. They hang from trees, pergolas and porches, and climb along slopes and terraces. They grow in poor rocky soil where little else flourishes. To get the most out of the land, the Minhotos train their vines to grow upwards, on trees, houses and hedges, leaving ground space for cabbages, onions and potatoes. This free-wheeling system made it difficult to modernise grape production, but for many years the larger vineyards have been using a system of wire-supporting crosses called *cruzetas*.

The *vindima*, or grape harvest, is still done by hand and is a wonderful sight to behold. Harvesting takes place in September and October and lasts until early November. It can be a hazardous task, requiring towering 30-rung ladders to get at the elusive treetop grapes, although most vines now are trained at tractor height. In the hilly country, men still carry huge baskets of grapes weighing as much as 50kg (110lb) on their backs. On some back roads, squeaky ox-carts transport the grapes to wine-presses. In these modern times, however, the fruit is generally transported in trucks.

While harvest is still a festive occasion, it no longer involves quite the

Main attractions
Braga
Barcelos
Viana do Castelo
Vila do Conde
Peneda-Gerês National Park
Ponte de Lima
MIEC

Map on page 280

Decorations for the Braga folklore festival.

> **Tip**
>
> The Comissão de Viticultura da Região dos Vinhos Verdes in Porto can provide information on *vinho verde* wine routes and estates to visit (http://rota.vinhoverde.pt).

unbridled merrymaking of yore. In the old days, workers used to perform a kind of bacchanalian dance, their arms linked, stamping on the grapes with their bare feet. It was said that this was the only way to crush the fruit without smashing the pips and spoiling the flavour of the wine. This was often accompanied by music and clapping, glasses of spirits and a good deal of sweat. Nowadays, mechanical extractors often remove the pips, and presses are generally used to crush the grapes, although treading still takes place in a few vineyards.

There is a second style of agriculture here which is even more distinctive and unique to this region of Portugal. It is known as dune agriculture, and involves digging small depressions in the actual sand dunes, which then capture the moisture from the sea mist and protect the crops from the sometimes strong winds. These sandy allotments are traditionally fertilised by dried seaweed, which many people believe contributes to the consistently high quality of the produce that is grown here. The seaweed is harvested in early autumn, collected by enormous nets and then spread out to dry in the sunshine.

BRAGA

Some people still refer to **Braga** ❶ somewhat wistfully, as "the Portuguese Rome". In Roman times, as Bracara Augusta, it was the centre of communications in north Lusitania. In the 6th century two synods were held here. Under Moorish occupation, Braga was sacked and the cathedral badly damaged, but in the 11th century the city was largely restored to its former eminence by Bishop Dom Pedro and Archbishop São Geraldo. The archbishop claimed authority over all the churches of the Iberian peninsula, and his successors retained the title of Primate of the Spains for six centuries.

Like a Renaissance prince, one of his successors, Archbishop Dom Diogo de Sousa, encouraged the construction of many handsome Italian-style churches, fountains and palaces in the 16th century. Zealous prelates restored many of these works in the subsequent two centuries, but often with unfortunate results. Braga lost its title as ecclesiastical capital in 1716, when the patriarchate went to Lisbon. But it is still an important religious centre, and the site of Portugal's most elaborate Holy Week procession.

A visit to Braga usually begins at the **Sé** (Cathedral; www.se-braga.pt, which was built in the 11th century on the site of an earlier structure destroyed by the Moors. Of the original Romanesque building there remains only the southern portal and the sculpted cornice of the transept. Although it has been greatly modified by various restorations, the cathedral is still imposing. The interior contains some fine tombs, including those of the founders, Count Henri and his wife Teresa, a granite sculpture of the Virgin, an 18th-century choir loft and organ case, and richly decorated chapels and cloister.

Of particular interest is the **Tesouro da Catedral** (Cathedral Treasury), with a fine collection of 15th-century vestments and silver chalices and crucifixes dating from the 10th and 12th centuries.

Nearby, with plain west walls set off by an 18th-century fountain, is the **Paço Arquiepiscopal** (Archbishop's Court), built in the 14th century and reconstructed several times. The palace now houses the Public Library, with city archives dating back to the 9th century and comprising 300,000 volumes and 10,000 manuscripts. On the western side of Praça Agrolongo stands one of Braga's Rome-inspired churches, **Nossa Senhora do Pópulo**, built in the 17th century and remodelled at the end of the 18th. It is decorated with *azulejos* depicting scenes from the life of St Augustine.

The **Museudos Biscainhos** (www.visitportugal.com/en/content/museu-dos-biscainhos) just across the way is a 17th-century mansion with lovely gardens and fountains. It houses the municipal museum with an impressive collection that includes 18th-century tiles, ceramics, jewellery and furniture.

The city has been digging into its past in recent years and uncovered such riches as Roman baths, a sanctuary called Fonte do Idolo and the remains of a house: Domus de Santiago. An archaeological museum, the **Museu de Arqueologia D. Diogo de**

Splendid wooden doorway of Braga Cathedral.

Funicular to the monastery, Braga.

Sousa (www.visitportugal.com/en/content/museu-d-diogo-de-sousa) displays these finds, with fascinating exhibits including mosaic flooring dating from the 1st century AD. The museum is a short walk from the ruins of the above-mentioned **Termas Romanas** (http://bragaromana.cm-braga.pt), dating from the 2nd century AD.

Five minutes' walk east of the Sé is the gorgeous blue *azulejo*-tiled **Raio Palace**, the 18th-century home of merchant João Duarte de Faria. In 2015 the house re-opened as the **Centro Interpretativo Memórias da Misericórdia de Braga** (www.scmbraga.pt/cimmb-palácio-do-raio), a museum housing sacred art, sculpture, ceramics and jewellery.

BOM JESUS

There are many other churches and chapels of interest in the centre, but the best known is **Santuário Bom Jesus** ❷ (http://bomjesus.pt; free) which is conspicuously set on the wooded Monte Espinho, about 5km (3 miles) outside Braga. This popular pilgrimage centre is remarkable for its grandiose Baroque stairway and the view from its terrace of the Rio Cávado valley with the mountains in the distance. The double flight of stairs is flanked by chapels, fountains and often startlingly bizarre figures at each level, representing the Stations of the Cross.

If you don't wish to climb the steps, there is a funicular (daily 9am–8pm, until 7pm in winter) and a winding road to the top. There, among oak trees, eucalyptus, camellias and mimosa, stands the 15th-century church, rebuilt in the 18th century. In its **Capela dos Milagres** (Chapel of Miracles) are votive offerings and pictures left by past pilgrims. Several hotels, souvenir shops and restaurants are also located in the vicinity of the sanctuary.

BARCELOS: COCK AND BULL

Just northwest of Braga is the charming market town of **Barcelos** ❸, on the north bank of the Rio Cávado. Barcelos has 15th-century fortifications, a 13th-century church and a 16th-century palace, but more than that, it has one of the best markets in the country.

Feeding the hens.

Traditional dancing in Viana do Castelo.

Every Thursday, traders and artisans display their crafts, textiles and other goods in the centre of town. There are also plenty of food stalls to ensure you won't go hungry.

It was here that the late Rosa Ramalho, the most famous folk-art sculptress in Portugal, created her world of fanciful ceramic animals and people – a style that has been continued by her granddaughter. Head to the **Feira de Artesanato** to browse local crafts including copperware, handmade rugs, wooden toys, bright cotton tableware, and, of course, the *galo de Barcelos* – the ubiquitous Barcelos cockerel.

A monument, the so-called Senhor do Galo cross, is the most apt reminder of the extraordinary legend that lies behind the rooster's elevation to Portugal's unofficial national emblem (see page 221). There is an excellent pottery museum, the **Museu de Olaria** (www.museuolaria.pt), featuring traditional ceramics and pottery from all over the country, including the Azores.

VIANA DO CASTELO

A lively fishing and shipbuilding port at the mouth of the Rio Lima, **Viana do Castelo** ❹ was called Diana by the Romans. This was the centre of Portugal's wine trade until the port declined in the 18th century and Porto became pre-eminent. There is a good deal to see in the centre of Viana, as well as beyond: the town is home to several of the region's most enticing sweeps of sand. In the central Praça da República there is a beautiful 16th-century fountain and the remarkable Misericórdia hospital, with a three-tiered facade supported by caryatids.

There is also a museum here, the **Museu do Traje** (Costume Museum), with two floors of colourful traditional costumes. Nearby stands the handsome 15th-century parish church with a Gothic portal and Romanesque towers.

The town is dominated by **Monte Santa Luzia** ❺, home to a flamboyant 20th-century church built in Byzantine style. To get here, hop on the funicular railway (Jan–Feb and Nov–Dec Tue–Fri 10am–noon and 1–5pm, Sat–Sun 10am–5pm, Mar–May and Oct Mon–Fri 10am–noon and 1–5pm, Sat–Sun 9am–6pm, June–Sept daily 9am–8pm). Alternatively, energetic souls can climb the stairs just past the hospital. To the west of the town, the Baroque Nossa Senhora da Agonia church is the site of a popular pilgrimage each August. Dancers, musicians and other celebrants, wearing vivid embroidered traditional costumes, come from all over the Minho to take part in the three-day *festa*, which is among Portugal's most spectacular.

Moving to the waterfront you'll come to the **Gil Eannes** (www.fundacaogileannes.pt): a former naval hospital ship, now a floating museum dedicated to the ship's former function, which was mainly servicing the cod fishermen in Greenland and Newfoundland. Across the river is the enticing **Praia**

There is no escaping the Barcelos cockerel.

An old gate in Braga.

> **Fact**
>
> Walk or cycle along the Ecopista, heading east from Valença to Cortes (13km/8 miles). This former railway track has been converted to a signposted paved pathway and is flanked by beautiful countryside, including bubbling streams, vineyards and mountains. For details visit www.ciclovia.pt.

de Cabedelo beach, accessible via a five-minute ferry ride from the harbour (hourly May–Sept). There are more good beaches nearby, including at the small resort of Carreço, just 5km (3 miles) to the north.

COASTAL ROUTE FROM PORTO

An alternative route into the Minho is by driving up the coast from Porto and returning by the inland route. The Atlantic beaches are generally broad, with fine sand, but the sea is cold and rough. A fishing town and resort, **Vila do Conde** ❻, is the site of the vast Convento de Santa Clara, which was founded in 1318, the 16th-century parish church of São João Baptista, and a lovely 17th-century fortress. Travellers are welcome to watch how fishing boats are made and to visit the lace-making school and museum, the Museu das Rendas de Bilros (free). Nearby, **Póvoa de Varzim** ❼ is another popular fishing port-resort, with an 18th-century fort and a parish church. There is also a casino and a modern luxury hotel, the Axis Vermar, with heated swimming pools and tennis courts. Further north, **Ofir** ❽ is a delightful seaside resort set amid pine forests. Just across the Rio Cávado lies the town of **Esposende** ❾ with the remains of an 18th-century fortress. There are many new, often garishly painted, houses in towns and villages along the way, which have often been built by emigrants returned from France, Germany and elsewhere.

ALONG THE RIO MINHO

Continuing northwards, beyond Viana do Castelo, the road leads to **Caminha** ❿ on the banks of the Rio Minho, an attractive town with echoes of its past as a busy trading port. The church, dating from the 15th century, has a beautiful ceiling of carved wood. There are several lovely 15th- and 16th-century buildings near the main square.

At the estuary of the Minho, the road turns inland and follows the river, which forms the border with Spain. **Valença do Minho** ⓫ is a bustling border town with shops and markets. Spaniards come here regularly to purchase items that include table linen

The unusual grain stores of Soajo.

and crystal chandeliers. The Portuguese, on the other hand, cross the border to Tui or Vigo to buy canned goods such as asparagus and artichokes, as well as clothing. The old town of Valença is still fairly intact, with cobbled streets and stone houses with iron balconies, surrounded by 17th-century granite ramparts. The ancient convent, with a splendid view of the Minho and of Spain, is now a *pousada*.

From **Monção** ⓬, a fortified town known for its spring water and classy *vinho verde*, you can either take the road south through the heart of the Minho, or continue along the riverside and cross over the mountains of Serra da Peneda and sense the isolation. Either way, the routes meet at Ponte da Barca.

THE MOUNTAIN ROUTE

Follow the river as far as **Melgaço** ⓭, another fortified town, and turn inland for **Castro Laboreiro** ⓮, an ancient settlement with an 11th-century castle, which is most renowned for a large breed of working dog that was introduced to protect the villagers from marauding wolves.

Take the road from here to **Senhora da Peneda** ⓯ to find an amazing Bom Jesus-style church in the middle of nowhere. A long flight of steps ascending to the church is adorned with 14 chapels, each containing a tableau depicting a major event in the story of Christ.

Dramatic mountain scenery opens up as you pass through a number of villages, including Rouças and Adrão, to meet the road outside the village of **Soajo** ⓰, where there is a colourful market on the first Sunday of the month. Of particular interest here are the communal *espigueiros*, granite grain stores built on mushroom-shaped legs, and grouped around a threshing floor.

The road onward leads southeast to **Lindoso** ⓱ (the name comes from *lindo* meaning beautiful) and a finely situated border castle keeping watch for invaders from Spain. Below the castle ramparts lies another cluster of *espigueiros*. Return from Lindoso on the road to Ponte da Barca. You will see lush countryside, crisscrossed by rivers with medieval stone bridges; simple white churches with elaborate granite doorways and windows; and, of course, unending vineyards. Due to the high population density, the land has been divided and subdivided for generations, so the average property now consists of just a hectare or two.

The road now passes **Arcos de Valdevez** ⓲, an attractive hillside town built on the banks of the Rio Vez, with a magnificent view of the valley. Just to the south, **Ponte da Barca** ⓳, on the south bank of the Rio Lima, has a lovely 15th-century parish church and an old town square, but the principal attraction is the fine arched bridge, after which the town is named, built in 1543 and often restored.

This is a possible starting point for a visit to the stunning **Peneda-Gerês**

Capela das Malheiras chapel, Viana do Castelo.

> **Fact**
>
> Guimarães' Festival of St Walter, the Festas Gualterianas, dates from the middle of the 15th century. This three-day celebration, on the first weekend in August, includes a torchlight procession, a fair with traditional dances, and a medieval parade.

National Park (see box for a suggested route). Covering a vast 703 sq km (272 sq miles), the park encompasses wild plains with grazing cattle, pine-clad mountain ranges and lush forests. It is the wettest region of Portugal, and there are streams and rivers and a flourishing plant life with some 17 species found nowhere else, as well as extensive forests of oak and pine. Wild ponies, deer, wolves, golden eagles, wild boars and badgers also live within the boundaries.

The park encompasses fascinating ancient villages with stone houses, cobbled streets and a predominance of elderly women dressed in black. You may fish, go horse riding, hike and mountain climb amid the breathtaking scenery. There are also dolmens, perhaps 5,000 years old, and milestones that once marked the old Roman road to Braga.

The bustling, central little spa town of **Vila do Gerês** ⑳ (also called Caldas do Gerês) has plenty of places to stay and a popular spa centre (www.termas-dogeres.pt). There are also some good hiking trails surrounding the town; detailed maps are available at the tourist office. Nearby, tiny **Rio Caldo** is the park's centre for water sports, including kayaking, waterskiing and rowing.

THE LIMA VALLEY AND THE SOUTH

Here you might turn westwards, along the beautiful valley of the Lima River, which the Romans believed to be the *Lethe:* the mythical River of Forgetfulness. The area has numerous great estates or *solares*, which stand as a tangible reminder of the glories of the old empire. Some are now guest-houses, and arrangements to visit or stay in these manors should be made beforehand if possible (see page 121).

Ponte de Lima ㉑ is one of the loveliest towns in Portugal, mainly because of its location on the south bank of the Lima and its picturesque historic centre. There is a popular market, held every other Monday, resembling a splendidly colourful "tent city" on the river bank. It sells everything from local cheese to cotton underwear.

Enjoying watersports in the national park.

⊙ PARQUE NACIONAL DA PENEDA-GERÊS

It is easy to make a round trip of the Peneda-Gerês National Park by car, taking in some of the most spectacular scenery on both sides of the border. From Ponte da Barca take the road east towards Lindoso, past the hydro scheme to the border at Madaleina. Cross into Spain – there are no formalities – and continue alongside the reservoir until you come to a right turn signposted Lobios and Portela do Homen. Take this turn and you eventually cross back into Portugal.

On the Portuguese side you have a choice: continue straight down the "main" road to the old spa town of Caldas do Gerês then towards Braga, or, shortly after crossing back into Portugal, take the right turn down the road which follows the Vilarinho reservoir to Campo do Gerês, which has an excellent visitor centre portraying traditional life in Vilarinho das Furnas, the village submerged by the reservoir. Then drive towards Covide, passing a well-stocked craft shop, then west to Vila Verde. Of the two options, the latter is the more interesting. Roads can get very busy at weekends in summer, and at peak times the park authority may impose traffic restrictions.

If you plan on camping in the national park, be sure to use a designated site, or you could be faced with a hefty fine. Tourist offices have lists of official sites which are, generally, of a very high standard.

The town faces a magnificent Roman bridge with low arches, and remains of the old city wall still stand. A 15th-century palace with crenellated facade now serves as the town hall. Across the river, the 15th-century **Convento de Santo António** has beautiful woodwork, including two Baroque shrines.

Continuing towards Viana do Castelo, you pass more manor houses, such as the Solar de Cortegaça, with its great 15th-century stone tower. This is a working manor, with wine cellars, a flour mill and stable.

GUIMARÃES: BIRTHPLACE OF A NATION

A busy manufacturing town noted mainly for textiles, shoes and cutlery, **Guimarães** ㉒ still possesses many reminders of its past glory as birthplace of the Portuguese nation. Around the year 1128, an 18-year-old boy named Afonso Henriques proclaimed independence for the region of Portucale from the kingdom of León and Castile. In the field of São Mamede, near Guimarães, the young Afonso Henriques defeated his mother's army, which was battling on behalf of Alfonso VII, king of León and Castile.

Guimarães has long been the centre of the Portuguese linen industry. It still produces high-quality, coarse linen from home-grown flax naturally bleached by the sun. The region is also known for its hand embroidery.

A good place to begin a tour is at the 10th-century **castelo** on the northern side of town. It is believed that Afonso Henriques was born here in 1110, the son of Henri of Burgundy, Count of Portucale, and his wife Teresa. The castle is a large mass of walls and towers on a rocky hill with a magnificent view of the mountains. The dungeon and fortifications were restored many times. Early in the 19th century, the castle was used as a debtors' prison; it was restored again in 1940. At the entrance stands the small Romanesque chapel of **São Miguel do Castelo** with the font where Afonso Henriques was baptised in 1111.

Heading into town, you pass the 15th-century Gothic **Paço dos Duques**

> **Tip**
> A cable car (www.turipenha.pt) links the historic centre of Guimarães with the summit of the nearby Penha mountain. It covers the distance of 1700 metres (5577ft) in just 8 minutes, offering amazing views of the city.

The Roman bridge at Ponte de Lima.

Statue of Afonso Henriques at Guimarães.

Vineyards at the church of Palmeira de Faro.

de Bragança (www.visitportugal.com/en/node/138306). This massive granite construction consists of four buildings set around a courtyard and has been completely restored. Outside stands a fine statue of Afonso Henriques by Soares dos Reis. Visitors may also view the splendid chestnut ceiling of the Banquet Hall, the Persian carpets, French tapestries, ancient portraits, porcelain and documents.

The Rua de Santa Maria, with its cobblestones and 14th- and 15th-century houses, leads to the centre of town. On the left lies the **Convento de Santa Clara**, built in the 1600s and now used as the town hall.

The church of **Nossa Senhora de Oliveira**, dating from the 10th century, was rebuilt by Count Henri in the 12th century and has undergone several restorations. Still visible are the 16th-century watchtower and 14th-century western portal and window. The church takes its name from a 7th-century legend of an old Visigoth warrior named Wamba who was tilling his field nearby when a delegation came to tell him he had been elected king. Refusing the office, he drove his staff into the ground, declaring that not until it bore leaves would he become king. It turned into an olive tree and the church was later built on the spot.

Adjacent to the church of Oliveira, the convent now holds the **Museu de Alberto Sampaio** (www.cm-guimaraes.pt/museus/poi/museu-de-alberto-sampaio), displaying the church's rich treasury of 12th-century silver chalices and Gothic and Renaissance silver crucifixes, as well as 15th- and 16th-century statues, paintings and ceramics.

The busiest square in Guimarães is the Largo do Toural. Just beyond, the **Igreja São Domingos** was built in the 14th century and still has the original transept, rose window and lovely Gothic cloister. The latter houses the **Museu Martins Sarmento** (https://msarmento.org), named after the man who was responsible for the excavation of the Citânia de Briteiros (see page 289) and displaying objects from that site and other *citânias* (ancient Iberian fortified villages) of northern Portugal, as well as collections of Roman inscriptions, ceramics and coins.

The nearby **Plataforma das Artes e Criatividade**, located in a splendidly converted market, is a multifunctional centre hosting art exhibitions, cultural and social events. It also houses the **Coleção José de Guimarães** (www.ciajg.pt) with an interesting collection of African, Precolombian and ancient Chinese art. On display are also works by the local artist José Maria Fernandes Marques, better known as José de Guimarães.

Continuing along the broad garden called the Alameda da Resistência ao Fascismo, you reach the **Igreja São Francisco**, founded in the 13th century. There is little left of the original Gothic structure, but the sacristy has impressive 17th-century gilt woodwork and ceiling, as well as some striking *azulejos*.

High on the outskirts of the city stands **Santa Marinha da Costa**, founded as a monastery in the 12th century and rebuilt in the 18th century. The church is functional and can be visited. The cells of the monastery, which were badly damaged by a fire in 1951, have been restored and turned into a luxury *pousada* (www.pousadas.pt). A 10th-century Mozarabic arch and vestiges of a 7th-century Visigothic structure are visible in the cloisters, and the veranda is decorated with magnificent 18th-century tile scenes and a fountain.

CITÂNIA DE BRITEIROS

After the Briteiros exhibit at the Martins Sarmento museum, you could visit the original site, 11 km (7 miles) north of Guimarães. At first, the **Citânia de Briteiros** ❷❸ (daily 9am–5pm, until 6pm Apr–Sept) appears from a distance to be nothing more than piles of stones on a hillside, but it is in fact one of Portugal's most important archaeological sites. Here are the remains of a prehistoric fortified village said to have been inhabited by the Celts. It was discovered in 1874 by archaeologist Francisco Martins Sarmento.

Near the summit, two round houses have been reconstructed. Also visible are the remains of defensive walls, ancient flagstones and the foundation walls of more than 150 houses. The houses were circular with stone benches running around the walls. A large rock in the centre supported a pole which would in turn have held up a thatched roof. Several of the houses are larger, with two or more rectangular rooms, presumably the homes of prominent members of society. The town evidently had an efficient water system: spring water flowed downhill through gutters carved in the paving stones to a cistern and a public fountain.

About 14km (8.7 miles) southeast of Guimarães lies the small town of Santo Tirso ❷❹. Here, world-famous architects and Pritzker Prize winners Álvaro Siza Vieira and Eduardo Souto de Moura teamed up again (they had previously collaborated on London's Serpentine Gallery) to renovate the town's **Museu Municipal Abade Pedrosa** (http://mmap.cm-stirso.pt). Converting a historic Portuguese monastery, the architects added a two-storey (one above and another underground) modern wing with a white-rendered facade, a flat roof covered with traditional red tiles, and an interior decorated with white marble.

Occupying the second floor of the old monastery, the Museu Municipal comprises an interesting archaeological collection including sculptures, ceramics and coins found in the region and dating from prehistoric to medieval times. Meanwhile, the new wing contains the **International Museum of Contemporary Sculpture** (MIEC; http://miec.cm-stirso.pt; free) with works by Portuguese as well as international artists. It also has a pleasant café and an auditorium.

Traditional honeypots for sale. Bee keeping is a practice well established in most regions, producing a variety of honeys from wild lavender to orange blossom.

Restored houses of the ancient settlement Citânia de Briteiros.

Bragança countryside.

TRÁS-OS-MONTES

Isolated by distance and mountains, Trás-os-Montes has developed unique cultural and agrarian facets that distinguish it from the rest of Portugal.

To most Portuguese, the remote northeastern province of Trás-os-Montes ("behind the mountains") could be on the other side of the moon. Lisboetas are inclined to look at it as if from a vast distance – albeit with fierce affection. The word *"trás"* – "back" or "behind" – fits the region like a glove. Before Portugal joined the EU, this region was backward in almost every aspect: cut off from the rest of the country by mountains, poor road and rail systems, and grinding poverty that drove the workforce of almost every village to migrate to urban areas, or emigrate to the more advanced economies of northern Europe, or overseas. Now, improved roads, better communications and farming subsidies have led to rapid improvements in living standards, although pockets of poverty still exist.

REGIONAL DIFFERENCES

There has been higher emigration from the north of Portugal than from the south, and one of the principal reasons is the division of land. The south is an area of *latifúndios* – large landholdings – while the north has *minifúndios*, or smallholdings. A farmer's land in the north is often insufficient to provide him and his family with a living; the terrain, with its steep-sided valleys

and high mountains, also makes farming here a challenge.

A more subtle factor affecting Portugal's conservative north is the Church. While all Portugal is Roman Catholic, the sheer remoteness of the northeast corner has meant that national government has little impact, while tradition and religion predominate. This has particularly influenced education, particularly; not so long ago the only educated man in a village was the priest, whose wisdom and opinion would be sought on every matter ranging

Main attractions
Parque Natural do Alvâo
Atei
Montalegre
Chaves
Montesinho
Bragança
Rio de Onor
Miranda do Douro

Map on page 292

Goats in Portugal are used mainly for their milk.

Who will buy?

from the spiritual to aspects of crop harvesting.

Geographically, Trás-os-Montes covers the extreme northeast corner of the country, from Bragança in the north to the Rio Douro in the south and west to Chaves and Montalegre. Climatically, the region is different, too. Cut off from the influence of the Atlantic, it is hotter and drier in summer and colder in winter, especially in the far northeastern Terra Fria, the cold lands. Trás-os-Montes remains one of the most interesting areas of the country, for its towns, its countryside and its historical connections.

ENTERING THE REGION

You can enter the region, which includes the Alto Douro, from a number of directions. Northern border crossings from Spain are at Vila Verde da Raia, on the road leading south to Chaves (this is a historical invasion route – employed by the armies of Napoleon in the early 1800s); at Portelo, in the Parque Natural de Montesinho; from the east at Quintanilha, east of Bragança; and at Miranda do Douro and Bemposta, where the Douro forms the frontier. From inside Portugal, the main routes into the region are from Porto or Lamego via Vila Real; or from Guarda via either Torre de Moncorvo or Freixo de Espada à Cinta.

This itinerary enters the region at Vila Real and follows a meandering route to absorb the sights and atmosphere of the area without ignoring the major points of interest.

SERRA DE ALVÃO

Two scenic routes lead north out of Vila Real, one on each side of the high Serra da Padrela – to Chaves in the north, and Bragança in the northeast. But the adventurous traveller may strike northwest into the rugged Serra de Alvão, and be treated to one of the most lavish vistas the country has to offer. The road leads through the **Parque Natural do Alvão**, an exceptionally beautiful and pristine natural park with mountains, a river and a wide range of flora and fauna. Continue across the Rio Olo to **Mondim de Basto** ❶ on the banks of the

TRÁS-OS-MONTES | 293

Rio Tâmega. There it forms the border between Trás-os-Montes and the Minho.

Granite gives way to slate – many of the houses are roofed by it – and in the high passes you can hear the rushing of mountain waters and the tinkle of goat bells. In the winter there is snow here, but at other times of the year you are likely to encounter a profusion of wild flowers and pine forests. Pine resin, which is used in the manufacture of paints and turpentine, is a major product of this area.

A side trip of some 12km (8 miles) from Mondim de Basto will take you to **Atei** ❷, a delightful little village containing numerous archaeological remnants of Roman occupation. From here a curious subterranean passage of either Roman or Arab construction (opinions vary) leads down to Furaco on the banks of the Tâmega.

Leaving Mondim de Basto, the road winds northwards to Cabeceiras de Basto, in Minho province, at the head of a small "peninsula" that juts up into Trás-os-Montes. Stop at the imposing Baroque Mosteiro Refóis before heading into the high Serra de Cabreira and back into Trás-os-Montes at Póvoa.

BARROSO DISTRICT

You soon join the main Braga–Chaves road that runs beside the gigantic expanse of lake formed by **Barragem do Alto Rabagão** ❸, a huge dam, but here again another side trip could take you north – to Montalegre, the towering Serra do Larouco, and the primitive villages of the Barroso district.

As the largest town in the area, **Montalegre** ❹ might be considered the capital of Barroso. Given a charter in 1273 by King Afonso III, and restored and expanded in turn by King Dinis and King Manuel I, Montalegre is thought to have enjoyed its status from a much earlier time, for the pillory in the centre of town carries the coat of arms of King Sancho I, who reigned from 1185 to 1211.

The town commands a view over an extensive area – understandably it has been a military centre for centuries. Montalegre is rich in archaeological finds. Lusitanians, Romans, Suevi and Visigoths were all here, and the magnificent four-towered castle was much used during the many wars that Portugal fought against Spain. At 21 metres (69ft) high, it is now a national monument.

The north of the region is home to the Serra do Larouco, the second-highest range of mountains in the country (after the Serra da Estrela), with a number of passes leading into Spanish Galicia.

The district of Barroso stretches from the foothills of the Serra do Larouco southeast towards the city of Chaves. There is no absolute boundary, but it would include such villages as Meixido, Padornelos and Tourém. If you can close your eyes to the "emigrant architecture" – uncontrolled modern housing that is built with money saved by the Portuguese who work abroad – you will find in these settlements a sense of history utterly remote in time.

Monastery ruins of Pitoes das Junias, Peneda Gerês National Park.

Sweeping vista across Montalegre.

The ancient houses are built of enormous granite or slate blocks. Doors, windows and balconies are of weathered antique wood. Until recently, many houses were thatched. Once common, dirt streets are rapidly becoming paved, and electricity has only recently been installed. Almost every church is Romanesque, with the typical facade rising to a twin-columned peak to house the church bell.

For centuries the people of Barroso lived out their lives cut off from the outside world. They developed their own customs, songs, festivals and habits. In many corners of the world under similar circumstances local people may treat outsiders with suspicion or alarm, but this is certainly not the case in Barroso. It is hard to imagine a more warm-hearted, hospitable people, willing to share the peculiarities of their daily lives with those who come to visit them.

COMMUNAL BULLS

One of the region's most colourful festivals is the annual **Chega de Touros**, an inter-village competition. The name means "The Arrival of the Bulls". Each village takes enormous pride in its own bull, a communally owned animal bred especially for the purpose of inseminating the various cows owned by the individual farmers. This bull, by both tradition and breeding, is the biggest and fiercest animal imaginable, intended as much to gain the honours at the annual competition as it is for stock purposes.

Held in June, July and August, the Chega is essentially a bullfight, where the bull of one village is pitted against another in a fierce battle. Each animal is decorated and fêted by his villagers, and paraded to the accompaniment of noisy bands and crowds. The fight itself is in deadly earnest, with the champions of each bull goading their animal into combat. The fight continues until one animal is injured, or turns and runs. The victor is then led away by his villagers with much celebration.

At the end of the season there will be a regional champion, and this is the lucky animal who will be put out to pasture with the region's cows.

A rustic doorway in the Barroso district.

WINE OF THE DEAD

Boticas ⑤ is the place to drink *vinhos mortos*, "wine of the dead". In order to protect their wine stocks from the French during the Peninsular War in the early 1800s, the villagers buried it in the ground. When it was later retrieved, the wine was found to be much improved. The practice is still followed, with good results. To sample another regional drink, make a short diversion west to the spa village of **Carvalhelhos** ⑥. The spring water here is particularly sweet and is sold all over the country. Most refreshing is *com gas*, the sparkling version.

CHAVES

Chaves ⑦, just a few kilometres down the road from Barroso, seems a world away. An ancient city, the fortified Lusitanian village of the present site was captured by the Romans in AD 78. The Emperor Flavius founded the city of Aqua Flaviae there, inaugurating the still-popular hot springs and baths. Chaves is now a bustling town with a population of about 41,000. An agricultural and textile centre, it is famous for its *presunto*, or smoked ham (see page 296); you can taste it, with a glass of wine, at Faustino's (www.adegafaustino.pt), a former winery that claims to be the largest taverna, or *tasca*, in Portugal.

The town is also well known for its natural spa, which was first discovered and developed by the Romans. The town's Parque Termal (Largo das Caldas; www.termasdechaves.com) offers a wide range of treatments said to cure everything from arthritis to obesity. You can also join the queue waiting for a mug full of the steamy water.

Situated on the Rio Tâmega, Chaves commands a strategic position in a wide valley that extends from the Spanish frontier into the heart of Trás-os-Montes. Just about every invader who set his heart on Portugal, or chunks of it, routed his armies through this channel. Here the Romans built one of the largest of their bridges in the Iberian peninsula. Completed in AD 104, it has 20 arches, is 140 metres (459ft) in length, and is still very much

Dom Afonso, standing proud in the centre of Chaves.

The modern town of Chaves was once known to the Romans as Aquae Flaviae.

Eat

Presunto (smoked ham), the local gourmet delicacy of Chaves, is traditionally kept for one year in salt, paprika, wine and garlic, before being well smoked for around eight weeks, then eaten raw. It's available in every restaurant.

Home to Bragança Castle, Trás-os-Montes means 'behind the mountains'.

in daily use. In the middle of the bridge are two inscribed Roman milestones. Chaves means "keys" in Portuguese, but the ancient Aqua Flaviae was later shortened to Flavias, and local mispronunciation may have produced the current name.

Sights include the parish church, rebuilt in the 16th century; and the former Bragança ducal palace, now the **Museu Região Flaviense** (Tues–Sun 10am–1pm, 2.30–6.30pm, in the Praça de Camões. It also has other branches around town (same hours as above), including the **Museu de Arte Sacra da Região Flaviense** (Rua da 3ª Ordem), the **Núcleo Museológico Ferroviário** (Rua da Linha do Comboio) and the **Museu Militar** (in Torre de Menagem). Prior to the formation of Portugal, the fortified city was a part of the original county of Portucale. Several of Portugal's early kings added significantly to its castle, one of the most important in the land.

A second castle, also once an integral part of the defences of this strategic valley, still stands at **Monforte** ❽, about 12km (8 miles) to the northeast.

EAST FROM CHAVES

Heading east towards Bragança you will pass the old town of **Vinhais** ❾. Its castle is barely more than a ruin, although there was a significant population here. The town is set high in the Serra de Montesinho, on the south flank of the **Parque Natural de Montesinho** ❿, a wildly rugged park of heath-like scenery, the habitat of rare wolves, boars and foxes, as well as many varieties of flora and fauna. The area survives on agricultural pursuits, particularly vines, woodwork, weaving and basket-making.

To explore the region, first stop at the tourist office in Bragança (Avenida Cidade de Zamora; www.cm-braganca.pt) and ask for a book about the park, which contains a detailed map of the area. Be aware that not all of the roads are paved. Whichever direction you take, you will have a journey through spectacular country.

A mountain, Cidadela, rises behind Vinhais. Over it passed the Roman road that led from Braga to Astorga; today this ancient route is rich in archaeological discoveries. In the 11th and 12th centuries there was a general movement by the population of this area towards the more fertile farmlands of the south. To prevent this, various monasteries were founded and encouraged by the early rulers of the region to develop their own agriculture and cottage industries. One of the most important of these was the **Mosteiro de Castro de Avelãs** ⓫, a few kilometres west of Bragança. Parts of the church of the Benedictine abbey have been incorporated into the present-day parish church.

BRAGANÇA: A FASCINATING CITY

With a population of some 35,000, **Bragança** ⓬ is the administrative capital, a university town, and also an agricultural trade centre (for livestock, vineyards, olives and grains). It has a thriving textile industry, and has been famous for its ceramics since prehistoric times (in a nearby cave at Dine, archaeologists have found pottery dating from the Palaeolithic period).

Known as Brigantine to the Celts and Juliobriga to the Romans, Bragança received its first *foral* (royal charter) from King Sancho I in 1187 – when the family from which the dukes of Bragança are descended started building their feudal castle there. The Braganças – still pretenders to the throne of Portugal – provided the land's kings and queens consistently from 1640 until the formation of the republic in 1910, and the emperors of Brazil from 1822 to 1889. In 1662, Catherine of Bragança, daughter of the first Bragança king João IV, became queen to Charles II of England, thus renewing the long alliance between the two nations. Since the fall of the monarchy, a foundation, the Fundação da Casa de Bragança, has managed all royal properties, including the family's 16th-century ducal palace in Vila Viçosa.

Bragança's ancient castle still stands – with a Princess' Tower full of ghosts. The keep of the castle houses the **Museu Militar de Bragança** (military museum; tel: 273 322 378; Tue–Sun 9am–noon, 2–5pm). You can also see

A statue and fountain in Bragança. The city was originally a Celtic settlement known as Brigantion.

Bragança Castle is an excellent example of civic Romanesque architecture.

ⓞ MONTESINHO

The stunning Parque Natural de Montesinho (see page 296) has a tangible feeling of being stuck in a time warp. The dramatic countryside is stippled with ancient villages that preserve their age-old customs, and many still bear their ancient Roman or Visigothic names. The protected area covers 751 sq km (290 sq miles), but you don't have to have your own vehicle to explore it, as this is great hiking country as well. There are at least a dozen well-marked hiking trails running throughout the park, which vary in difficulty. Coroa (1,273 metres/4,175ft) and Montesinho (1,486 metres/4,874ft) are the highest points. Pick up a route map at one of the park information offices and follow the waymarks. Don't forget to carry drinking water with you. For details, visit www.montesinho.com.

an unusual medieval *pelourinho* (pillory), its shaft piercing a granite boar. Also within the castle walls, you will find the 12th-century five-sided Domus Municipalis, the oldest municipal hall in Portugal. The town walls, with their 18 watchtowers, are still largely intact, and the city has a fine cathedral and fascinating museum of archaeology, furniture and ethnography, the **Museu do Abade de Baçal** (tel: 273 331 595; Tue–Sun 9.30am–noon, 2–6pm), in what used to be the Bishop's Palace.

Another fascinating museum is the **Museu Ibérico da Máscara e do Traje** (tel: 273 381 008; Tue–Sun 9am–1pm, 2–5pm), with a display of colourful ribboned costumes and masks worn during the annual Carnival and similar festivities. The **Centro Ciência Viva** (www.braganca.cienciaviva.pt; Tue–Fri 10am–6pm, Sat–Sun 11am–7pm) celebrates the city's economic reliance on silk from the 15th to the 19th centuries, while the **Centro de Arte Contemporânea Graça Morais** (http://centroartegracamorais.cm-braganca.pt; Tue–Sun 10am–6.30pm), has a permanent exhibition of paintings by local artist Graça Morais, as well as regular temporary exhibitions featuring Portuguese and Spanish contemporary artists and sculptors. The **Centro de Fotografia Georges Dussaud** (tel: 273 324 092; Tue–Sun 9am–12.30pm, 2–5.30pm) showcases beautiful photography of Trás-os-Montes by French photographer Georges Dussaud.

EXCURSIONS NORTH

Basing yourself in historic Bragança makes it relatively easy to make short day trips out into the surrounding region. First, to the north, in the furthest corner of Portugal, there is **Rio de Onor** ⑬, a tiny village that straddles the border with Spain. It took a rare presidential visit for the village to acquire its first bus service. The people of Rio de Onor developed their own dialect and intricate communal social system. In their music and folk dances a common instrument is the *gaita-de-foles* – a bagpipe, with Celtic associations similar to those of Scotland and Ireland.

A good time to visit the villages that extend in an arc from Vinhais, across

A farmer in the Rio do Onor region of Portugal.

Bragança, and down as far as Miranda do Douro and Freixo de Espada-à-Cinta, is between Christmas Day and Epiphany (6 January), when the local population celebrates a number of feasts connected with the Christian calendar – but incorporating ferocious masks and bizarre costumes. These celebrations date back to the dawn of time, when the agrarian people of these pastoral regions practised fertility rites and paid more than passing attention to magic.

Carnival, in February, is another good time to visit. Forty days before Easter the masks and costumes come out again, and you cannot be sure if it is the Christian spirit or the bogeyman that dominates the season. As in so many places, the Catholic Church incorporated pagan elements in order to appease the local people, and the rites became entangled.

EXCURSIONS SOUTH

South of Bragança you may head towards the Spanish frontier at **Miranda do Douro** ⓮. This fortified town sits above a craggy gorge overlooking the Douro. Like many of the country's border towns, it has suffered a turbulent history in its attempts to keep out the Spanish. These days invaders from across the river are welcomed with open arms – provided they bring a supply of euros.

Fifteenth-century houses with granite doorways, a 16th-century cathedral with a sequence of gilded wood altarpieces, an excellent folk museum, the **Museu da Terra de Miranda** (Tue 2–6pm, Wed–Sun 9am–1pm, 2–6pm), and the medieval Rua da Costanilha make it a worthwhile stop.

It is possible to make a circular tour by following the road on to the quiet town of **Mogadouro** ⓯, which nestles in the shadow of a 12th-century castle built by King Dinis on earlier Roman foundations.

On the subject of castles, don't miss the impressive ruins at **Algoso** ⓰, on the way back to **Vimioso** ⓱. Since the 12th century, this fortress has guarded the area surrounding its lofty perch – a hill called Cabeça da Penenciada – while 500 metres (1,650ft) below, the Rio Angueira flows westwards to the Rio Maçãs.

The church at Miranda do Douro.

The striking coastal location of São Vicente.

MADEIRA

The Madeira archipelago has a feel that is distinct from mainland Portugal. Its beauty is varied, from the flowery elegance of Funchal to the remote inland craters.

The discovery of the Madeiran archipelago, 608km (378 miles) west of Morocco, was an early triumph for the ambitious seafarers inspired by Prince Henry the Navigator. In 1418, while sailing south to colonise the West African coast, the caravels of João Gonçalves Zarco and Tristão Vaz Teixeira found shelter on a low-lying island they called, in gratitude, Porto Santo (Holy Port). Two years later they returned, to discover a large mountainous island 37km (23 miles) to the southwest, which they named Ilha da Madeira – the Island of Wood. Madeira Island and Porto Santo remain the only two inhabited islands in the archipelago.

Modern explorers will find that Madeira is still a wild and beautiful place to visit. Its great forests have sadly gone – burnt down by the first settlers with fires that got out of control and are said to have raged for years – but humans have contributed more modest wonders to an Atlantic island whose natural splendour has earned it such titles as "God's Botanical Gardens" and "The Floating Flowerpot".

THE CITY OF FUNCHAL

A statue of Gonçalves Zarco now stands as a central landmark in **Funchal** ❶, the capital of Madeira and home to more than a third of the 270,000 islanders. The city squats in the centre of a wide bay on the sunnier south side of the island, its name inspired by the wild fennel *(funcho)* that the discoverers found growing on the surrounding plain. Behind it rises a natural amphitheatre of terraced hills and mountains that provide shelter from the northeasterly winds that frequently blow over the island – rain, storms and consolatory rainbows are the price you pay for Madeira's splendid verdant landscape. The island's geographic conditions bring another hazard: wildfires.

Main attractions
Funchal
Blandy's Wine Lodge
Pico do Arieiro
Santana
Curral das Freiras
Porto Santo

Map on page 302

Dancers at the Funchal Spring Flower Festival.

Madeira

The most recent, in August 2023, killed three people and displaced almost a thousand. Increasingly high summer temperatures, dry woodlands and strong winds are to blame for these devastating phenomena.

Cruise-ship passengers and tourists with limited time usually settle for the two essential Madeiran experiences, the Monte toboggan ride and tea at Reid's Palace Hotel. The first of these involves taking the cable car or driving up to **Monte** ❷, a cool and leafy hilltop resort with *quintas*, sanatoriums and the **Monte Palace Tropical Gardens** (http://montepalace.com). The nearby twin-towered church of Nossa Senhora de Monte contains the tomb of Emperor Charles I of Austria. From here you can descend to Funchal by *carro de cesto*, a kind of wicker sofa attached to wooden runners that is guided 2km (1.2 miles) down the steep lanes by a pair of drivers wearing boaters and white flannels. This unique form of transport was invented by an English resident looking for a speedy way to get down to his office from his *quinta*.

Tea at **Reid's Palace Hotel** is far less strenuous, and simply involves climbing into a wicker armchair and ordering a pot of Earl Grey tea and some crustless cucumber sandwiches. A world-famous five-star hotel with a prestigious site overlooking Funchal harbour, Reid's was opened in 1891 to cater for the growing number of well-to-do visitors to the island – particularly the British, who liked to stop over en route to and from their colonies.

The British presence on the island has proved influential in many ways – besides endorsing Madeira's reputation as a refined holiday destination acclaimed for its civility and hospitality. Their fondness for cane furniture, acquired in East Asia, stimulated the island's wicker industry centred on the eastern town of Camacha (see page 307). Another important cottage industry, the production of an intricate and understandably expensive kind of embroidery *(bordados)*, is indebted to an Englishwoman, Elizabeth Phelps, who introduced it in the 1850s to supplement local incomes after disease devastated the island's vines, with disastrous effects on the islanders' living standards. Rua dos Murcas is the best place to buy.

More recently, there has been another presence on the island that has hit the headlines: Cristiano Ronaldo. Recognised as one of the world's top footballers – and honoured as the sport's highest-ever goal scorer by FIFA in 2023 – Ronaldo is now Madeira's most famous native son, and just about everywhere you go in the capital, you will see his face staring out from mugs, T-shirts and dishcloths. It's an image that also reminds visitors that Madeira has moved on from its bygone image of starched British gentility. The **CR7 Museum** (Av. Sá Carneiro/Praça do Mar Nº27; http://museucr7.com), dedicated to Ronaldo, displays a wax figure of the footballer and more than 100 of his trophies. Interactive screens show

São Lourenço Fortress in Funchal.

Harvesting grapes in Madeira.

important moments from Ronaldo's career and his best goals, and you can even have your picture taken with Ronaldo's very own digital avatar.

LOMQUATS AND SCABBARD FISH

Funchal's true pleasures are woven into the everyday life of the city. A visit to the **Mercado dos Lavradores** (Workers' Market), a cornucopia of good things, costs nothing – unless, of course, you are tempted to buy some lomquats, tomarillos, pittangas or any of the many other exotic fruits and vegetables grown on the island.

Venture into the *mercado's* inner halls and you can gaze in safety upon the gloriously ugly *espada* (scabbard fish) that frequently features on Madeiran menus (not to be confused with the equally common traditional dish called *espetada* – beef cooked on a skewer over a wood fire scented with laurel twigs). Despite its vicious teeth and eel-like appearance, *espada* tastes good and is something of a rarity as it is only caught here and off the coast of Japan. The most important catch in the archipelago, the fish lives at a depth of up to 760 metres (2,500ft) and is hunted year-round by fishermen from **Câmara de Lobos** ❸, just west of Funchal. They use lines with baited hooks and flies spaced at regular intervals that can be more than 1.6km (1 mile) in length.

For a rewarding insight into Madeira's past, there are several places worth visiting: the oldest wine lodge, **Blandy's Wine Lodge** (www.blandyswinelodge.com; charge for tours) on Avenida Arriaga, dates in part from the 16th century, and the best way to explore is to join a tour where the process behind the famed Madeiran wine production is explained; tastings are also offered. There is also a wine shop offering more than 250 wines from Madeira, mainland Portugal and international wineries.

Inaugurated in the early 1500s, Funchal's **Sé** (Cathedral) is the oldest sacral building on the island, well worth visiting for its Flemish paintings and amazing cedar ceiling. Others churches of interest include **Igreja de São João**

Wine for tasting at Madeira Wine Festival, Funchal.

Go tobogganing through the streets of Funchal.

◉ MADEIRAN WINE

Madeira's fortunes have long been entwined with those of its famous sherry-like drink, and the names of English, Scottish and Irish immigrant families such as Leacock, Cossart, Gordon and Blandy have become synonymous with the island's history. In the 18th century it was discovered that long sea voyages through the heat of the tropics, far from spoiling the wine, improved its quality. This lengthy process of maturation has now been replaced by the *estufagem* system, whereby young wine is stored in hothouses *(estufas)* for several months. Four main types of Madeira are produced today: a dry Sercial and medium-dry Verdelho, both ideal as aperitifs, and the richer Bual and dark, sweet Malmsey, which are both often served with desserts.

Evangelista (Church of St John Evangelist), a fine example of a Mannerist temple, dating from the 17th century, and **Igreja de São Pedro** (Church of St Peter) from the 18th century. The latter took almost 150 years to complete and boasts a valuable collection of antique paintings, jewellery and furniture. The 15th-century **Convento Santa Clara** (Santa Clara Monastery) is open for cheap guided tours (10am–noon, 3–5pm; ring the bell to enter).

For a photographic glimpse into the past, check out the **Madeira Photography Museum** (https://cultura.madeira.gov.pt/museu-de-fotografia-da-madeira-atelier-vicente-s) in Rua da Carreira, which finally re-opened its doors re-opened in 2019 after years of renovations and houses a collection of old photographs of life on the island as recorded since 1865 by the Vicente family. Continue your history lesson at the **Museu Quinta das Cruzes** (Calada do Pico 1; https://mqc.madeira.gov.pt/en), the former residence of João Gonçalves Zarco, who discovered Madeira and became its first governor. The *quinta* is now packed with art treasures and the attractive gardens stay open throughout the lunch break. They are one of several exotic oases around the city, which include the **Boa Vista Orchids** and, the largest, **Jardim Botânico** (Botanical Gardens), on Caminho do Meio.

Housed in a beautiful 17th-century palace at Rua Mouraria 31, the **Museu de História Natural do Funchal** (https://cultura.madeira.gov.pt/museu-de-historia-natural-do-funchal.html documents the fauna and flora of the island.

Most of Madeira's hotels are located on the west side of the capital – only a short bus or taxi ride from Funchal's main square**, Praça do Município**. Decorously paved with black and white stones, this is bordered by imposing buildings with whitewashed facades and dark basalt outlines that remind visitors how Church and State have lorded it over this Portuguese outpost. A Jesuit church and college, founded in 1569, fills its north side (www.colegiodosjesuitas.pt). The college is now a vibrant cultural centre where monthly fado concerts are held, as well as local food and wine tastings. The 18th-century **Câmara Municipal** (Town Hall; http://cm-funchal.pt) to the east was once the palace of the Conde de Carvalhal. The count's country residence was at **Quinta do Palheiro Ferreiro**, 8km (5 miles) east of Funchal, which is now a 320-hectare (800-acre) estate owned by the Blandy family, with magnificent gardens open to the public (www.palheirogardens.com).

On the south side of Praça do Município, the former Bishop's Palace houses Madeira's principal art museum, the **Museu de Arte Sacra do Funchal** (Funchal Museum of Sacred Art; https://masf.pt). Among its exhibits is a fine collection of 15th- and 16th-century Flemish paintings acquired during the island's profitable trade in sugar with Flanders. "White gold" was the spur that provoked Madeira's rapid colonisation – by the 1450s merchants from Lisbon had established lucrative plantations on

> **Tip**
> Madeira's network of buses provides an excellent way of travelling around the island, if you don't feel like driving. Buses serve virtually every corner of the island, originating from Funchal's various privately run bus terminals. Major companies include EACL (www.eacl.pt), SAM (www.sam.pt) and Rodoeste (www.rodoeste.com.pt). Tickets can be bought on board and timetables are available at Funchal's main tourist office.

Shopping for fresh produce in the Mercado dos Lavradores.

> **Fact**
>
> The maintenance paths running alongside the irrigation channels, or *levadas*, that water the terraces provide 3,200km (2,000 miles) of long, level walks – a pleasant surprise on this mountainous island – into the silent heart of Madeira, with the stream of water serving as a faithful companion.

Taking in the view in Curral das Freiras.

the island, worked by slaves brought over from Africa and the nearby Canary Islands, 416km (258 miles) to the south. By the 17th century, most of Madeira's terraces had been given over to producing its eponymous fortified wine, originally derived from Cretan vines introduced to the island by Henry the Navigator. Among these was the sweet *malvoisie* grape, which gave rise to the malvasia or malmsey wines that so besotted Europe in the 16th century. In Shakespeare's *Henry IV*, Falstaff is accused of selling his soul for "a cup of Madeira and a cold capon's leg".

For exquisite tiles, check out the delightful little **Casa-Museu Frederico de Freitas** (http://casamuseuff.blogspot.com) on Calçada de Santa Clara, which has an exhibition of tiles from around the world, including Turkey, Syria and Holland, as well as other beautiful decorative arts dating from the 16th century.

A little over 30 minutes away from Funchal in the **Calheta** district is the award-winning **MUDAS - Contemporary Art Museum** ❹ (https://museus.madeira.gov.pt/DetalhesMuseu?museuId=1) designed by architect Paulo David. Wonderfully integrated into the rugged coastal landscape, it contains around 400 art pieces from the 1960s to the present day. The museum hosts various exhibitions, concerts, plays and lectures. It also houses a library, a shop, a café and a restaurant. It can be reached from Funchal by Rodoeste bus.

WINE ROUTES

Madeira wine travels and keeps well and few visitors leave without a bottle or two. Funchal has many invitingly fusty wine lodges and tasting bars where you can indulge in some serious research. **HM Borges** (www.hmborges.com) on Rua 31 da Janeiro is worth seeking out, while **Barbeito Wine Lodge** (www.vinhosbarbeito.com) on Estrada da Ribeira Garcia is a smaller traditional producer with a tasting room and shop. The most comprehensive initiation into the history and production of Madeira wine is provided by Old Blandy's Wine Lodge (see page 304).

Take any road out of Funchal, and the arduous work required to produce the island's wines, fruit and other crops soon becomes apparent. The true heroes of Madeiran history are its farm labourers and their enslaved predecessors, who over the centuries toiled to win cultivable land from the island's steep and irregular terrain. Workers resolutely sculpted the island with staircases of tiny stone-walled fields – sometimes built by suspending men on ropes from above, with baskets of soil carried up from the river beds far below. These *poios*, or terraces, are fed by a phenomenal network of irrigation channels, known as *levadas*, that today run for thousands of kilometres, including 40km (25 miles) through tunnels.

PEAKS, CLIFFS AND VILLAGES

Even without the terracing that has transformed the island's landscape into a precipitous work of art, Madeira would be staggeringly attractive. A range of volcanic mountains runs east–west across the island, rising to a central conference of peaks, of which the highest is **Pico Ruivo** ❺ at 1,862 metres (6,109ft). The nearby summit of **Pico do Arieiro** ❻, which can be comfortably reached by car, provides a physical and spiritual high point. From here, providing you have prayed away the clouds, you can follow an exhilarating on-top-of-the-world path across the peaks to **Achada do Teixeira**.

From all sides of these central mountains, deep ravines run seawards to boulder-strewn beaches where small villages have grown up – most spectacularly at **Ribeira Brava** ❼ and **São Vicente** ❽, directly opposite each other on the south and north coast respectively. The ridges above them invariably culminate in sheer cliffs that are among the highest in the world. If you have the head for it, a viewing platform at **Cabo Girão** enables visitors to contemplate a vertical drop of 580 metres (1,900ft).

Along Madeira's wild north coast, narrow roads have been stitched into the cliffsides, threading through tunnels, round hairpin bends and under waterfalls that provide a free and unexpected car wash. **Porto Moniz** ❾, a weather-beaten town on the island's northwestern tip, with several small hotels, fish restaurants and volcanic rock pools, provides a welcome goal for adventurous motorists searching for the raw side of Madeira.

Other popular ports of call are the village of **Santana** ❿, on the northern coast, where the islanders' traditional A-shaped thatched cottages have been colourfully restored, with a couple open for visitors; the forest resort of **Ribeiro Frio** ⓫ on a winding road that traverses the island between Funchal and Santana; and, closer to the capital, the wicker-making centre, **Camacha** ⓬, towards the east of the island.

For all this natural drama, Madeira is a fundamentally benign and relaxing island. Blessed with fertile soil, abundant water and an equable subtropical climate, the countryside is graced with a profusion of native plants and flowers that have been supplemented by exotic

Basket-making is a traditional industry in Camacha.

A classic A-shaped cottage in Santana.

imports. **Quinta Vigia**, the gardens of the regional president's residence; (www.madeira.gov.pt) on Avenida do Infante in the capital, is home to bird of paradise flowers among other stunning exotics. The island is a heaven for walkers and the botanically inclined, with the mountain pass at **Boca da Encumeada** and the **Parque das Queimadas** popular starting points for hikers.

Two-thirds of the island is a protected area, and the **Laurisilva forest**, which occupies one-fifth of the land between 330 metres (1,000ft) and 1,300 metres (4,250ft), is a UNESCO World Heritage Site.

OFF THE BEATEN TRACK

Like all good islands, Madeira has plenty of secrets. An easy and worthwhile trip from Funchal is up to **Curral das Freiras** ⓭ (Corral of the Nuns), a secluded crater-like valley that until the late 1950s could only be reached by the narrow mountain paths that still snake down its sides. It gets its name from the nuns of Funchal's Santa Clara Convent, who fled here in 1566 when French pirates sacked the capital. Another pleasant surprise lies to the west of Ribeira Brava – a plateau of austere and often misty moorland known as the **Paúl da Serra**, where a tiny white statue, Nossa Senhora da Serra, supervises the grazing sheep and cows.

The east side of Madeira is less mountainous and is consequently the most developed part of the island. Here you can find the airport, two golf courses, stretches of intensive farmland and **Machico** ⓮, which can claim to be Madeira's second city even though it only has about 21,000 inhabitants, one high-rise hotel and a seafront commandeered by a sandy football pitch.

In the northeastern corner of the island the mood changes again as the land narrows to a low-lying, sandy peninsula called **Ponta de São Lourenço**, reached through a tunnel to the north of Machico. Here Caniçal was, until 1981, the island's principal whaling station.

Continue to the end of the headland, which offers good views and blustery walks, and you will often meet old men selling souvenirs carved from redundant stocks of whalebone.

PORTO SANTO AND OTHER ISLANDS

The arid landscape of Ponta de São Lourenço provides a foretaste of that found on Madeira's neighbouring island, **Porto Santo** ⓯. The sleepy world of Porto Santo is a relatively accessible one, connected daily by ferry (two hours) and aeroplane (15 minutes). The island is a complete contrast to Madeira: while the former has a surplus of mountains, water and vegetation but no beaches to speak of, Porto Santo has just a few parched volcanic hills and a south coast that is one long, 7km (4-mile) stretch of unspoilt sand. It is as if God were planning to add beaches to Madeira but, like a builder who leaves a pile of sand outside your front door then disappears, he somehow forgot.

Porto Santo is blessed with unspoilt beaches.

This divine oversight is a blessing both for beach lovers and for connoisseurs of small-island life, as well as wind- and kite-surfers who hold competitions here. Plagued by rabbits and erosion, and vulnerable to attack by pirates, Porto Santo has always been ignored in favour of its lush and fertile neighbour, but it is nevertheless well worth a visit.

The capital, **Vila Baleira** ⓰, makes a virtue out of such inertia, and has only recently made efforts to cash in on its most famous resident, Christopher Columbus. The explorer was among the many sugar buyers who came to the islands in the 1470s, and later married the daughter of Porto Santo's first governor, Bartolomeu Perestrello. It is a leafy and attractive town with a palm-shaded main square and a tempting beach.

During the summer, holiday-makers from Funchal and mainland Portugal flock to Porto Santo, giving it the semblance of a seaside resort. But even at the height of the season there is space enough to wander along its magnificent beach. And, if it's your thing, to enjoy the island's 27-hole golf course.

Porto Santo is linked underwater to another separate group of islands, the barren **Ilhas Desertas**. Only 16km (10 miles) southeast of Madeira, they rise as high as 480 metres (1,570ft) and can easily be seen from the main island's southern shores. Despite repeated attempts over the centuries, settlement of the two islands – **Deserta Grande** ⓱ and **Bugio** ⓲ – has proved impossible. They are now a nature reserve where sea birds, wild goats, venomous black spiders and a colony of monk seals live in curious harmony. The Ilhas Desertas can sometimes be visited by boat trips from Funchal, and if you are interested in wildlife and wilderness regions it is worth enquiring at the tourist office.

Another set of islands also belongs to the Madeiran archipelago and is even more inhospitable than the Ilhas Desertas. Known as the **Ilhas Selvagens**, these lie 215km (135 miles) south of Madeira. Despite being closer to the Spanish Canaries, they remain under Portuguese jurisdiction.

Shops and small cafés await, close to the hiking trails.

Holy pilgrimage at Convento de Nossa Senhora da Esperanza.

THE AZORES

Time seems to have stood still in the beautiful Azores islands. Way out in the Atlantic Ocean, they have a character of their own, yet are redolent of Portugal's maritime history.

The nine islands of the Azores floating in the Atlantic Ocean are gratifyingly rich in romantic history, cryptic legend and stunning natural beauty. You cannot ignore their volcanic origins – deep craters or calderas are their most outstanding feature. But greenery and trim, patchwork fields impose order and a surprising gentleness. With their tall cliffs and farm-quilted countryside, their tiny homesteads sprinkling the lush landscape, the islands are a magical presence in a volatile ocean.

To Portuguese explorers, who first mapped them in the 15th century, the Azores (Açores in Portuguese) became vital stepping stones in an expanding empire. Christopher Columbus, returning from his momentous 1492 voyage to America, took on water at the eastern island of Santa Maria. For centuries the Azores have offered a safe haven and restful stopover for other mariners.

This remote island group has an extra dimension if you share the view that the 650km (400-mile) -long archipelago's two tiny, westernmost islands, Flores and Corvo, more than a third of the way across the Atlantic, mark the true outermost limit of Europe. The islands are meteorologically important to weather forecasters – an Azores High (high-pressure area) extending to the east means fine weather for western Europe.

ORIGINS

The name Açores was bestowed on the archipelago by Gonçalo Velho Cabral who, with Diogo de Silves, landed at Santa Maria in 1427. These daring seafarers mistook the many buzzards there for hawks, which are called *açores* in Portuguese. But from myth, fable and fanciful charts, another legend persists. Here, some believe, is the lost Atlantis, from Plato's account of a sunken empire. Yet chroniclers wrote that all the islands were uninhabited when the Portuguese arrived.

Main attractions
Ponta Delgada
Caldeira das Sete Cidades
Furnas
Santa Maria
Angra do Heroismo
São Jorge
Horta
Graciosa

Map on page 312

Hot ferrous waterfall in São Miguel.

Thermal springs in Furnas village, São Miguel.

In 1439, settlement officially began on the seven then-known islands (Flores and Corvo were not discovered until 1452), through the efforts of Prince Henry the Navigator. His colonisation policy was so zealous that he offered land to Flemish farmers (the connection was through his sister, Isabel, who was married to the Duke of Burgundy, ruler of Flanders). Prince Henry not only foresaw the role of the islands in his larger purpose of African colonisation but, in his businesslike way, realised they could be profitable, and so organised the planting of wheat and sugar cane.

Throughout Portuguese history, the islanders have held themselves apart from Lisbon, and have often chosen an opposing path. During the 19th-century War of the Two Brothers – the Miguelist Wars between two sons of King João VI – islanders supported the liberal Dom Pedro IV against his absolutist brother, Dom Miguel, who had the support of most of Portugal.

Hardy islanders today still live by farming and fishing. There's a significant dairy industry. You will see cows milked on steep hillsides, their milk occasionally still carried in churns by farmers on horseback. But there are more cerebral pursuits, too, and from the Azores have emerged many of the finest poets, novelists and philosophers in Portuguese culture. One of several daily newspapers, *Açoriano Oriental,* is among the oldest titles in Europe. The islands' identity was established long ago; autonomous government came in 1976, two years after the coup that toppled Salazar's dictatorship (see page 70).

ISLAND ATTRACTIONS

The Azores are gradually attracting more tourists, but still remain off the radar. Great for walking holidays, they are full of pleasant surprises, and invite the visitor to explore. In other words, a dream world for anyone seeking unspoilt nature, tranquillity and the chance to "get back to basics". What they are not, though, are bland resorts for sun worshippers. There are relatively few sandy beaches, and these are mostly volcanic black. The weather is mild (the winter averages 14°C/57°F, summer 23°C/74°F) but except for June to September, it is often wet and windy.

Island pleasures are unpretentious and relaxed. You will discover awe-inspiring scenery of stunning beauty, luxurious vegetation with exotic plants (around 60 of 850 species are endemic), enchanting lakes amid extinct craters, tranquil hill country with rolling fields and lush meadows, magnificent coasts lined by picturesque villages and historical towns, and spectacular hydrangea hedges crisscrossing the landscape.

There is also much to see in the daily working life, which still has a rather traditional aspect. Entertainment is generally limited to discos and bars. Custom and religion are served by frequent *festas*, and the striking Baroque churches carved from basalt.

You can see the relics of a long tradition of whaling, and will encounter the sons and grandsons of whaling men – and, in summer, numerous emigrant families on annual trips home. The Azores are worth a visit even if you only have time to see São Miguel. The Government Tourist Office *(Turismo)* is very friendly and helpful, and the Portuguese Tourist Board will provide plenty of information (see page 329).

The islands are ideal for walking. The more ambitious can climb Pico (Peak) on Pico island: at over 2,300 metres (7,550ft), this is Portugal's highest mountain, but there are numerous less demanding hikes. Additionally, an expanding number of sports facilities range from deep-sea fishing, whale-watching and diving to golf and tennis.

The islands divide naturally into three groups: São Miguel and Santa Maria in the east; Terceira, São Jorge, Graciosa, Faial and Pico in the centre; and Flores and Corvo to the west.

SÃO MIGUEL

São Miguel ❶ is perhaps the most varied of the islands. It is also the largest, measuring 65km by 16km (40 miles by 10 miles), and the most populated, with nearly half the archipelago's population of 246,000.

On the south coast, the capital of **Ponta Delgada** ❷ sprawls behind the

Tip
The main tourist office in the Azores is on Avenida Infante Dom Henrique, in Ponta Delgada, São Miguel island, www.visitazores.com.

A flower vendor in Ponta Delgada.

ESPÍRITO SANTO CULT

On the island of Terceira, gaudy chapels *(impérios)* reflect the islanders' ardour for the Espírito Santo cult, which originated in medieval Germany and was promulgated in Portugal through the teachings of the 17th-century Jesuit priest, António Vieira, and brought to the Azores by early Portuguese settlers. On Whit Sunday, the day of the Holy Spirit, there are processions in towns and villages throughout the island, and many villages have regular Sunday celebrations. A child is usually crowned as an 'emperor', and bears a sceptre, overseeing the ensuing festivities. Local people believe that worship of the Holy Spirit – whose insignia, a crown, sceptre and a white dove, are kept in the *impérios* – will protect their communities from volcanic eruptions, earthquakes, and damage from storms.

A banana tree on the Azores island of San Miguel.

Milk cows grazing on a pasture overlooking the Atlantic.

waterfront – the Avenida Infante Dom Henrique – with its arcades and 18th-century city gates. The town is dramatically set off against numerous small volcanic cones rising on the distant hills. City sights include several fine Baroque churches, among them the 16th-century parish church, Igreja Matriz de São Sebastião. Also of architectural interest are the Palácio da Conceição, which houses the government; and the curious Baroque Casa de Carlos Bicudo with its mermaid facade.

For a view that overlooks the city, head for the **Reduto da Mãe de Deus**, where in 1944 an ill-informed anti-aircraft battery shot at an aircraft carrying General Eisenhower on his way home. There's a good museum, the **Museu Carlos Machado** (http://museucarlos-machado.azores.gov.pt, in the 16th-century Convento de Santo André (there are two other branches in the Church of the Jesuite College and the Santa Bárbara Centre on Rua Dr. Carlos Machado), with exhibits on the island's natural history and ethnography, as well as folk art, paintings and sculpture.

In the west of the island are the enchanting twin lakes within the **Caldeira das Sete Cidades** (Cauldron of the Seven Cities). This is best viewed from Vista do Rei (The King's View), but you will be able to spot only one sleepy village in the crater. In sunlight, one lake is blue, the other green – stemming, legend has it, from the tears of a princess forced to part from her shepherd lover. A half-day circuit of the island might lead past pineapple plantations (visitors welcome) just north of the capital, on to Sete Cidades and the promontory of **Ponta dos Mosteiros**, eastwards to Capelas and its tobacco fields, and finally to the historical town of **Ribeira Grande**. Further east are the Caldeiras da Ribeira Grande, a small spa in picturesque surroundings, and the tea plantations of Gorreana (http://gorreana.pt).

Eastwards from Ponta Delgada, past sandy beaches, are the potteries of **Lagoa** and the diving centre at Caloura, and, beyond, the attractive town of **Vila Franca do Campo** with three ornate Baroque churches. The municipal museum has a good collection of musical instruments and pottery, including clay ocarinas. Above Vila Franca, the pilgrimage chapel of **Senhora da Paz** affords a splendid view over the south coast. Just offshore, accessible from the pretty harbour, is the tiny crater island of **Ilheu**, with a natural seawater swimming pool.

Northeast and inland, past the crater lake of Lagoa das Furnas, is the village of **Furnas** ❸, with hot springs and boiling mud cauldrons that give off the rich stink of sulphur. But here, too, is the famous **Terra Nostra** botanical park (www.parqueterranostra.com) with more than 2,000 different trees, a volcanically heated lake you can swim in, and a pleasant hotel and restaurant, the **Terra Nostra Garden Hotel**. The dish of the house is *cozido à Furnas* – meats and vegetables steamed in underground ovens. For a picnic, you can boil your own eggs in the hot springs beside the crater lake.

SANTA MARIA AND TERCEIRA

The island of **Santa Maria** ❹, only 17km by 9km (10 miles by 5 miles), has peaceful fields and red-roofed whitewashed houses in a southern Portuguese style (initially settlers came from Algarve and Alentejo). Today there are some 6,000 inhabitants. Apart from the underlying volcanic massif, there is also sedimentary rock, and the beaches therefore are a shining gold, in bright contrast to the more usual volcanic black. Santa Maria is the driest, sunniest island, often called the "Algarve of the Azores". Just north of the airport in Anjos is the reconstructed church, where Christopher Columbus once knelt in prayer. The main town is **Vila do Porto**. The nearby Centro de Interpretação Ambiental Dalberto Pombo (t https://parques-naturais.azores.gov.pt/pt/parques/2/centro/3) displays several collections on the island's natural heritage.

In the central group, **Terceira** ❺ (29km by 17km/18 miles by 10 miles) derives its name from the fact that it was the third island in the archipelago to be discovered. All the settlements on Terceira stretch along the coastline, while the unpopulated interior of the island – a wild and rugged landscape partly covered with native brushwood of tree heather, juniper and mosses – is often enveloped in clouds.

Terceira is distinguished by its capital, **Angra do Heroísmo** ❻, which is, deservedly, on UNESCO's World Heritage list – it is undoubtedly the most beautiful town in the archipelago. Once the capital of the Azores, it was granted its heroic title by Queen Maria II, the daughter of Dom Pedro IV, whose regency the island stoutly supported. Severely damaged by an earthquake in 1980, Angra has largely recovered. Its cathedral (constructed between 1570 and 1612 and considered the largest temple of the archipelago), plus several churches, castles and palaces, are of considerable interest. The municipal museum, **Museu de Angra de Heroísmo** (https://museu-angra.cultura.azores.gov.pt), is a good place to learn more about the island's history. A

Typical whitewashed houses on Santa Maria.

Hot springs, or furnas, on San Miguel.

Looking down on the red roads of São Jorge.

The colourful city of Angra do Heroismo, on Terceira.

circuit of the island encompasses stunning views of green patchwork fields subdivided by stone walls. Terceira's most boisterous *festas* are around 24 June, the day of São João (St John the Baptist), and include *touradas à corda*, the running of rope-restrained bulls.

FROM SÃO JORGE TO CORVO

Beautiful **São Jorge** ⑦, 56km (35 miles) long by only 8km (5 miles) wide, rises abruptly from the sea and culminates in a mountain ridge that is often shrouded in mist. Besides its glorious natural setting, São Jorge affords magnificent views of all the central islands. Almost all the villages are set on small coastal plains *(fajãs)* at the foot of tall cliffs; some hamlets can only be reached via narrow footpaths. This island is another excellent choice for walkers. The Fajã da Caldeira de Santo Cristo natural reserve is also a surfer's Mecca and the only place in the Azores where clams grow. **Velas** ⑧, with stunning views across to Pico, is the main town and a good base to explore the island and to buy the excellent local cheese. Among its main attractions are several churches, an 18th-century Baroque town hall and natural pools.

Faial ⑨ rises almost symmetrically on all sides to the central **Caldeira**, an eerie crater with a depth of some 300 metres (1,000ft). Faial's epithet, "Blue Island", was inspired by its hydrangea hedgerows running like blue ribbons over the countryside in June and July – a stunning sight for people used to seeing these bushes only in neat parks and gardens.

The lively capital of **Horta** ⑩ is extremely pleasant, with some interesting museums and churches. Its harbour is a port of call for transatlantic sailors, with each crew commemorating their journey by painting a picture on the *mole* (breakwater). It is said that this ritual secures divine protection for the rest of the journey. The famous **Peter Café Sport** is a well-known meeting spot for sailors, seamen and even spies, which has been in business since 1918. It includes a small **museum** dedicated to the art of scrimshaw – beautifully ornate nautical scenes engraved on the teeth and bones of sperm whales. **Ponta dos Capelinhos** is a dramatic contrast to the lively town and flowery countryside: here, in 1957–8, an undersea volcanic eruption rumbled and grumbled and left a legacy of vast, grim dunes of dark cinder. The **Porto Pim Whale Factory Museum** (Fábrica da Baleia; www.oma.pt) provides an interesting insight into what used to be one of the island's main industries.

Graciosa ⓫ is as gracious as its name suggests, with soft sloping hills and peaceful villages scattered over the island. Yet it also has a volcanic heritage: in Caldeira do Enxofre you may descend 182 stone steps to a huge cavern (furna) with a sulphurous subterranean lake. In the small, tidy capital of **Santa Cruz** ⓬ it becomes obvious why Graciosa was known as the "White Island": all its houses are traditionally whitewashed. Graciosa is home to the archipelago's smallest seabird, the endemic Monteiro's storm petrel, which nests on the islets off the coast.

The towering peak which gives the island its name is the main reason to visit **Ilha do Pico** ⓭, but a look round the island reveals fertile countryside in the east and bizarre rocky regions (called *mistérios*) in the west, which have been flooded by lava comparatively recently. In the sheltered enclosures between dry-stone walls, grapes are grown to produce the local wines.

In **Lajes** ⓮, a small whaling museum, the **Museu dos Baleeiros** (www.museu-pico.azores.gov.pt) recalls the all-too-recent past, when men went out hunting the giant creatures: Herman Melville's *Moby Dick* is set in these waters. Rising to over 2,350 metres (7,700ft), majestic Pico is the highest mountain not only in the Azores but in the whole of Portugal. To climb the main peak (this is best done in summer), you will need proper gear and a reliable route-finder.

Ilha das Flores ⓯ (17km by 12km/10 miles by 7 miles) does not abound in flowers, as its name suggests. But it is the most humid island of the Azores, its wet climate accounting for the lush evergreen vegetation. Flores offers some wild landscapes that are quite different from those of the other islands: basalt predominates, in the form of high-lying, boggy plateaux where waterfalls plummet down over steep rock faces. In the capital, **Santa Cruz**, there is the charming ethnographic Museu das Flores (www.museu-flores.azores.gov.pt), in a converted convent, with displays about life on the island and interesting, quirky artefacts.

From Flores, a boat runs daily, weather permitting, to **Ilha do Corvo** ⓰ (corvo means crow in Portuguese), which measures only 6km by 3km (4 miles by 2 miles). It is the smallest and quietest island in the archipelago, with the 430 inhabitants all living in **Vila Nova**, which is the only village. Corvo's prime sight is a tranquil lake embedded in an isolated crater, whose swampy islets reputedly resemble a map of the Azores. The voracious birds after which the island was named can still be seen around the shores.

> **Where**
> Between April and October, daily whale-watching trips are organised (see www.visitazores.com for details) by Espaço Talassa in Lajes, on Ilha do Pico (www.espacotalassa.com). Trips last around three hours and are preceded by a multimedia presentation (on dry land) all about the creatures you are hoping to see.

View of Horta harbour with Pico Mountain at dusk.

Ponte de Lima azulejo.

PORTUGAL

TRAVEL TIPS

TRANSPORT

Getting there 320
    By air 320
    By rail 320
    By road 320
Getting around 321
    By car 321
    By air 321
    By train 321
    By bus 322
    Boat trips 322
    Transport in Lisbon 322

A – Z

Accessible travel 323
Admission charges 323
Accommodation 323
Budgeting for your trip 323
Children 323
Climate 324
Crime and safety 324
Customs regulations 324
Eating out 324
Electricity 324
Embassies 325
Emergencies 325
Etiquette 325
Festivals and holidays 325
Health and medical care 326
LGBTQ+ travellers 326
Media 326
Money 327
Nightlife 327
Opening hours 328
Postal services 328
Religious services 328
Shopping 328

Sports 328
Telephones 329
Tourist information 329
Tour operators and
    travel agents 330
Visas and passports 330
Website and apps 330
Weights and measures 330
Women travellers 330

LANGUAGE

Getting by 331
Basic communication 331
    Greetings 331
    Telephone calls 331
    At the hotel 331
Eating and drinking
    in a restaurant 332
Menu decoder 332
    Entradas (Starters) 332
    Peixe (fish) 332
    Carne (meat) 332
    Salada (salad) 332
    Doces (desserts) 332
    Basic commodities 332
Health 332
Sightseeing 333
Shopping 333
    Shops 333
Travelling 333
Numbers 333

FURTHER READING

Portuguese works 334
Books about Portugal 334
Other Insight Guides 334

TRANSPORT

GETTING THERE

By air

Scheduled flights

TAP Air Portugal (www.tap.pt) is Portugal's national airline and it has wide international links. Flights, particularly from Paris, can get very heavily booked in the summer (July/August) and around Christmas and Easter.

Many major airlines make non-stop direct flights to Lisbon from capital cities in Europe and other continents. There are several flights a week from New York, Los Angeles and Boston.

You may also, from some countries, fly directly to Porto in the north, Faro in the south and to Madeira and the Azores. Links with London are particularly good. Budget airlines also operate between the UK, Lisbon and Porto, including Easyjet (www.easyjet.com), Ryanair (www.ryanair.com) and Vueling (www.vueling.com).

Visitors from the USA and Canada can travel, among others, on Air Canada between Toronto and Porto and Lisbon; between Los Angeles and Terceira, Azores; and between Boston and Lisbon, Porto, and Ponte Delgada, Azores; as well as various routes between Portugal and the rest of Europe.

Between regular airlines and charter companies the choice is considerable – and ticket prices vary a great deal.

Charter flights

Because Portugal is a popular tourist destination, charter flights from Britain and continental Europe to Lisbon and Faro are frequent in summer, less so in winter. There are similar flights from the United States. Although primarily intended for holiday-makers buying a complete package, including accommodation, spare capacity is sold off as seat only, and often at a discounted rate.

Airports

In Lisbon and Porto the international airports are on the outskirts of the city. Taxis will take you to the city centre. All have meters and lists of charges for out-of-town journeys. The website for Portugal's airports is www.ana.pt. In Lisbon, airport taxis cost around €20 and drivers are entitled to charge an excess for luggage over 30kg (66lb). The easiest way to reach the town centre, if you don't have much luggage, is the Metro extension, which was completed in 2012. The red line runs from Aeroporto, and you can change at S. Sebastião for the blue line to Restauradores or Baixa-Chiado, which will take around 35 minutes; trains run from 6.30am to 1am. The Aerobus (www.aerobus.pt) runs from the yellow bus stop outside the airport every 20 minutes from 8am to 9pm and takes about 20 minutes to the centre of town, and can be quicker than a taxi when traffic is heavy. Tickets allow you a free day's travel on the city's transport system. There are also several public Carris buses (705, 722, 744, 783 and night bus 208) which connect the airport with the city; however, luggage dimension limits apply (50x40x20cm). Porto and Faro also have bus services to their city centres and good air links with each other.

Aeroporto de Lisboa
www.aeroportolisboa.pt/pt
Aeroporto Dr Francisco Sá Carneiro (Porto)
www.aeroportoporto.pt
Aeroporto de Faro
www.aeroportofaro.pt/pt/fao/home
Aeroporto da Santa María (Azores)
www.ana.pt/en/sma/home
Aeroporto da Madeira (Madeira)
www.aeroportomadeira.pt

By rail

Nowhere in Portugal is yet linked to the superfast TGV system, but there's a busy international (and national) train service run by the national railway company, CP (Comboios de Portugal), as well as a daily train, the Sud Express.

There are also routes between northern Spain and Portugal. Vigo to Porto takes around 2 hours. Once in Portugal, you have a good, fast north–south route (Porto–Lisbon–Faro) as well as slow, scenic rides, if you care for them, especially in the north.

Special tickets

Various discounts are available, including for groups, seniors, students, youths and children. Eurail offers train passes: check www.thetrainline.com/trains/rail-passes/eurail for more details.

By road

By car

Good roads link Portugal with its Spanish neighbour at numerous border points. Main east–west routes to Lisbon are from Seville via Beja; from Badajoz via Elvas; from Salamanca via Viseu (via the IP5 highway).

If driving from England, using the channel ferries, or the Channel Tunnel, allow three days; or, via Plymouth–Santander or Portsmouth–Bilbao, allow two.

By bus

Flixbus (www.flixbus.co.uk operates buses between Paris and Lisbon. Although cheap, it may not be as cheap as a no-frills carrier. Tickets tend to be open, so make sure you book a seat for the return journey. Contiki (www.contiki.com) offer a range of travel packages aimed at young people.

GETTING AROUND

By car

Thanks to EU funding, many of Portugal's roads have improved considerably over the past decade or so. However, many rural routes continue to be poorly maintained and narrow. In the cities, traffic can be heavy, especially in rush hour, and towns can be difficult to negotiate. The best plan is to find a car park and walk. Remember to drive on the right, giving priority to traffic on your left.

You will need a blue zone parking permit to park in most major cities. You can acquire these free of charge from the local police. Do not park within 18 metres (60ft) of a road junction, 15 metres (50ft) of a bus or tram stop. Park facing the same direction as the moving traffic on your side of the road. Car parks are increasing in number and are obviously the most secure option.

Seat belts are compulsory in both front and rear seats, and children under 12 below 150cm tall must travel in the back. Talking on a mobile phone while driving is also illegal. Offending against these and other regulations is subject to heavy on-the-spot cash fines. Watch out for compulsory dipped-headlight signs on motorways in the north. By law you should also have a red warning triangle and a fluorescent yellow jacket in the car (provided in rental cars). If you break down, 24-hour assistance is available via the Automóvel Clube de Portugal (www.acp.pt).

The alcohol limit is 0.5g/litre, or 0.2g/litre for those with less than three years' driving experience. Driving over the limit will result in steep fines and possibly having your license revoked. There are four categories of highway:

AE are motorways on which tolls are levied (120kph/75mph speed limit)
IP are *itinerários principais* (main trunk roads, 100kph/62mph)
IC are *itinerários complementares* (complementary trunk roads, 100kph/62mph)
AN are *estradas nacionais* (main roads, 90kph/53mph)

The speed limit in urban areas is 50kph (30mph).

Car hire

To get the best car hire deals, book in advance with internet-based brokers, like Holiday Autos (www.holidayautos.com). Alternatively, the major international car hire companies have offices at the airport, including Hertz, Avis, Alamo and Europcar – along with several local, generally less expensive, companies. Reliable local choices include Amoita (www.amoita.com) and Guerin (www.guerin.pt); the latter has offices at Faro and Lisbon airports, as well as in the cities of Porto and Lisbon.

To rent a car in Portugal, most agencies require you to be at least 21 years old and to have had a valid driving licence for a minimum of one year. An international driving permit is not necessary for EU citizens but can be useful for those coming from elsewhere.

By air

TAP Air Portugal is the national airline. There are daily services between Lisbon, Porto, Faro, Madeira and the Azores.

The airline TAP Express (a rebranded Portugália) also operates a solid domestic and international service, and has a good reputation.

By train

Trains in Portugal range from the comfortable and speedy alfa *rápidos* to the painfully slow *regionais*. Generally, the most efficient routes are the Lisbon–Coimbra–Porto and the Lisbon–Algarve lines. Algarve trains depart from Gare do Oriente. Santa Apolónia is where to catch trains to northern and central Portugal. *Rápidos* (alfa) are fast and punctual and cost more. Some *rápidos* have first-class carriages only; others have a very comfortable second class as well. Next in line are the *directos intercidades*, which make more stops and travel more slowly. These have both first- and second-class compartments; second-class here is likely to be less comfortable than in the *rápidos*.

Finally, the *semi-directos*, and especially the *regionais*, seem to stop every few metres and take longer than you could have believed possible. On *directos*, *semi-directos* and *regionais*, second-class seats are not assigned, and the train company, **Comboios de Portugal (CP)**, has no qualms about issuing more tickets than seats if the need arises. If you want to be certain of a seat, board early. On rural routes, trains are almost always regional. Carry cash on regional lines – it's often not possible to buy tickets in advance or by card.

Oriente Station was designed by Santiago Calatrava.

Furthermore, to reach more remote – or even not-so-remote – destinations, it may be necessary to change trains, and timetables are seldom coordinated. Unless you are catching *rápidos* (and *intercidades*), which are punctual, leave yourself plenty of time between transfers. Note also that only the international trains like the Sud-Expresso and the Faro–Porto Comboio Azul have restaurant cars.

Stations in Lisbon

There are four main railway stations in Lisbon. Cais do Sodré and Rossio are commuter stations. International and long-distance trains to the north and east leave from Santa Apolónia, just to the east of Praça do Comercio. Trains south to Alentejo and the Algarve leave from Gare Oriente.

Stations in Porto and Coimbra

Porto and Coimbra each have two railway stations. Porto's São Bento and Coimbra A are located in the respective town centres. Most long-distance trains, however, arrive and leave from Porto's Campanhã station and Coimbra B station, outside the cities, and there are shuttle services between the central and outlying stations.

By bus

Bus networks are privately run. The major carriers are Rede Expressos (www.rede-expressos.pt), Rodonorte (www.rodonorte.pt) and Eva Transportes (www.eva-bus.com).

Except for routes between major cities, the bus is often faster than the train, and the system is certainly more extensive. This is particularly true in the north and between the smaller towns in Algarve and Alentejo.

There are quite a few private bus lines which specialise in particular areas of the country. Often they have more direct routes to smaller towns. Many travel agencies can book tickets on a private line, or may even run their own.

Boat trips

Boat trips are offered in a variety of vessels, traditional and modern, on the country's three main rivers, the Tejo, Douro and Minho. Many are privately run, so tourist offices do not necessarily have all the information. Hotels, particularly in the Douro region, should be able to tell you all the options.

Rio Tejo Seaventy organises cruises from Alcântara docks (www.seaventy.pt).

Rio Douro Boats depart from the Cais de Ribeira in Porto. Trips range in length from an hour to several days, visiting quintas and stopping en route. The largest operating company is **Douro Azul** in Porto (www.douroazul.pt). Living Tours (www.living-tours.com) offers short and multi-day cruises. **Portowellcome** in Vila Nova de Guia also organises trips (www.portowellcome.com). Bluedragon City Tours (http://bluedragon.pt) offer walking, bike, and Segway trips, including food and wine tours.

Transport in Lisbon

Trains

Commuter trains to Cascais (stopping in Carcavelos, Estoril and other towns along the western coast) depart from Cais do Sodré station, west of the Praça do Comércio. Trains depart roughly every 15 to 20 minutes; the journey to Cascais (the end of the line) takes 35–40 minutes.

Trains to the northwestern suburbs, including Sintra, leave from the Rossio station at 15-minute intervals. The trip to Sintra takes about 45 minutes and operates from Campolide.

Buses and trams

The city bus company, Carris (www.carris.pt) runs an extensive system of buses, trams *(eléctricos)* and funiculars. Bus stops are clearly marked by signposts or shelters. All stops display a diagrammatical map of the bus route; many have a map of the entire city system.

Pre-World War I trams ply the smaller, steeper streets where buses are unable to navigate. Some of them are quite beautiful, inside and out; they are slower and cheaper than the buses and are a good way to see the city. The tram is also supplemented with some larger, more modern vehicles operating along the riverside.

Carris also runs three funiculars and an elevator. The Santa Justa Elevador is near the Rossio. One funicular climbs the steep Calçada da Glória from Praça dos Restauradores, another connects Rua de São Paulo with Largo Calhariz, and the other links Largo da Annunciada with Rua Câmara Pestana. You pay on board, or they are covered by Carris tickets and passes.

Tickets and passes

It is worth considering buying a Viva Viagem or 7Colinas card. These cost €0.50, are valid for one year, and you can charge them up repeatedly. You thus pay less per journey than you do if you buy regular tickets. They can be charged so that they're useable only on the Carris network, or so that they can be used on the Carris and the Metro networks. Buying tickets for each journey works out more expensive. Don't board the bus without paying, as ticket inspectors appear from time to time and the fine is steep.

The Carris information kiosks scattered all over the city provide information and sell tickets and passes. Two of the most convenient kiosks are in Praça da Figueira, near the Rossio, and near Eduardo VII Park.

Metro

The Metro is useful for travel in the central zone of the city and travelling to/from the airport. The system is easy to use and cheap. You can buy single tickets and validate them at the machines next to the ticket booths. Carris kiosks and Metro stations also sell a one-day Bilhete Carris/Metro ticket valid for buses, trams, funiculars and the metro. Alternatively the Viva Viagem or 7Colinas cards may be charged so that they are valid on the Metro. A planned extension, linking up the green and yellow lines, began construction in 2019 and is due to be completed by the end of 2024.

Taxis

In all Portugal's cities, taxis are plentiful and cheap. They are either cream-coloured or black with green roofs. In the city, they charge a standard metered fare, with no additions for extra passengers. (They carry up to four people.) Outside city limits, the driver may use the meter or charge a flat rate per kilometre, and is entitled to charge for the return fare (even if you don't take it). You should tip taxi drivers between 5 and 10 percent.

A

Accessible travel

Portugal is gradually catering more to travellers with disabilities and there is a handful of organisations that may be able to advise you further. Tourism For All (Adelino Amaro da Costa 14 Loja – Ouressa 2725-208, Mem-Martins, tel: 964 631 583, www.tourism-for-all.com) offers a wide choice of itineraries, including city breaks, overnight trips, accommodation and tours. They speak English. Ourico do Mar (tel: 968 573 135; www.ouricodomar.com) offer wheelchair-accessible holiday accommodation, with wheelchair-accessible transport in the Algarve. Newer and larger hotels generally have disabled-accessible rooms and adapted toilets, and museums and major sights are gradually providing ramped access.

Admission charges

Portugal's museums and galleries are relatively inexpensive, ranging from around €3–10 for an adult ticket. Over-65s and students generally pay half price upon proof of identification. You can expect to pay in the region of €15–30 for entrance to theme parks and water parks. Both Lisbon and Porto offer discount cards: the Lisboa Card (www.lisboacard.org) and the Porto Card (www.portocard.city), which offer substantial discounts on multi-sights and unlimited travel on public transport. For more information, check the respective tourist offices.

Accommodation

Accommodation ranges from 5-star luxury hotels with fantastic facilities to basic private rooms for rent, or from boutique, charming converted mansions, to glamping-style yurts in the middle of the North Portugal countryside. Hotels in Portugal offer great value when compared with places elsewhere in Europe. This is particularly the case at the luxury end of the market.

Pousadas and manor houses

It's well worth trying to stay in some *pousadas* while you are in Portugal, as these are a speciality of the country, the like of which you won't find elsewhere. *Pousadas* are national inns in architecturally special buildings, which provide stylish and comfortable accommodation, usually in great settings. They are to be found in most parts of the country–some in historic castles, some in converted convents or grand country houses– and the majority serve excellent regional food.

For reservations, contact the *pousadas* directly or call the central number (tel: 218 442 001; www.pousadas.pt or check www.pousadasofportugal.com).

Guesthouses

Portugal has some very charming, modest guesthouses. These often have a lot of local character, and are well located, but are well kept and appealing. Bed and breakfasts in private homes are designated by an official TER symbol on a metal plaque and the logo of the State Tourist Office (Direcção-Geral do Turismo); there are three categories:
TH *Turismo de Habitação*: in houses of architectural merit.
TR *Turismo Rural*: characteristic rural houses.
AT *Agroturismo*: houses forming part of a farm estate.

Hotels

Hotels in Portugal come in several guises:

Hotels offer amenities such as restaurants and room service. All rooms have bathrooms.
Albergarias are essentially hotels offering 4-star comfort and meals.
Estalagems are very similar but may be 4- or 5-star.
Residencials have star gradings and are like small hotels but generally do bed and breakfast only. They usually have an "R" on a sign outside.
Pensãos are more basic, and again do bed and breakfast only. You can find 4-star *pensãos*, but the majority offer fewer comforts than that.

B

Budgeting for your trip

Portugal remains one of the cheapest countries in southern Europe for tourists. Some average costs are:
A beer: €1.50–3
A glass of house wine: €1.50
Main course at a budget/moderate/expensive restaurant: €8/€10/€20
Double room in a cheap/moderate/deluxe hotel: €50/€80/€100–200
Taxi journey from Lisbon airport to the centre: €20
Single bus ticket or metro ticket: €1.80

C

Children

Like its neighbour, Spain, Portugal is a seriously child-friendly country. Children are made welcome just about everywhere, including hotels, restaurants and bars. There are plenty of kiddie-geared activities on offer as well, particularly in Algarve, with water parks, boat trips and beaches. Watch the strength of the sun in summer, however, and always ensure your child is wearing a hat and plenty of sunblock. Most hotels can supply a cot if notified in advance, and babysitting is generally provided at 4- and 5-star hotels. Otherwise, tourist offices may be able to recommend babysitting services. Children's meals are not always available, but most restaurants are happy to provide a smaller portion. On public transport, children under three travel free while 4- to 12-year-olds pay half fare (on trains only; full fare on Metro and buses). Discounts are available for over-65s on the Metro.

Climate

Summer (June–September)

Summers are generally hot throughout the country with endless days of sunshine. Average high temperatures in Lisbon in July sit at around 28°C (82°F). The north also enjoys warm summers, but with greater rainfall (51mm in September in Porto). Some inland areas experience extremely high temperatures in summer – Alentejo in the south and the Upper Douro in the north often top 40°C (104°F) for long periods. Algarve in contrast tends to be moderately hot in summer (31°C/88°F), enjoying the benefit of cooling westerlies. July and August are peak holiday season in Portugal and are correspondingly busier and more expensive.

Winter (November–March)

Southernmost Algarve enjoys mild winters with many fine sunny days and average highs of 16°C (60°F) in January. Sheltered, south-facing beaches provide ideal sun traps throughout the year, though evenings might have a chill in the air.

Around Lisbon, winters are mild with an unpredictable mixture of sunny and showery days, while in the northern and central regions winters are rainy and surprisingly chilly (average highs of 9°C (48°F) in Bragança in January). In the mountains it's even colder, and variable snow falls on the Serra da Estrela and mountains to the north and east between November and February (sometimes enough for ski enthusiasts, although conditions are far from ideal).

Shoulder season (April, May & October)

April, May & October are in many ways the best months to visit Portugal, with far smaller crowds, mild temperatures and only moderate rainfall (44mm in Lisbon in May) making hiking and sightseeing very pleasant. Porto sees average highs of 21°C (70°F) in October.

What to wear

Given the variable weather in northern Portugal, it is sensible to pack for all possibilities – it can rain in Porto at any time of year, while summers in the Douro vary from warm to very hot. Lisbon is often windy, so bring layers for the evenings, even in summer. Modest clothing is recommended for visiting religious buildings.

Crime and safety

Portugal has a well-deserved reputation for non-violence, and crime rates are low. However, petty theft and muggings can be a problem in some of the more run-down areas of Lisbon and Porto, close to some of the larger shopping centres, and some of the major resorts. Foreign-registered cars or cars obviously rented may be targets for thieves if left unattended in out-of-the-way locations.

Use your common sense and the usual degree of attention, and, as in most places, take special care walking around late at night in resorts and in the larger cities.

Stolen property

In the event of theft, report it to the police within 24 hours to reclaim insurance. In Lisbon the main Policia de Segurança Pública (PSP, tel: 213 421 623; www.psp.pt) station dealing with foreigners who have been robbed is at the Palacio Foz, in the Praça dos Restauradores.

Lost property

All lost property on buses and trams will be held at the Customer Care department at Campo Grande station for two days, then forwarded, along with other items handed to the Lisbon police, to Olivais police station, Praça Cidade Salazar (Mon–Fri 9am–12.30pm and 2–4pm, tel: 218 535 403. At the airport, you can enquire about your lost property by calling tel: 218 444 530. There is also a lost and found official website (https://perdidoseachados.mai.gov.pt/) but only in Portuguese.

Customs regulations

You can bring currency up to €10,000 into the country without declaration. The duty-free allowance for travellers over 17 years of age from non-EU countries is 200 cigarettes and 1 litre of spirits or 4 litres of wine. EU residents can bring in 800 cigarettes, plus 10 litres of spirits, 20 litres of beverages with alcohol content below 20 percent, 90 litres of wine or 110 litres of beer.

E

Eating out

Eating establishments in Portugal run from cosy family-run cafés to Michelin-starred restaurants via Lisbon's must-visit kiosk cafés and food markets. A classic way to start the day is with a pastry or sandwich and a coffee at a *pastelaria* (bakery). Lunch (noon–3pm) tends to be a bigger and more varied affair, with many cafés and restaurants offering an economical *prato do dia* (dish of the day). Portuguese eat dinner earlier than their Spanish neighbours, between around 7.30–10pm. In restaurants you will usually be brought bread, butter and sometimes fish pâté before your meal – it's not free, but you will only be charged for what you eat. Tipping is not traditional in Portugal beyond rounding up to the nearest euro or round number, although up to 10 percent is increasingly expected in tourist areas.

Electricity

Mains voltage is 220V, which is fine with equipment intended for 240V. Plugs are the European two round-pin variety. Adaptors are sold at airports, hardware stores and supermarkets.

Embassies

Embassies are listed in phone books (under *Consulado* or *Embaixada*). Most are in Lisbon, Porto or Faro.

Embassies in Lisbon:
Australia
Avenida da Liberdade, 200, 2°
Tel: 213 101 500
Canada
Avenida da Liberdade, 196-200, 3°
Tel: 213 164 600.
Republic of Ireland
Avenida da Liberdade, No. 200, 4°
Tel: 213 308 200.
South Africa
Avenida Luís Bivar, 10/10 A
Tel: 213 192 200.
UK
Rua de São Bernardo, 33
Tel: 213 924 000
US
Avenida das Forças Armadas, 16
Tel: 217 273 300.

Emergencies

To contact the emergency service (police, ambulance or fire) dial **112** (toll-free). Most operators speak at least two foreign languages, usually including English.

Etiquette

The Portuguese are usually courteous and hospitable. Taking a short while to learn and use the language basics will serve you well (see page 331).

If you are invited to someone's house, it is polite to bring flowers for the hostess or a small toy or sweets if there are young children.

There are orderly queues at bus stops. Be sure to respect them.

For some reason, stretching in public (on the street or at the table) is considered rude. Otherwise, use common sense and a smile and you shouldn't go far wrong.

F

Festivals and holidays

January
1 January: New Year's Day (national holiday).
20 January: Festa das Fogaceiras in Santa Maria da Feira – young girls in traditional dress carrying castle-shaped *fogaças* cakes on their heads.

February
February/March (depending on date of Easter): Carnaval celebrated all over Portugal, but especially in Lisbon, Loulé, Nazaré and Viana do Castelo.

March
Late March/early April (week preceding Easter): Semana Santa (Holy Week). Celebrated nationwide, with local variations such as Senhor Ecce Homo festival in Braga featuring barefoot, torch-bearing, hooded penitents.

April
25 April: Dia da Liberdade (Liberty Day) celebrates the 1974 revolution.
Late April: Ovibeja Agricultural Fair. Nine-day Beja fair, nightly concerts.

May
1 May: Labour Day
3–5 May: Feira das Cantarinhas. Fair of traditional handicrafts in Bragança.
Early May: Queima das Fitas, Coimbra. Local students go mad with parades, fado and the burning of gowns.
Early May: Festa das Cruzes. Festival of the Crosses in Barcelos, with concerts nightly.
13 May: Fátima Romaris. Celebrates the vision of the Virgin at Fátima.

June
10 June: Portugal Day.
12–13 June: Festa de Santo António. Celebrated all over the country, but especially in Lisbon.
Mid-June: Corpus Christi celebrations, Monçao. A procession and a battle between the forces of good and evil.
23–4 June: Festa de São Joao (John the Baptist), celebrated especially in Porto, Aveiro and Braga. In Porto large parties are held where people are hit over the head with inflatable mallets.
29 June: Festa de Sao Pedro (St Peter). Music, dancing and processions.
Late June: Feira Nacional da Agricultura, Santarém. Features horse racing, bullfights and bull-running in the streets.
Late June: Festa de São Gonçalo, Amarante. A large procession with single people exchanging phallic-shaped cakes as love tokens.
Late June: Festas Populares. Huge Alentejo country fair in Évora.
Late June: Rock in Rio, Lisbon. Huge rock festival.

July
First weekend of the month Festa do Colete Encarnado, Vila Franca de Xira, has bull-running in the streets; and Festa dos Tabuleiros, Tomar (every four years: 2023, 2027, etc), showcases a procession of girls dressed in white, balancing large trays of bread and wheat on their heads.
Mid-July: Festival Marés Vivas. Cool music festival in Porto.

August
Early August: Festival do Sudoeste, Zamujeira do Mar. Large music festival with international stars.
Mid-August: Festival do Marisco, Olhão. Celebration of shellfish.
15 August: Feast of the Assumption.
20 August: Romaria da Nossa Senhora da Agonía (Our Lady of Sorrows), Viana do Castelo. Parade of floats, music, fireworks and lots of drinking.
Mid-August to 21 September: Feira de São Mateus, Viseu. An agricultural fair featuring bullfights, fado and folk dancing.
Late August: Folkfaro, Faro, Algarve. Lots of live folk music.

September
8 September: Nossa Senhora da Nazaré, Estremadura. Folk dances, bullfights and processions.
Late September: Feiras Novas, Ponte de Lima, the Minho. Huge market and fair.

October
5 October: Republic Day.
13 October: Fátima Romaris, Fátima. Celebrates the vision of the Virgin; similar to the May festival.
Late October: Feira de Santa Iria, Faro, Algarve. Honouring St Irene with music and a fun fair.

November
1 November: All Saints' Day.

December
1 December: Independence Day.
8 December: Feast of the Immaculate Conception.
25 December: Christmas Day.

Fado restaurant in Lisbon.

H

Health and medical care

For Visitors to Portugal should check the most up-to-date guidance at www.gov.uk/foreign-travel-advice/portugal/entry-requirements.

The Portuguese health service has reciprocal emergency-treatment arrangements with EU countries. EHIC cards are being phased out for UK citizens in favour of the UK Global Health Insurance Card (UK GHIC); if you have an existing EHIC card, it will remain valid until its expiry date. GHIC cards are available online at www.ghic.org.uk. It is also advisable to have additional health insurance.

Beware of sunburn; use sunscreen (bring it from home as it is much more expensive in Portugal).

Tap water is generally safe but not always palatable, so it is best to use bottled water *(água mineral)*.

Insect bites (usually by mosquitoes) can be a problem in the summer, so bring repellents. In the countryside, snakes are not uncommon but they are rarely a problem: apart from one species of viper in the north, other venomous snakes have fangs at the back of their mouths, so even if they were to strike, it is unlikely to do you any major harm. There is no rabies in Portugal.

Useful numbers

Ambulance Tel: 112 (emergency number)
INEM (Instituto Nacional de Emergência Médica; www.inem.pt)
Tel: 213 508 100 (Lisbon)
Portuguese Red Cross
Tel: 213 913 900

Linha Vida (for information on drug use and abuse)
Tel: 1414

Chemists

When closed, all chemists *(farmácias)* have a list on their doors highlighting the nearest one that is open. Newspapers also publish a list of chemists that stay open late.

Hospitals

Every town has a **centro de saúde** (health centre), some with 24-hour emergency service.

Lisbon

There are half a dozen large hospitals in Lisbon. The following have accident and emergency departments:
Hospital Cruz Vermelha, Rua Duarte Galvão, 54 (situated behind the zoo), tel: 217 714 000; www.hospitalcruzvermelha.pt.
Hospital de Santa Maria, Avenida Prof. Egas Moniz (in the Cidade Universitária area not far from Sete Rios), tel: 217 805 000 for general enquiries or 217 805 111 for emergencies; www.chlc.min-saude.pt.
Hospital São Jose, Rua José A. Serrano, tel: 218 841 000; www.chlc.min-saude.pt.
Hospital da Luz Torres de Lisboa, Rua Tomas da Fonseca, Torres de Lisboa, tel: 217 104 400; www.hospitaldaluz.pt/torres-de-lisboa/pt.

Porto

Centro Hospitalar do Porto, Largo Prof. Abel Salazar, tel: 222 077 500; www.chporto.pt.

Private clinics

Lisbon

Clinica de Santo António, Avenida Hospitais Civis Lisboa, 8, Reboleira, 2720 Amadora, tel: 214 999 380; www.lusiadas.pt

Porto

Hospital CUF Trindade, 115 Rua Da Trindade, tel: 222 075 900; www.cuf.pt/hospitais-e-clinicas/hospital-cuf-trindade.

L

LGBTQ+ travellers

In a country heavily influenced by the Catholic Church, attitudes towards LGBTQ+ people are not as tolerant as elsewhere in Europe. Lisbon is the most important city in Portugal's LGBTQ+ scene and offers a number of bars and clubs catering to a LGBTQ+ crowd. In certain enclaves of the Algarve, such as "the Strip" in Albufeira, LGBTQ+ visitors will find accommodating bars and restaurants.

The website www.portugalgay.pt contains a travel guide with information in English and other languages.

M

Media

Newspapers & magazines

Portugal has several daily newspapers, two of which – *A Bola* and *O Jogo* – are dedicated solely to football!

The principal general newspapers are now published in both Lisbon and Porto and tend to have a regional bias, as indicated: *Diário de Notícias* (Lisbon), *Jornal de Notícias* (Porto), *Público* (Lisbon and Porto) and *Destak* (Lisbon, Porto and Coimbra).

Weeklies include the *Expresso* (up to *Sunday Times/Observer* standard). The *Anglo-Portuguese News* is a website including news and listings and *The Portugal News* (www.theportugalnews.com) likewise provides local and international news, plus listings and classifieds. In the Algarve, *The Resident* is a popular weekly English newspaper primarily aimed at the local expat community.

Television

RTP, the state-owned corporation, operates several national television channels (including Rtp 1, Rtp 2, Rtp3 news channel and Rtp Memória), two regional stations and one international (RTP Madeira, RTP Azores, RTP Internacional). There are also two commercial stations (**SIC** and **TVI**).

Films are transmitted in the language of origin, with subtitles, as are many serials and documentaries. There is a high content of soap operas (many Brazilian) and quiz shows. Most hotels have satellite/cable TV, which will include Sky News, Eurosport, CNN and CNBC.

Radio

There are four national and five regional **RDP** (state-owned) radio stations as well as more than 300 local radio stations. Among them are Antenna 1, which broadcasts

World Music

In Portugal you can hear local music played on unusual instruments and rooted in deep traditions, and you can hear world music, brought in from the former colonies in Africa and Latin America.

Festas have kept alive local folk groups, which show no signs of dying out, and modern musicians often turn to these roots for inspiration, from the Arabic-inspired songs of Alentejo to the bagpipe wails of Trás-os-Montes. There is a rich variety of instruments, notably the *guitarra portuguesa*, a 12-string instrument that has several versions, and the four-string *cavaquinho*, the ancestor of the ukelele. There is also a strong a capella tradition, and you may hear student groups break into song in the streets of Porto or Coimbra.

Brazilian music has come to the fore in recent years, and Portugal is a good place to hear it. You can also seek out venues with music from Africa, or from Cabo Verde, a small Atlantic island and former colony with a disproportionate number of talented singers, such as Cesaria Évora.

popular music and news, and Antenna 2, a classical music station. Meanwhile, Antenna 3 plays contemporary and alternative music. There are also commercial radio stations, among them **TSF** and **RR**, which offer a similar mix of news and popular music.

Money

Currency

The euro is the national currency of Portugal. It is divided into 100 cêntimos (cents) which is the basic unit of currency. The smallest coin is the 1 cêntimo piece; and the largest is the 2 euro coin. Notes go from 5 to 500 euros. The symbol for the euro is € and is written before the figure, eg €7.50 is 7 euros 50 cêntimos.

Exchange

While you may want to buy a small amount of euros before you leave home, you will get a better exchange rate if you wait until you are in Portugal. Once you have bought euros, however, it may be costly to re-exchange them for foreign currency. The most economical policy is to change money as you require it.

Money is best changed at banks, rather than at hotels or travel agencies. Outside normal banking hours, ATMs (cash machines), usually called *Multibanco*, are widely available and there are currency exchanges at Lisbon's Santa Apolónia railway station as well as at the airports. ATMs taking all the major cards, including credit cards, are widespread throughout the country.

Credit cards

Major credit cards can be used in most hotels, restaurants and shops, but check in advance to avoid embarrassment. Country restaurants and *pensãos* may only accept cash. It is increasingly difficult to exchange traveller's cheques in Portugal.

Tipping

A tip of 5–10 percent is sufficient in restaurants and for taxi drivers. Barbers and hairdressers expect to receive the same.

N

Nightlife

Portugal's nightlife is liveliest in Lisbon, and Lisbon's nightlife – from fado to great bars and discos – throbs in three main areas: in the picturesque district of Bairro Alto, a tightly knit grid where tiny bars spill into the streets, providing a party atmosphere; in the Cais do Sodré area behind the Avenida 24 de Julho; and around the reclaimed dockside at Alcântara.

Look out, too, for events in the **Fundação Calouste Gulbenkian** (http://gulbenkian.pt) and the **Centro Cultural de Belém** (www.ccb.pt). The **Coliseu dos Recreios** (www.coliseulisboa.pt) in Rua das Portas de Santo Antão is the main venue for popular music performances. Major theatrical events are staged in the **Teatro Nacional Dona Maria II** (www.tndm.pt) in Rossio Square and in the Casino-Auditorio (www.casino-estoril.pt) in Estoril. The **Teatro Camões** in the Parque das Nações (www.cnb.pt) is the main home of La Companhia Nacional de Bailado, the national ballet company.

The **Teatro Nacional São Carlos** (http://tnsc.pt/) in Chiado is the city's opera house, which has a winter season. The **São Luís Teatro Municipal** (www.teatrosaoluiz.pt) is the capital's principal classical music venue, but look out for concerts in romantic settings, such as the São Roque church, and at Sintra and the palace at Mafra.

Tickets for many events can be obtained from the fifth floor of the Fnac department store in Chiado.

The Orquestra Nacional do Porto is a major national orchestra, and Porto has a prime classical music venue in the striking **Casa da Música** (www.casadamusica.com) as well as the **Auditório Nacional Carlos Alberta** (www.tnsj.pt); and popular music is staged at the Coliseu de Porto (www.coliseu.pt).

The Orquestra do Algarve (www.orquestradoalgarve.com) holds concerts throughout the year and there are a number of festivals along the coast. **Loulé** has a renowned jazz festival.

There are a number of music festivals around the country throughout the summer, including the annual **Festival do Sudoeste** in the Alentejo and the biennial **Rock in Rio** in Lisbon.

Any town or village is lively until late on the night of a festival but at other times of the year the tourist towns and resorts in **Algarve** are among the few places to keep late hours; here summer visitors like to stay up until the early hours. Lagos, especially, is a fun party town.

For a list of what's going on where, the best place to look is *Time Out* (www.timeout.com), which has extensive listings for Lisbon and Porto; they also produce a free print magazine. Try *Trippin* (https://trippin.world/destination/lisbon) for more curated recommendations.

Music

Although Portugal's nightlife usually comes to an end fairly early, music—in fado houses, concert halls and nightclubs alike—tends to start fairly late, around 10pm.

The Portuguese musical tradition is much broader than simply fado. Folk music, very different from fado, is surprisingly vibrant in Portugal, as is jazz. There are several Lisbon nightclubs devoted only to African music, which are the places to go to hear the latest in African-influenced sounds.

O

Opening hours

Most stores open for business Monday–Friday 9 or 10am–7pm (with some taking a lunch break 1–3pm) and Saturday 9am–1pm, and are closed Sunday and holidays. Some shops in central Lisbon are open on Saturday afternoon and some malls and supermarkets are open on Sunday and all day during the week.

Major **banks** are open Monday–Friday 8.30am–3pm.

Museums usually open 10am–6pm, and are closed on Mondays or Tuesdays.

P

Postal services

Postal services, both international and domestic, are generally reliable and efficient. Allow five days for delivery within Europe. For next-day delivery within Portugal, use *correio azul*, an internal express service.

The post office also provides services such as express mail (*expresso*), postal money orders (*vales*), general delivery (*poste restante*), registered mail (*registos*), insurance on packages (*seguro*), and telephone and scanning services.

Post offices are open Monday–Friday 9am–6pm; smaller branches close for lunch from 12.30–2.30pm. In district capitals, the main branch is usually open on Saturday morning. Mail is delivered Monday to Friday.

To buy stamps, stand in any queue marked *selos* (stamps). To mail or receive packages, you need to go to the queue marked *encomendas*.

Be certain to write Via Aérea on all airmail items. To send large parcels home, if speed is not important, consider the less expensive alternative of surface mail. For details visit www.ctt.pt.

R

Religious services

Portugal is a Catholic country with around half of the more traditional north's population attending Sunday Mass (fewer in Lisbon and the south of the country). Many of the country's festivals have their roots in religion and Fátima attracts some 300,000 pilgrims every May and October, the most important months on this site's calendar. Although around 80 percent of the population is Catholic, the Portuguese are, overall, very tolerant of other religions.

S

Shopping

What to buy

Portuguese handicrafts range from hand-carved toothpicks to wicker furniture to blankets and rugs. The most famous items are ceramic tiles (azulejos – see page 162) and pottery, Arraiolos rugs, embroidery and lace (see page 220). The beautiful Vista Alegre porcelain and Atlantis crystal bear comparison with the best in the world.

Pottery Different varieties of ceramic work are produced all over the country; in Alentejo, for example, you will find examples of *barro* pottery, a simple brown clay, sometimes decorated, sometimes glazed. Decorations on ceramics tend to be paintings of fruit or flowers, or sometimes scenes of rural life. Fine pottery from around Coimbra often carries animal motifs, and looks quite intricate in comparison with the simple Alentejano decorations. Further north, blue-and-white glazed pottery appears.

Rugs Arraiolos rugs, by contrast, come from only one place, the one from which they take their name: Arraiolos, in Alentejo. (They are, however, sold in other parts of the country, especially in Lisbon.) The art of designing and stitching these rugs probably goes back to the Middle Ages.

Sports

Participant sports

Golf

The standard of golf courses in Portugal is very high. Those in the Estoril/Sintra area and in Algarve are particularly popular. Among useful and comprehensive websites are www.portugalgolfe.com and http://algarvegolf.net.

Water sports

There are few facilities for hiring equipment outside Algarve. In the Lisbon area you will find surfboards and other equipment for hire at the beaches. For sailing, there's **the Cascais Naval Club** (www.cncascais.com). Windsurfers head for the long beaches and wild waves at Guincho, farther out. For deep-sea fishing, check with the local tourist office.

In Algarve, all the larger tourist beaches and towns have some facilities. Near Lagos, there are windsurfing and waterskiing facilities at Luz, São Roque (Meia Praia) and Alvor beaches; the latter two also have sailing facilities. Praia da Rocha has sailing, windsurfing and waterskiing facilities; sailing and windsurfing are

---

Public Holidays

1 January New Year's Day
February Shrove Tuesday
March/April Good Friday
25 April Anniversary of the Revolution (1974)
1 May Labour Day
10 June Portugal and Camões Day
early/mid-June Corpus Christi
15 August Day of the Assumption
5 October Republic Day
1 November All Saints' Day
1 December Restoration of Independence
8 December Day of the Immaculate Conception
25 December Christmas Day
Local municipal holidays are as follows:

Aveiro – 12 May
Beja – 17 May
Braga – 24 June
Bragança – 22 August
Castelo Branco – 24 April
Coimbra – 4 July
Évora – 29 June
Faro – 7 September
Guarda – 27 November
Leiria – 22 May
Lisbon – 13 June
Porto – 24 June
Portalegre – 23 May
Santarém – 19 March
Setúbal – 15 September
Viana do Castelo – 20 August
Vila Real – 13 June
Viseu – 21 September

practised at Armação de Pera, near Albufeira. Vilamoura has extensive water sports facilities, as does Vale do Lobo. The wild coast near Sagres is particularly popular with surfers.

Walking & hiking
The many national parks in central and northern Portugal are ideal for walking and hiking: the Serra da Estrela and Peneda-Gerês and Montesinho National Parks are three of the best. The beaches and cliffs along the Algarve coast are also excellent for walking, as are the hills around Mogadouro in Trás-os-Montes. Various local organisations offer hiking and climbing excursions.

Horse riding
There are stables all around the country where horses can be hired. Algarve in particular has a number of riding centres. Most of the horses you will encounter are at least in part Lusitano, a famous and sure-footed Portuguese breed. Adventure centres in northern Portugal also offer horse riding trips, such as around Campo do Gerês in the Minho.

Spectator sports

Football
Football dominates Portuguese sporting life. From the 10-year-olds playing in the street to the hundreds of professional, semi-pro and amateur teams, to the massive coverage the sport is given on TV and in the papers, football in Portugal is inescapable.

The three most important teams in the country are FC Porto, from Porto, and Benfica and Sporting, from Lisbon. Just about everyone in Portugal, no matter where they are from, is a loyal fan of one of the three.

The football season stretches from August to June. Tickets for the big three teams are difficult to get, as there are many season-ticket holders. In Lisbon, try the ticket kiosk located in Praça dos Restauradores; elsewhere, try the stadiums themselves. Games are held across the weekend, with the big clubs also playing European fixtures midweek.

Bullfighting
Portuguese bullfighting is different from the Spanish variety. It is considered less violent because the bull is not killed in the ring (however, it is killed later, out of public view). Nonetheless, it is bloody enough to disturb many people. The star Portuguese bullfighters are on horseback, the horses beautifully bedecked and highly trained. A striking aspect of the Portuguese *corrida* is the team of *forcados* – eight unpaid local men, colourfully dressed in short coats, tight pants, waistbands and stockings – who face the bull bare-handed in an exhibition of pure machismo.

Bullfighting is popular primarily in Ribatejo (just outside Lisbon) and in Lisbon itself. The season runs from spring to autumn. In Lisbon, *corridas* are held in the Campo Pequeño bullring. There is also a ring in Cascais. The most famous bullfights, however, are held in Santarém and Vila Franca da Xira, northeast of Lisbon (take the train from Santa Apolónia.)

Ribatejo festivals, which are frequent in the summer, almost always feature bullfighting and the freeing of bulls in the streets.

T

Telephones
All **phones** are equipped for international calls and most accept coins.

MEO or NOS sim cards can be bought at kiosks and many shops. Instructions for using the phone are written in English and other major languages. You can also make calls (international and local) from post offices. Go to the window for a cabin assignment and pay when the call is finished. Many of the internet cafés in the larger cities also have several telephone booths. In general they can be found near train stations.

Many village stores and bars in Portugal have metered telephones. Phone first, pay later, but be prepared to pay more than the rate for call-box or post-office calls. As elsewhere, calls made from hotels are higher still.

For US phone customers, useful numbers are:
AT&T: tel: 800 800 128 (international toll free access code).
Verizon: tel: 800 837 4966 (customer service).
Sprint: tel: 817 698 4199 (customer service).

> ### Time Zone
> GMT (summer time March–October GMT +1); the Azores are 1 hour behind continental Portugal.

Mobile phones
Mobile phone (cellphone) use is widespread, with the main local operators being Vodafone, MEO and NOS. You can buy a pre-paid SIM card to insert in your phone. You can also buy a pay-as-you-go cheap local phone at the airport or numerous mobile phone shops, which can be cheaper than roaming for non-EU citizens.

Tourist information
The national tourist office (ICEP) has offices in Lisbon, Porto and at Faro airports. Most towns have *Turismo* (tourist offices), which are generous with maps and information. Some of the smaller ones close at weekends off season. Regional capitals have separate city and regional offices. Portugal's official website is www.visitportugal.com.
Albufeira
Rua 5 de Outubro
Tel: 289 585 279
Aveiro
Rua João Mendonça, 8
Tel: 234 420 760
Azores
Rua Ernesto Rebelo, 14
Horta, Faial
Tel: 292 200 500
Beja
Rua Capitão João Francisco de Sousa
Tel: 284 311 913
Braga
Avenida da Liberdade, 1
Tel: 253 262 550
Bragança
Avenida Cidade de Zamora
Tel: 273 381 273
www.cm-braganca.pt
Castelo Branco
Avenida Nuno Álvares, 30
Tel: 272 330 339
www.cm-castelobranco.pt
Coimbra
Largo da Portagem
Tel: 239 488 120
www.centerofportugal.com
Cascais & Estoril
Praça 5 de Outubro – Cascais
Tel: 912 034 214
www.visitcascais.com

Évora
Praça do Giraldo, 73
Tel: 266 777 071
www.cm-evora.pt
Faro City
Rua de Misericórdia, 8
Tel: 289 803 604
www.visitalgarve.pt
Guimarães
Largo José Maria Gomes
Tel: 253 421 221
www.guimaraesturismo.com
Lagos
Praça Gil Eanes
Tel: 282 763 031
Lisbon
Lisboa Welcome Centre, Rua do Arsenal, Praço do Comercio
Tel: 210 312 700
www.visitlisboa.com
Ask Me Lisboa
Palacio Foz, Praça dos Restauradores
Tel: 213 463 314
Madeira
Avenida Arriaga, Funchal 18
Tel: 291 211 902
www.visitmadeira.pt
Porto City
Rua Clube Fenianos, 25
Tel: 223 325 167
www.visitportoandnorth.travel
Setúbal
Casa da Baía
Av. Luísa Todi, 468
Tel: 265 534 402
www.mun-setubal.pt
Tomar
Avenida Dr. Cândido Madureira
Tel: 249 329 823
www.centerofportugal.com
Viana do Castelo
Praça do Eixo Atlântico
Tel: 258 098 415

Portuguese tourist offices abroad
Ireland
70 Upper Leeson Street, Dublin 4
Tel: +353 1 669 9100
Spain
C/Lagasca, 88 - 4º, 28001 Madrid
Tel: +34 915 77 35 85
United Kingdom
11 Belgrave Square, London, SW1X 8PP
Tel: +44 20 7235 5331
United States
757 Third Avenue, Suite 1703, New York, NY 10017
Tel: +1 646 2731231

Tour operators and travel agents

There are numerous travel and tour companies that offer comprehensive packages. Most are booked via the internet, including the following:

Portugal: www.portugal.com. A wide range of accommodation options, including *pousadas*, manor houses and rural stays, as well as packages that include sightseeing, including week-long tours of Lisbon and northern Portugal.

Lisboa Sightseeing: www.lisboasightseeing.com. Offers custom-designed tours of the capital, including boat tours, jeep safaris of the surrounding countryside and sightseeing days in Porto.

Affordable Tours: www.affordabletours.com. A US-based company that offers a variety of reasonably priced tours.

Riviera Travel: www.rivieratravel.co.uk/escorted-tours/tours-to-portugal. Escorted tours and cruises of the region.

Saranjan Tours: www.saranjan.com. Customised tours including a 7-day cooking school, bicycle tours and market and craft fairs tour.

V

Visas and passports

European Union nationals may enter Portugal with a national identity card. Citizens of Australia need only a valid passport for a three-month stay; the same applies to Americans, Canadians and UK citizens staying for less than 90 days in any 180-day period. For longer stays, check the Portuguese Embassy's website (http://londres.embaixadaportugal.mne.gov.pt/en) to find out what type of visa or work permit you may need.

All other non-EU visitors must show a valid passport when entering Portugal, and this will be stamped with a tourist visa valid for up to 90 days. No one with a tourist visa is permitted to work.

Bureaucracy is a serious problem, so you should apply for an extension at least one week before your time runs out.

Visas or extended-stay visas can be obtained at any Portuguese consulate abroad, or contact the Serviço de Estrangeiros (Foreigners' Service) at Avenida António Augusto de Aguiar, 20, Mon–Fri 8.30am–7pm, www.sef.pt (although this service appears to be extremely challenging to use).

The British office that deals with extensions to visas is at the Portuguese Consulate, 3 Portland Place, London W1B 3HR, tel: 020 3433 3624.

W

Website and apps

Tourist board websites:
www.visitportugal.com
www.visitportoandnorth.travel
Accommodation:
www.pousadas.pt
www.solaresdeportugal.com
www.manorhouses.com
Hostunusual.com/destinations/portugal
Apps:
Visit Portugal travel guide (official tourist board app)

Weights and measures

Portugal uses the metric system of weights and measures.

Women travellers

Women travelling alone should take the normal precautions, although incidences of sexual assault and violence are low. Bag snatching is more of a problem and women should avoid carrying a bag late at night in quieter areas. The north tends to be more conservative; in smaller villages it may be more prudent for unmarried couples to check in under the same name.

LANGUAGE

GETTING BY

If you speak Spanish you will be able to read Portuguese and understand some, but certainly not all, of the spoken language. There are also slight similarities with written, but little with spoken, French. For most English-speakers, however, Portuguese, which has many nasal sounds, is not easy to follow.

Many Portuguese speak a second language, and most have the tolerance and courtesy to help resolve problems or queries. At the tourist offices and in virtually all hotels and many restaurants you will find the major European languages are spoken. Yet learning just a few simple words and phrases in Portuguese will certainly enhance your visit.

BASIC COMMUNICATION

yes sim
no não
thank you obrigado/a
many thanks muito obrigado
all right/okay de acordo/está bem
please faz favor, por favor
excuse me faz favour (to get attention)
excuse me com licence (to get through a crowd)
excuse me desculpe (sorry)
wait a minute espere um momento
can you help me? pode ajudar-me?
certainly com certeza
can I help you? posso ajudálo/a?
can you show me? pode mostrar me?
I need... preciso...
I'm lost estou perdido/a
I'm sorry desculpe-me
I don't know não sei
I don't understand não comprendo
do you speak... fala...
English inglês
French francês
German alemão
please speak slowly faz favor de falar devagar
please say that again diga outra vez, se faz favor
slowly devagar
here/there aqui/ali
what? o quê?
when/why/where? quando/porquê/onde?
where is the toilet? onde fica a casa de banho? (or more politely: pode-me indicar onde fica a casa de banho?)

Greetings

hello (good morning) bom dia
good afternoon/evening boa tarde
good night boa noite
see you tomorrow até amanha
see you later até logo
see you soon até já
goodbye adeus
Mr/Mrs/young lady/girl senhor/senhora/menina
pleased to meet you muito prazer em conhecê-lo/lá
I am English/American sou Inglês/Americano (a)
I'm here on holiday estou aqui de férias
how are you? como está?
fine, thanks bem, obrigado

Telephone calls

I want to make a telephone call quero fazer uma chamada
the area code o indicativo
the number o número

Questions

where is...? onde é...?
when...? quando...?
how much...? quanto custa?
is there...? há...?
do you have...? tem...?
at what time...? a que horas...?
what time is it? que horas são?
do you have a...? tem um...?

can you get this number for me? podia fazer-me uma chamada para este número?
the line is engaged está ocupada
no one replies ninguém atende
the operator a telefonista
hello? está lá?
may I speak to... posso falar com...
hold the line please não desligue, faz favor
who is that? quem é?/de onde fala?
may I leave a message? posso deixar um recado?
I will phone later ligarei mais tarde

At the hotel

do you have a room available? há algum quarto disponível?
I have a reservation tenho uma reserva
single/double room um quarto individual/duplo
twin/double bed camas individuais/cama casal
with bathroom com casa de banho
for one night para uma noite
two nights para duas noites
how much is it per night? qual é o preço por noite?
with breakfast? com pequeno almoço incluindo?
does it have air conditioning? o quarto tem ar condicionado?
it's expensive é caro
can I see the room? posso ver o quarto?
what time does the hotel close? a que horas fecha o hotel?
dining room sala de jantar
what time is breakfast? a que horas é servido o pequeno-almoço?
please call me at... acorde-me às...
the bill please a conta por favor
can you call a taxi please? chame um táxi por favor?
key a chave
lift elevador
towel toalha
toilet paper papel higiénico
pull/push puxe/empurre

☕ Drinks

coffee (black and strong) *um café*
coffee with milk *um café com leite*
large, weak coffee with milk *um meio de leite/galão*
tea (lemon) *um chá (de limão)*
orange juice (bottled) *sumo de laranja*
orange juice (fresh) *sumo de laranja natural*
mineral water (still) *agua sem gás; (fizzy) agua com gás*
chilled/room temperature *fresca/natural*
red (mature)/white wine ("green") *vinho tinto (maduro)/branco (verde)*
bottle/half bottle *garrafa/meia garrafa*
beer *cerveja*
milk *leite*
cheers! *saúde!*

EATING AND DRINKING IN A RESTAURANT

can we have lunch/dinner here? *podemos almoçar/jantar aqui?*
we only want a light meal *queremos apenas uma refeição ligeira*
a table for two/three... *uma mesa para dois/três...*
may we have the menu? *a ementa se faz favor*
we should like... *queríamos...*
what do you recommend? *que recomenda?*
what is this? *o que é isto?*
do you know what this is in English? *sabe o que é isto em Inglês?*
what wine do you recommend? *qual é o vinho que recomenda?*
not too expensive *não muito caro*
I'll have that *quero aquilo*
is it good? *É bom?*
well-cooked/rare *bem passado/ mal passado*
grilled *grelhado*
fried *frito*
boiled *cozido*
vegetables *legumes*
spoon *colher*
fork *garfo*
knife *faca*
would you like some more? *deseja mais?*
no thank you – no more *obrigado – não desejo mais*
yes please *sim, mais faz favor*
I enjoyed that *gostei muito*
we have finished *acabámos*

the bill please *a conta se faz favor*
toilets (ladies/gents, men/women) *casa de banho (senhoras/senhores, homens/mulheres)*

MENU DECODER

Entradas (Starters)

amêijoas ao natural clams with butter and parsley
camarão prawn
gambás langoustines
pasteis de bacalhau dried-cod fishcakes
presunto smoked ham
rissois de camarão shrimp pies
santola recheada dressed crab

Peixe (fish)

arroz de polvo octopus with rice
atum grelhado grilled tuna
bacalhau á Brás fried dried cod with fried potatoes and scrambled eggs (there is an almost endless variety of dishes with dried cod)
caldeirada de peixe fish stew
ensopado de enguias eels with fried bread
lagosta lobster
linguado sole
lampreia lamprey
lulas recheadas stuffed squid
robalo sea bass
rodovalho halibut
salmão salmon
salmonete red mullet
salmonetes á moda de Setubal grilled red mullet
sardinhas grelhadas com pimentos grilled sardines and peppers
savel shad
truta trout

Carne (meat)

arroz à moda de Valência kind of paella
arroz de pato duck with rice
cabrito assado roast kid
carne assada roast beef
churrasco pork cooked on a spit
coelho à caçadora rabbit stew
cozido à portuguesa variety of boiled meats and vegetables
feijoada dried beans with rice and various smoked meats
frango de carril roast chicken with a hot sauce
frango na pucara chicken casserole
leitão assado roast sucking pig
peru turkey

porco pork
tripas à moda do Porto tripe with dried beans
vitela veal

Salada (salad)

alface lettuce
cebola onion
cenoura carrot
pepino cucumber
tomate tomato

Doces (desserts)

arroz doce sweet rice
fruta fruit
gelado ice cream
laranja orange
leite creme type of custard
maça apple
marmelada quince marmalade
papos de anjo small butter cakes with syrup
pasteis cakes
pera pear
pudim flan crème caramel
queijo cheese
uvas grapes

Basic commodities

açucar sugar
alho garlic
azeite olive oil
azeitona olive
manteiga butter
pão bread
pão integral wholemeal bread
pimenta pepper
sal salt
vinagre vinegar
sande (fiambre/queijo/misto) sandwich (ham/cheese/mixed)

HEALTH

is there a chemist's nearby? *há uma farmácia aqui perto?*
where is the hospital? *onde fica o hospital?*
I feel ill *não me sinto bem*
it hurts here *tenho uma dor aqui*
I have a headache *tenho dor de cabeça*
I have a sore throat *dói-me a garganta*

☕ Sopas (Soups)

caldo verde cabbage and potato
canja chicken broth
creme de marisco seafood soup
sopa de coentros coriander, bread, and a poached egg

I have a stomach ache *tenho dores de estômago*
I have a fever (temperature) *tenho febre*
call a doctor *chame um médico*
take this prescription to the chemist *leve esta receita para a farmácia*
take this note to the hospital *leve esta carta para o hospital*
danger! *perigo!*
look out! *cuidado!*
help! *socorro!*
fire! *fogo!*

SIGHTSEEING

what should we see here? *o que podemos ver aqui?*
what is this building? *que edifício é este?*
where is the old part of the city/town? *onde fica a zona antiga da cidade/vila?*
when was it built? *quando foi construída?*
what time is there a Mass? *a que horas se celebra a missa?*
when is the museum open? *qual o horário do museu?*
is it open on Sunday? *está aberto no domingo?*
how much is it to go in? *quanto custa a entrada?*
free admission *entrada gratuita*
can I take pictures? *posso tirar fotografias?*
photographs are prohibited *é proibido tirar fotografias*
follow the guide *siga o guia*
we don't need a guide *não precisamos de guia*
where can I get a plan of the city? *onde posso obter un mapa da cidade?*
how do I get to...? *como se vai para...?*
can we walk there? *podemos ir a pé?*

SHOPPING

what time do you open/close? *a que hora abre/fecha?*

can I help you? *posso ajudar?*
I'm looking for... *procuro...*
we are just having a look around *queremos ver o que há*
how much does it cost? *quanto custa?*
do you take credit cards? *aceitam cartões de credito?*
have you got...? *tem...?*
can I try it on? *posso experimentá-lo?*
this is not my size *não é a minha medida*
too small/big *é muito pequeno/muito grande*
it's expensive *é caro*
I like it/don't like it *gosto/não gosto*
I'll take this *levo este/a*

Shops

bakery *padaria*
barber *barbearia*
bookshop *livraria*
butcher *talho*
chemist *farmácia*
department store *armazém*
dry cleaner *lavandaria a seco*
fishmonger *peixaria*
grocer *mercearia*
hardware store *drogaria*
optician *oculista*
post office *correios*
shoe shop *sapataria*
shopping centre *centro comercial*
stationer *papelaria*
tobacconist *tabacaria*

TRAVELLING

airport *aeroporto*
arrivals/departures *chegadas/partidas*
boat *barco*
bus *autocarro*
bus station *centro camionagem*
bus stop *paragem*
car/hire *carro/a lugar*
customs *alfândega*
driving licence *carta de condução*
flight *voo*
motorway *auto-estrada*
railway station *estação de comboio*

⏰ Days of the week

Sunday domingo
Monday segunda-feira
Tuesday terça-feira
Wednesday quarta-feira
Thursday quinta-feira
Friday sexta-feira
Saturday sábado

return ticket *bilhete de ida e volta*
single ticket *bilhete de ida*
smokers/non-smokers *fumadores/não fumadores*
ticket office *bilheteria*
toll *portagem*
train *comboio*

NUMBERS

1 *um/uma*
2 *dois/duas*
3 *três*
4 *quatro*
5 *cinco*
6 *seis*
7 *sete*
8 *oito*
9 *nove*
10 *dez*
11 *onze*
12 *doze*
13 *treze*
14 *catorze*
15 *quinze*
16 *dezasseis*
17 *dezassete*
18 *dezoito*
19 *dezanove*
20 *vinte*
30 *trinta*
40 *quarenta*
50 *cinquenta*
60 *sessenta*
70 *setenta*
80 *oitenta*
90 *noventa*
100 *cem*
200 *duzentos*
1,000 *mil*

FURTHER READING

PORTUGUESE WORKS

Luís de Camões Author of Portugal's best-known piece of literature, the epic poem *The Lusiads*, written in 1572 and celebrating the Portuguese Era of Discoveries.

Eça de Queiroz (1845–1900) is one of Portugal's best-known authors. His most popular work is *The Maias*, about a wealthy Lisbon family in the early 20th century. Other titles include *The Tragedy of the Street of Flowers* and *The Crime of Father Amaro*.

Eugénio Lisboa has edited a number of books of poetry and short stories, including *The Anarchist Banker and Other Portuguese Stories*, and *Professor Pfiglzz and His Strange Companion*.

Fernando Pessoa (1888–1935) is second only to Camões in the list of illustrious Portuguese poets. He wrote under other names: Alberto Caeiro, Ricardo Reis and Álvaro de Campos, transforming his style with each. His *Book of Disquiet* contains his disturbing meditations around Chiado.

José Saramago (1922–2010) received the Nobel Prize for Literature in 1998, hastening the translation of his works into English. *Journey to Portugal* is a good place to start, a wonderful travelogue full of detailed insight. *Baltasar and Blimunda* and *The Year of the Death of Ricardo Reis* are also recommended.

Miguel Torga's autobiography, *The Creation of the World*, recalls his Trás-os-Montes childhood, a boyhood in Brazil and return to qualify as a doctor and work in his native village, where *Tales from the Mountain* and *More Tales from the Mountain* are set.

BOOKS ABOUT PORTUGAL

Backwards Out of the Big World: A Voyage into Portugal by Paul Hyland. Following in the steps of Henry Fielding from Lisbon to the Spanish border, Hyland brings a new insight into the country.

Birdwatching Guide to the Algarve by Kevin Carlson. Where to go and what to see.

A Concise History of Portugal by David Birmingham. A standard, with many illustrations.

In the Lands of the Enchanted Moorish Maiden, edited by Mandi Gomez. These 11 "exhibition trails" on Moorish Portugal cover "Christianised" mosques, palaces, fortifications and urban settlements between Coimbra and Algarve.

The Last Kabbalist of Lisbon by Richard Zimler. Set in Lisbon in 1506, when "New Christian" Jewish converts were being murdered.

Prince Henry The Navigator: A Life by Peter Russell. A portrait of the king as Renaissance man.

The Portuguese Seaborne Empire 1415–1825 by C.R. Boxer. An enthralling work full of awkward truths and compelling anecdotes.

Portugal's Struggle for Liberty by Mário Soares. By Portugal's most eminent political figure – a long-serving president and a key personality in post-revolution events.

The Portuguese: The Land and Its People by Marion Kaplan. A revised and updated edition to the revealing, readable and entertaining portrait.

A Small Death in Lisbon by Robert Wilson. Excellent novel of life in Portugal.

Portuguese Voyages 1498–1663: Tales from the Great Age of Discovery, edited by Charles David Ley. Contemporary accounts of the great sea voyages.

Republican Portugal, a Political History 1910–1926 by Douglas L. Wheeler. A fascinating account of the period between monarchy and dictatorship when Portugal endured 45 successive governments.

The Taste of Portugal by Edite Vieira. Recipes, history and folklore.

Hunting Midnight by Richard Zimler. After the success of *The Last Kabbalist of Lisbon* (see above), Zimler has set this fictional tale of bigotry and betrayal in 18th- and 19th-century Porto.

The Migrant Painter of Birds by Lidia Jorge. A beautifully crafted poetic novel by this feminist novelist about a girl from a Portuguese farming family and her absent father.

The High Mountains of Portugal by Yann Martel. The Canadian novelist's most celebrated work since *Life of Pi* explores grief in three stories set in different times and places across Portugal.

Night Train to Lisbon by Pascal Mercier. A thrilling depiction of life in Portugal both pre- and post-democracy.

⊙ Send us your thoughts

We do our best to ensure the information in our books is as accurate and up-to-date as possible. The books are updated on a regular basis using destination experts, who painstakingly add, amend and correct as required. However, some details (such as opening times or travel pass costs) are particularly liable to change, and we are ultimately reliant on our readers to put us in the picture.

We welcome your feed back, especially your experience of using the book "on the road", and if you came across a great new attraction we missed.

We will acknowledge all contributions and offer an Insight Guide to the best messages received.

Please write to us at:
**Insight Guides
PO Box 7910
London SE1 1WE**
Or email us at:
hello@insightguides.com

OTHER INSIGHT GUIDES

Other Insight Guides titles available to the Iberian Peninsula include *Insight Guide Spain*, *Insight Guide Southern Spain*, *Insight Guide Pocket Portugal* and *Insight Guide Pocket Lisbon*.

CREDITS

PHOTO CREDITS

Adam Jones 83
Alamy 45, 78, 79, 80, 119, 218B, 249, 289B
Apa Publications 295T, 315T
Art Archive 48, 49
Biblioteca Nacional, Lisbon 58, 59, 64
Corbis 30, 57, 61, 63, 69, 71, 72, 84, 86L, 86R, 102/103T, 118L, 310, 314B, 317
Dreamstime 125, 126, 180, 187, 189B, 212B, 229B
Fotolia 10T, 11BL, 54, 109, 143, 197T, 205, 210, 219B, 233, 273T
Getty Images 70, 73, 85
Gil Galvin/Apa Publications 181T, 192T
iStock 8ML, 8MR, 9ML, 10B, 12MR, 12B, 13TL, 13MR, 13TR, 13BL, 16/17, 20, 21B, 22, 23, 32, 44, 65, 76, 77, 90, 92, 93, 98, 104/105, 106, 111, 124, 127, 128, 130/131, 134/135, 140, 142T, 146, 147B, 149B, 153T, 154B, 154T, 165, 168B, 169, 171, 179B, 183, 186, 189T, 195T, 195B, 203, 204B, 206B, 207B, 208B, 211T, 218T, 223, 224, 242, 260, 261B, 262B, 271T, 271B, 273B, 274, 277BL, 293B, 303B, 304B, 304T, 306, 307B, 308, 311, 314T, 315B

Lydia Evans/Apa Publications 9TR, 9MR, 9ML, 11TL, 11TR, 21T, 24, 25, 26, 35, 46, 47, 52, 81, 88, 91, 94, 95, 96, 97, 99, 103ML, 103BR, 103BL, 107, 113, 116, 120, 121, 129, 136, 137T, 137B, 145T, 145B, 148, 150, 152, 155, 156, 157T, 157B, 158B, 159B, 162/163T, 162BR, 162BL, 163TR, 164, 166, 168T, 172B, 173, 176, 177, 179T, 181B, 182, 185B, 188B, 188T, 191, 192B, 196T, 196B, 197B, 199, 201, 202, 206T, 209B, 216T, 220/221T, 220BR, 220BL, 221BR, 221BL, 221TR, 222, 225B, 225T, 226, 227B, 227T, 228T, 228B, 230T, 230B, 231B, 235, 237, 239, 240, 241, 243, 245B, 246B, 247, 250, 251, 252, 253, 254, 255, 256T, 256B, 257T, 258, 259, 261T, 263T, 263B, 264, 265, 267, 270, 272, 275, 276BL, 277ML, 277BR, 279, 282B, 283B, 284, 285, 286, 288T, 289T, 290, 291, 294, 295B, 297T, 297B, 298, 318, 320, 321, 322/323, 330/331
Mark Read/Apa Publications 108, 110, 112R, 158T, 159T, 172T, 174T, 207T, 208T, 209T, 212T, 214T, 221ML, 229T, 236, 246T, 262T, 277TR, 281T, 282T, 283T, 292, 299

Mary Evans Picture Library 51
Museu da Cidade, Lisbon 34, 37, 63, 64, 62
Museu da Marinha, Belem 53, 67
Museu de Evora, Evora 117R
Museu Militar, Lisbon 28/29, 36, 60, 62
Museu Nacional de Arte Antiga, Lisbon 40, 43, 50, 56, 114, 117L
Phil Wood/Apa Publications 112L, 147T, 149T, 163ML, 231T, 303T, 307T
Pictures Colour Library 9TL, 141, 213, 248, 287, 301, 313
Press Association Images 68
Public domain 82, 118R
Scala 115
Shutterstock 1, 4, 8BL, 9MR, 12ML, 14/15, 18/19, 27, 31, 33, 38, 39, 74/75, 87, 89, 100, 101, 102B, 103TR, 122/123, 132/133, 142B, 151, 153B, 163BR, 163BL, 170, 175, 178, 185T, 190, 193, 194, 198, 204T, 211B, 214B, 216B, 217, 232, 234, 238, 245T, 266, 276/277T, 276BR, 278, 281B, 288B, 293T, 296, 300, 305, 309, 312, 316B, 326
TopFoto 66
Turismo de Portugal 167, 174B, 215, 219T, 316T

COVER CREDITS

Front cover: National Palace of Pena *Shutterstock*
Back cover: Praia dos Pescadores Algarve *Shutterstock*
Front flap: (from top) Carvoeiro beach *Shutterstock*; Alentejo wine *Shutterstock*; University library in Coimbra *Shutterstock*; The
architecture of Guimaraes *Shutterstock*
Back flap: Bom Jesus do Monte Monastery *Shutterstock*

INSIGHT GUIDE CREDITS

Distribution
UK, Ireland and Europe
Apa Publications (UK) Ltd;
sales@insightguides.com
United States and Canada
Ingram Publisher Services;
ips@ingramcontent.com
Australia and New Zealand
Booktopia;
retailer@booktopia.com.au
Worldwide
Apa Publications (UK) Ltd;
sales@insightguides.com
Special Sales, Content Licensing and CoPublishing
Insight Guides can be purchased in bulk quantities at discounted prices. We can create special editions, personalised jackets and corporate imprints tailored to your needs.
sales@insightguides.com
www.insightguides.biz

Printed in China

This book was produced using **Typefi** automated publishing software.

All Rights Reserved
© 2025 Apa Digital AG
License edition © Apa Publications Ltd UK

First Edition 1992
Ninth Edition 2025

No part of this book may be reproduced, stored in a retrieval system or transmitted in any form or means electronic, mechanical, photocopying, recording or otherwise, without prior written permission from Apa Publications.

Every effort has been made to provide accurate information in this publication, but changes are inevitable. The publisher cannot be responsible for any resulting loss, inconvenience or injury. We would appreciate it if readers would call our attention to any errors or outdated information. We also welcome your suggestions; please contact us at:
hello@insightguides.com

www.insightguides.com

Editor: Siobhan Warwicker
Author: Imogen Malpas
Picture Editor: Tom Smyth
Cartography: original cartography Colourmap Scanning, updated by Carte
Layout: Ankur Guha
Publishing Technology Manager: Rebeka Davies
Production Operations Manager: Katie Bennett
Head of Publishing: Sarah Clark

CONTRIBUTORS

This new edition of *Insight Guide: Portugal* was commissioned and copyedited by **Siobhan Warwicker**.
Imogen Malpas thoroughly updated the book, building on the work of **Abigail Blasi** for the last edition. Thanks also go to **Chloe Da Veiga Pinto** for her input.

This edition builds on the original book put together by **Alison Friesinger Hill**, **Thomas Hill**, **Ruth Rosengarten**, **Jean Anderson**, **Scott Carney**, **Katherine Barrett Swett**, **Sharon Behn**, **Marvine Howe**, **Deborah Brammer**, **Jeremy Boultbee**, **Jenny Wittner**, **Nigel Tisdall**, **Brian and Eileen Anderson**.

ABOUT INSIGHT GUIDES

Insight Guides has more than 50 years of experience in publishing high-quality, visual travel guides. We produce hundreds of full-colour titles, in both print and digital form, covering more than 200 destinations across the globe, in a variety of formats to meet your different needs.

Insight Guides are written and updated by local authors, whose expertise is evident in the extensive historical and cultural background features. Each destination is carefully researched by regional experts to ensure our guides provide the very latest information. All the coverage in **Insight Guides** is independent; we strive to maintain an impartial view. Our inclusions are carefully selected to guide you to the best places in a destination, so you can be confident that when we say a place is special, we really mean it.

Legend

City maps
- Freeway/Highway/Motorway
- Divided Highway
- Main Roads
- Minor Roads
- Pedestrian Roads
- Steps
- Footpath
- Railway
- Funicular Railway
- Cable Car
- Tunnel
- City Wall
- Important Building
- Built Up Area
- Other Land
- Transport Hub
- Park
- Pedestrian Area
- Bus Station
- Tourist Information
- Main Post Office
- Cathedral/Church
- Mosque
- Synagogue
- Statue/Monument
- Beach
- Airport

Regional maps
- Freeway/Highway/Motorway (with junction)
- Freeway/Highway/Motorway (under construction)
- Divided Highway
- Main Road
- Secondary Road
- Minor Road
- Track
- Footpath
- International Boundary
- State/Province Boundary
- National Park/Reserve
- Marine Park
- Ferry Route
- Marshland/Swamp
- Glacier   Salt Lake
- Airport/Airfield
- Ancient Site
- Border Control
- Cable Car
- Castle/Castle Ruins
- Cave
- Chateau/Stately Home
- Church/Church Ruins
- Crater
- Lighthouse
- Mountain Peak
- Place of Interest
- Viewpoint

INDEX

A
accommodation 323
  Douro Valley 268
  manor houses 121
  pousadas 120
Adam, Robert 111
Adega Regional 175
Afonso, Duke of Bragança 49, 184
Afonso Henriques 36, 37, 38, 41, 46, 108
  and Guimarães 287
  and Lamego 271
  and Porto 259
Afonso III 41, 189, 211
Afonso IV 41, 43
Afonso, Jorge 116
Afonso V 49, 54, 55
Afonso VI 60
Africa
  Angola 70, 90
  early exploration of 50, 52
  food from 90
  the Congo 53
African music 25
agriculture 42
  Algarve 184
  Madeira 306
  maize 126
  Minho 279
  regional differences in land holdings 291
air travel 320, 321
Albufeira 191
Albuquerque Afonso de 53, 108
Alcácer-Quibir, battle of 56, 59, 193
Alcañices 41
Alcañices, Treaty of 42
Alcobaça 228
  Cistercian abbey 38, 228
Alentejo 199
  agriculture 199
  Alter do Chão 214
  architecture 109, 201
  beaches 215
  Beja 217
  Castelo de Vide 212
  crafts 210, 220
  Crato 214
  Elvas 210
  Estremoz 201, 207, 220
  Évora 34, 199, 201, 202, 203
  Évoramonte 207
  Florda Rosa 214
  food and drink 218
  getting around 199
  getting there from Lisbon 202
  history 201
  Marvão 199, 212
  megalithic monuments 207
  Mértola 218
  Miróbriga 215
  Monsaraz 211
  Montemoro-Novo 203
  Nisa 214
  pastimes 202
  politics 201
  Portalegre 211
  Porto Covo 215
  Pulo do Lobo (Wolf's Leap) 218
  Reguengos 211
  Sines 215
  Vila Nova de Milfontes 215
  Vila Viçosa 201, 209
  wines 10, 100, 218
Alfonso IX of León 41
Alfonso VII 37
Alfonso VI of León 36
Algarve 21, 183
  Albufeira 191
  Alcantarilha 191
  Alcoutim 190
  Alte 196
  Armação de Pêra 192
  Barril 188
  Cabo de Santa Maria lighthouse 187
  Cabo de São Vicente 194
  Cacela Velha 189
  Castro Marim 189
  crafts 185
  Estói 197
  Faro 186
  Fuzeta 188
  getting around 186
  golf 190
  history 183
  Ilha da Armona 188
  Ilha de Tavira 189
  Key routes and places 185
  Lagos 185, 192
  Loulé 11, 185, 197
  Luz 193
  Martim Longo 190
  Monchique 195
  Monte Gordo 189
  Olhão 102, 187
  Olhos d'Agua 191
  Porches 192
  Portimão 192
  regional specialities 184, 197
  Rocha da Pena 192
  rural villages 195
  Sagres 194
  salt pans 128
  Sanlucar de Guadiana 190
  Santa Luzia 188
  São Lourenço 190
  Silves 196
  Tavira 185, 188
  theme parks 191
  Vilamoura 191
  Vila Real de Santo António 189
  Vila Romana de Milreu 197
  west coast 194
Algés 165
Algoso 299
Alijó 272
Aljezur 195
Aljubarrota, battle of 44
Almeida, Helen 119
Almendres 207
Almourol 45, 224
Almovavids 36
Alpiarça 224
Alquevadam 210
Alter do Chão 214
Alvão 292
Amarante 269
ancient Lusitania 35
Andeiro, João Fernandez 44
Anes Bishop Martinho 150
Anglo-Portuguese alliance 44, 46
Angola 70, 90
Angra do Heroísmo 315
Anthony of Padua, St 150
Anunciação, Tomás Joséda 118
Aquário Vasco da Gama (Dafundo) 165
Aqueduto da Amoreira 210
architecture 107
  Alentejo 109, 201
  azulejos 110, 162
  Baroque 109
  Gothic 108
  Mannerism 110
  Manueline 108
  modern 112
  neoclassical 111
  Pombaline 111
  Renaissance 110
  Rococco 111
  Romanesque 107
  Romanticism 111
  Trás-os-Montes 293
Arcos de Valdevez 285
Arrábida 180
  Serra da 11
Arrifana 195
art 114
  azulejos 110, 162
  Flemish artists 114, 115
  frescoes 114
  Grão Vasco 116
  Mannerism 116
  Modernist 118
  Neoclassical 117
  polyptych of St Vincent 114
  portrait painting 117
  Renaissance 116
  Romanticism 117
  sculpture 115
arts and crafts 220
  Alentejo 210, 220, 328
  Algarve 185
  Barcalos cockerel 221, 283
  Colchas (linen bedspreads) 256
  Handicrafts Fair (Estoril) 167
  Madeira 303
  Portalegre 211
Atalaia 216
Atei 293
Aveiro 245
Azores 311
  Angra do Heroísmo 315

INDEX

beaches 312, 313
Caldeira 316
Caldeira das Sete Cidades 314
climate 313
Corvo 311, 312
culture 312
discovery of 50, 52, 312
Espírito Santocult 313
Faial 316
Flores 311, 312
food 90
Furnas 315
government 312
Graciosa 317
Ilha das Flores 317
Ilha de Pico 313
Ilha do Corvo 317
Ilha do Pico 317
Ilheu 315
Ponta Delgada 313
Ponta dos Mosteiros 314
Santa Maria 311, 315
São Jorge 316
São Miguel 313
Terceira 313, 315
Vila Franca do Campo 314
azulejos (tiles) 110, 162

B

Bairrada 99
Barcelos 221, 282
barcos rabelos 276
Baroque architecture 110
Barragem de Castelo do Bode 255
Barragem de Santa Clara 216
Barragem de Valeira 271
Barragem do Alto Rabagão 293
Barroso district 293
Barroso, Durão 72
Batalha 108, 227
beaches
  Alentejo 215
  Azores 313, 315
  Cascais and Estoril 167, 169
  Faro 187
  Figueira da Foz 248
  Ilha de Tavira 188
  Lagos 193
  Madeira 307
  Minho region 283
  Mira 248
  north of Sintra 175
  Portinho da Arrábida 180
  Praia da Barra 248
  Praia da Rocha 192
  Praia de Carvoeiro 192
  Quiaios 248
  Silver Coast 223, 230
Beckford, William, Sketches of Spain and Portugal 82
Beira Alta 251
Beira Baixa 255
Beiras 24
Beja 217
Belmonte 253
Beresford, Marshal William Carr 63
Bernard of Clairvaux St 36
birds 129, 187, 190
  Ilha Berlenga 232

boar hunting 129
boats
  barcos rabelos 259, 265, 276
  caravelas 259, 265
boat trips 322
Boca do Inferno (Cascais) 169
Borba 209
Bordalo Pinheiro, Rafael 118
Borrow, George 83
Boticas 295
Braga 280
  architecture 110
  Bom Jesus church 285
  cathedral 281
  Festas de São João 103
  history 34, 281
  Museu Dom Diogo de Sousa 282
  Nossa Senhora do Pópulo 281
  Palácio de Arzobispo 281
  Palácio dos Biscainhos 281
  Termas Romanas 282
Bragança 292, 297
Bragança regime 60
Brazil 61, 63, 64
  food from 90
bread 94
Bright, Peter 100
Buçaco 244
  Hotel de 100, 245
Bugio 309
bullfights 11, 329
  Cascais 168
  Chega dos Toiros (Trás-os-Montes) 294
  Nazaré 230
  Vila Franca de Xira 223
Buraco dos Mouros 197
Burgau 193
buses 320
  Lisbon 322
  Madeira 305
Byron Lord 83
  Childe Harold 82, 171

C

Cabo Carvoeiro 232
Cabo da Roca 175
Cabode São Vicente 195
Cabo Espichel 180
Cacilhas 177
Caetano Marcelo 70, 73
Caldas da Rainha 220
Caldas de Moledo 270
Caldas de Monchique 195
Caldas de Rainha 231
Caldeira (Azores) 317
Cambra 255
Caminha 284
Camoes, Luís Vaz de 21, 46, 56, 57
Carcavelos 166
Carlos I 67, 148, 169
Carlotta Joaquina 64
Carmona, General Oscar 68
Carnival 299
Carvalhelhos 295
Casa de Diogo Cão (Vila Real) 274
Cascais 166
Castelo Branco 220, 256
Castelo de Vide 213
Castile 44, 46, 49

Castilho, João 229
castles 45
  accommodation in 120
  Algoso 299
  Almourol 10, 45, 224
  Alpiarça 224
  Bragança 297
  Castelo Branco 256
  Castelo de São Jorge (Lisbon) 151
  Castelo dos Mouros (Sintra) 173
  Castro Laboreiro 285
  Évoramonte 208
  Guimarães 10, 45, 286
  Lamego 45, 271
  Mértola 219
  Monsanto 257
  Montemoro-Novo 202
  Montemor-o-Velho 248
  Óbidos 232
  Ourém 226
  Palmela 121, 177
  Porto de Mós 227
  Santiago do Cacém 215
  São Filipe (Setúbal) 178
  Sesimbra 180
  Silves 196
  Tomar 225
  Vila Viçosa 201, 209
Castro de Avelãs, Mosteirode 297
Castro, General Pimentade 68
Castro Laboreiro 285
Castro Marim 189
Catherine of Bragança 47, 60, 297
Cavaco Silva, Aníbal 72
caves 227
Caxias 166
censorship 68
Cetóbriga 179
Charles II, British king 47, 60, 297
Chartists 65
Chaves 292, 293, 295
cheese 95
children 323
churches and cathedrals
  Alte 196
  Basilica da Estrêla 110
  Bom Jesus 111, 282
  Braga cathedral 281
  Capela dos Ossos 187
  Cathedral 186
  Clérigos (Porto) 110
  Coimbra 108, 240
  de São João Evangelista 305
  de São Pedro 305
  Évora cathedral 205
  Guarda cathedral 251
  Igreja São Francisco 288
  Lagos 193
  Lamego 116, 271
  Lisbon 151
  Mafra church and library 175
  Misericórdia 206
  Misericórdia (Aveiro) 247
  Montemor-o-Velho 248
  Nossa Senhora da Assunção (Cascais) 168
  Nossa Senhora da Conceição (Tomar) 110
  Nossa Senhora da Conceição Velha 147

INDEX | 339

Nossa Senhora da Graça 206
Nossa Senhora da Nazaré 230
Nossa Senhora da Rocha 192
Nossa Senhora de Guadalupe 193
Nossa Senhora de Oliveira 288
Nossa Senhora do Pópulo 281
Portalegre 211
Porto 115, 261, 262
Romanesque 107
San Domingos Cathedral (Aveiro) 247
Santa Engrácia 110, 153
Santa Madalena (Falperra) 111
Santarém 223
Santo António da Sé 150
São Francisco (Capela dos Ossos) 206
São Lourenço 190
São Miguel do Castelo 287
São Pedro de Balsemão 271
São Roque 155
São Vicente de Fora 152
Setúbal 178
Silva Cathedral 196
Tavira 188
Tomar 226
Vila Nogueira de Azeitão 181
Vila Real 274
Viseu 116, 253
Citânia de Briteiros 33, 289
climate 125, 324
coastline 127
coffee 95
Coimbra 235, 243
architecture 107
Arco de Almedina 239
Baixa 239
Casa de Sobre-Ripas 238
churches 108, 238, 240
Colégio de Santo Agostinho 238
fado 235
Fonte das Lágrimas 240
getting around 226
Igreja de São Bartolomeu 240
Igreja Santiago 240
Jardim Botânico 240
Jardim da Manga 239
Mosteiro Celas 240
Mosteiro de Santa Cruz 239
Núcleo da Cidade Muralhada 239
Quinta das Lágrimas 42, 240
railway stations 322
Sé Nova (New Cathedral) 238
Sé Velha (Old Cathedral) 108, 238
shops 240
Torre de Anto 238
university 55, 235, 236, 237
Coimbra question 64
Colares 175
colonies 53
Columbano 118
Columbus, Christopher 309, 311
Conímbriga 10, 236, 243
Constantine, Roman emperor 34
Córdoba, Muslim 35
Costa, Afonso 68
Costa Cabral António, de 65
Costa da Caparica 177, 179
Costa Nova 248
Covilhã 253

crime 324
Cristo Reimonument (Almada) 177
Cromeleque do Almendres 207
Crusades 38, 46, 51
Cunhal Alvaro 232
Curia 245
currency 327
customs regulations 324

D

Dafundo 165
Dahomey 71
Dãowines 99
Delgado, General Humberto 69
Deserta Grande 309
desserts 95
Dias Bartolomeu 52
Dinis, king 42, 145, 152, 274
palace at Erstremoz 208
Douro river 127, 259, 265, 267, 276
Douro Valley 10
accommodation 268
Alijó 272
Amarante 269
Barragem de Valeira 272
Caldas de Moledo 270
Casa do Douro 270
Castelo Melhor 273
climate 267
Foz Côa 10
getting there 268
Lamego 270
Mateus 274
Mesão Frio 270
Muxagata 273
Panóias 273
Peso da Régua 267
Pinhão 268, 271
Ponte de São Gonçalo 269
port wine production 267, 276
Régua 270
Sabrosa 273
São João da Pasqueira 271
Vila Real 274
Douro wines 100
driving 320
car hire 321
drugs (illegal) 26
Duarte 49

E

Eanes, Gil 52
eating out
reader 332
economy 23, 71
Edward VII, British king 159
El Cid 270
electricity 324
elevadores
Lisbon 322
Elvas 210
embassies 325
emergencies 325
emigration 24, 25, 291
English visitors to Portugal 82
Ericeira 175
Ericeira, count of 61
Esposende 284
Estoril 166

Estréla 126, 253
Estremadura
Batalha 108
Óbidos 232
Porto de Mós 227
Santarém 224
Tomar 110, 225
Estremoz 201, 207, 220
etiquette 325
European Union 23, 24, 72
Évora 199, 201, 202
cathedral 205
history 34, 203
Jesuit University 205
Museu de Arte Sacra 205
Museu de Évora 205
Palácio de Dom Manuel 207
Templo Romano 204
Évoramonte 207

F

fado 25, 85, 235, 327
Faial (Azores) 316
Falperra Santa Madalena 111
families 26
Faro 186
Museu Marítimo 187
Museu Municipal 187
Museu Regional do Algarve 187
Fátima 226
Fátima, Our Lady of 79, 80, 102
Chapel of Apparitions 227
Fauna 129
Felipe I (Felipe II of Spain) 56, 59
Felipe II (Felipe III of Spain) 60, 178
Felipe III (Felipe IV of Spain) 60
Fernandes Pacheco, Lopo 150
Fernandes, Vasco 116
Fernando I 44, 47
Fernando I of León 36
Ferreira Antónia Adelaide 272
Ferreira, wines 100
festivals and events 11, 103, 327
Carnival 11, 299
Chega dos Toiros (Trás-os-Montes) 294
Estoril Music Festival 167
Feira de São João (Évora) 207
Festa do Sudoeste 102
Ribatejo 11, 223
São Mateus (Viseu) 254
Terceira (Azores) 316
Fielding, Henry 156
Figueira da Foz 248
fishing industry 127
flora 128
Florda Rosa 214
Florentino, António 114
Flores (Azores) 311, 312
Flower, Frederick William 262
Fóia 195
food and drink 91
Football 329
Forester, Baron Joseph James 47, 272
forest fires 129
forestry 26, 129
Forrester, Joseph James 101
Fortalaza de Sagres 194
Franco, General Francisco 68

INDEX

Franco, João 67
French Revolution 63
Fronteira Marquêsde 61
Funchal 301

G

Galicia 35
Gama, Vasco da 52, 57, 89, 108, 145
Garrett, Almeida 65, 260
gay travellers 326
geology 126
Geraldes, Geraldo 38
Geraldo, São 281
Gilbert of Hastings, bishop of Lisbon 46, 150
Gil Eannes 283
Goa 53, 108
Golden Triangle 166
gold trade 61
golf 167, 190, 328
　Algarve 190
　Golden Triangle 167
Gomes, General Costa 70
Gonçalves Zarco, João 301, 305
Gothic architecture 108
Graciosa (Azores) 317
granite 126
Grão Vasco 116
Gruta da Santa Margarida 180
Grutas de Alvados 227
Grutas de Santa António 227
Grutas Mira de Aire 227
Guarda 251
Guimarães 288
　castle 10, 45, 287
　churches 287
　Convento de Santa Clara 288
　museums 287
　Paço dos Duques de Bragança 288
Guimarães, Conde de Castro 168
Gulbenkian, Calouste 160

H

health and medical care 326
health care 326
Henri of Burgundy 36
Henrique, Cardinal 56
Henry the Navigator 47, 49, 51, 52, 54, 89
　and Madeira 49, 89, 301
　and Porto 262
　and the Algarve 193
　and the Azores 312
　and Viseu 253
　in the polyptych of St Vincent 114
Herculano, Alexandre 65
history 33
　Alentejo 201
　Algarve 183
　Anglo-Portuguese alliance 44, 47
　Azores 311
　Black Death 43, 44
　Braga 281
　Bragança 297
　Bragança regime 60
　British military occupation 63
　Cascais 168
　Castelo Branco 256
　Chartists 65
　Chaves 296
　Coimbra 236
　Conímbriga 243
　coup (1974) 70, 119
　cultural development 64
　empire building 60
　First World War 68
　great earthquake (1755) 62
　Lamego 271
　liberal revolution 63, 118
　Lisbon 34, 145
　Miguelist wars 64, 67
　Moors 35, 38, 41, 56
　Óbidos 232
　Peninsular War 47, 63, 67, 269
　Phoenician traders 33, 144
　Porto 259
　prehistoric culture 33
　Reconquista 35, 38, 41
　Renaissance 55
　republicanism 67
　Romans 33, 34, 144, 183
　Salazar dictatorship 68, 73, 80
　Spanish rule 59
　split with Spain 36
　Viseu 253
horses
　Alter Stud Farm 214
　Escola Portuguesa de Arte Equestre 11
　horse riding 329
Hospitallers 36, 38
hospitals 326
humanism 55
Hundred Years War 44

I

Iberian union 56, 59
Idanha-a-Velha 256
Ilha Berlenga 232
Ilha do corvo (Azores) 317
Ilha do Pessegueiro 215
Ilha do Pico (Azores) 317
Ilhas Desertas 309
Ilhas Selvagens 309
Ilheu (Azores) 315
India 52, 53
Inês de Castro 43, 240

J

Jesuits 61, 62
Jesus Santos, Luciade 226
Jews 54, 62
　in Tomar 226
João I 44, 47, 49, 108, 114
　and Batalha 227
　and Évora 201
João II 50, 54
João III 55, 56
João IV 60, 180
João V 61, 110, 145, 175
João VI 63, 64, 117
John of Gaunt 44, 46
John of God St 203
John Paul II Pope 226, 227
José 181
José, king 62
Julius Caesar 144, 217

K

Knights of St John (the Hospitallers) 36, 38
Knights Templar 36, 38, 43
　disbanding of 43
　in Tomar 225
Koolhaas, Rem 112

L

Lagos 192
Lamego 270
landscapes 21
language 331
Larouco Serrado 293
Leonor Teles 44
liberal revolution 63
　and art 118
limestone 127
Lindoso 285
Lisbon 21, 143, 154
　Agua da EPAL 153
　Aguas Livres Aqueduct 111, 153, 155
　Alcântara 157
　Alfama 143, 144, 150
　Amoreiras shopping centre 112
　architecture 107, 111, 144
　Arco Rua Augusta 147
　Arqueológico do Carmo 154
　Arquivo Nacional da Torrede Tombo 161
　Art, Architecture and Technology 159
　Avenida da Liberdade 160
　Bairro Alto 154
　Baixa 143, 147
　Basílica da Estrêla 110, 156
　Belém 143, 144, 157
　bullring (Campo Pequeno) 161
　Calouste Gulbenkian 112, 119, 160
　Câmera Municipal 148
　Campo Grande 161
　Casa dos Bicos 147
　Castelo de São Jorge 151
　cathedral (Sé) 150
　Centro Cultural de Belém 158
　Centro de Arte Moderna 160
　Chafariz do Rei 148
　Chiado district 112, 154
　Cidade 161
　Colecção Berardo 158
　Convento do Carmo 154
　earthquake (1755) 62
　Eduardo VII 160
　Elevador de Santa Justa 154
　English Cemetery 156
　English visitors' views of 83
　Escola de Artes Decorativas 151
　Estação Santa Apolónia 153
　Estacção do Rossio 149
　Expo '98 144, 154
　fado 10, 85, 87, 327
　Feira da Ladra 153
　festivals 11, 102, 103
　fountains 111
　history 34, 144
　hospitals 326
　Jardim Botânico 155

INDEX | 341

Jardim Zoológico de Lisboa 161
Largo das Portas do Sol 151
Mãe d'Agua das Amorerias 155
Marinha 157
Mayer 160
Militar 153
Miradouro de Santa Luzia 151
Monteiro-Mór 161
Monument to the Discoveries 119
Mosteiro dos Jeronimous 94, 109, 157
Museu de Arte Sacra 155
Nacional de Arquelogia 157
Nacional de Arte Antiga 117, 156
Nacional de Arte Contemporânea 119
Nacional do Azulejo 153
Nacional dos Coches 158
Nacoes 154
nightlife 327
northern hills 159
Nossa Senhora da Conceição Velha 147
Nossa Senhora da Graça 152
Oceanário de Lisboa 154
Paço dos Condes de Almada 149
Padrão dos Descobrimentos (Monument of the Discoveries) 158
Palácio de Belém 158
Palácio de São Bento 156
Palácio dos Marquêses de Fronteira 161
Palácio Foz 149
Palácio Nacional da Ajuda 159
Panteão Nacional 153
pastéis de Belém (custard tarts) 94
Pavilhão do Conhecimento 154
Planetário 157
Pombaline 112
Ponte 25 de Abril 144, 157, 177
Ponte Vascoda Gama 112, 177, 144
Praça da Figueira 149
Praça do Comércio 112, 147, 148
Praça Dom Pedro IV (Rossio) 149
Praça do Municipio 148
Praça dos Restauradores 149
Praça Marquès de Pombal 159
Rotunda 159
Royal Palace of Ajuda 111
Santa Engrácia 110, 153
Santo António da Sé 150
São Jorge 10
São Roque 110, 155
São Vicente de Fora 152
siege of (1147) 46
stations 322
Tagus (Tejo) river 127
Teatro de São Carlos 154
Teatro Nacional 149, 327
Teatro Nacional São Carlos 327
Time Out Mercado da Ribeira 148
Torre de Belém 158
tourist office 147
trains 165, 171
Trajoe da Moda 161
university 55, 145, 161
Vasco da Gama Tower 154
wines 100

zoo 161
literature 65
censorship 69
lost property 324
Loulé 327
Lourosa 255
Luís I 65, 168
Lupi, Miguel, Sousa Martins'
Mother 118
Lusitania 34, 144
Luso 245

M

Macau 53
Machado Bernardino 68
Madeira 301
  Achada do Teixiera 307
  agriculture 306
  beaches 307
  Boa Vista Orchids 305
  Bocada Encumeada 308
  buses 305
  Cabo Girão 307
  Camacha 307
  Câmerade Lobos 305
  Câmera Municipal 305
  Casados Azulejos 305
  Curral das Freiras 308
  discovery of 52, 301
  food 90
  Funchal 301
  História Naturaldo Funchal 305
  Institutodo Bordado Tapeçeriae Artesano 303
  Jardim Botânico 305
  Laurisilva forest 308
  Machico 308
  Mercado dos Lavradores 304
  Monte Palace Tropical Gardens 303
  Monte toboggan ride 303
  MUDAS - Contemporary Art Museum 306
  Museu de Arte Sacra 305
  Museude Fotografia Vicentes 305
  Old Blandy's Wine Lodge 304
  Parque das Queimadas 308
  Paúl da Serra 308
  Pico do Ariero 307
  Pico Ruivo 307
  Ponta de São Lourenço 308
  Porto Moniz 307
  Praça do Município 305
  Quinta das Cruzes 305
  Quinta do Palheiro Ferreiro 305
  Reid's Palace Hotel 303
  Ribeira Brava 305
  Ribeiro Frio 307
  Santana 307
  São Vicente 307
  wine 304
Mafra 175
magazines 326
Magellan Ferdinand 52, 273
maize 126
Malacca 53
Malhoa José 118
Manini Luigi 244
Mannerism
  architecture 110

art 116
manor houses 121
Manuel I 54, 55, 109, 152, 226
Manuel II 67
Manueline architecture 108
Manueline painting 116
Marceneiro Alfredo 86
Mardel Carlos 111
Maria I 82
Maria II 64, 65, 315
Mariza 25, 87
markets
  Lisbon 147, 154
  Loulé 197
  Mercado dos Lavradores (Madeira) 304
  Ponte de Lima 286
Marranos 26
Martin, St 77, 80
Marto Jacinta and Francisco 227
Marvão 212
Mateus 274
media 326
megalithic sites 33
  Alentejo 207
Melgaço 285
Melville Herman Moby Dick 317
Mértola 219
Mesão Frio 270
Methuen, Treaty of 61
MFA (Armed Forces Movement) 70
Mickle William 83
  translations of Camoes 46, 57
migrant workers 24
Miguelist wars 312
military-monastic orders 37, 42
Minho region 279
  Barcelos 282
  Braga 281
  Caminha 284
  Citânia de Briteiros 33, 289
  coastal route from Porto 284
  grape harvest 279
  Guimarães 45, 289
  Lima Valley 279
  Monção 285
  mountain route 285
  Valença do Minho 284
  Viana do Castelo 11, 47, 283
Mira 248
Miranda do Douro 299
Miróbriga 215
mobile phones 329
Modernism
  architecture 112
  art 119
Mogadouro 299
Monção 285
Mondego river 127
Mondim de Basto 292
money 327
Monsanto 257
Montalegre 293
Monte Clérigo 195
Montemoro-Novo 202
Montemor-o-Velho 248
Monte Santa Luzia 283
Montesinho, Parque Natural de 296, 297
Moors 38, 41, 56
mountains 126

INDEX

Alvão 292
Arrábida 180
Cidadela 296
Estréla 11, 125, 126, 253
Larouco 293
Monchique 194
Moutinho, Pedro 87
museums and galleries
  Académico 237
  admission charges 323
  Alberto Sampaio (Guimarães) 288
  Amadeo de Souza-Cardoso (Amarante) 269
  Arqueologico Martins Sarmento (Guimarães) 288
  Arte Contemporânea 112, 264
  Arte Sacra 305
  Baleeiros (Azores) 317
  Beja 217
  Bragança 299
  Carlos Machado (Azores) 314
  Casada Música 264
  Casa das Histórias Paula Rego (Cascais) 169
  Casa do Infante (Porto) 262
  Centro Ciência Viva (Bragança) 298
  Centro de Arte Contemporânea Graça Morais (Bragança) 298
  Centro Português de Fotografia 262
  Ciência 237
  Condes de Castro Guimarães (Cascais) 168
  CR7 Museum 303
  Design e da Moda 147
  Dom Diogo de Sousa (Braga) 281
  Erstremoz 209
  Francisco Tavares Proença Júnior (Castelo Branco) 256
  Grão Vasco (Viseu) 254
  Guarda 252
  Guerra Junqueiro (Porto) 261
  Guy Fino (Portalegre) 212
  Ibérico da Máscara e do Traje (Bragança) 298
  Institutodo Bordado Tapeçeriae Artesano 303
  Judaico de Belmonte 253
  Machado de Castro 238
  Mar Dom Carlos (Cascais) 169
  Mértola 219
  Militar de Bragança (Bragança) 297
  Monográfico de Conímbriga 243
  MUDAS – Contemporary Art Museum 306
  Municipal Museum Abade Pedrosa (Santo Tirso) 289
  MUDE (Design Museum) 147
  Museo do Douro (Régua) 270
  Museu de Fotografia Vicentes 305
  Museu do Vinho da Quinta Nova (Pinhão) 271
  Museu Militarde Bragança (Bragança) 298
  Museu Municipal (Lagos) 193
  Olaria (Barcelos) 283
  Oriente 156

Peniche 232
Plataforma das Artes e Criatividade (Guimarães) 288
Port Wine Museum 263
Região Flaviense (Chaves) 296
Românico 263
Santarém 223
Sebútal 179
Terra de Miranda (Miranda do Douro) 299
Viana do Castelo 283
Vila Viçosa 209
music and dance 327
  African 25
  Alentejo 202
  fado 10, 25, 85, 327
  folk music 327
  Noites de Queluz 172
Muslim Portugal 38
Muxagata 273

N

Napoleon 63
narcissi 128
Nasoni, Nicolau 110
national parks and nature reserves
  Ilhas Desertas 309
  mountain parks 11
  Parque Arqueológico do Vale Côa 272
  Parque Nacional Peneda-Gerês 11, 126, 129, 279
  Parque Natural da Arrábida 180
  Parque Natural da Ria Formosa 187
  Parque Natural das Serras de Aire e Candeeiros 127, 227
  Parque Natural de Montesinho 296, 297
  Parque Natural do Alvão 292
  Reserva Natural das Dunas de São Jacinto 248
  Reserva Natural do Sapal 190
  Serra da Arrábida 11
Nazaré 230
Negreiros, José Almada 119
Neoclassicism
  architecture 111
  art 117
newspapers 326
nightlife 327
Nisa 214
Noronha, Maria Teresa de 86
Nossa Senhora da Conceição Velha 147

O

Óbidos 231
  Pousada do Castelo 120
Odeceixe 194
Odemira 216
Oeiras 166
Ofir 284
Olhão 187
  Festival do Marisco 102
Oliveira Bernardes, António 163
Oliveira do Hospital 255
olive trees 125
Omar Khayyám, Rubiyat 36

opening hours 328
Ourém 226
Ourique 217

P

Paço dos Duques de Bragança (Guimarães) 287
Pais Gualdim 225
Pais, Sidónio 68
Palácio de Arzobispo (Braga) 281
Palácio dos Biscainhos (Braga) 281
Palácio Episcopal (Castelo Branco) 256
Palmela 121, 177
Panóias 274
parks and gardens
  Boa Vista Orchids 305
  Coimbra 240
  Dom Infante Pedro (Aveiro) 247
  Eduardo VII 159
  Évora 207
  Jardim Botânico 155, 305
  Jardim Botânico da UTAD 274
  Jardim Orquídea 308
  Monte Palace Tropical Gardens 303
  Palácio Episcopal (Castelo Branco) 256
  Quinta da Bacalhoa 181
Parque Arqueológico do Vale Côa 272
Parque Nacional 126
Parque Nacional da Peneda-Gerês 279
Parque Nacional Peneda-Gerês 11, 126, 129, 286
Parque Natural das Serras de Aire e Candeeiros 127, 227
Parque Natural de Montesinho 296, 297
passports 330
patron saints 80
Pedro and Inês 43
  tombs of 115, 229
Pedro I 44
Pedro II 60
Pedro IV 64
Pedro V 65
Pegões 202
Pena Palace 173
Pena Palace (Sintra) 109, 173
Peneda-Gerês Parque Nacional 129, 279, 286
Penha Longa Atlantic 167
Penhas da Saúde 253
Peniche 232
Peninsular War 47, 63, 67, 269
people 23
Pereira, Nuno Alvares 44, 154, 228
Peso da Régua 267
Pessoa Fernando 69, 119
Phelps Elizabeth 303
Philippa of Lancaster 47, 108, 173
Phoenician traders 33, 144
Pinhão 268, 271
Pires, Tomé, Suma Oriental 55
politics 201
Pombal Marquisde 61, 101
Ponta de Sagres 194
Ponte 25 de Abril (Lisbon) 144,

INDEX | 343

157, 177
Ponte da Barca 285
Ponte de Lima 286
Ponte de São Gonçalo (Amarante) 269
Ponte Vasco da Gama (Lisbon) 112, 144, 177
pork 93
port 47, 97, 260
  and Pinhão 268
  and the Douro Valley 267
  barcos rabelos 259, 276
  Colheitas 98
  dynasties 47, 101
  Port and Duoro Wines Institute (Porto) 260
  port-wine lodges (Porto) 264, 265
  Solardo Instituto do Vinhodo Porto (Lisbon) 157
  Solardo Vinho (Porto) 260, 263
Portalegre 212
Portas de Beja 218
Portimão 192
Portinho da Arrábida 180
Porto
  and the Douro Valley 268
  architecture 110, 112
  Arte Contemporânea 112, 264
  barcos rabelos 265
  Cais da Ribeira 263
  Câmara Municipal 260
  Casada Música 112, 264
  Casa do Infante 262
  Casa Serralves 112
  Centro Português de Fotografia 262
  Church of Clérigos 110
  Estação São Bento 261
  Feitoria Inglesa 111, 261
  food and drink 260
  Gaia Cable Car 264
  Misericórdia 115
  Museu Serralves 264
  Nacional Soares dos Reis 263
  Palácio de Bolsa (stock exchange) 262
  Palácio do Bispo 261
  Ponte de Dona Maria Pia 263
  Ponte Dom Luís I 263
  Port and Douro Wines Institute 262
  Port Wine Institute 260
  port-wine lodges 264, 265
  Port Wine Museum 263
  Praça da Batalha 262
  Praça da Liberdade 260
  railway stations 322
  Romântico 263
  Rua Santa Catarina 262
  Santa Clara 261
  São Francisco 261, 262
  São João Novo 262
  São Lourenço 261
  Sé 261
  Solardo Vinhodo Porto 263
  Torre dos Clérigos 262
  wine trade 47, 260
Porto Covo 215
Porto de Mós 227
Porto Santo 301, 308
Portugal

food 89
Portuguese empire
  and food 91
  Brazil 52, 61, 63, 64
  colonial wars 70
  in Africa 51, 53, 70
  independence granted to colonies 71
  Salazar era 69
postal services 328
pousadas 10, 120
Póvoa de Varzim 284
Praia de Cabedelo 284
prehistoric culture 33
Prester John 50
public holidays 325, 328
Pulo do Lobo (Wolf's Leap) 218

Q

Queiroz, José Maria Eçade 218
Queluz 171
Queluz Palace 171
Quillinan, Dorothy 82
quintas
  Aveleda 269
  Bacalhoa 181
  Madeira 304, 306
  Sintra 174
  Torres 181

R

radio 326
Ramalho, Rosa 283
Reconquista 35, 38, 41
Régio, José 212
regional differences 291
Rego, Paula 119
Régua 270
Reguengos 210
religion 26, 77
  All Saints' Day 78
  All Souls' Day 78
  and northeast Portugal 291
  and republicanism 67
  and Salazar 73
  and the Colonies 53
  Counter-Reformation 56
  cult of Our Lady of Fátima 79, 80
  cult of the dead 80
  Easter 78
  Jesuit missionaries 61
  Jews and New Christians 26, 54, 62, 226
  midnight baptism 77
  military-monastic orders 37, 42
  miracles 79
  procession of the dead 78
  religious art 114
  religious services 328
  saints 77, 78
  shrines 79, 80
  the Inquisition 54, 56, 64
Renaissance 55
  architecture 109
  art 116
republicanism 67
Reserva Natural das Dunas de São Jacinto 248
Reynolds, Sir Joshua 117

Ribatejo
  Alpiarça 224
  Santarém 223
  Vila Franca de Xira 223
Rio Caldo 286
Rio de Onor 298
rivers 127
  Douro 127, 259, 265, 276
  Guadiana 199
  Lima 127
  Minho 284
  Mondego 127
  Tâmega 295
  Tejo 127, 255
  Vila Nova de Gaia 259
  Zêzere 255
Rocha dos Soidos 197
Rococco architecture 111
Rodrigues, Amália 85, 86
Romanesque architecture 107
Romans 34, 145, 183
Romanticism
  architecture 111
  art 118
Ronaldo, Cristiano 303
ruby port 98
rural communities 24

S

Sabrosa 273
Sagres 194
saints 77, 78
  John of God 203
  Vincent 115, 194
Salazar, António de Oliveira 68, 73, 80, 86
  and art 118, 119
Saldanha, Duke of 65
Salema 193
salt cod 52, 92
Sancho I 184, 293, 297
Sancho II 41, 184
Sandeman, George 101
Santa Luzia fortress (Elvas) 210
Santana Lopes, Pedro 72
Santar 255
Santarém 224
Santiago do Cacém 215
Santos, António Machado 68
Santos, Armandinho and Jaime 86
Santo Tirso 289
São Francisco church 114
São João da Pasqueira 271
São Jorge (Azores) 316
São Julião da Barra 166
São Martinho do Porto 231
São Miguel (Azores) 313
São Pedro de Balsemão 271
São Pedro de Sintra 172
São Salvador do Mundo 271
sardines 92
saudale 86
sculpture 115
Sebastião, Dom 56, 59, 152, 193
Senhora da Peneda 285
Septembrists 65
Sequeira, Domingos António 117
Serpa 218
Serra da Estrela 11, 125, 126
Serra do Buçaco 244

INDEX

Sesimbra 180
Setúbal 178
   Church of Jesus 108, 178
   São Filipe chapel 163
Severa Maria 86
shopping 240, 328
shrines 79, 80
   Nossa Senhora do Cabo 180
   Our Lady of Fátima 79, 80, 102, 226
Silva Porto, António 118
Silver Coast 223, 230
Silves 183, 184
Sines 215
Sintra 83, 172
   Casa Museu Anjos Teixeira 173
   Coastal excursions from 175
   getting there 171
   Henrique Calado Riding Ring 11
   Hotel Lawrence 172
   Museu das Artes de Sintra 173
   Museu Ferreira de Castro 172
   museums 173
   News Museum 173
   Palácio de Monserrate 174
   Palácio de Seteais 174
   Palácio Nacional 109, 172
   Parque da Pena 173
   Pena Palace 111, 173
   Queluz Palace 171
   Quinta da Capela 175
   Quinta da Regaleira 174
   Quinta de São Thiago 175
Sintra Vila 172
Siza Viera, Alvaro 112
Soajo 285
Soares, Mário 71
socialism 64, 67
   socialist reforms 71
Sócrates, José 72
Solares de Portugal 121
Sortelha 253
soups 94
Sousa, Archbishop Dom Diegode 281
southern
   Alentejo 216
Southey, Robert 82, 180
Souza-Cardoso Amadeo 119
Spain
   Castile 44, 47, 49
   Portugal's split with 36
   Portugal under Spanish rule 56, 59
Spanish Civil War 68
spices 90
   trade in 53, 61
Spínola, General Antóniode 70
sports and activities
   Autódromo do Estoril 167
   bullfights 329
   Cruz Quebrada soccer stadium 165
   football 329
   golf 167, 190
   horse riding 169, 329
   walking & hiking 329
   water sports 329
Suevi people 35
Sufism 36
Symington family 101

T

Tâmega river 293
Taveira Tomás 112
Távora Fernando 112
tawnyport 98
taxis 322
telecommunications 329
television 326
Terceira (Azores) 313, 315
Termas de São Pedro do Sul 254
Terzi Filippo 110
the Inquisition 56
Theodomirus 77
time zone 329
tipping 327
Tomar
   Convento do Cristo 110, 116, 225
   Nossa Senhora da Conceição 110
Tomar Convento do Cristo 109
Tomás, Admiral Américo 69
tomatoes 90
Tordesillas, Treaty of 52
Torralva, Diogode 110
touring Portugal 137
tourist offices 329
tours 330
trains 320, 321
   Lisbon 165, 322
   stations 322
trams
   Lisbon 322
Trancoso 253
transport 320, 322
   Boticas 295
   Lisbon 322
   trains 322
Trás-os-Montes 24, 137, 292
   Algoso 299
   architecture 293
   Atei 293
   Barroso district 293
   Bragança 292, 296
   Carvalhelhos 295
   Chaves 292, 293, 295
   Chega dos Toiros 294
   climate 292
   emigration from 291
   entering the region 292
   Mogadouro 299
   Mondim de Basto 293
   northern villages 298
   Rio de Onor 298
   Serra de Alvão 292
   Vinhais 296
Tróia 179

U

unemployment 25
universities 55
   Coimbra 55, 235, 236, 237
   Évora 207
   Lisbon 55, 145, 161
   Porto 263

V

Valença do Minho 284
   Pousada de São Teotónio 120

Vaz Teixeira, Tristão 301
Vendas Novas 202
Viana do Castelo 284
   festa 11
Vicente, Gil 56
Vieira, Antonio 313
Vieira, Domingos 117
Vieira, Francisco 117
Vila do Conde 284
Vila do Gerês 286
Vila Franca de Xira 223
Vila Fresca de Azeitão 181
Vilamoura 191
Vila Nogueira de Azeitão 181
Vila Real 274
Vila Romana de Milreu 197
Vila Viçosa 201, 209
Vimioso, Conde di 86
Vincent, St 115, 194
Vinhais 296
Viriathus 34
visas 330
Viseu 253
   cathedral 116, 253
Viseu, Duke of 55
Visigoths 35
Vista Alegre 248
Vouzela 255

W

walking & hiking 329
water sports 328
Waugh, Evelyn 82
weights and measures 330
Wellington, Duke of 47, 63
Whitehead, Sir John 111
whiteport 98
wildlife 129
Windsor, Treaty of 44, 47, 261
wine and wineries 100
   Alentejo 100, 219
   Algarve 184
   Borba 209
   Boticas 295
   Chaves 295
   Curia wineries 245
   Madeira 304, 306
   Maria da Fonseca Winery (Vila Nogueira de Azeitão) 181
   Mateus Rosé 273
   Minho grape harvest 279
   Quinta da Aveleda 269
   regions 99
   vinho verde 99, 270, 285
women 24
   fadistas 85, 87
   travellers 330
work 25
World War I 68
World War II 69, 80

Y

young people 24

Z

Zacuto, Abraham 54
Zambujeiro Dolmen 207
Zamora, Treaty of 37